S. Stevens (Samuel Stevens) Hellyer

Principles and Practice of plumbing

S. Stevens (Samuel Stevens) Hellyer

Principles and Practice of plumbing

ISBN/EAN: 9783337106607

Printed in Europe, USA, Canada, Australia, Japan

Cover: Foto ©ninafisch / pixelio.de

More available books at **www.hansebooks.com**

TECHNOLOGICAL HANDBOOKS.

PRINCIPLES AND PRACTICE

OF

PLUMBING.

BY

S. STEVENS HELLYER,

Author of " The Plumber and Sanitary Houses," and " Lectures on the Science and Art of Sanitary Plumbing."

WITH ILLUSTRATIONS.

LONDON: GEORGE BELL AND SONS,
YORK STREET, COVENT GARDEN.

1891.

CONTENTS.

CHAPTER I.

PLUMBERS' TOOLS . . . . PAGE 1

CHAPTER II.
LEAD AND SOME OF ITS USES.

Lead ores—Lead mines—The process of extracting the lead from the ore in a reverberatory furnace, and running it into pigs—Properties of lead—Lead under heat—Action of oxygen on lead—Of water—Of acid—Manufacture of lead pipes and castings—Patents for milled lead—Lead funnel pipe made by hand—Weight of lead pipe as required by certain water companies—Sizes of lead sheets —The annual production of lead 5

CHAPTER III.
TIN AND ITS ALLOYS.

Tinning of metals—Tinstone—Production of tin—Plumbers' solder—Fine solders—Blow-pipe solder—Solders and their melting-points 13

CHAPTER IV.
SOLDERING APPARATUS AND FIRE-PLACES.

Cotton and Johnson's patent "Torch" lamp—The "Self-acting Blowing-lamp"—The "Blow-pipe" lamp—Briggs' patent "Solderer" lamp—Plumbers' stoves . . . 17

CHAPTER V.
Lead Burning.

The "Chalumeau Aer-hydrique"—The airo-hydrogen blow-pipe and apparatus—Briggs' patent "solderer"—Lining tanks for chemical purposes—Use of the copper-bit . . 20

CHAPTER VI.
Lead Laying.

Advantages of lead—A table of relative strengths of lead for various purposes 25

CHAPTER VII.
Lead Laying (*continued*).

The bossing up of breaks and corners—Lead coverings to cornices—Channel cutting—Lead dowels 29

CHAPTER VIII.
Lead Laying (*continued*).

Cesspools and their sockets—Setting out and bossing up of roof-cesspools—Counter-sinking—Overflow-pipes . . 37

CHAPTER IX.
Lead Laying (*continued*).

Dormers—Cheeks and sills—Drips in gutters and flats—Splayed edges to drips 42

CHAPTER X.
Lead Laying (*continued*).

Flats—Warping of boards—Setting out the rolls—Long gutters—Wood tilt—Deep gutters 47

CHAPTER XI.

LEAD LAYING (*continued*).

Hips—Ridges—Fixing of a wood-roll—Bossing down the end of a hip-roll—Intersection of the hips with the ridge—Hips to Mansard roofs—Laps or passings—Lead bays to sloping roofs 50

CHAPTER XII.

LEAD LAYING (*continued*).

Wood-rolls—The undercloak and overcloak—Bossed ends—The lay-down—Seam rolls—Copper tacks—Domes and ogee-shaped roofs—Seam rolls on high pitched roofs—Lead bays 55

CHAPTER XIII.

LEAD LAYING (*continued*).

Step-flashings — Rubble-work — Secret gutters — Soakers — Number of soakers required for the side of a roof . . 63

CHAPTER XIV.

LEAD LAYING (*continued*).

Lead tacks—Welted tacks—Tacks to straight-flashings—Secret tacks—A torus—Lead valleys—Single welts—Double welts—Snow-boards 68

CHAPTER XV.

JOINT MAKING.

Essential points for good joints—Length of joints—Joint wiping with or without an iron—Solder for making joints—Shaving and tinning the pipes—Fitting and fixing the pipes—A table of the lengths of joints . . 74

CHAPTER XVI.

Joint Making (*continued*).

Underhand joints—Upright joints—Lead collars—Use of the splash-stick—Overcast joints 82

CHAPTER XVII.

Joint Making (*continued*).

Block joints—A lead flange—Close-fitting jointing—Flange-joints—Taft-joints—Branch-joints—Mitre-joints—The branch-pipe to fit inside the main-pipe 88

CHAPTER XVIII.

Joint Making (*continued*).

Copper-bit joint—" Tinker's joint "—Ribbon joint—Overcast ribbon joint—Blow-pipe joint—Astragal jointing . . 98

CHAPTER XIX.

Elbow Joints and Pipe Bending.

Elbow joint—Elbow mitre joint—Pipe bending—Evil of reducing the strength of a pipe—Contracting the bore of a pipe—Water dropped upon a hot pipe—Hand dummy—Long dummy—Overbending of a pipe—Bobbins and followers—Double bend—Bending light lead pipes—Use of sand for bending funnel pipes 102

CHAPTER XX.

Non-cleansing Plumbers' Traps.

Traps made by hand—D-trap, under sinks, lavatories, and elsewhere—Syphon or round pipe trap—D-trap compared with the anti-D—Narrow-band D-trap—Helmet D-trap—Experiments with a D-trap—Bell trap—Traps with mechanical seals—Check valves 111

CHAPTER XXI.

SELF-CLEANSING PLUMBERS' TRAPS.

PAGE

Principles on which traps should be constructed—S-trap—Half S-trap—Anti-D-trap—Quantity of water allowed by the water companies—Experiments with an anti-D-trap—Results of experiments with the above traps—Anti-D-traps for sinks—Tests with a half S-trap . . . 121

CHAPTER XXII.

THE LOSS OF WATER-SEAL IN TRAPS.

Ways in which the water-seal of a trap may be lost—Tests to show the loss of the water-seals of various traps—Round pipe trap—D-trap—Narrow-band D-trap—Eclipse trap—Bower trap—Anti-D-trap—Tests for syphonage and back pressure—Arrangement of trap vents—Test showing the value of an anti-syphoning pipe . . . 131

CHAPTER XXIII.

LOSS OF WATER-SEAL IN TRAP, AND TRAP VENTILATION.

Syphonage—Back-pressure—Use of the anti-syphoning pipe—Increase in the bore of a soil pipe, or waste, carried up to the roof—Experiments with an anemometer—"Anti-syphoning trap-vent"—U-shaped and V-shaped round pipe traps—"Emptage" trap—Evils in the fixing of the vent-pipe off a round pipe trap (to prevent momentum)—Loss of seal by evaporation—Loss of seal by a blow-down of air in a pipe 147

CHAPTER XXIV.

LINING CISTERNS AND SINKS WITH LEAD.

Cisterns in confined places—Strengths of lead for wood cisterns—Lining tanks for chemical purposes—Dimensions of a cistern for cutting out the lead—Lining of a wood cistern—Sides—Ends—Bottom—Soldering of the upright angles—Of the bottom—Lining a wood sink—Strengths of the lead—Use of oak cappings 156

CHAPTER XXV.
Pipe-Fixing.

Rounding and straightening of pipes—Use of the plumb-line—Fixing by lead tacks—Danger of fixing by wall-hooks in place of face-tacks for service pipes—Pairs of tacks in preference to double tacks—Soldering of tacks to pipes—Method of fixing where the pipes are much exposed to the sun's rays—Chases for pipes—Horizontal pipes—Fixing of service pipes to prevent pipe-freezing—Use of cocoa-nut fibre—Position of service pipes with regard to drain-pipes 163

CHAPTER XXVI.
Rain-water and Rain-water Pipes.

Disconnection of the rain-water from the soil drain—Storage of rain-water—Filtration of rain-water—Stoppage of rain-water pipes—Use of rain-water shoes—Rain-water used for flushing the drains—Rain-water heads—Socket tacks 169

CHAPTER XXVII.
Soil Pipes and their Disconnection and Ventilation.

Seamless lead pipe—Advantages of lead soil pipe over iron—Fixing iron soil pipes—Outside a house—Inside a house—Coating and painting of iron pipes to protect them from rust—The jointing of iron pipes as compared to the jointing of lead pipes—Outside soil pipes as compared with inside soil pipes—Sizes of soil pipes—Connection of branch soil pipes—Foot ventilation—Mica valves—"Mushroom" air-inlets—Cowls—Position of soil pipe terminals—Connection of lead soil pipe with iron drain—"Duck's foot" bend 175

CHAPTER XXVIII.

HISTORY OF WATER-CLOSETS.

PAGE

Primitive closets: Italy, France, Scotland, Spain, Germany, England—Extracts from a book, published in 1734, called "The London Art of Building"—Extracts from other books—First patent for a water-closet in 1775—Alexander Cumming's closet, 1775—Samuel Prosser's closet, 1777—Joseph Bramah's closet, 1778, the first valve-closet—Pan closets—Improvements in pan closets in 1796—In 1826 188

CHAPTER XXIX.

WATER-CLOSETS (*continued*).

Evils of the pan closet—"Wash-out" and "wash-down" classes of closet—"Water-battery" wash-out closet—Advantages of "wash-down" closets over "wash-out" closets—Seat-action flushing arrangement—Hopper closet—Plug or plunger closet—Trapless closets . . . 198

CHAPTER XXX.

WATER-CLOSETS (*continued*).

Closets in public buildings—In private houses—Advantage of valve closets—Valve closets used as slop sinks—Overflow arrangements—"Optimus" valve closet—Use of lead safes or trays—Copper-hinged flaps for the ends of overflow pipes 208

CHAPTER XXXI.

WATER-CLOSETS (*continued*).

Connection of an earthenware closet or an earthenware closet-trap to a lead soil pipe—Value of traps separate and independent of the "fitting"—Connection of a lead trap to a lead soil pipe—Connection of earthenware to lead by Portland cement—A flanged connection—Elastic closet cement 214

CHAPTER XXXII.

WATER-CLOSETS (*continued*).

PAGE

Open closets—Inclosed closets—Water supply to closets—Water-waste preventing cisterns—Valve and regulators and waste-preventing supply-valves to valve closets—Ventilation of w.c. apartments 220

CHAPTER XXXIII.

SLOP-SINKS AND DRAW-OFF SINKS.

Water-closet and slop-closet combined—Slop-sink waste pipes kept separate from soil pipes—Disconnected from soil drains—Sinks for hospitals—Hot-water draw-off sink-wastes—Of lead, with expansion joints *outside* the house—Of cast iron with expansion joints, and galvanized wrought iron with screwed joints *inside* the house—Traps fixed under slop-sinks—Flushing cisterns for slop-closets and sinks—Material of which sinks should be made—Pantry sinks 224

CHAPTER XXXIV.

SCULLERY SINKS.

Material for scullery sinks—Use of draining-boards—Sink with two compartments for washing vegetables—Waste-pipe and disconnecting-trap—Grease intercepting traps—In country house—In town houses—" Flush-out " grease-trap 232

CHAPTER XXXV.

BATHS AND LAVATORIES.

Overflow arrangements—Secret overflows—Use of a bath in washing out the drain—Lead safes and their overflow pipes—Plug and washer—Tip-up basins—One trap to one basin—Waste-pipes from baths and lavatories—Bath fixed in a dressing-room—Combination baths . . . 238

CHAPTER XXXVI.

URINALS.

Need of copious flushes—Automatic flushing cisterns—Pedestal closets as urinal basins—Lip urinals—Basins with wide fronts 248

CHAPTER XXXVII.

WATER, AND ITS STORAGE.

Water tested by a qualified analyst—Storage of water—Cisterns: Lead-battened, slate, earthenware, galvanized wrought iron, lead-lined—Action of water upon lead pipes—Action of water upon lead generally—Positions of cisterns—Cistern safes—Positions of waste-pipes as regards cisterns 251

CHAPTER XXXVIII.

HOUSE DRAINS.

Drains above ground—Underground—Inside a house—Outside a house—Essential features of a good drain—Stoneware pipe drains and their joints—Laying a drain—Cast-iron pipe drains and their joints—Sizes of drains—Access chambers—Drain flushing 262

CHAPTER XXXIX.

HOUSE DRAINS (*continued*). DISCONNECTION AND VENTILATION.

Value of disconnection—Valve flaps—Manhole drain-syphon Ventilating drain-syphon—Buchan's disconnecting-trap—Value of a water-drop in a disconnecting-trap—Pipe shafts—"Drain-sentinel" disconnecting-trap and chamber—Channel pipes—Manholes, and their fresh air inlets—"Combination" cast-iron disconnecting trap—Scott-Moncrieff's cast-iron trap and chamber—John Smeaton, Son and Co.'s cast-iron manhole and trap combined—Ventilation of drains—Tests with a model house-drain—Ventilating pipes and their terminals 270

PLATE I.

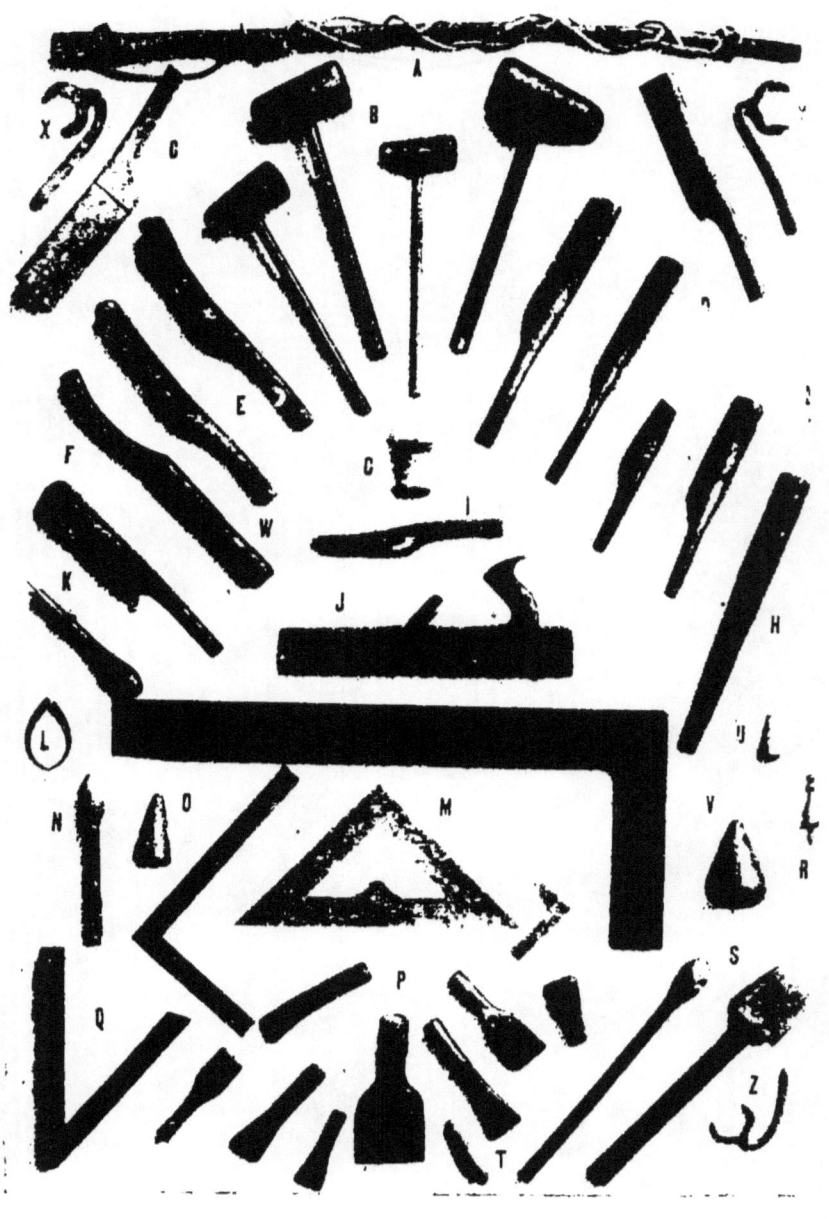

To face p. 1.

PRINCIPLES AND PRACTICE OF PLUMBING.

CHAPTER I.

PLUMBERS' TOOLS.

IF a man may be judged by his appearance, much more may a workman be judged by his tools.

In these days of strong competition the man in any trade or profession who does not provide himself with the best tools, the most efficient appliances obtainable, for executing his work expeditiously and efficiently, does himself a great injustice.

It is true that some men may become so skilled in their work that they can do what they want to do—can execute their work—with very poor instruments; can, in fact, do better work with poor tools than unskilled men can do with good tools: but no inexperienced man, no improver, no student-plumber, should remain content with his kit—his bag of tools—until it contains a perfect tool for any and every piece of work he may be called upon to execute.

Many a piece of work has been wanting in finish—in

execution—quite as much from want of proper tools as from lack of skill in the use of them.

For executing difficult and important pieces of work a man may show almost as much skill and intelligence in the selection of his tools as in the execution of the work.

Apart from the pleasure of working with the tool best suited for the work, there is the great economy of labour attending it; hence men indifferent to the tools they use often work much harder and take longer time over their work than the men who select their tools with intelligence.

To possess a perfect tool for any and every piece of work a poor plumber may be called upon to execute in the course of his life-labour would indeed mean a large kit; but it does not mean that he should daily burden his shoulders with a bag too heavy to be borne. The tools, the full kit,[1] up to the amount of his knowledge and experience,

---

[1] How the public are amused when "Punch" or the Press try to "show up" the British Workman! But I fancy the B. W. gets the larger fun out of such caricaturing. What an ass the public is! The man who writes the skit from his easy chair only wants pen and ink to do *his* pretty piece of work; but the poor plumber, or the poor carpenter, for their work, may want any *one* of a kit or a chest of tools that would raise a sore on the back of a donkey to carry them, and would need the air to be scented with carrots to get him along. And yet plumbers and carpenters are often sent for by intelligent householders to come and remedy some defect in the house, without giving them the smallest clue for what they are wanted. And so directly they present themselves, prepared to do any one of half-a-dozen things, they find they have not equipped themselves for the work required; and, to the astonishment of the householder (and their friends the caricaturists), the B. W. has to return to his shop again for tools or things which he could easily have brought with him at first, if only he had been properly told why he was sent for. The other day the author heard of a plumber having been sent for "to repair a service-pipe," and when he arrived upon the scene, and could find no leakage in any of the pipes, he was told that there must be "something wrong with the service-

can be kept at his house or at his lodgings, and his bag made to contain the tools necessary for the work in hand.

Not only should a plumber possess a full and complete set of tools, but he should become thoroughly accustomed to the use of each one of them, for his dexterity in their use will greatly depend upon the way he handles them.

It is only necessary for the skilled in any art to see how a man handles his tools to at once gauge the ability of that man.

The man who takes pride in his tools—who at some trouble keeps them clean and nice—is almost certain to take pride in his work; and, taking pride in his work, he is never likely to rest contented with himself until he can execute it with efficiency.

Instead of illustrating a tool here and a tool there throughout the many pages of this work, they are chiefly shown on Plates I. and II. And in order to give a faithful representation of the many and various tools used by a plumber, I asked one of my intelligent foremen to arrange his bag of tools on a board, or on two boards, and get them photographed; and I think the reader will agree with the writer, that only a plumber could have arranged and grouped such tools with so much artistic merit.

On looking at the plates I notice one omission, viz., the plumbers' bag. The big hammer is there, but not the bag! He has been a foreman so long that he does not now care to carry the bag about with him; or perhaps the bag has only been omitted from want of space.

pipes, as the gaslights jumped up and down dreadfully, and the water must somehow have got into the gas-pipe"; for some friends had told them that the jumping light was caused by water.

EXPLANATION OF PLATE I.

- A. Cutting-out knife.
- B. Set of mallets—four sizes.
- C. Hornbeam dresser.
- D. Set of box-wood dressers—five sizes.
- E. Half round box-wood dressers—two sizes.
- F. Large size box-wood dressers.
- G. Chalk-line, and piece of chalk standing on the reel.
- H. Pulling-up stick, for pipe bending.
- I. Small size box-wood dresser.
- J. Lead-cutting plane.
- K. Key-hole saw.
- L. Calipers.
- M. Set of four squares.
- N. Small hand-dummy.
- O. Box-wood turn-pin, also called tan-pin.
- P. Set of box-wood chase-wedges—eight sizes.
- Q. Bevel.
- R. Plumb-line.
- S. Hand-dummies—egg-shape and wedge-shape.
- T. Drawing-knife, for trimming and cutting.
- U. Turn-pin, small size, of box-wood.
- V. Turn-pin, 3-in., of box-wood.
- W. Bossing-stick, box-wood.
- X, Y, Z. Spanners, three kinds.

EXPLANATION OF PLATE II.

- A. Set of steel chisels, diamond points, and spikes.
- B. Fine and coarse rasps, and plumbers' brush.
- C. Iron ladles, two sizes.
- D. Two hatchet copper-bits.
- E. Set of screw-drivers—three sizes.
- F. Snips, and screw-hammer.
- G. Iron and steel bolts for pipe-bending, and resin-box.
- H. Spirit-level.
- I. Splash-stick, shave-hook, draw-knife, and two chipping-knives.
- J. Compasses and scriber.
- K. Cutting-plyers.
- L. Copper-bit-straight, and long dummy with wire handle.

PLATE II.

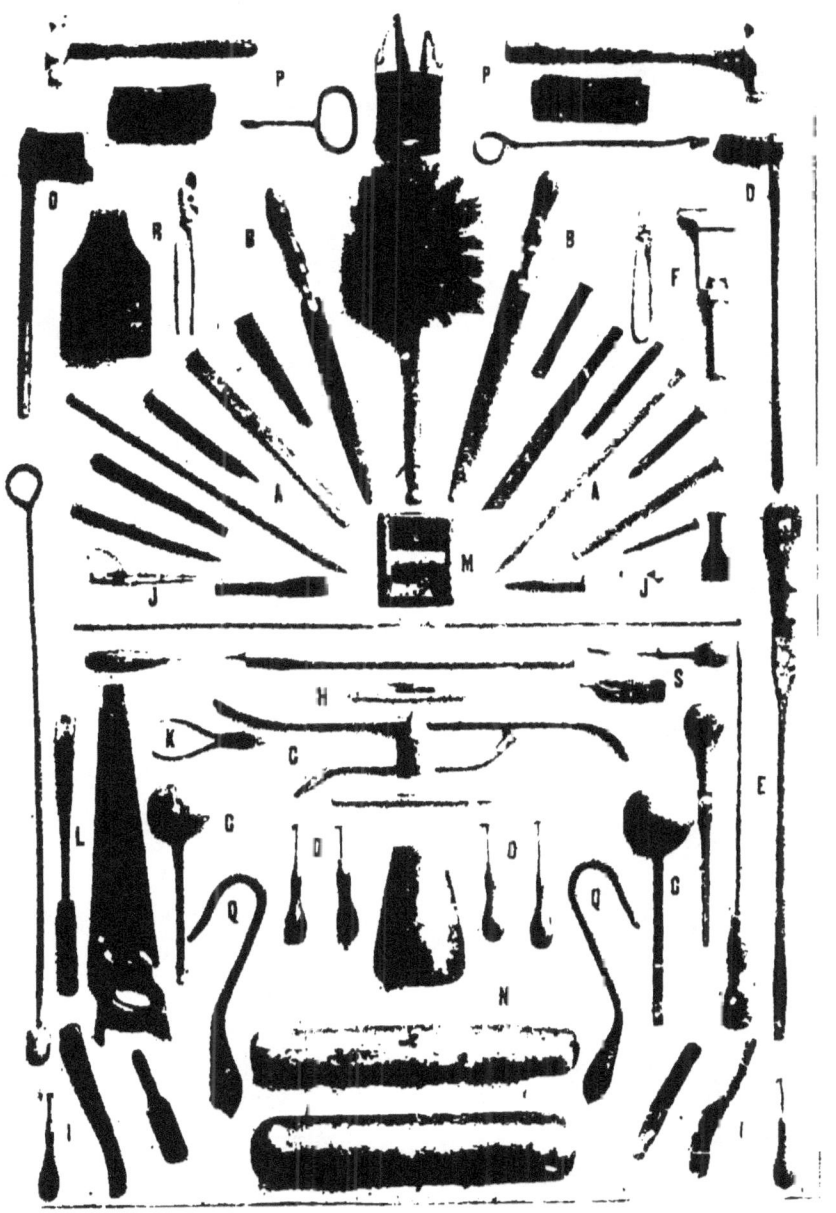

To face p. 4.

M. Looking-glass.
N. Mandrels and large turn-pin.
O. Set of shave-hooks.
P. Large hammer and small hammer, soil-pot, card-wire, pot hook, quench-hook, and felt.
Q. Irons, two sizes.
R. Gas-plyers and drifting-plate.
S. Spoon-hook and tie.

CHAPTER II.

LEAD, AND SOME OF ITS USES.

FOR the next edition of my work, "The Plumber, and Sanitary Houses," my son, Mr. Bertram Hellyer, has searched through the records of the Patent Office and worked up a brief history of the apparatus invented from time to time for the manufacture of sheets and pipes; and as he has worked in other interesting matter I make some extracts from it, as some who read this work may not read that.

"Lead can certainly claim a history of no mean length, though it would be impossible to say definitely when it was first used. The Romans, obtaining it in England and Spain, used it to a large extent for water-pipes, using a solder of an alloy of lead and tin.

"Of lead ores the two principal are galena, a compound of lead and sulphur, in the form of sulphide of lead, and cerusite, or carbonate of lead. Galena, by far the most important and most widely distributed, is of a dark metallic nature, chiefly containing, besides lead, sulphide of silver.

"Of lead mines, perhaps the chief of Great Britain are those of Derbyshire and Cornwall in England, Flintshire in

Wales, Dumfries in Scotland, Wicklow in Ireland, and the Laxey mine in the Isle of Man. In Europe: Carinthia in Austria, Sala in Sweden, the Harz in Germany, those of Saxony, and particularly those in the south of Spain. Lastly, the American mines."

To procure the metal from the galena, the ore is roasted in a furnace under the influence of the oxygen of the air till all the sulphur is burned away and the lead remains.

Through the kindness of one of the largest lead manufacturing houses in the world I am enabled to give an

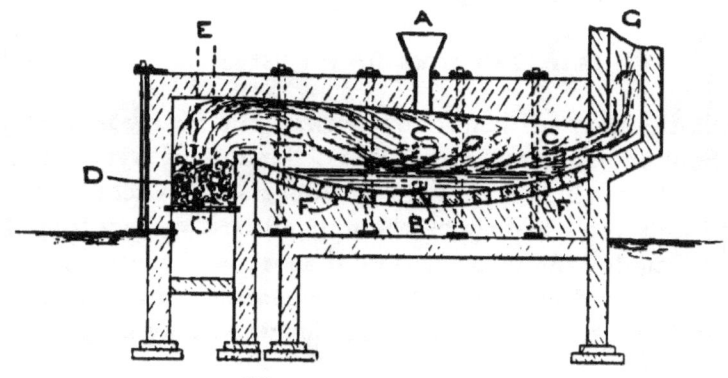

Fig. 1.—VIEW OF A REVERBERATORY FURNACE.

illustration (fig. 1) of one of their reverberatory furnaces in Wales.

"At the front and back of the furnace there are three openings, C C C, of the same dimensions, formed by strong cast-iron door-frames, with an inward inclination; these openings are used for raking the ore, to expose as much surface as possible to the influence of the oxygen. At the front of the furnace will be found the tap-hole, B, and at the back of this is the lead-pot, into which the lead is run. In the roof is an opening, A, through which the charge of ore is placed in the furnace from a hopper above. The fire, D, is charged with coal at the back, and cleared at the front. Above and in front of the ash-pit is a flue, E, which carries off any vapour. At the opposite end of the furnace are two rectangular flues, which are connected with a common flue, G, which runs direct to the stack: these flues are provided with dampers, with which they are regulated. Over the brick bottom of the furnace is spread a quantity of grey slags, F F, which act as an excellent furnace bottom.

"The furnace is built of best Buckley fire-bricks, and is braced together with wrought-iron standards and tie-rods. The quantity used to charge the furnace has increased of late years, and is now 29 cwts. of ore [in England, as far as I can ascertain, except in Cornwall, the charge is never so much as this], which is thrown through the hole in the arch by the hopper above. It is then evenly spread over the bed, and frequently, and at times constantly, stirred for about two hours. The furnace temperature is regulated by the damper, and the doors are left partially open in order to admit the requisite quantity of air. At the end of the two hours the grate is cleared from clinker, coal is thrown on the fire, and the damper opened a little so as to expose the charge to a higher calcining heat.

"This operation takes about an hour: more coal is then thrown on the fire, and the doors of the furnace are closed till the charge has melted, which takes about half-an-hour. The doors are again opened, and a few shovelfuls of lime are thrown upon the charge to thicken the unreduced portion, which is then allowed to cool and calcine for an hour. Again the fire is charged, the damper raised, and lime added, till the whole charge of ore is thoroughly melted.

"At the end of eight hours the charge is quite ready to be withdrawn or tapped: the doors of the furnace are opened, the slag thickened with lime, the plug taken out of the tap-hole, and the lead is run out into the lead-pot ready to receive it, and ladled out into pig-moulds. A pig is a piece of solid lead about 2 ft. 3 in. long, 5 in. wide, and 3 in. deep, but it varies in size and shape—of the under side—and therefore in weight, according to the mould of the manufacturer, and may weigh about 1 cwt., $1\frac{1}{4}$ cwt., or $1\frac{1}{2}$ cwt.

"Lead is run down into pigs for better transit. Two men are engaged with each furnace, one at the front, the other at the back.

"The ores generally worked in Flintshire furnaces, such as we have described, yield from 75 per cent. to $81\frac{1}{2}$ per cent. of lead per ton of ore. The fumes from the flues are swept out periodically, and worked in the furnaces in conjunction with the ores; they give from 40 per cent. to 50 per cent."

To speak briefly of its **properties**, pure lead is a pale bluish-grey metal, having the qualities of softness and plasticity in a very high degree, whilst the absence of elasticity is very strongly marked. Under heat it melts at 612° Fahr.; at a bright red heat it emits vapours, and at a white heat it boils. Exposed to ordinary air it becomes tarnished, but the thin film formed increases very slowly. Lead rapidly takes up **oxygen** with formation of protoxide, which is produced in two forms, massicot and litharge. With respect to the **action of water on lead**, absolutely pure water has no action on lead by itself, but in presence of pure oxygen it rapidly attacks lead, forming hydrated oxide, which is soluble in water as an alkaline liquid. As all soluble lead compounds are poisons, it follows that lead cisterns and pipes must contaminate pure water; but again, the presence in the water of even small proportions of bicarbonate or sulphate of lime prevents its action on lead, though all impurities by no means act in like manner; for instance, nitrate and nitrite of ammonia intensify the action of water on lead. Acids have little or no effect in the action of water on lead, though the stronger acids—such as nitric acid—have a slowly-taking-place effect which becomes more noticeable if the temperature is raised.

I feel compelled to say something on the manufacture of lead pipes and castings before finally dismissing this " weighty " topic from our minds.

Quite late into this century in the cities of London and Westminster, and other parts of England as well as on the Continent, the manufacture of lead pipe formed the principal work of many a plumber in many a plumbery, and very expert ye plumbers of ye olden time were in producing pipes of various strengths, and in sizes from $\frac{3}{4}$ in. to 7 in., to suit the needs of the times. By the kindness of M. Poupard, of Paris, I have in my possession some graphic illustrations showing French " plombiers " at work in an old Paris " plomberie," casting sheets and plates, and in the manufacture of lead pipes, together with the various apparatus used ; the arrangements being similar to those that obtained favour in England before hydraulic power was adopted in the making of the sheets and pipes. A competent authority has written me a most interesting letter on the manufacture of sheet lead and lead pipes, from which I make the following extracts :—

" My family have preserved a continuous history of the lead trade, and I find that the first rolling-mill was erected by our firm in 1797 at Newcastle-on-Tyne. I can't specify what width the sheets were rolled ; however, lead was not usually rolled for many years after. Iron had been treated in that way, as it is a metal so easily manipulated. The earliest record I can find of the manufacture of pipe is this extract : ' 1810. This year pipe was first manufactured at our Chester works, and the price was £6 15s. above that of pigs.' It does not say that it was made by hydraulic power, but I am under the impression that hydraulic power was not introduced until some considerable time later.

"I remember being at Pompeii some years ago and seeing some pieces of pipe made by the old Romans from lead; they were evidently made from sheets very smooth and thin, and had been soldered up the sides, and were as perfect as when first put in.

"The Romans, during their occupation of Britain, worked the lead mines in Cumberland and Wales. I have seen several pigs of lead here in London and at Newcastle with the name of the Roman emperor Hadrianus on them, who was in Britain in 119 A.D., and who built the Roman wall from Newcastle to Carlisle. These pigs are beautifully cast, much the same weight as those in use now, and the letters clearly and sharply cut. I cannot say whether they were cast in sand, iron, or bronze moulds."

From the records of the Patent Office it appears that the earliest patent for milled lead dates back as far as 1687, the entry reading, "Manufacture of milled lead for sheathing and preservation of ships, or any other thing." There is no actual mention of rolling lead for many years, although there is a patent of 1749 for casting lead to be used for milling, and one in 1759 for rolling "all malliable metal." In several patents for rolling metals towards the end of the eighteenth century, only iron is actually specified, but other metals seem to be understood as being treated similarly; whilst in 1839 there is a patent for "Improvements in rolling lead and other soft metals," proving from its very title that lead had previously been rolled. With regard to lead pipes, I find that there is a patent in 1820 for "Certain improvements in machinery for manufacturing lead and other metal into pipe and sheets." The apparatus was operated by hydraulic pressure, and this is the first mention of hydraulic power being used, bearing out the evidence of the letter above.

PLATE III.

To face p. 10.

Up to within about the last quarter of a century, and for three-quarters of a century previously, **cast sheet lead** was manufactured very largely by my predecessors at the Lead Works, 21, Newcastle Street. The size of the sheets chiefly made was about 20 ft. by 7 ft. But directly I could make my voice heard, I used it in condemning cast sheet lead, on account of the varying strengths of a roof covered with it, some parts even of a single bay varying as much as 30 and even 50 per cent. in thickness. Some of the sheets in the last casting remained on our pile for about ten years, and were finally melted down and turned into sash-weights. Messrs. M. Hall and Co. write me that they still keep the appliances for casting sheets 13 ft. by 6 ft., though it does not pay to put them into operation for a smaller parcel than about 50 tons.

But though cast sheet lead is not now manufactured by hand, some plumbers still continue to make **lead funnel pipe** by hand, with a soldered seam either drawn or wiped; but though such a pipe when properly made may last a century or more, there can be no absolute certainty as to how long it will last unless you know the man who made it, and unless every inch of the seam can be seen; and even then it may look fair enough to the eye, but directly your back is turned it may set up some galvanic action and belie your opinion by rapidly oxidizing.

As seamless lead pipe of an equal substance all over can now be had of any size from $\frac{3}{16}$ in. up to 6 in., and of any strength, it is not necessary to describe how to make up pipes by hand, for not only are round pipes made by hydraulic pressure power, but also square and rectangular pipes.

The following table shows the weight of lead pipe—the *communication pipe*—per yard, as required by certain water companies:—

	⅜-in.	½-in.	⅝-in.	¾-in.	1-in.	1¼-in.
London, according to Metropolis Water Act	lbs. 5	lbs. 6	lbs. 7½	lbs. 9	lbs. 12	lbs. 16
Kent	—	5	7	9	12	—
West Surrey . .	4	5½	—	9	14	20
Caterham . . .	5	6	8	10	14	—
Colne Valley . .	5	7	9	11	16	—
Sevenoaks and Tonbridge . .	—	5	7	9	12	15

Weights of Services and Wastes.

	½-in.	¾-in.	1-in.	1¼-in.	1½-in.	2-in.
Strong service pipe, *per yard*	lbs. 4½	lbs. 7¼	lbs. 10½	lbs. 14	lbs. 18	lbs. 24
Service pipe (light), *per yard*	3¼	5⅜	8½	12	16	21
Waste pipe, *per yard*	—	—	—	12	16	21
"Warning pipe" — pipes "discharging with an open end," minimum strength, as per Metropolis Water Act, 1871, *per yard*	3	5	7	—	—	—

Lead pipe can be encased with block tin to any strength required.

Milled lead and seamless **lead pipes** are manufactured in the following cities and towns, viz.:—Birmingham, Bristol, Chester, Derby, Dee Bank, Glasgow, London, Leeds, Manchester, Newcastle, Plymouth, Shrewsbury, and St. Helens.

The **width** of the sheets varies with some of the different manufacturers; the usual width up to within the last few

PLATE IV.

To face p. 12.

years has been with most of them 7 ft., the length being 33 ft. Many houses now make their sheets 7 ft. 6 in. in width, and even 8 ft., and at St. Helens sheets are milled even up to 9 ft.

The production of lead in the United Kingdom for the five years including 1885 to 1889 averaged about 37,000 tons—the returns for the year 1890 are not yet published. It is impossible to estimate the consumption of lead in the United Kingdom, but according to the imports and exports it appears to be something like 140,000 tons per annum.

One firm manufactured at its various works as follows, viz., for 1890 :—

	Sheets.	Pipe.
London	10,566	5,219
Chester	2,712	2,144
Newcastle	4,464	2,546
Liverpool	2,380	836

Pig lead was imported for the year 1890 to the extent of 158,649 tons, exported to 55,536 tons. It is imported from Australia, Germany, Greece, Mexico, and Spain.

CHAPTER III.

TIN AND ITS ALLOYS.

THE Latin for tin is *stannum*, whence the chemical symbol "Sn." It has a specific gravity of 7·291, and melts at 442° F. Alloyed with lead it forms pewter and solder; with small portions of antimony, copper, and bismuth, it forms block tin, Britannia, etc.

Pure tin does not tarnish in the air, as plumbers very well know. It is proof against acids and liquids, such as vinegar, lime juice, etc., etc. Copper saucepans, baths, slop-sinks, or any kind of copper vessel, only require to be scoured and made clean and bright for melted tin to readily tin upon them; though, for removing the last film of oxide which so soon forms upon well-cleaned and well-brightened copper, it is necessary to sprinkle powdered sal-ammoniac upon the parts to be tinned; or to rub a piece of sal-ammoniac over the copper—a piece being held in a pair of tongs for the purpose—before passing the melted tin over it with a wisp of tow. Wrought iron and cast iron can also be tinned, the process being very similar to that of copper tinning. The articles to be tinned are thoroughly cleaned and washed with sulphuric acid, and then heated up to the melting point of tin, when the fluid tin is rubbed on the bright surface of the iron with a ball of cotton or a cork.

Sal-ammoniac is applied during the operation to keep the surface of the metal free from oxidation. Tinned iron articles which are deficient in tin oxidize more rapidly than iron without any tin coating, owing to a galvanic reaction, caused by the contact of the tin and iron.

Tinstone, which is the only ore of tin found in sufficient quantity to be the subject of mineral exploration, is found in many places; the oldest known deposit is in Cornwall, where it occurs in veins or small strata, from whence large supplies of some of the purest tin used still comes to London. It bears the well-known mark of the *Lamb and Flag*. Plumbers' solder and fine solder have been made in the firm, of which I am now the head, for a century and a half, of Truro tin. But for many years past large quantities of tin have been brought into London from Australia, the Straits Settlements, and the islands of Banca and Billiton, as shown by the following statistics.

The Cornish production is somewhere about 9,500 tons per annum.

	During 12 months ending 31st Jan., 1887.	During 12 months ending 31st Jan., 1888.	During 12 months ending 31st Jan., 1889.	During 12 months ending 31st Jan., 1890.	During 12 months ending 31st Jan., 1891.
	tons.	tons.	tons.	tons.	tons.
Shipment from the Straits Settlements to London	11,053	20,520	16,215	18,673	14,200
Shipment from Australia to London . . .	6,455	5,833	6,319	5,942	5,050

Plumbers' solder is usually made out of two parts of lead and one of tin, but for seam or angle soldering, as well as for flange joints, and for upright joints, solder a little richer not only looks better, but it works better. Sixty-five per cent. of soft pig lead to 35 per cent. of Truro tin makes good wiping solder. It is generally made in *casts*, consisting of eight bars, and weighing about 7 lbs. per bar, from prints stamped in a large level bed of prepared casting sand; or the tin and lead, being well mixed into good alloy, is run into moulds made in flasks of sand. In the illustration, fig. 2, A shows the top, and B the bottom of a *cast* of solder. A stick of fine solder is shown at C.

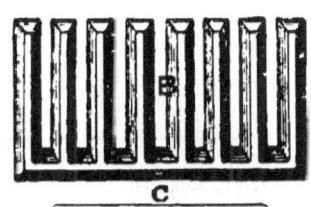

Fig. 2.—Showing the Upper and Under Side of a Cast of Solder, and a Stick of Fine Solder.

Fine solder, for soldering with a copper-bit, is made out of about eight parts of tin to seven of lead. When the two metals have been well heated and well mixed in a melting-pot, the alloy is run out with a ladle into *sticks* (into small U-shaped grooves sunk in iron plates) about 18 in. long, ½ in. wide, and ⅜ in. thick. A stick of fine solder is illustrated at c, fig. 2, and when it is of good quality it gives forth a crackling noise most pleasant to the ear of the plumber, when he bends it to forecast its fluidity for flowing round a jointing when heated by a copper-bit or blowing-lamp.

Blow-pipe solder is made with about 7½ per cent. more tin than fine solder, or fine solder is melted down in a pot and further enriched by adding from 5 to 10 per cent. of tin to it, as circumstances may require. It is then run out with a small ladle upon faced iron plates into thin narrow strips about $\frac{3}{16}$ in. wide, $\frac{1}{12}$ in. thick, and 18 in. long.

A Table of Alloys with Tin, and their Melting Point.

SOLDERS.	Tin.	Lead.	Melts at
Plumbers' solder.	1	2	441° F.
Copper-bit solder ("*poor*") .	1	1	370° F.
Do., or Fine solder("*good*")	65 %	35 %	—
Blow-pipe solder.	2	1	340° F.
	3	2	334° F.
	3	1	356° F.
	1	5	511° F.
	1	10	541° F.

Soft solders (extracted chiefly from Appleton's "Dictionary of Mechanics").

Tin.	Lead.	Bismuth.	Melts at
5	3	3	202° F.
3	2	5	212° F.
1	2	2	236° F.
2	2	1	242° F.
4	4	1	320° F.

CHAPTER IV.

SOLDERING APPARATUS AND FIRE-PLACES.

1.

COTTON and Johnson's patent "Torch" is a very useful means of getting a good flame for making joints with a blow-pipe.

2. The "Self-acting Blowing-lamp," illustrated in fig. 3, is all that a plumber wants in many cases for melting his solder, for making small joints and for repairing jobs. For working in confined places, it is better to have the hinged wind-guards, D, made to take off. The lamp is a French invention, with some improvements made upon it in England. It is made in several sizes and used for various purposes.

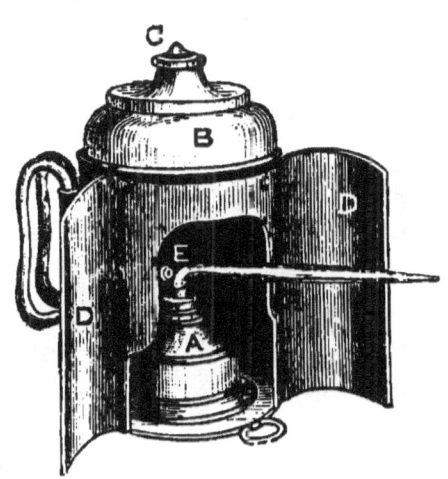

Fig. 3.—SELF-ACTING BLOWING-LAMP.

An upright joint, or branch joint, of any size can be made with it in from five to twenty minutes, depending, of course, upon the size of the joint and the skill of the joint-maker. Underhand joints from $\frac{1}{2}$ in. to 2 in. are easily enough made with the heat from such a lamp, but for underhand joints upon large pipes it is not so well suited.

The lamp is not so well suited for soldering sinks and

cisterns as well-heated pots of solder. For making **wiped joints**, etc., **plumbers' solder** should be run out into thin strips, say about ¼ in. thick, 1 inch wide, and 15 or 18 in. long. This solder is quickly melted upon well-heated jointings from the flame of such a lamp. With a well-directed blast a bulb of solder is soon formed upon the pipings, and heated up to the consistency of wiping. If the joint is too large to wipe round, the cold parts can be heated up as the wiping proceeds.

The lamp, A, should be filled with methylated spirit, and the wick (common lamp-cotton) should be kept well in front of the jet, E, to prevent the blast from jumping. The boiler, B, should never be more than half-filled with methylated spirit, and the safety-valve, C, should be loosened and cleaned from time to time, to prevent it sticking and bursting the boiler.

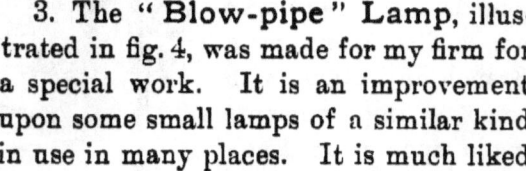

Fig. 4.—BLOW-PIPE LAMP.

3. The "**Blow-pipe**" **Lamp**, illustrated in fig. 4, was made for my firm for a special work. It is an improvement upon some small lamps of a similar kind in use in many places. It is much liked by those who have worked with it. The lamp, A, is filled with common lamp-cotton, and this is saturated with benzoline. A powerful blast is obtained by blowing through the india-rubber tubing, C, which can be of any length, and which is blown by the solderer, or his mate, or it can be blown by bellows attached to the tubing, or any air-forcing machine, and the lungs of the plumber saved. The solder is melted upon the jointings as explained in the other lamps, Art. 2.

4. Briggs' patent "**Solderer**" is an apparatus of much

SOLDERING APPARATUS AND FIRE-PLACES. 19

more value to the plumber for making joints, etc., than either of the two lamps described in the two preceding paragraphs. A general view of the apparatus is shown in fig. 5, with the flame from the burner melting a thick stick of solder upon a branch joint. The apparatus is made in two sizes, the largest being furnished with two burners or jets, one for **soldering** and one for **lead**

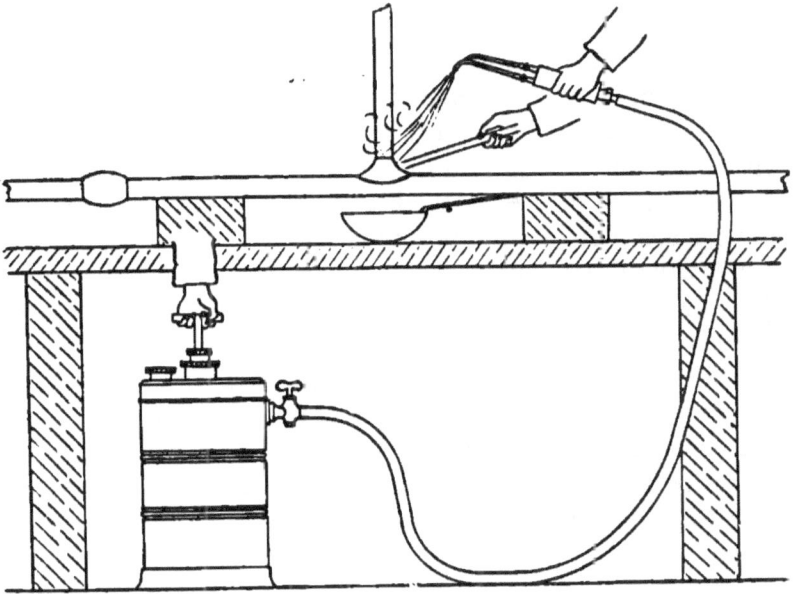

Fig. 5.—View of the Patent "Solderer."

burning. The apparatus, which has been in use in my works for two or three years, has given great satisfaction. The "Solderer," partly filled with absorbent material, is charged with a small quantity of benzoline, which, mixed with air pumped into the cylinder, will supply sufficient gas to make a large number of joints, and an occasional supply, say a pint, of benzoline, is all that is required to keep the machine in constant working condition. No evaporation takes place when out of use, as the cylinder is hermetically sealed.

5. The following description of **fire-places** is extracted from my book, "Lectures on the Science and Art of Plumbing." "A good fire-place is essential where a large amount of soldering is wanted—if it is to be expeditiously done. In jobbing work, where the plumber cannot use a modest stove in the house, he prefers *going* to the devil—a well-known fire-grate—rather than go into the kitchen for his heat, to be *sent* to such a quarter by the cook. The *heat* in kitchens is generally too great for men with 'metal' to stand it. If the plumber happens 'to be without a devil'—a position 'devoutly to be desired,' I should say, by others as well as plumbers—he can easily make a fire-place with a few bricks.

"**A plumbers' stove** is shown in the view which heads Chapter I., and it is a great improvement on the old fire-grate. But the plumber, especially the jobbing plumber, can, if he chooses, be independent, in a large majority of cases (except in new buildings), of fire-places, pots, ladles, and irons, and I recommend him to take up his independency in this matter by using lamps," described in Arts. 2 and 3, or the patent "Solderer," Art. 4.

CHAPTER V.

LEAD BURNING.

THE following description of lead burning is taken from my "Lectures."

1. "A very valuable method of soldering metallic substances was invented in France, in 1838, by the Count de

Richemont. This airo-hydrogen blow-pipe was called by the inventor the 'Chalumeau Aer-hydrique.' The English patent for this invention was taken out in the name of Luke Hebert, in 1838. But Mr. Mallet claims to have used a similar apparatus prior to 1833. The soldering done by this instrument is improperly called *autogenous* soldering. As I shall speak simply of lead joinings— though it is used for uniting various metals—I shall speak

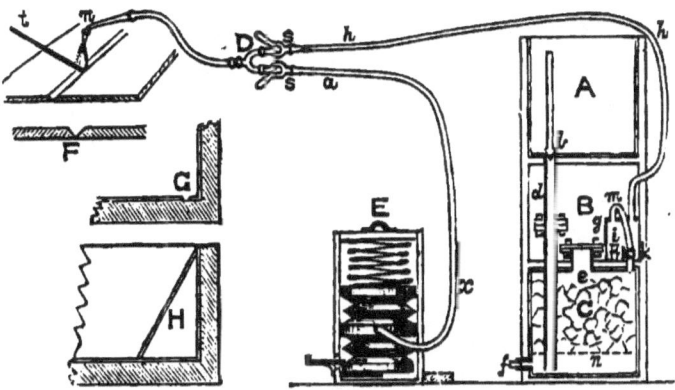

Fig. 6.—AIRO-HYDROGEN BLOW-PIPE AND APPARATUS.

of it as **lead burning**, the name by which it is known in the trade.

"An apparatus complete is illustrated in fig. 6, from one of those now in the possession of my firm. It consists of a self-acting and self-regulating gas generator, A B C, for giving a continuous current of hydrogen gas, through the forked-shaped blow-pipe, D, and of a pair of bellows, E, for supplying atmospheric air (through the same blow-pipe) for the combustion of the gases. The organist found to his cost that the organ-blower played an important part in producing his music, and the burner, or solderer, will find, in using this apparatus, that his burning will depend much upon the blower.

"A good steady stream of **air** is required to be sent through the tubing, $x\ a$, for the proper **combustion of the gases.** Stop-cocks are fixed at s s, in the forked-shape piping, D, to regulate the current of **hydrogen** from the gas generator, and the stream of air from the bellows. The bent jet-tube can have any sized nozzle, n, screwed to it to suit the work to be done. The india-rubber tubings, a and h, connecting the bellows and hydrogen gas holder with the blow-pipe, can be of any length to suit circumstances. The **gas generator** is divided into three nearly equal compartments, as shown in the section, A B C. It is about 12 in. by 13 in., and stands just 3 ft. high. The upper and lower reservoirs, A and C, are lined with lead, the lower one, C, being made air-tight. The metals and pipings are united without solder—*i.e.*, by fusion of the metals. A plug is fixed, as shown at b, in the upper reservoir, A, over the communicating-pipe, d, to the lower reservoir, C.

"Diluted sulphuric acid, of the specific gravity $1{\cdot}16$, is put into the upper reservoir, A; and the lower reservoir, C, is filled with zinc clippings through the aperture, e, which is afterwards made air-tight. f is a leaden tube, closed by a cork, and through which the saturated acid is discharged; g is a safety chamber, into which the hydrogen generated in the reservoir, C, is conveyed by means of a tube, m; k is a stop-cock fixed in the tube, m; i is a tube fixed in the safety-chamber, G, with a cork stopper, which acts as a safety-valve to prevent explosion; P is a perforated false bottom, which supports the zinc clippings in the lower reservoir, C; n is the brass jet-tube, screwed to fit the various-sized nozzles through which the gaseous mixture escapes.

"The **apparatus**, fig. 6, is **charged**, when in use, by putting 7 lbs. of zinc clippings into the lower reservoir, C, through the aperture, e, 3 quarts of water and $1\frac{1}{2}$ pints of sulphuric acid into the upper reservoir, A. A pint of acid is added about every two hours. The zinc lasts eight or ten days. The saturated acid should be drawn off after each usage.

"Very *intense* and *forcible* jets of flame can be obtained by this **airo-hydrogen blow-pipe**, at any rate sufficient to melt strong platina wire. For neat burning, it is important to have the right flame-jet. When applied to a bit of shaved lead, the heated point becomes immediately as bright as silver. The following test will indicate with certainty if the mixture and the force of the current be duly regulated; *e.g.*, when the hottest and most reductive point of the interior flame is applied to a piece of shaved lead, the heated point becomes immediately as bright as silver, and the flame itself assumes a violet tint, produced by the volatilization of a small portion of the lead. When there is too much or too little air, the heat is not so *intense* or *pointed*, and the melting spreads over a larger surface owing to its being heated more slowly.

"Two pieces of lead can be united when they only butt against each other, as shown at F, but it is better in many cases to make one piece lap over the other. The parts to be united should be shaved bright (the width required for the burning), and a narrow strip of thin lead, as shown at *t*, shaved bright, should be held in the left hand for supplying the lead required for filling up the uneven space of the joining, or for making a raised seam. In lining cisterns and sinks, for burning under this process, the sides and ends should turn on to the bottom a little, say, $\frac{1}{2}$ in. to $1\frac{1}{2}$ in., and **butt** against each other, as shown at G, so as to get a **flat surface burning** for uniting the bottom with the sides; and the sides of the cistern should be connected with the ends, or the ends with the sides, on the vertical faces, in a **diagonal line**, for the outer edge of the overlaps of the lower piece to form a base to burn upon."

2. Briggs' patent **Solderer**, illustrated in fig. 5, is also much used for **lead burning**. (Chap. IV. Art. 4.)

3. For **lining tanks** for chemical purposes the plumber should be extremely careful to see that he obtains sheets manufactured from **refined pig lead**.

4. For a plumber to fully furnish himself with the knowledge essential to the efficient execution of every piece of work that comes within his vocation may well overwhelm the young student plumber with some concern for his competence, both of brains and money, in after life. But **lead burning** is so **useful** an **art**, that in addition to his other accomplishments he should endeavour to add to them the knowledge of uniting pieces of metal with a metal of the same kind.

5. Lead burning is especially adapted for joining the edges of two pieces of lead together where it would be difficult to lap the lead properly to keep out the weather, as in covering cornices, carved wood pinnacles and finials, balustrades, etc. And for lining tanks with lead for chemical works, where it is absolutely essential that no solder be used, it is the only method of joining the several pieces of lead together. Lead pipes for chemical works should also be united by burning them together with lead, and this the skilful lead burner can very well do.

6. Two pieces of lead can easily be burnt together with the aid of a hatchet-shaped **copper-bit**. To do this, shave the edges to be united, put a piece of brown paper under the joining, and pull a copper-bit—heated nearly red-hot—along the edges, using a narrow strip of thin lead, well shaved, for making good the seam. The tinned edges of the copper-bit should be preserved as much as possible, and they should be brightened up, by pulling the end of a stick of fine solder over them, before commencing the burning.

CHAPTER VI.

LEAD LAYING.

1.

OF all the metals for covering roofs there is none so yielding, so accommodating to the skilful worker, as lead. With it he can cover almost any form of woodwork on roof, spire, or turret. Turned, moulded, or carved wood finials and pinnacles, as well as balustrades, carved wood crockets, and moulded cornices, only require time for the manipulator of lead to so cover them that they shall stand the weather and last for centuries. The plumber can cover with lead a wood ball of any size, if not as quickly, yet as dexterously, as a cook covers an apple with dough.

2. Then as to the durability of lead. Iron rusts away, cement cracks and falls down, zinc perishes and vanishes, and tiles and slates break here and there about the roof, and so come and go, but the well-laid lead goes on for ever. Upon its surfaces on the roofs of old abbeys and cathedrals, crows that live a century rub their beaks when hatched, and clean their bills when they go to the place where they caw no more. And when the time comes for its renewal, its sale as old lead often realizes 40 per cent. of its original cost, including the cost of the labour both of laying it and removing it. Of what other roof-covering can the like be said?

3. The durability of leadwork on the roofs of houses, churches, and abbeys, is often diminished as much from want of a knowledge of the principles on which it should be executed as from a want of skill in the art of executing it.

Like the members of many a poor family, many a nail, many a tack, is often left to bear a weight that can only be borne for a short period, when nail and tack let go their hold, and the lead and its insufficient supports slip away together.

Elevated though the pieces of lead often are to the very highest positions, their tendency is ever downwards; and unless they are well secured to their places by the plumber, no matter how clever the bossing may be, they will soon begin to drop away; until, finally, losing all hold upon their surroundings, they sink right down, and give place to other pieces.

If it were not the tendency of human nature to forget, it would hardly be necessary to remind a plumber of the specific gravity of lead. He knows its weight well enough when he is tugging up a ladder with a roll on his shoulder; and, also, when he is lifting a large piece into its position; but when it is there he often becomes forgetful, and insufficiently secures the lead in its place.

4. To succeed in laying lead well and efficiently, it is not only necessary to secure it properly, but it must also be rightly bossed and equally distributed; and not left thick in one place and thin in another, as is too often the case.

Happy would be that monarch who could so regulate the affairs of his nation that there should be no want or complaining in his streets. And though this might mean neither poverty nor riches to any of his subjects, it would mean some comfort to them all. The skilful plumber can so manipulate his lead, that in his efforts to benefit the poverty-stricken places he need not beggar the richer parts; and when his work is done, he can rejoice that he has left his breaks and corners—his bossings—of an even thickness right throughout.

5. Every schoolboy knows that from nothing you can take nothing. It is, therefore, useless to attempt to work

a piece of lead of a certain superficial area into a place of much larger area, and expect to leave it the same thickness in the latter as it was in the former. And yet some men often try this, with the result that lead $\frac{1}{8}$ in. at starting is thinned down at the finishing to $\frac{1}{36}$ in., with, perhaps, a "bird's-eye" (a little hole) here and there,—often screened from sight by a bit of "touch." "The last tap did it, sir," used to be the croaking cry of a plumber who was fairly good at internal work, but who, off and on, for twenty years had been trying to learn the art of bossing.

6. In leadwork, wherever the need may be, the worker rejoices in the use of a metal that, *presto* like, can be passed from one place to another; that can be worked by the skilled from the place of plenty to the place of poverty. To do this without causing distress on any part of the lead operated upon is the plumber's privilege, as it is his duty.

7. There is no difficulty in bossing up a corner, or in working up a break, to any height required; though a height of 6 in. is generally sufficient for flats and gutters. For cesspools, where the angles are not allowed to be soldered, the corners and breaks may have to be bossed up to a height of 15 in., or even higher. Nor is there any difficulty in doing this or in bossing up out of a piece of flat sheet lead a lead jar or lead vase 3 ft. high.

8. The difficulty in working lead is when it can only be bossed on one of its sides, when the tools cannot be used on both faces to keep the lead smooth and free from buckling and creasing, when bossing it into recesses, and into the internal angles of deep moulded cornices, etc.

9. In breaks, hollows, drips, and recesses, and such-like places, where the parts to be covered are of much greater area than the surface of the lead standing directly over or round about such parts, the plumber should take some pains to compute the extra lead required, and then see where he can best draw it from.

10. It has been said that an artist has more than two eyes; the plumber must often wish for a greater sight than he is blessed with, to see where he can get a supply to meet his wants. He can leave on lobes and extra widths, here and there, in his piece of lead, when cutting it out; and he can generally manage to work up feeders from the margins; but, like Oliver Twist, he ever cries for "more."

11. In robbing Peter to pay Paul—in drawing lead from one part to drive it into another—care must be taken not to thin the roadway along which the extra lead has to travel, for it is easier to work up contingents—supplies of lead—through lead $\frac{1}{4}$ in. thick than through lead half that thickness. It is also easier and quicker to work up supplies of lead in the form of wavelets than in the form of driblets; for the lead particles travel better in masses, and in rounded forms, than in detachments or thin lines—better in the shape of a walnut than a wafer.

12. It is no mark of competency to polish up or overdress a piece of work. The skill of the worker is shown at a much earlier stage. Finish off the work without toolmarks, but leave burnishings to the incompetent.

13. The great absence of that noisy music that ever denotes the whereabouts of the plumber when he is on a building, rather proves that he had "no part or lot" in that house which was put together without sound of tool or hammer; but though the plumber can do but little on a roof without making himself heard, he can, when he possesses the skill, so complete his work that no mark of the hammer or any such tool shall be left upon it, and this is the "Hall mark" of a master of his craft.

TABLE *showing relative strengths of Lead in so many pounds per superficial foot for various purposes, and in three gradations.*

	For very great durability.	For great durability.	For fair durability.
	lbs.	lbs.	lbs.
Flats and gutters	8	7	6
Valley gutters	8	7	6
Ditto, where there would be no traffic, and would be screened from the sun . .	7	6	5
Hips and ridges	7	6	5
Tacks to hips and ridges . .	8	7	6
Dormer cheeks	7	6	5
Dormer sills and tops . . .	8	7	6
Torus, curb, and apron-flashing	7	6	5
Step flashings	6	6	5
Wide flashings	7 or 6	6	5
Cover flashings (under 9 in.)	6	5	4
Soakers	5	4	3

CHAPTER VII.

LEAD LAYING (*continued*).

Breaks, Corners, and Cornices.

1.

To boss up a **corner** out of a flat piece of lead, for the stand-up on each side to reach a height of 6 in., and to be of equal thickness all over, a surplus of lead equal to 6 in. by 6 in. must be got rid of. But to boss or work up a **break** for the sides to be of equal height, 6 in., lead just that size (6 in. by 6 in.) is wanted. When, therefore, these two pieces of work are near each other, as they often are, the surplus lead of the corner should be bossed into the want of the break, or as much of it as practicable.

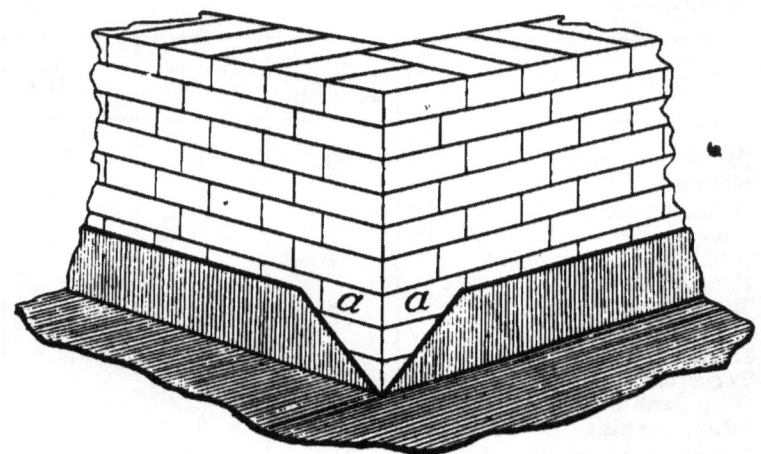

Fig. 7.—SHOWING TRIANGULAR VACANCY IN A CUT BREAK.

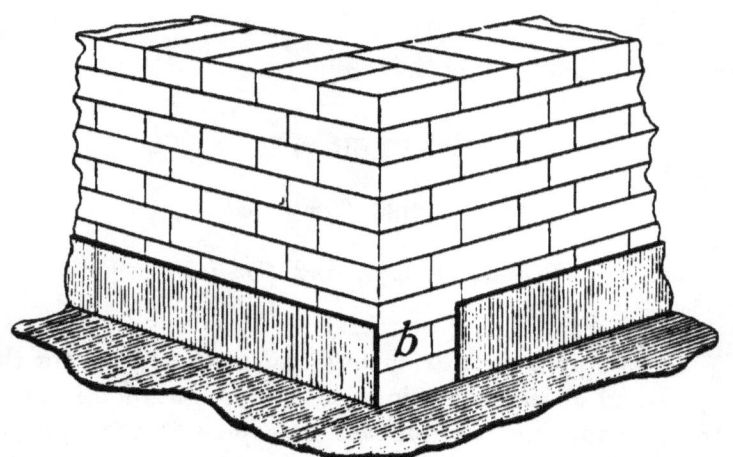

Fig. 8.—SHOWING A SQUARE VACANCY IN A CUT BREAK.

2. If instead of bossing up the break the lead were cut down the angle with a knife, and the sides turned up,

there would be a triangular vacancy on each side of the line of the vertical angle of the break, as shown at *a a*, fig. 7. Or, if instead of cutting the lead down the line of the angle, it were cut through the stand-up part of one of the sides, parallel with the edge of the stand-up of the other side, and along the end of the latter, parallel to and on the line of the horizontal angle, there would be a vacancy 6 in. by 6 in., as shown at *b*, fig. 8.

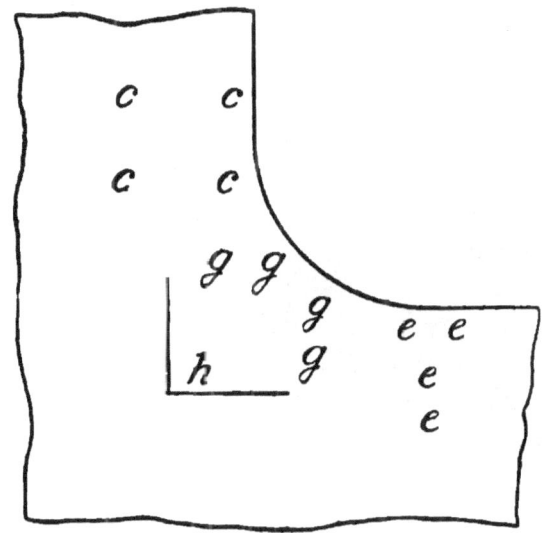

Fig. 9.—SHOWING LEAD FOR BOSSING UP BREAK.

3. The **lead for bossing into a break** is drawn from an extra width of turn-up left for the purpose, as shown in figs. 9 and 10. Some prefer to boss the lead into the break from round about the top, *g g g g*, chiefly using a bossing-stick for the purpose. But this means a tedious bossing of from about an hour-and-a-half to three hours, depending upon the ability of the worker.

By pulling and curling or twisting round the ends a little at *c c* and *e e*, and pouching up the lead at the break at *g g h*, a large amount of lead can be drawn from the sides and worked in waves, with the side of the big mallet, to the break. And in this way, as well as drawing down lead from round about the top, *g g*, the break can be knocked up pretty quickly.

The lead should be pulled up hard at about *g g* with the left hand; and with the right hand, by a series of quick heavy blows with the side of the big mallet (the large end being kept chiefly outwards), lead should be gathered at

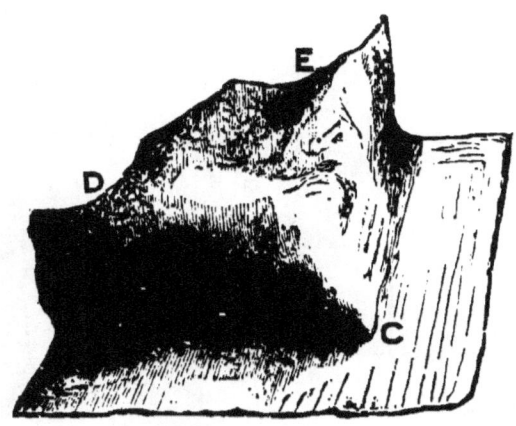

Fig. 10.—Break partly Bossed up.

about *e e e*, and driven round into the break. By repeating this process several times, on both sides of the break, where practicable, and by keeping hard at the work, to keep the lead warm by the friction from a quick succession of blows, it will soon be found that enough lead has been gathered round about the break, as shown in fig. 10, to complete it with a bossing-stick, working the lead down from D and E into the angle of the break, somewhat after the shape of a cocoa-nut, which gives a reserve of lead for working into the angle just before squaring up the sides. When completed, the lead in every part of the break should be left equal in thickness to any other part of the sheet.

To afford plenty of lead for bossing up a break, it is better to cut the piece of lead of which it is to be made much larger than the place it is to fit into, and to set it out for its position, and perform any other bossings upon it, after the break has been bossed up.

In drawing the lead from the sides, care must be taken not to weaken the lower part of the stand-up, or any part of the horizontal angles, or the bottom.

4. To **boss** up a **corner** 6 in. high out of 7 lbs. lead, means half-an-hour's hard labour for the plumber, even if he gets through it in that time, especially if the lead be at all hard; and though no great skill be required to accomplish it, much labour may be saved by intelligent bossing. Some men work hard and do not get up such a corner in an hour.

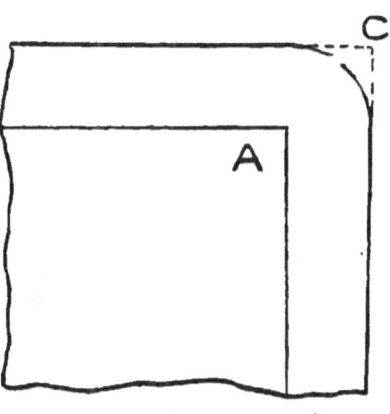

Fig. 11.

5. To avoid unnecessary bossing in working up a corner, it is better to cut off the surplus lead, the corner marked c in fig. 11. Having chalked in the lines on each side of the corner, to show the place of the turn-up, get a straight-edge, or piece of quartering, and lay it down on the line chalked in, and so placed that you can just see the line all the way down; and then, with your mate kneeling upon the quartering at one end and you at the corner end, pull up the side—the stand-up—as hard as you can. Do the same with the other side or end, and cut in the horizontal angles with the hornbeam dresser, using the big hammer

or big mallet to drive it in, and square up the sides. One blow ought to be enough for each dresser length; to repeat the blows only tends to weaken the lead in the angle, where it ought to be kept strong.

6. The horizontal angles next the corner may be just marked in with the edge of the dresser or chase-wedge, though the lead thickens more readily when free from tool-marks, and with a correct eye no such marks are necessary.

7. Begin the bossing upon the projecting or pouched

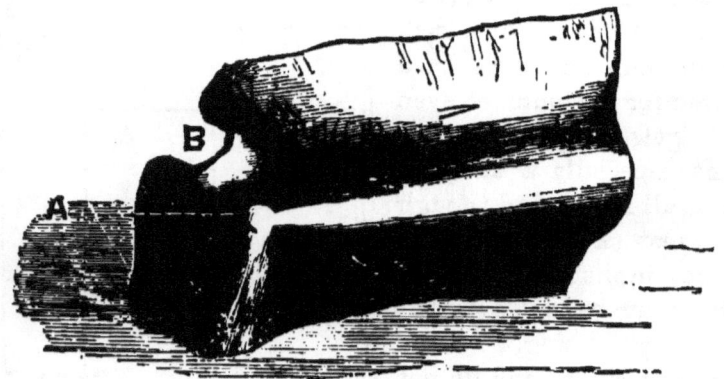

Fig. 12.—SHOWING CORNER PARTLY BOSSED.

corner, standing out like a donkey's ear, about $1\frac{1}{2}$ in. up from the bottom, as shown at A, fig. 12. Work in a little hollow with the thin edge of the bossing-stick, and boss the bulb or surplus lead downwards to thicken the bottom and stiffen the corner and horizontal angles, to prevent the former pulling over in the further bossing. Then drop the bossing-stick, and take two mallets and knock up the corner, keeping the lead circular all the time. When the stand-up is bossed up high enough, the corner should be squared up with two dressers, and finished off.

8. As the durability of **lead coverings to cornices** depends so much upon its freedom to expand and contract,

the pieces of lead should never be put on in very long lengths; and instead of soldering the ends of the pieces together, especially when the weathering of the cornice is outwards, the ends should be seam-welted, or turned over rolls.

9. When a cornice is too wide for the rain to drain to the front, a **channel**, as shown at A, fig. 13, should be cut in the stone top, next the face of the wall, and the top of the cornice weathered back into it. When the stone cornice is deep enough, shallow sinkings can be made where the rain-water is to be taken away, and the lead dressed down into them. The stone channel can often also be so worked that, when the cornices are of great length, a drip may be formed in them here and there. Where the stone is not thick enough to admit of this, the weathering from the edge of the channel should be outwards, and the edges of the lead on this part seam-welted, and the edges in the channel burned or soldered.

10. When the **edge** of the lead is left to **sail over** beyond the cornice, it is nearly always in need of dressing up, for it so frequently gets knocked about with ladders, etc.; nor is the edge of the top of the stone cornice so well protected from the weather as with a turned-down edge.

11. When the **edge** of the lead top is **turned down** over the edge of the fillet of the stone or wood cornice, great care should be taken to carry it down below the bottom edge of the fillet for the rain to run off, or drain away, clear of the mouldings. When the edge of the lead is only just turned round the top edge of the fillet, or when it is dressed round under the bottom edge and into the cyma, the washings of the top run and drain round upon the lead into the mouldings, and down over the walls, leaving dirty stains behind them.

12. The lead at the back of the cornice should be made to stand up against the face of the wall, just high enough

to protect the lower joints of the wall from rain splashes, as shown at A, fig. 13. A separate **lead cover-flashing**

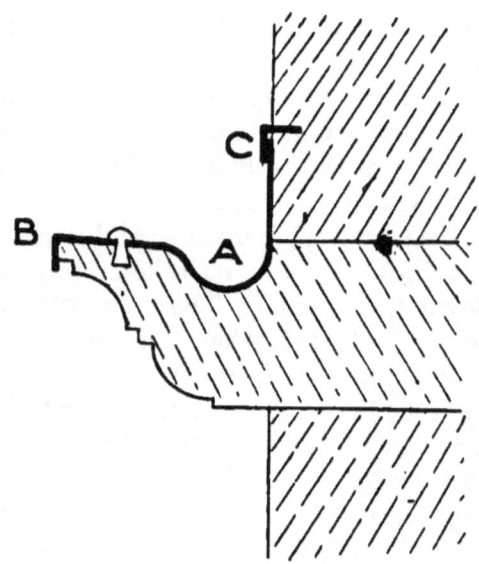

Fig. 13.—SECTION SHOWING LEAD COVERING TO A STONE CORNICE.

(to give better freedom to the lead on the cornice) should be fixed to the stand-up, as shown at C, where practicable.

13. To keep the lead top in position, and to prevent the

Fig. 14.—DOT-MOULD.

wind blowing it up, a few inches back from the front edge, and at intervals of about every 2, 3, or 4 ft., according to circumstances, **lead dowels** should be run into the stone cornice, with hemispherical heads over them (fig. 13) to keep down the lead. These lead dowel-dots are easily run into the stone with molten lead, and formed by using the tool shown in fig. 14. Around the aperture in the lead top for pouring the lead through to the dowel, a little necking should be bossed up to keep out the rain-water, in case the burning should not be perfect when the dot is run in.

CHAPTER VIII.

LEAD LAYING (*continued*).

Cesspools and their Sockets, and Overflows.

1.

PERHAPS no piece of work varies so much in size and shape as a **roof-cesspool**. Many a young plumber, and old plumber too, for that matter, has found to his chagrin that when the many-sided cesspool has been made, and he comes to put it into its place, it is too large or too small, or that he has canted or splayed the wrong side, or that some sides are too deep and others too shallow. And so materials and labour are wasted, or the cesspool is bungled into its place to tell its own tale to every beholder.

2. When a many-sided **cesspool** has to be **bossed** up out of one piece of lead, and the sides are all various in shape and height, it may tax the skill of a good plumber to make it so that it shall fit in every part exactly; but when the angles are allowed to be **soldered**, as they mostly are, it only requires care in setting out to make a cesspool to fit almost any position.

3. Great accuracy is required in taking the dimensions and in **setting out the cesspool** on the piece of lead of

which it is to be made. As it is desirable to have as little soldering as possible, the several ways of cutting out the corners should be computed, to see which way will give the least **angle-soldering**. Great care should be taken to see that the plan of the cesspool—the bottom—is correctly lined out on the piece of lead with a chalk-line before lining or marking in the sides, as no two angles may agree and every one of them may be more or less out of square.

4. Supposing the dotted lines A B, C D, and E F, in fig. 15, to show the bottom of a cesspool, and that the end 1 has to stand up square, with a return of $1\frac{1}{2}$ in. for the rebate of the gutter; that the side 2 stands up vertically 12 in., and then turns back upon the roof 6 in.; and that the side 3, with its return or extended length for the end, A B, C D, stands up 18 in. next a vertical wall, the diagram, fig. 15, shows the best way of cutting out the lead and preparing it for turning up and soldering. The cleats—the parts hatched in the diagram—are simply for the purpose of holding the lead in its place during the angle-soldering; and in order that they may be broken off very readily when the soldering is done, an arrow-shaped groove should be cut with the point of the shavehook along the dotted line next the cleat, and this groove should be well soiled.

5. In fig. 15 the angles of the bottom are all shown square; but whether obtuse or acute, it is easy to mark an exact plan of the bottom of the cesspool on the piece of lead from which the cesspool is to be cut out, by the aid of a bevel; and, in fact, any form of angle, vertical or horizontal, can readily be taken with this instrument and marked upon the lead.

In taking the dimensions of the place that the lead cesspool is to fit into, always allow, in measuring the length and width, etc., of the bottom, for the two thicknesses of the lead of the sides; this is sometimes forgotten, and when the cesspool is made, like some pompous personage, it is found too big for its place.

6. As there is no difficulty in reducing the end of a lead **socket-pipe** to fit into the socket (from which its name is derived) of a cast-iron rain-water pipe—Chapter XXVI.—and especially as it is generally difficult to give a socket-pipe much fall, it is better that it should be of a larger size than the rain-water pipe, for in great storms, where the cesspool is shallow and the socket-pipe small,

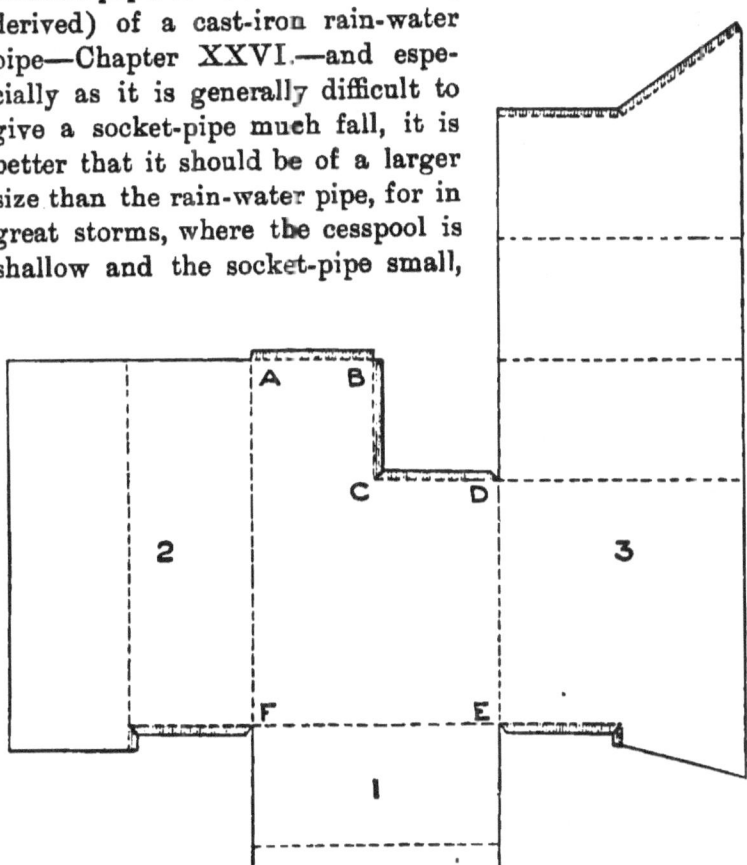

Fig. 15. CESSPOOL SET OUT READY FOR SOILING AND SHAVING.

the water is delivered into the former quicker than it can be taken away by the latter.

7. When the socket-pipe goes out of the bottom of a cesspool there is no difficulty in making the **soldered**

joint. Nor with good arrangement and care should there be any great difficulty in soldering it to any part of the cesspool;—on the face of one of the sides, or bird's-mouth (half on the bottom and half on the side); or partly on the bottom and partly on each of two sides. But when a plumber has had an experience of wiping such joints on cold frosty days, he will know that there is no time to go to sleep over the making of them.

8. The **countersinking** for the jointing should be about ¾ in. deep, and 1¼ in. wide at the top, and the lead of the cesspool well dressed down into it, as shown in section, fig. 16. The end of the pipe should be *rounded* over and dressed down tightly into the countersinking, and not tafted back at right angles, *i.e., flat.* The joint will then not only be stronger, but it will be easier wiped, as the cloth can then be pressed well down upon both edges (the pipe edge and the cesspool edge) at the one wiping. The interior of the pipe should be well soiled from its mouth to a few inches downwards, and the margins round the countersinking should also be well soiled.

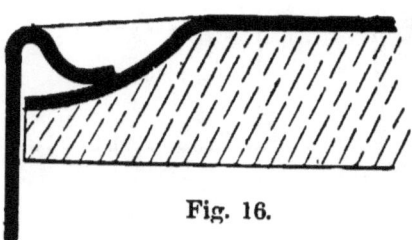

Fig. 16.

9. The edge of the **shaving** on the end of the pipe should be on the ridge or highest part of the rounded edge, and that on the bottom and side, or sides, of the cesspool, at the edge of the countersinking. To get true edges and an equal width of soldering, shave the edges with the shaving half of a pair of compasses. The mouth of the pipe should be well plugged with some dry wood shavings wrapped over with paper to prevent the solder running down the pipe.

10. **To make the joint**, splash or pour on the metal

very rapidly, and get a good body of solder all over and round about the connection; and, with the aid of a properly heated iron, wipe the upper part (the part in the vertical face), first rubbing the iron well over the outer edge, as the solder cools quicker on the upper part and outer edge than on the bottom and inner edge. When the joint is

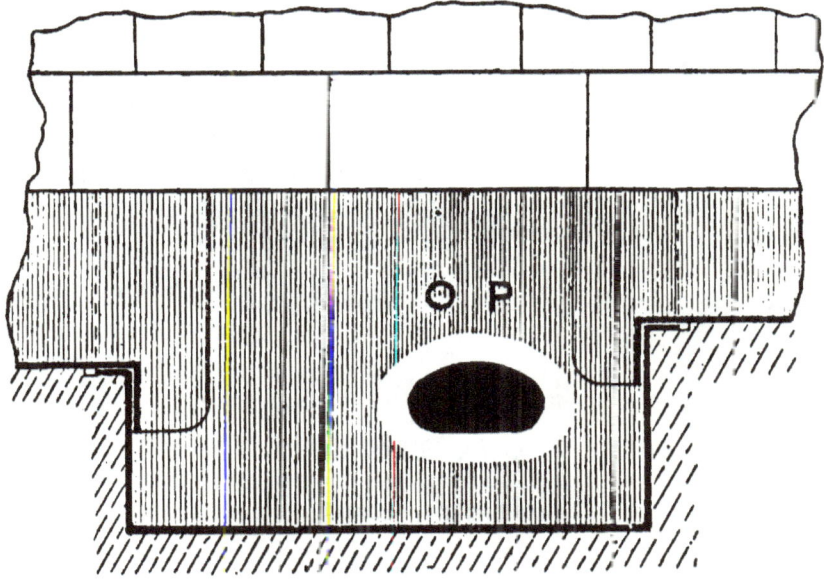

Fig. 17.

wiped, never forget to break up the surplus solder into pieces whilst it is hot, for easy removal.

11. An **overflow-pipe** or **spout**[1] should be fixed to every cesspool where practicable, especially to mansions and churches in the country, where the socket-pipes are liable to get stopped up with leaves, etc. Even if there were no

---

[1] It is difficult to see the wisdom of calling rain-water pipes *spouts*, for though they are generally conspicuous enough, they are silent conductors, and nobody ever sees what is passing through them.

necessity to fix such pipes, it would be a pity in many instances to do away with them; for a gargoyle gives an architect a happy way of relieving the nakedness of flat surfaces and unbroken cornices, as well as affording a means of protecting the walls and rooms of the house from damage by an overflow of rain-water from the cesspool.

To get the best results from such spouts in case of stoppage of the socket-pipe, and to avoid a great reduction in the depth of the cesspool, the mouth of the overflow-pipe should be considerably enlarged, and its lower part flattened, as shown at O P, fig. 17. Of course it is important to fix the overflow-pipe so that the lower part of its mouth shall stand well below the lowest gutter which empties into the cesspool. This is not always done by men, who forget the purpose for which the overflow is fixed.

CHAPTER IX.

LEAD LAYING (*continued*).

Dormers and Drips.

1.

DORMERS are built in a great variety of sizes and shapes, and are placed in all sorts of positions; and they are treated and covered in a great variety of ways. So full of mouldings, wings, and flying ornaments are they at times, especially on the Continent, that one wonders, when looking at them, whether the building has been erected for the sake of the dormers, or the dormers for the building. In these days, when houses are "run up" for one's own occupation, and not for his grandson's, the services of the poor plumber are not much required in connection with dormers, especially when there is much ornament upon them. Zinc is the metal chiefly used. They are made entirely of zinc, or their exteriors are covered with zinc.

2. Dormers are sometimes covered with copper, but oftener with lead. The tops are sometimes covered with slate, but much oftener with tiles, and the sides with lead or zinc; but now that hip and valley tiles are so much in use, the dormer is often handed over to the carpenter and tiler, though the plumber is generally wanted for the cills, if not for the saddle-pieces—the pieces at the apex of the valleys.

3. **Each side of a dormer** may be covered in one piece of lead, or, where this would make too large a piece, two or more pieces should be fixed, and be lapped horizontally, or seam-welted down the middle. To take the weight of the cheeks off the slates or tiles, instead of turning the lead round to flash the roof, it is better to fix soakers, and to let the cheeks form a cover-flashing to them, trimming the edges of the cheeks about 1 in. up from the slates or tiles. If the top edge of the piece or pieces can be turned over upon the edge of a board, and copper nailed, the lead will be held up in its place much better than by soldered-dots, though it may be necessary to fix a secretly soldered lead-tack here and there, at the back of the cheek, to keep it in its place. It is better for such tacks to be kept near the top of a piece, when they have to carry any great weight, for the lead to be suspended upon the tack, like a coat held up by its loop, rather than that the lead should rest upon the tack; for in the latter case the cheek sags down upon the tack, and folds over it in a most unsightly way. Where the cheeks are returned upon the front faces of the uprights their vertical edges can generally be closely nailed with copper nails, and welted. Their lower ends are sometimes bossed round the ends of the sill. In such cases the

wood arrises should be rounded off a little to prevent the sharp edges cutting the lead during the bossing.

4. The **sills**, when of deal, are generally covered with lead; but in any case it is better for a piece of lead to be fixed right under the sill, and for it to be turned up inside, and copper nailed.

5. A **drip**, whether in a gutter or flat, should not be less than $1\frac{1}{2}$ in. deep, and is better 2 in.; and when there is more than one drip, they should not be more than 10 ft. apart.

6. The edge of the upper end of a lead gutter or of a lead bay—*i.e.*, the underlap—should be bossed up and **rebated** its thickness, and $1\frac{1}{2}$ in. wide, into the boards of the drip of the gutter or flat next above it, as shown at *a*, fig. 18. The end of the gutter, which empties into the lower gutter—*i.e.*, the overlap, should be

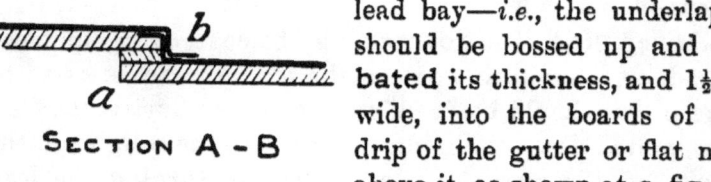

Section A - B

Fig. 18.

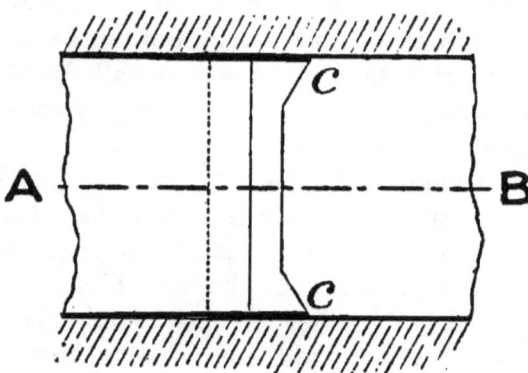

Fig. 19.

worked down into the bottom corners of the drip with care, and made to lay upon the bottom of the gutter, as shown in section *b*, fig. 18, and on plan *c c*, fig. 19.

7. To work the lead down into the corners of a drip, fold over the end of the stand-up upon the part to be bossed down into the corner, and, with two or three sharp blows of the mallet, knock the fold—the lead doubled down—into the corner. Then, with the side of the big mallet, work a supply of lead round into the drips from the upper edge of the stand-up; and as this is worked along with the drifting-plate (R, Plate II.) at the back, to give a smooth surface to work the lead against, the part which had been folded down will open up to the wall again. Having drawn a good supply of lead in this way, on both sides, any further lead required can be worked up from the end of the lead gutter by the mallet and a blunt chase-wedge, and the drip finished off neatly with the sharp one, leaving the lead in the corners of about the same thickness it is in any other part of the gutter.

It is important that, during the whole of the time the lead is being worked into the corner of the drip, the mate should press down hard, with his shoulder upon the holding-down stick, on the edge of the stand-up, directly over the corner.

8. If it is preferred, the lead can be worked up into the corners in waves from the edge of the lay-down upon the gutter bottom; but it will take much longer time this way than by drawing the supply down from the stand-up. As it is easier to work a supply of lead through thick lead than thin, be careful to keep the thoroughfares strong, and work up the supplies in rounded forms, as if you had a Scotch scone, or a section of an orange, or half a walnut, or a tobacco pouch underneath the lead. To prevent friction of two faces of lead, a drifting-plate (R, Plate II.) placed between the two surfaces is very helpful, especially when the lead is wanted to be driven into any place.

9. With splayed edges to the drips the bossing is, of course, much easier; and where there are likely to be

driving rains, and the drips are 2½ in. deep, it is desirable to have splay-drips, as the laps at the sides are greater than with square-drips.

10. In the North it is the custom to finish off the lead at the drip about ½ in. or 1 in. up from the bottom of the gutter, as it is alleged that the wordwork is liable to be rotten, by the water drawn up by capillary attraction, when the overlap is made to lay down upon the bottom of the gutter; but in the South, where some of the most experienced and the most skilful plumbers in the world are to be found, the drips are treated as shown in fig. 19. And no one has ever seen the ends of old gutter boards rotten where the lay-down has been properly done; and one is, therefore, inclined to think that capillary attraction is greater in the North than in the South, or that there is a lack of skill somewhere, for the turn-down of the North only requires about half the skill of the lay-down of the South. With the latter there is a better lap at the sides, a better finish, and a better protection of the gutter boards from the moisture of a saturated atmosphere. And if there are no heavy mists in Scotland, there are some cold winds to blow up between such open lappings. I think it must be conceded, even by the plumbers of the North, that a lay-down to a drip and a roll keeps a house warmer than the simple turn-down over the edge of a drip, and the short covering to a roll.

CHAPTER X.

LEAD LAYING (*continued*).

Flats and Gutters.

1. TO prevent the **boards warping** and curling up at their edges, by the heat of the sun upon the lead flat, they should be of narrow widths and well seasoned; and they should be **nailed down at each edge**, for it not only spoils the appearance of a lead flat to see board-markings showing up through it, but it is detrimental to the lead.

2. The boards should be laid to run the way of the **fall**, and where the place to be covered is of great length, the flat should be so constructed that the drips shall not be more than 10 ft. apart. The fall should not be less than 1½ in. in 10 ft., and the drips about 2 in. deep.

3. The plumber in **setting out the rolls** should so arrange them that where there are skylights, chimneys, or other projections through the flat, the rolls shall come in at the corners of such obstacles, so as to do away with as many breaks as he can; but due regard must be paid to the general appearance of the flat, and the symmetry of the rolls.

4. In planning the position of the rolls, the width of the sheet from which the lead is to be cut should be considered, for it prevents much waste to **split a sheet down the middle**; but the rolls should not be more than about 2 ft. 9 in. apart, and a sheet 7 ft. wide, when split down the middle, will do this very well. (Chap. XII., Art. 20.)

5. The lead in *wider* widths than about 2 ft. 9 in. between the rolls is not so durable as in *narrower* widths.

Under the rays of the sun the middle part of a bay is drawn up to a height sometimes of several inches; and when the rolls are not too far apart, and proper freedom has been allowed for **expansion and contraction,** the lead will go back to its bed again at night, often with a loud report. (Rolls, Chap. XII.)

6. The **rolls** should be continued to **butt with** the

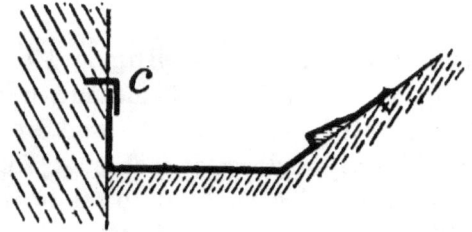

Fig. 20.

end of the drip, or cut off in a line with the face of the gutter. When they are cut off short, ½ in. or so back

Fig. 21.

from the arris of the drip, or arris of the gutter, the wet is sure to get in through the lap at the end of the roll, and rot the woodwork.

7. **A long gutter** with a sloping roof on each side, fig. 21, should have its lowest end only just wide enough for a snow-shovel to move in, as with several drips, and a fall of 1½ in. between the drips, the gutter at its upper end will be too wide for one piece of lead. When the width of a gutter exceeds about 2 ft. 6 in. or 3 ft., especially if ex-

posed to the sun, a roll should be fixed down the middle to reduce the width of any one piece of lead. The drips (Art. 5, Chap. IX.) should not be less than 1½ in., and are better 2 in. deep. They should not be more than 10 ft. apart.

8. The **wood tilt** or edge of the springing should be kept up about 3 or 3½ in. from the sole of the gutter, and the lead continued up to go under the slates or tiles 6 in. beyond it, as shown in figs. 20 and 21. In roof-gutters to churches, where heavy falls of snow often remain for some

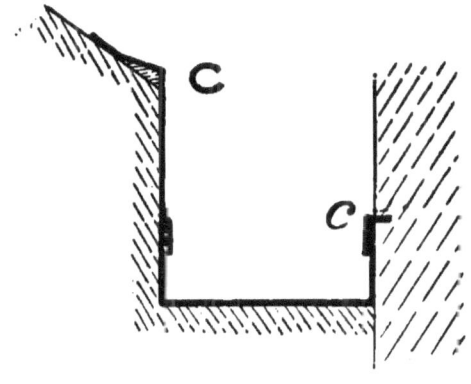

Fig. 22.

time before they are cleared, the springing should be kept up 4 or 5 in. from the bottom of the gutter, and the drips should be deeper, 2½ in. or 3 in. deep.

9. When in **deep gutters** a side or the sides of a gutter are vertical, and of wood, to be covered with lead, it is better to fix apron-flashings to them, rather than continue up the stand-up of the gutter to flash itself, as shown at c, fig. 22. This apron-flashing, when more than about 9 in. deep vertically, should be welted at the ends, and not lapped. (Chap. XIV., Art. 15.)

10. Where flats and gutters abut against brick or stone

walls, or other vertical faces, the lead should be turned up against such faces to stand a height of 6 in., as shown at *c*, fig. 22, so that, with a proper cover-flashing over the **stand-up**, there may be no risk from rain-splashings, rain-water, or snow-water. In some positions, where the sun has access to one part of a flat, or one part of a gutter, and not to another, snow is often melted into little pools where it cannot run away; and in such cases, where the stand-up is very low, or where the drips are shallow, the snow-water finds an easy way into the interior. (Chap. XIV., Art. 18.)

CHAPTER XI.

LEAD LAYING (*continued*).

Hips and Ridges, and Laps and Passings.

1.

HIPS AND RIDGES.—Like the Siamese twins, it is difficult to separate the one from the other. The hip should be divided into equal parts, but no piece of lead should exceed 10 ft., and is much better about one-third less. The width to go round the roll can easily be taken by a strip of lead, and marked with a chalk-line upon the lead, allowing 6 in. on each side—or whatever width may be specified—for the lay-down upon the slates.

2. The **wood-roll** should be so fixed that the wings or roof-flashing may key well under it, and for this purpose the bottom of the roll must be kept up about $\frac{1}{2}$ in. above the line of the top of the slates. When the roll has been fixed higher than necessary, and the plumber cannot get the carpenter to lower it, he should not attempt to make

two horizontal angles, as in forming the one he will destroy the trueness of the other. What he has to do is to see that the lead clips the roll very tightly, and that he secures it there by a proper tacking of the wings.

3. To avoid indentations and tool-marks the lead should be carefully dressed over before it is turned up. Two lines should be struck upon the face of the lead, to show where the wings on both sides of the roll are to be turned up, and a chalk-line should be struck midway between these lines to show the middle part of the roll. The **sides** or wings should then be **turned up** at right angles, and the roll angles cut in with the hornbeam dresser and big hammer. At any part of the hip or ridge where there is to be any bossing, at a roll-end or intersection, the angles should not be cut in.

4. **In fixing the lead in its place**, with the plumber at one end of it and his mate at the other, the turned-up lead (looking like a trough gutter) is lifted up at one end and banged down with a considerable degree of hardness, and then the other end is treated in a similar way. After one or two bangs, the middle chalk-line being kept true with the middle of the roll, the wing on one side of the roll is pressed down with the hands, and then the wing on the other side, and the angles driven in under the roll.

5. Great care should be taken to cut the **angles** in truly, and this is readily done by keeping the edge of the dresser (the hornbeam dresser) straight, and pressing its side, as a guide, tight against the roll at every stroke of the big hammer or big mallet. If this is done properly there will be no necessity to use the dresser upon the roll, and the hip will look as straight and smooth as a gun-barrel. When the hip is conspicuous from the ground, the underlap should be countersunk into the roll.

6. The top end, or **underlap**, of each piece of lead should be nailed with about half-a-dozen *strong* copper

nails, or *stout* iron clout nails; but in most cases the nails to the ridge-lead may be a couple less. The laps to the ridge should be 6 in., but they may be a little less to the hip, though 6 in. laps throughout are best.

7. In **bossing down the end of a hip roll**, be careful not to split the lead at the top of the roll-end, or in the angles of the roll. If the roll be a large one, 3 in. or larger, take off the arris the keenness of the end of the wood-roll with a pocket-knife, chisel, or rasp, and boss down the lead with a small mallet, beginning a little way out from the end of the roll, in order to work back an extra thickness upon the top of the roll-end, to strengthen that part for the further bossing. Open out the lead at its end with your hands, and work it back towards the roll. In continuing the bossing keep the lead from buckling, using a dummy inside if necessary, and remember that all that is wanted is a disc of lead not equal in area to half the surplus lead at your command.

8. To work down the overcloak at the **intersection** of the hips with the ridge, be careful to have an extra width of lead round about such points, and see that there are no nail-heads in the underlaps to cut through the lead at the points of the bossing. Lift up the end of the overlapping ridge-piece and bang it down several times, as if you would drive and jerk all the lead into the many corners before you begin the bossing. And then when you begin the bossing, with a small mallet, keep the underside of the lead up from the ridge, as by this means, when the bossing is nearly done, you can work the extra lead which this will give you round to the underside of the roll at the very place it is wanted, to thicken the lead in the corners of the intersections, and to keep it there. This is best done with a box-wood dresser and mallet, the mate pushing up the side or wing all the time with his stick. The lead for working up into the intersections can be drawn from the margins

and from the end of the ridge, working it up towards the end of the bossing with the blunt chase-wedge, and finishing it off with the sharp one and box-wood dresser.

9. The sides or wings should be secured in their positions by **lead tacks** 2½ in. or 3 in. wide, of a strength 1 lb. to the superficial foot stronger than the lead of the hips and ridges, and about 2 ft. 6 in. apart to the former, and 3 ft. 6 in. apart to the latter. The tacks should be nailed by two stout clout nails to the wood hip; and in trimming the edges of the sides they should be notched into them, to give a straight line to the edges, and turned down upon the lead about ¾ in. Where there is likely to be any traffic, or where there are great winds, the turn-round of the tack would be better welted. (See Tacks, Chap. XIV.)

10. To secure lead **hips** to Mansard roofs, or to roofs of **great pitch**, where the lead is nearly vertical, a lead tack, of a sufficient width to clip round the roll and about 6 in. long, should be **soldered** or burned to the underside of the lead, and the tack turned round upon the wood-roll, and secured on both ends by stout copper screws, three or four to a side. The wood-roll should be countersunk to receive the thickness of the solder and of the tack, which should be of 8 lb. lead, to further add to the support of the lead hip, and to prevent the appearance of any tack on the external face of the roll. The tacks should be not more than about 2 ft. 6 in. apart, to hips of 7 lb. lead.

11. **Laps or Passings** generally.—Hips and ridges, curb and step-flashings, and narrow apron-flashings, should have a lap of 6 in., though for step-flashings and hips, where the roof has a sharp pitch, a little less suffices. In narrow cover-flashings to the stand-up of flats and gutters, a lap in the flashing of 4 in. is all that is necessary; for the lap of the flashing upon the stand-up of the flat or gutter, 2½ in. or 3 in. will do very well.

The overlap in cover or horizontal flashings to flats and

gutters should be cut in a line with the edge of the overlap of the drip. In exposed positions the edge of the overlap should be made to stand northwards or eastwards, and not towards the south-west, for the driving rains to drive between the laps. (See Welts, Chap. XIV., Art. 16.)

12. For **lead bays to roofs**, where there are no drips, and the sides are too long to cover in single lengths, the **lap**, when the fall is about 1 ft. in 3 ft., should not be less

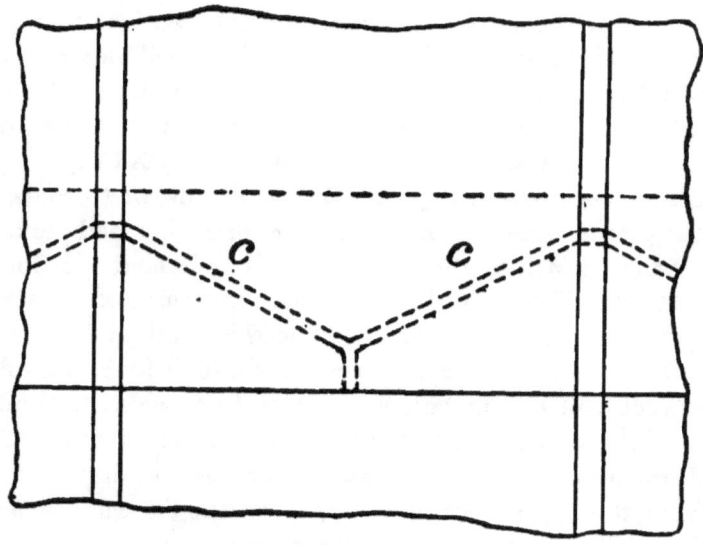

Fig. 23.

than about 12 in.; and even with such a lap capillary attraction is so great that it is better to cut condensation channels in the boarding, and dress the underlap into them, as shown by the dotted lines c c, fig. 23. The contact between the two surfaces will thus be broken, and the capillary attraction retarded. The capillary attraction between the surfaces of the roll-laps can easily be interrupted, if not entirely prevented, by making a hollow ring round the underlap of the roll, about 8 in. or 9 in. up from the edge of the overlap, as shown in fig. 23. In the case of a wood-roll, a hollow, $\frac{3}{4}$ in. wide and $\frac{1}{2}$ in. deep, can be cut with a gouge, and the underlap dressed down into it; and in the case of a seam-roll, a hollow ring can be formed in the roll with a chase-wedge.

CHAPTER XII.

LEAD LAYING (*continued*).

ROLLS AND BAYS.

Wood-Rolls—Bossed Ends—Intersections—Seam-Rolls—Copper Tacks and Lead Bays.

1. FOR flats and lead coverings to **roofs** with **slight falls**, wood-rolls are better than seam-rolls, as the former not only resist foot traffic better, but are easier to dress up again when damaged, and they are also cheaper.

2. For lead coverings to **roofs with a high pitch**, as cathedrals and churches, etc., where the weight of the lead ever tends to drag the bays downwards, seam-rolls are stronger and more durable than wood-rolls, and they have also a much better appearance.

3. With **wood-rolls** there is nothing to support the lead overcloak except its clip round the roll, which on the southern side of a roof is ever being loosened by the heat of the sun. But with **seam-rolls** the overcloak is *welted* to the undercloak, and there is not only this clip of the edges, but there is also the friction of the two faces of the turned roll, the *grip* of the overcloak upon the undercloak over the entire roll, and which will never be entirely re-

linquished, no matter how hot the sun may be upon the leads. Then the side of the overcloak is further held in position by being welted and bound together with the undercloak by *copper tacks*. A well-tacked and a well-turned seam-roll will last for centuries.

4. For keeping out the rain, a seam-roll need not be so large as a wood-roll when covered. A *seam-roll* $1\frac{1}{2}$ *in. diameter* is large enough for most roofs; $1\frac{1}{4}$ in. is better for small roofs and domes.

5. A **wood-roll** should be **deeper** than it is **wide**, as shown in section, fig. 24, to give room for the lead of the overcloak to key well under it. If a wood-roll on a flat, when covered, measures about $1\frac{3}{4}$ in. across, and stands about 2 in. high, it will look bold and answer very well.

6. The **undercloak** should be turned up round the roll and terminated just under the shoulder on the opposite side, *i.e.*, about $1\frac{1}{4}$ in. or $1\frac{1}{2}$ in. beyond the middle of the top of the roll, and its edge feathered off with a rasp or shavehook, and nailed with strong copper nails (or iron clouts) about 9 in. apart. In some cases it is insisted upon that the undercloak shall be continued down to the bottom of the roll, and it must be conceded that this gives more friction of the two faces, for holding up the overcloak side of the bay. But many plumbers are content simply to turn up the undercloak to reach about one-third round the roll, instead of about two-thirds or three-fourths.

7. The **overcloak** should be drawn tightly round the roll and well keyed under it, and a lay-down should be left upon the flat 1 in. or $1\frac{1}{4}$ in. wide (depending somewhat upon the size of the roll), as shown at A, fig. 24.

In turning the overcloak round the roll keep the lead free from bruises and tool-marks. Press the stand-up round with your hands, and then with a round roll of wood and big hammer drive the lead in under the roll as far as it will go. Then with the edge of the wood dresser complete the angle, keying in the overcloak tightly. If this is properly done there will be no need to use the dresser upon the upper part of the roll.

8. **Bossed Ends.**—The expert finds no difficulty in working down the end of a roll, either the butt end or the open end, though some men never become adepts at it.

9. To boss down the **end** of the **overcloak** of a 1½ in. or 2 in. roll ought not to be a work of more than five minutes, though many men are content if they accomplish it in a quarter of an hour, and some men take half-an-hour.

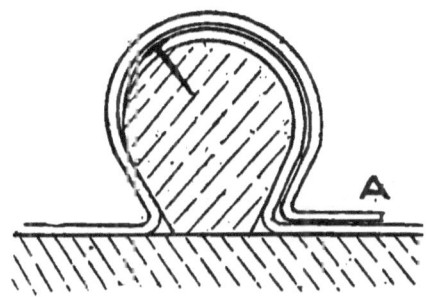

Fig. 24.

Instead of bossing down a lot of surplus lead to cover a disc 1¾ in. diameter with a bossing-stick, or tapping it down with a very little mallet over a dummy held up under the lead, open out the end of the lead roll with your hands, and work the lead round the roll-end with the large end of the small mallet, working the surplus lead off to the lay-down side of the roll. A quick succession of blows, like the rat, tat, tat, tat of a doctor's knock upon a door, and the thing is done. Then finish off the end with a box-wood dresser and mallet, and turn to the more difficult work of bossing down the other end of the roll, the end next the wall.

10. To boss and dress the overcloak round the **end of a roll** where it **butts** against a wall. Before laying the bay, boss and prepare the end to fit about half way round the roll, leaving all the surplus lead you can for working into the other half *in situ*. Pouch up the overcloak, for the corner to slide in over the roll, a few inches away from the end, when putting the bay into its place. The roll having been turned and completed, the overcloak of the butt end will then be ready for completion. Press and work down with your hands a good supply of lead from the stand-up, and any further lead required can be worked up in waves from the lay-down in the flat. With care and a little skill the lead right in the corner can be left just as thick as in any part of the bay.

11. The important thing to be observed for working the overcloak over the junction of many rolls, is to see that enough lead is left upon the piece for working up under the rolls at their points of **intersection**.

12. Before beginning the bossing, where practicable, lift up the overcloak and bang it down as hard as possible a time or two, for it to take the shape of the rolls. Pouch up the lead between the rolls, and work the pouches up into the intersections, using a mallet and also a chase-wedge for the purpose. It is also advantageous to keep the overcloak a little way up from the rolls, just at the intersections, as towards the completion of the bossing it will afford some spare lead for working round to the under part of the roll, where it is likely to be much wanted. The end of the lead over the top of each roll can be cut down as far as the line for the trimming, and a circular hole made to prevent it splitting farther. This will give greater freedom to the lead for working it down upon the flat, and for working it up under the rolls.

13. The **edge** of the **lay-down** should be trimmed to run parallel with the roll. A slovenly trimmed edge is a

disgrace to the plumber. One of the legs of a pair of compasses stuck into a narrow wood guide, about 2½ in. or 3 in. long, as shown in fig. 25, and the point of the other half of the compasses for scribing upon the lead, will give a good line to cut to. The wood guide is drawn down in the angle of the finished roll, and the trimming-line is scribed upon the lay-down of the overcloak, the pair of compasses being held at right angles with the roll.

14. The side of the lead bay which is to form the **undercloak** of a **seam-roll** should be turned up about 3¾ in. (dependent, of course, upon the size the roll is to be), and should be made perfectly true in the entire length of its edge and horizontal angle. To get rid of any irregularity in the edge of the stand-up, run a lead-plane over it, J, Plate I.

15. **Copper tacks** for securing the lead in its place should be fixed against the stand-up, with their bottom ends turned round and screwed into the boarding, into which they should be countersunk, as shown at C T, fig. 26. The tack is shown secured to the boarding directly under the turned roll in

Fig. 25.

figs. 26 and 27, but in practice this cannot always be managed. The top ends should be well notched down into the edge of the stand-up of the overcloak, and turned round upon the opposite face for a depth of about ½ in., to well clip the lead, as shown by the thick line in fig. 26. The tacks should be cut out of about 22 oz. copper, *i.e.*, about $\frac{1}{32}$ in. thick, and should be about 3 in. wide. The number of the tacks in a roll, *i.e.*, their distance apart, must depend upon the weight they have to carry, and upon the pitch of the roof. In sharp pitches there should be a tack about every 18 in., with three stout copper screws to each. For a slight slope a tack every 2 ft., or every 2 ft. 6 in., with the same number of screws, three to a tack, gives good security.

16. Having secured the stand-up of the undercloak, turn up the stand-up for the **overcloak** in the bay next to it, and see that it stands about 1¼ in. higher than the undercloak. Bring the two stand-ups together and welt them. In turning the edge of the overcloak over upon the edge of the undercloak, to form the welt, care must be taken to leave a space of about ¼ in. between the edge of the undercloak and the place of the folding, for when the roll is formed the overcloak will describe a larger circle than the undercloak. Where this is not provided for, the horizontal angle of the overcloaking bay will be drawn up from the boarding, and to get it down again the lead on that side of the roll will be much weakened.

17. The **roll** can be **turned** with the use simply of a mallet and a box-wood dresser, but it is very helpful to turn the welted edge round upon a piece or length of wood-roll; and the roll is

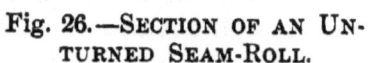

Fig. 26.—SECTION OF AN UNTURNED SEAM-ROLL.

also useful to drive against the lower part of the stand-up, to give it a rounded form. One or two sharp blows of the big hammer or mallet upon the wood-roll suffices for this. Instead of turning the roll and finishing it off bit by bit, it is better to turn the entire length over together gradually. And the less it is dressed and knocked about the quicker it will be finished, and the better will be its appearance.

18. For **domes** and ogee-shaped roofs. Having symmetrically divided out the bays, and marked the exact positions of the rolls upon the roof, line out on a piece of lead the bay best to start with, and turn up its two sides, the undercloak and the overcloak. Then, without attempting to shape the bay to the form of the roof, take the piece of lead up to its place, and whilst your mate holds one end firmly over its position, lift up the other end and bang it down as hard as you can, keeping your hands upon the stand-ups when banging it down; then let your mate treat his end in the same way. Keep banging down

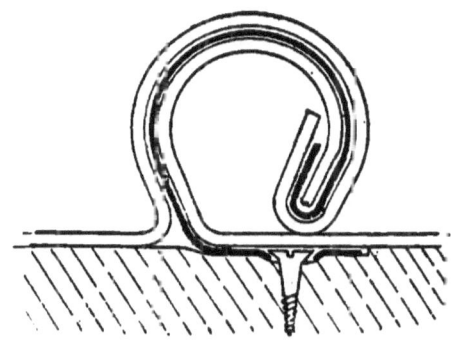

Fig. 27.—SECTION OF A SEAM-ROLL.

the ends in this way alternately, until the bay falls into its proper place, and the stand-ups stretch or contract as required. Square up the undercloak, and prepare the next bay in a similar way.

Bring the two bays together, welt the edges, and turn the roll, and so on till the dome or roof is covered.

19. To keep a **seam-roll of uniform size** right throughout its length, when one part is dressed into a concave and another over a convex, the stand-up of the former should be a little wider than that of the latter. It is important to remember this, especially where a seam-roll

has to be formed in a great hollow, or in an angle, as in turning the roll round into such recesses the stand-up contracts very much.

20. **Seam-rolls** on **high-pitched roofs** should not be more than 20 in. apart, or 2 ft. apart, so that **sheets** 7 ft. wide, or sheets 8 ft. wide, may be cut into three **bays**. And this will give great durability to the leadwork, as the tacks will be better able to support the lead in such narrow widths, and good freedom will be given for expansion and contraction.

Where it is important that the rolls should be kept even closer together than about 20 in., though such circumstances can scarcely occur, the bays can be cut across the sheet to any width required, and the width of the sheet, 7 ft. (or 8 ft.), made the length of the piece.

21. **Lead Bays.**—Apart from the support afforded by the rolls, and by the secret tacks of a seam-roll, each piece of lead on a flat with a great fall, each piece on the side of a sloping roof, and more especially each piece on a roof with a high pitch, should have a good means of keeping itself in position.

Where a portion of the top edge cannot be turned down into a notch cut in the boarding and nailed, a secret lead tack can generally be soldered to the underside of the lead, and the end of this tack pushed and wedged into an opening made in the roof-boarding for the purpose. Such tacks should be kept well up towards the top end of the piece of lead, for the bay to be suspended from it rather than rest upon it, as in the latter case the lead would in time buckle or sag down upon it, and show a fold or cord-crease on the surface of the bay.

CHAPTER XIII.

LEAD LAYING (*continued*).

Step-Flashings, Secret Gutters, and Soakers.

1.

FOR keeping out the rain on the sides of sloping roofs, where the slates or tiles butt against brick walls, or against chimneys, or other wall projections through roofs, **step-flashings** are generally fixed. The step-flashing may be complete in itself, *i.e.*, it may, and generally does, return upon the roof, to lay 6 in. upon the slates or tiles, as well as to stand up 6 in. against the wall, with the edges of its steps turned an inch into the joints of the brickwork. Or a step-flashing may simply have to cover the stand-up of a secret gutter, or the turn-up sides of soakers, terminating in these cases about ½ in. up from the slates or tiles.

2. Where a side of roof butts against a wall at an acute angle with the ridge, *i.e.*, where the rain in running down the roof runs towards the wall, **soakers**, or a **secret gutter**, should be fixed; for no matter what width of lay-down might be given to the step-flashing, it would not be wide enough to keep out the rain which would run under the lead only too readily, to rot the rafters if nothing worse.

3. Instead of fixing step-flashing, with a lay-down upon the slates or tiles, to **roofs much exposed** to driving rains from the south-west, it is better to fix soakers, with a simple cover step-flashing over them, to all walls, chimneys, and wall projections through roof.

4. The **width of** the lay-down of **step-flashing** upon

the slates or tiles should be 6 in., and the height of the stand-up against brickwalls 6 in. or 7 in. The height of a stand-up to a stone wall, where the joints are wide apart, should be an inch or two wider, from 7 in. to 9 in., according to circumstances.

5. In **rubble-work**, where the joints are irregular, and especially where the stones are not faced behind the flashing, it is better to fix the side-flashings in separate pieces, turning each step well into the joint of the stones.

6. Having turned up the side of a piece of lead (which should not be much more than about 7 ft. long) to stand against the wall, leaving 6 in. on the other side to flash the roof, chalk in a line about $2\frac{1}{4}$ in. up to mark the inner edge of the step—the water-channel line; and also chalk in another line, about $3\frac{1}{2}$ in. or 4 in. from the other line, to mark the outer edge. Take the turned-up piece of lead round to its place, and with a straight-edge placed against the face of the stand-up and along the bottom edge of the joint of the brickwork, scribe in a thin line (between the two lines chalked in to show the points of the edges) to mark where each step is to be turned.

Each step in the entire length of the piece of lead having been carefully marked, lay the back side of the stand-up down on a plank, and mark in with the point of one of the legs of a pair of compasses the diagonal lines between the steps. Cut the steps out with a pair of shears or with a sharp pocket-knife, leaving a piece of lead $\frac{3}{4}$ in. wide to each step, for turning into the joint of the brickwork. For stone walls—rubble-work—the turn-in of the separate pieces should be more, $1\frac{1}{4}$ in. or $1\frac{1}{2}$ in. The edges for turning into the joints can be turned with a small box-wood dresser, dressing and turning the lead back upon a wood dresser; but they are quicker and better turned with a proper turning tool, as fig. 28.

When the flashing has been nicely dressed up and the

turned edges of the steps well squared, take the lead to its place and fix it, securing each step with a lead wedge (or with a wood wedge where lead cannot be afforded); but in driving in the wedges be very careful not to knock the faces of the steps with any tool. Turn the lead tacks to keep the lay-down in its place, and come away, for he who dresses step-flashing against the face of a wall to show the irregularities of the brickwork behind it, is a fool for his pains.

7. A **secret gutter**, fig. 29, is a piece of lead, sometimes nearly invisible, fixed under tiles or slates on the sloping sides of a roof, where they butt against a wall. The sole of the gutter (C G) varies in width from about $1\frac{1}{2}$ in. to

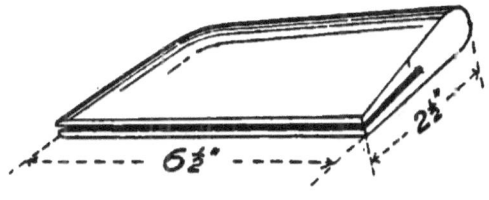

Fig. 28.

3 in., but in the former width it is difficult to get tools into it to form it. The bottom of the gutter on the roof side is formed by turning the lead over a narrow woodspringing or tilting-piece, about $\frac{3}{4}$ in. or 1 in. deep, and $1\frac{1}{2}$ in. or 2 in. wide; or it may be turned back upon a rafter and the edge welted, as shown in fig. 29. The lead is turned up against the wall 4 in., 5 in., or 6 in. high, according to circumstances, with a narrow cover-flashing over it, as shown at C F; or where the wall is of brick, it would of course be stepped.

Though a secret gutter be out of sight, it is not always out of mind, for its water-way, or water-course, often gets blocked up with bits of mortar, broken tiles, or other foreign matter, as leaves, etc. In most cases a simple

F

soaker worked in with each tile or slate, and a cover-flashing over it stepped into the joints of the brickwork, or grooved into the stone, is all that is necessary to make a roof sound and water-tight.

8. **Soakers** are not beer-logged beings, but pieces of lead (or zinc) for keeping out liquid. Quantity surveyors as well as plumbers often make great mistakes in calculating the quantity of lead required for soakers. Where a roof butts against a wall a soaker is used with each slate or tile. The soaker varies in size both in its length and width, according to the character of the roof, and the narrow or expansive ideas of the architects and plumbers concerned in the matter.

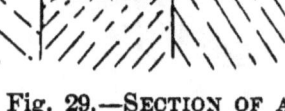

Fig. 29.—SECTION OF A SECRET GUTTER.

The soaker is usually turned up for one-half of its width to go under the slates, and the other half to stand up against the wall, and is cut out long enough to reach the rafter to which it is nailed (by the slater), and sometimes long enough for the end of the soaker next but one above it to lap a little over its edge, as well as to receive the long overlap of its next soaker. Soakers for slates are generally longer than those for tiles. As tiles are thicker than slates, the width of the stand-up of the soakers should be wider for the latter than for the former, even if a little less width be turned under the tiles to make up for the difference.

Soakers are generally cut out of 4 lb. sheet lead, when they are not of zinc, varying in size from 10 in. by 10 in., 10 in. by 9 in., 9 in. by 8 in., to even 9 in. by 7 in.

The number of soakers required to the side of a roof depends upon the number of the slates, which depends upon the lap to be given to the slates or tiles; and the length of the lap to slates and tiles depends upon the slope of the roof, and also upon the decision of the architect. In high-pitched roofs the laps can be less than in roofs of gentle slope.

To arrive at the number of soakers required, deduct the lap from the length of the slate or tile to be used, and see how many times half the remainder (the exposed surface of the tile) will go between the ridge and eaves, and the number of times will give the number of soakers; *e.g.*, the length from the eaves to the ridge is 20 ft., and the roof is to be covered with tiles $10\frac{1}{2}$ in. long, and to have a lap of 3 in.: $10\frac{1}{2}$ in. $-$ 3 in. $= 7\frac{1}{2}$ in., which $\div$ into two equal parts will give $3\frac{3}{4}$ in. into 20 ft., will go just 64 times, which will be the number of soakers required. Supposing the roof to be covered with slates 20 in. long with a $2\frac{1}{2}$ in. lap: 20 in. $-$ $2\frac{1}{2}$ in. $= 17\frac{1}{2}$ in., the half of $17\frac{1}{2}$ in. is $8\frac{3}{4}$ in., $8\frac{3}{4}$ in. into 20 ft. $= 27\frac{15}{35}$, giving 27 soakers and nearly the $\frac{15}{35}$th of another—which in practice would be 28 soakers as the required number. The scores of students who attempted this question in my written paper of questions in 1890, if they honour me by reading this, will see how much they were out in their answers.

CHAPTER XIV.

LEAD LAYING—(*continued*).

Etcetera.

1.

FOR securing hip, ridge, curb, and apron-flashings in their places, **lead tacks** should be fixed $2\frac{1}{2}$ in. or 3 in. wide, and of a strength 1 lb. to the superficial foot heavier than the flashing. One end of the tack should be nailed to the wood hip, ridge, or boarding with two stout iron clouts or three strong copper nails; and the other end should be turned round upon the face of the flashing about $\frac{3}{4}$ in., to well clip it.

2. A tack is rendered much stronger by welting its return edge to the flashing, as shown in section, fig. 30. Where the edge of the tack is not welted it should be notched its thickness into the edge of the flashing, to keep its position better, and also to give a straight edge to the trimming. When the **tack is welted**, the edge of the welting should be arranged to come exactly in a line with the edge of the flashing, especially when the flashing is much seen, to give a straight line to the edges of the flashing.

3. **Tacks** to **straight-flashings**—to gutter-flashing and to the stand-up of flats—may be of the same strength as the flashing. One end, about 1 in. deep, is turned down inside the stand-up of the gutter or flat, and the other end is made to clip round about $\frac{3}{4}$ in. upon the flashing, with its corners cut off for the sake of appearance. A tack about every 3 ft. or 3 ft. 6 in. answers very well.

4. Where, for the sake of appearance, it is desirable not to fix a thick tack under a flashing, as in the case of dormer cheeks, etc., and also for extra strength, **copper tacks** should be used, and their ends welted to the flashing.

5. A **secret tack** is a piece of lead or copper soldered at one end to the back or under side of a lead apron, dormer cheek, or bay, and nailed or screwed at the other end to the boarding. The tack should be of a size best suited for its work, and it may have to be so soldered that it shall pass through a horizontal joint or a vertical joint of the boarding; or a notch may be made in a board and the end of the tack pushed through, just where it is most wanted, and nailed or screwed on the inner side of the boarding.

6. A **torus** is chiefly fixed to the sides and ends of a roof-flat to give it an architectural finish; but it is often wrongly covered with lead. In some cases the ends of the lead bays are carried right round the torus and continued upon the slates! In others the apron-flashing is not only made to flash the slates, but is also continued up around the torus. In the former case the rain in time is sure to work its way through some of the many laps and rot the wood; and in the latter case the lead is sure to crack, and to get much out of shape with the expansion and contraction that will be constantly going on where it is much exposed to the sun.

In either of the foregoing methods it is difficult to fix tacks or means which shall keep the lead tight up against the under side of the torus.

7. The apron **curb** or lead **flashing** to the slates, should be fixed first, and this and the lead for the torus can be 1 lb. to the superficial foot lighter than the flats, supposing the latter to be 7 lb. lead. The apron-flashing can be fixed in lengths from 7 to 10 feet, and the ends bossed to

form the undercloaks and overcloaks to the hips, where the latter intersect with the curb. The apron should be nailed to the wood curb at its upper edge, and the lower edge, the lay-down upon the slates, should be held in position by lead tacks.

8. Where a **torus** is of **great length** it must be covered

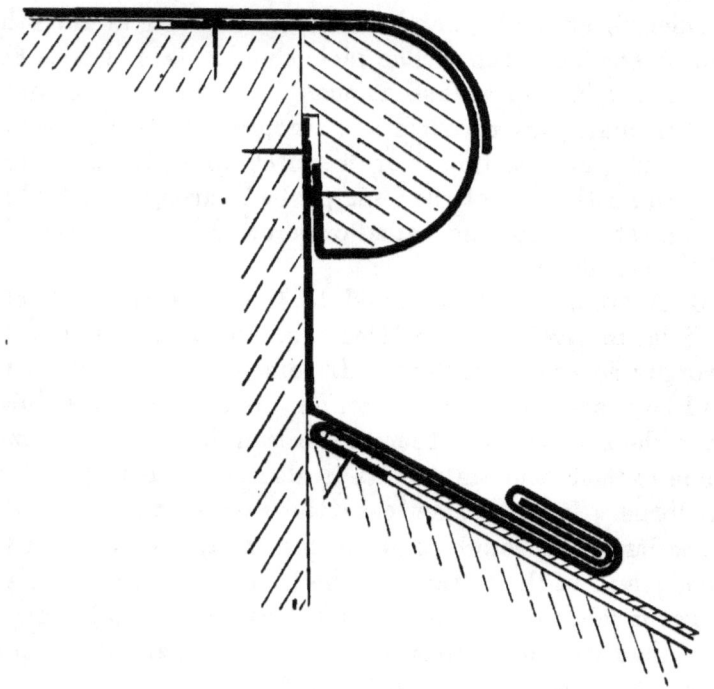

Fig. 30.—Lead Flashing to Torus.

in **pieces** 8 or 10 feet long. The lower part of the back of the torus must be rebated to allow for the thickness of the stand-up of the apron (unless that is carried right up to the surface of the wood-flat), and for the thickness of the turn-round of the covering to the torus.

The lead should be nailed to the lower part of the back side of the wood torus, and turned round to the front; the torus should then be fixed in its proper place and well nailed. The lead should then be tightly pulled round over the torus and dressed on to the edge of the wood-flat, into which it should be rebated and nailed, as shown in section, fig. 30.

9. The **ends** of the **lead bays** of the flat should be continued round to a little below the middle of the torus. For the sake of appearances, the end of the rolls should be spill-topped, *i.e.*, tapered down, but not to too fine a point, and the points should terminate just where the rounded part of the torus begins. Where seam-rolls are formed, the rolls may be continued round the torus to the edge of the bays.

10. Where there are no roof-runs, no roof-steps, or roof-ladders, **lead valleys** form a fair means for climbing from one roof to another.

11. The tilting-fillet or wood-springing is generally fixed about 3 in. up from each side of the wood valley; and the lead is laid in lengths from 7 to 10 ft., and carried up over the tilting edges to stand from 4 to 6 in. under the slates, according to circumstances.

12. When a roof of high pitch meets a roof of low pitch, the wood tilting-piece on the side of the valley of the latter roof should be a little deeper than ordinarily, deeper than if both roofs were of one pitch; and the edge of the valley gutter on the side of the lower roof should be turned round, as a further protection, and welted.

13. To the roofs of country mansions, where there is a good bit of traffic over them in repairing chimneys, slates, and parapets, and in clearing away the scattered leaves of autumn and the heavy snows of winter, it is better that the valley gutters should have **bottoms** to them, 6 or 7 in. wide. The laps in either case should not be less than 6 in.

14. A **single welt** is simply the edge of the lead turned

round an inch or less, or 1¼ in. or 1½ in. wide, to stiffen the edge of the lead, and to cover over the heads of the nails. The nailing behind the welt should be with copper nails, from 1 in. to 2 or even 3 in. apart, according to circumstances.

15. Flashings or aprons for covering vertical faces, when more than 9 or 12 in. deep, should have their edges **double-welted,** *i.e.*, seam-welted.

When deep-flushings are **lapped,** the woodwork near and about the laps, at the back of the flashing, will be subject to the decaying influences of dampness from great rains, and moisture from an almost daily evaporation of the condensation of the atmosphere between the two faces of the lead.

16. To **form a double-welt** (fig. 31) of long length, turn the edge of the undercloak back an inch, to stand out at right angles with the face of the lead. Cut or plane off the edge with a lead-plane, to make it an equal width throughout its whole length. Turn up the edge of the overcloak nearly double the width of the undercloak, and fix the piece of lead for the faces of the two stand-ups to stand close together, and parallel to each other. It is of great importance to leave a space of not less than about $\frac{3}{16}$ in. between the edge of the stand-up of the undercloak and the place of the folding of the overcloak, or in turning and flattening down the welt the angle of the bay of the latter will be drawn away from the boarding, and to get it back again the lead would be much thinned, perhaps split.

Fig. 31.—Section of a Double-Welt.

It will be much easier, and the edge will be straighter,

if, with a straight-edge held against the back of the stand-up, a shaving of lead be taken off with a shave-hook at the place of the folding.

In turning the edge of the overcloak over upon the stand-up or stand-out of the undercloak, do not dress the welt too tightly at the angle of the folding, as room must be left for the undercloak to work up into it during the turning of the welt, and in flattening it down, or back, upon the face of the bay.

17. To secure the welt—the bay—to the face of the woodwork do not drive in any nails, but fix secret copper tacks, as shown in section, fig. 31, and more fully described in Chap. XII., Art. 15.

18. Before leaving the subject of lead laying it may be well to say a word on **snow-boards**, though that is a work not quite within the plumber's province. The great object of snow-boards in gutters and flats is to provide a way of escape for melted snow. This is not always present to the mind of the carpenter, and his narrow-boards are often laid down in a way to frustrate the object for which they are fixed.

When the open spaces in the boarding run athwart the fall of the flat or gutter, the snow which falls between the boards readily forms itself into a number of ridges or obstructions in the way of the current; and a gutter in this way may be turned into a series of little snow-water ponds, some of which, on a sunny day, may become deep enough to overflow the sides of the gutter, or the drip, and run through into the roof, and cause some damage.

Where the boards are laid down the way of the current in a gutter or flat, with supports which have proper water-courses, the snow which falls through between the boards will leave water-channels for any melted snow to run freely away.

CHAPTER XV.

JOINT-MAKING.

1.
A FIRST brief in the bag of a young barrister can hardly delight him more than the first set of tools in the brand new bag does a young plumber. And the heart of the young barrister can hardly beat faster when he rises in court to make his first speech than beats the heart of the young plumber when he takes his cloth to wipe his first important joint in a shop full of quizzing joint-makers.

2. Though **the making of a good joint** in his first effort in a new shop may not mean so much to a young plumber as the making of a good speech in a new circuit to a young barrister, it means much. And no learner should relax his practice until he can make a perfect joint—underhand, upright, or branch—upon any size of piping, from $\frac{1}{2}$ in. to 6 in. diameter. And though great perfection in joint-making may not secure him a knighthood, it will secure him a good name among his fellow-craftsmen.

3. No wiped soldered joint is perfect which is not true in form, strong in body, clean at the edges, and free from solder inside.

4. For joints to waste-pipes, soil-pipes, and ventilating-pipes, at least two things are absolutely essential, viz.: (*a*) that the joint shall not only be sound, but shall *show* itself to be so; and that (*b*) it shall be **free from solder inside**, free from tears, spurs, strings, ribands, or droppings. The former for keeping in liquids and bad air, *i.e.*, both water-tight and air-tight; and the latter to keep the pipes

free from any place, points, or projections, in which hair, paper, or excrementitious matters could lodge, catch, or collect.

5. However **thick** the solder may be upon a joint, and however clean the wiping may be, if the solder has been **wiped beyond the edges** of the shaving in any part, *i.e.*, if the joint is not wiped clean at its edges, how is it possible to be quite sure that it is sound without testing it hydraulically or in some other powerful way.

6. If the makers of joints overwiped at their edges were present at the examinations, to say that they had used irons in making them, and that the **ends of the pipes** had been **tinned** previously to being coupled together, an examiner would perhaps be able to decide upon their soundness; but joints should be so wiped that they may be seen at a glance to be sound.

7. It is of the utmost importance that all joints to soil-pipes, waste-pipes, and ventilating-pipes, inside a house, should be so wiped that they can be readily **seen to be sound and reliable.** In pipes which are to be constantly charged with water—as service-pipes—defective joints will tell their own tale, graphically, before the plumber leaves the premises; but in foul liquor-carrying pipes, which are never so tested, the first intimation of any defect in the joints of soil-pipes may be a serious illness of one or more of the occupants of the house.

8. **Joints** being necessary **evils,** the utmost care should be taken to reduce them to the smallest minimum, and this is always done by the skilled in the art of joint-making. The solder is so well apportioned over the joint, the outer edge of the junction of the pipes is so well covered with solder, and the joint altogether is so cleverly, cleanly, and strongly wiped, that its durability will be co-extensive with the pipes on which it is made.

9. As some men can wipe a *long* joint easier and better

than a *short* one, and *vice versa*, a little latitude, or rather longitude, should be given them. But any great divergence from a good **standard length and strength** (Art. 24) should be strongly discouraged, especially among technical students, for to say the least it shows a strong need for further

Fig. 32.—UNDERHAND JOINT, TOO SHORT AND TOO LIGHT.   Fig. 33.—UNDERHAND JOINT, TOO LONG AND TOO HEAVY.

technological teaching when some students make an underhand or upright joint upon 4 in. pipes only 1 in. long, and others 5½ in. long. And yet such joints are not only made by students, they are also made by plumbers in different parts of the country, and fixed in our houses. This great difference in the strength of joints not only applies to joints made underhand or upright upon soil-pipes, etc., but also to branch joints. The joints illustrated in figs. 32 and 33, and 34 and 35, are taken from specimens sent to the City and Guilds of London Institute for examination. The Scotch plumbers are generally the chief sinners in making the short joint, though Aberdeen plumbers should be excepted, as they err on the other side; and the West of England plumbers the long and heavy underhand and upright joint; but as far as

Fig. 34.—BRANCH JOINT, TOO SHORT AND TOO LIGHT.

length is concerned some London plumbers could give eighths of inches and yet beat any record.

10. For plumbers arbitrarily to so prepare and make their joints, so shave their pipes, that one plumber uses 50 or 75 per cent. less solder, or 50 or 75 per cent. more **solder upon his joint** than another plumber, proves one or more of several things, viz., dishonesty or ignorance; waste or want of skill. *Dishonesty* if less solder has been put upon the joint *wilfully* than good strength requires; *ignorance* if the joint from *custom* has not been made strong enough for its work; *waste* if much more solder has been left

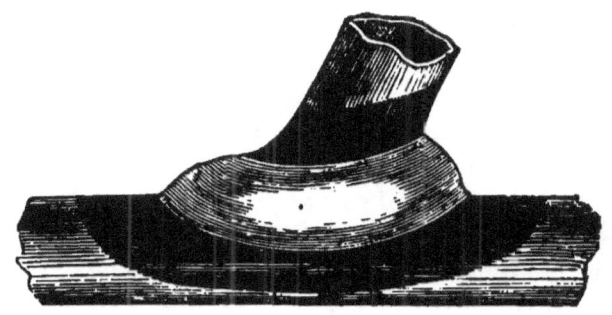

Fig. 35.—Branch Joint, too Long and too Heavy.

upon the joint, from want of thought, than circumstances require; *want of skill* if much less or much more solder has been wiped upon the joint than necessary, because the joint-maker, in his difficulty to make the joint, could not regulate the thickness of the solder in his wiping.

11. The *length* (Art. 24) of a joint being determined by the length of the **shaving of the pipes** to be joined together, there can be no difficulty in determining it exactly; but as the strength of a joint also depends upon the thickness of the solder wiped upon it—directly over the edge of the outer pipe—and this has to be done with metal in a fluid state very quickly, regulated only by the eye and

the feeling of the fingers through a cloth, the joint should be made a little heavier than absolutely necessary, so that its weakest part shall be equal to any strain it may have to bear—shall, in fact, be strong and durable.

12. If the joint-maker must economize, must use as **little solder** as will only just make the joint strong enough for its purpose, he had better save it in the length of a joint rather than in its thickness; for a joint *short* and *thick* is stronger than a joint *long* and *thin*.

13. The **strength of a joint** not only depends upon the quantity of solder upon it, but also upon the quality of it; and this may be deteriorated by the method in which the solder is both used and wiped upon the pipes.

14. The **solder** in the pot may be **poor** to start with, *i.e.*, it may have an insufficiency of tin in it; and then, in the process of making a joint, it may become poorer, that is, the solder of the joint may have parted with some of its tin. To pour on a lot of solder to get up a sufficient heat to wipe a joint without an iron means, *except to adepts*, that the solder finally left on the joint will be coarser than the first ladleful taken out of the pot (or, if a large joint, then the first few ladlefuls); as the richer solder of a pot keeps rising to the top.

15. **Tin** being of much less **specific gravity** (Chap. III.) than lead, and its melting-point being also much lower, the tin readily rises to the top, where the alloy is always richer than at the bottom (whether the pot stand over a fire or near the joint-maker), except at the moment when it is stirred, and it is of good heat. The *slow* joint-maker, trying to make his joint without the use of an iron, generally finds that he has no time to stir the solder every time he dips a ladleful from the pot; and so by the time he is ready to wipe his joint he is not only dipping coarser solder from the pot, he is also working with coarse solder upon the joint; for tin and the richer parts of the solder (being

more fluidal) have been ever running off and dropping away from the under part of the joint.

16. **When a joint wiped without an iron**, and wiped with solder which has parted with some of its tin, "sweats," where the water in the pipe oozes through the joint and stands like drops of dew here, there, and everywhere upon the solder, the man who made it, instead of lifting his eyebrows to the ceiling in wonderment, should sink into his boots for his self-assurance in discarding the use of an iron. Even to the eye a joint so wiped looks porous, and with the aid of a microscope the alloy shows most graphically where it has parted with tin, and become cellulose.

17. **When a joint is made with the aid of an iron**, less solder is taken from the pot to make it than when it is made without an iron. When sufficient solder has been roughly formed upon the joint, the hot iron is rubbed round the edges of the shaved parts of the pipe to insure good tinning, and to make the pipes hot, and the whole of the solder is so heated and wiped by a good joint-maker, that no part is allowed to cool and set in a manner to part with its tin.

18. **Solder** for making joints and for wiping purposes should only be **heated when it is wanted**, and it should never be heated to a higher degree of heat than required, *i.e.*, up to the point when a dry piece of wood put into it would smoke; but an observant mate ought to be able to tell at a glance when it is of the right heat, either by holding a ladleful near his face, or by passing the back part of the hand just over it. During the heating it should be frequently stirred with a ladle, as the tin rises to the top. When it is not stirred, and it is allowed to get to a red heat, it volatilizes.

19. To prevent matters accumulating upon any part of the jointings inside pipes, the **ends** of the **inner pipes** should

80   PLUMBING.

always be fixed the way of the current, as shown by the arrow and at A, fig. 36, and especially so in waste-pipes and soil-pipes, whether the joints are made upright or underhand, and also in the case of branch joints.

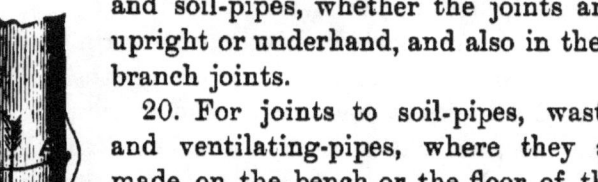

Fig. 36.

20. For joints to soil-pipes, waste-pipes, and ventilating-pipes, where they are not made on the bench or the floor of the shop, where they can be well got at and seen, the ends of the **pipes** should not only be **shaved** upon the **bench**, they should also be **tinned**, to prevent any foreign matter, as lime, mortar, or cement attaching itself to the shaved parts and tarnishing them, when carrying the pipes to their destination.

21. In **shaving** the ends of pipes, especially soil-pipes,

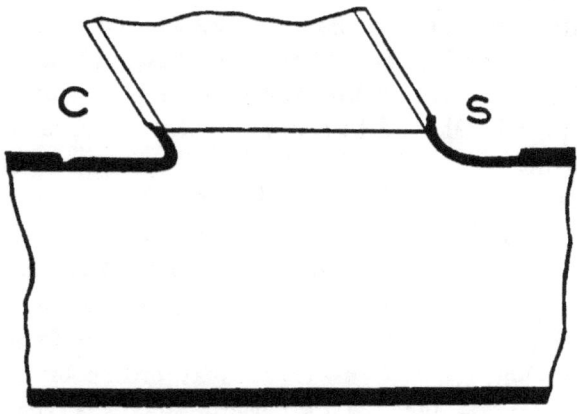

Fig. 37.—Showing where the Shave-Hook has weakened the Joint.

waste-pipes, and ventilating-pipes, and also in shaving lead, or any part of a pipe to be soldered, do not cut the shave-hook down into the lead to weaken it, as all that is required for the solder to readily tin upon it is a clean bright surface. This evil is somewhat exaggerated in the illustration, fig. 37, but it is not an infrequent thing to come across soldered angles, seams, and joints, not only made by students, but also by plumbers, where the shave-hook has removed half the original thickness of the lead or pipe, as shown at c and s.

22. When the ends of pipes are shaved *in situ*, where they cannot be well seen, it is a good plan to pull the point of the shave-hook round the ends, close to the junctions, and form one or two **concentric rings** upon them, to insure the solder adhering right round the jointing, as it is possible for a very fine line of the soiled surface to escape, not only the edge of the shave-hook, but also the notice of the shaver. Many faulty joints have been found some years after they have been made through such oversight.

23. In fitting and **fixing pipes together** to be soldered, see that they fit well and tightly together in every part of the jointing, so that there may be no possible place where the solder can run through to the interior of the pipes. And to prevent them shifting in the slightest degree, secure them well together. [In the examinations which have taken place in London in the last few years, more failures to complete a joint could be set down to poor fixing than poor wiping.]

24. In my "Lectures on the Science and Art of Sanitary Plumbing" I gave the following lengths for making upright and underhand joints, viz.: pipes $3\frac{1}{2}$ in. to 6 in., $3\frac{1}{2}$ in.; $1\frac{1}{4}$ in. to $3\frac{1}{2}$ in., 3 in.; and for smaller pipes a shorter length still. Recognizing the fact that, for easier wiping, most plumbers have a preferable length for certain joints, especially when they have to make them underhand, the following table might be treated as a standard length for joints. And the thickness of the solder upon the

G

external edge of the outer pipe should not be less than about $\frac{3}{16}$ in.

Size of Pipe.	Length of Joint.		Size of Pipe.	Length of Joint.	
	min.	max.		min.	max.
$\frac{1}{2}$ in.	$2\frac{1}{4}$ in.	$2\frac{3}{4}$ in.	$2\frac{1}{2}$ in. 3 in.	3 in.	$3\frac{1}{2}$ in.
$\frac{3}{4}$ in.	$2\frac{1}{2}$ in.	$2\frac{3}{4}$ in.			
1 in.	$2\frac{3}{4}$ in.	3 in.	$3\frac{1}{2}$ in. 4 in.	$3\frac{1}{4}$ in.	$3\frac{1}{2}$ in.
$1\frac{1}{4}$ in.	$2\frac{3}{4}$ in.	$3\frac{1}{4}$ in.			
$1\frac{1}{2}$ in.	$2\frac{3}{4}$ in.	$3\frac{1}{4}$ in.	$4\frac{1}{2}$ in. 5 in.	$3\frac{1}{2}$ in.	$3\frac{3}{4}$ in.
2 in.	3 in.	$3\frac{1}{4}$ in.	6 in.	$3\frac{1}{2}$ in. to 4 in.	

CHAPTER XVI.

JOINT-MAKING (*continued*).

Underhand and Upright Joints.

1.

BEFORE preparing the ends of pipes for joining together, well straighten and **round up the pipes**. Rasp off and feather the outer edge of the inner pipe, and scrape off the fringe or burr formed upon the inner edge by the rasping. Open the end of the outer pipe with a tan-pin (whether a large pipe or small one) for the inner pipe to enter it $\frac{1}{4}$ in. or $\frac{3}{8}$ in., without any contraction of the bore, and rasp off the outer edge. In "soiling" the ends of the pipes, soil over the interior end of the inner pipe (the parts brightened in cleaning off the edge formed by the rasping), to prevent the solder tinning upon it and running through to the inside in making the joint.

2. Having decided upon the length of the joint, and allowed for the entrance ($\frac{3}{8}$ in.) of the male end, scribe the

shaving-line round the pipe with the point of one of the legs of a pair of compasses, the point of the other leg being kept parallel with it, and drawn round upon the smooth surface of a piece of board, or held against the blade of a large saw placed tightly against the end of the pipe.

3. In making **underhand joints**, *i.e.*, joints to pipes fixed horizontally or at a slope, pour the solder upon the soiled parts of the pipes at the edges of the shaving, as well as upon the jointing, to make the pipes hot. [Some joint-makers prefer to pour the solder through a hole made in the lip of a ladle; but a better stream can be poured over the lip, with care and practice, as much or little can be poured just where it is wanted.] Pour the solder on very rapidly all round the jointing, conducting it to the underpart from both sides by letting it fall upon the cloth. In collecting the solder upon the jointing, and roughly forming it into shape, keep working it round and round

Fig. 38.—VIEW OF AN UNDERHAND JOINT.

the pipes, remembering that the solder has ever a great tendency to fall away from the underside, especially in the making of large joints. When sufficient solder has been formed upon the jointing, take the well-heated and well-cleaned iron and heat up the solder to a good consistency for wiping, draw the iron quickly round the underside, first on one edge and then on the other, and wipe the lower half, pressing well upon both edges in the wiping. Keep on wiping, and as you wipe keep the iron just in front of the cloth, bringing the ends of the wiping together somewhere on the upper part of the joint, to make a good and clean finish. In the case of small joints, when sufficient solder has been roughly formed upon the jointing, take the iron (unless you are a very expeditious joint-wiper, and can make the joint better without an iron) and rub it round upon the solder, first on one edge of the jointing and then on the other; then take the solder off upon the solder-cloth and heat it up into the form somewhat of a sausage-roll, place the middle part of the solder quickly against the underside of the jointing, and turn up first the outer half upon the ends of the pipes, and then pull up the inner half, and wipe the joint as expeditiously as you can, heating up the edges and the solder with the iron as required.

4. **An upright joint** is a soldered joint connecting two pipes (or two pieces, as a piece of brasswork and a piece of lead pipe) fixed in a vertical position. In fig. 42 two ends of $3\frac{1}{2}$ in. pipes are shown ready for making the joint. The ends of the pipes were soiled and tinned upon the bench before the pipes were fixed in their places. The pipes are brought out 2 or 3 in. from the wall, or a small hole is cut round the sides and back of the pipe (as shown at M^v, in fig. 44) for the ladle and the hand to go round the pipes to make the joint.

The edge of the outer pipe is well closed upon the end of the inner pipe to prevent the possibility of any solder running through the jointing to form a spur, or any such like evil inside the pipes. Some plumbers prefer not to close in the edge of the outer pipe. With a quick joint-maker this would make the better joint, as the solder between the two pipes would be of great value, but with slow and inexperienced plumbers the solder would be liable to run through and form spurs and ribands inside.

It must be evident to the most casual observer, that to make a joint in such a position, a great deal of solder will be wasted if means are not taken to catch the droppings of solder and falling pieces from the joint. Plumbers know this well enough, but do not always take the best means for saving the solder. They place pieces of board or slate round the pipe; or they tie some rags, or a wisp of straw, about the pipe, and catch the solder in this rude way; and, when the joint is made, they spend more time in picking off and picking up the solder than they did in making the joint.

5. Instead of building up or improvising a rough **means for catching solder** when making joints on vertical pipes, a proper instrument should be used, and this is very readily made and attached to the pipe, and with such means not a particle of solder need be wasted. Figs. 39 and 40 show pieces of lead cut with circular holes in the centre to suit two sizes of lead pipes. Fig. 40 shows the collar turned up, and clipped. These pieces of lead are called *collars;* they can be cut out of 5 lb., 6 lb., or 7 lb. remnants of lead to suit the various sized lead pipes. They should be

Fig. 39.—LEAD COLLAR.   Fig. 40.—PLAN OF A LEAD COLLAR WHEN TURNED UP.

kept well soiled all over, edges and all, to prevent the solder adhering to them.

With a well-arranged set of **collars**, which should be kept ready for use in all large jobs, a man ought not to take more than a minute or two in selecting the right collar, and fastening it upon the pipe, just where it is wanted, about 2 in. below the bottom edge of the joint, as shown at D, fig. 42. To secure the collar in its position upon the pipe, all that the plumber wants to do is to pull the collar *tightly* round the pipe and turn the points (*b*, fig. 39) one over the other to clip them, as shown in fig. 40, and D, fig. 42. He should then sprinkle a pinch of dust— which he can easily pick up in a building within a stride or two—to cover over any small space or opening which may be left between the collar and the pipe. As shown in fig. 42, the collar, when on the pipe, forms a dish for catching the falling solder. There is this additional advantage with such an arrangement, that the solder collecting in this dish keeps the pipes hot, thereby facilitating the making of the joint.

6. To make an upright joint, unless the plumber is well skilled in pouring with the ladle upon his cloth, he wants a splash-stick (illustrated in fig. 41) for **splashing the solder upon the pipes**. These splash-sticks are made of wood or iron, about 6 or 7 in. long, $1\frac{1}{4}$ in. wide in the spoon part, and $\frac{1}{8}$th to a $\frac{1}{4}$ in. thick. With care, there is no fear of the iron scratching the pipe, for the edges are well rounded. When the stick is made of wood, the smoke

Fig. 41.—SPLASH-STICK.

is apt to get into one's eyes, and interfere with the perfect sight just when it is most wanted.

7. In **making an upright joint**, splash the solder well upon the upper part of the jointing, round and round, at a little below E E, fig. 42; keep pulling up the solder from time to time with the splash-stick from the lower part of the jointing to the upper part, for the solder collecting in the dish will keep the lower part well heated. Splash on the solder rapidly, remembering that speed is the soul of joint-wiping, and roughly form the joint with the splash-stick. Then take the iron in one hand and the solder-cloth in the other, rub the iron over the solder, and pat it into its place with the cloth; then draw the hot iron right round the upper edge of the jointing, at the back, following it closely with the cloth. Do the same at the bottom edge, and then change hands with the cloth and iron, and

treat the front half in the same way, and the joint is made.
Before leaving the spot, and while the iron is still hot, rest
it in two or three places upon the solder collected on the
collar; pull the melting solder into the ladle, and the rest
of the collected solder on the collar will then come away in
sections, without waste or damage to the pipe.

8. An **overcast joint** is simply a wiped joint overcast
with an iron, to (*a*) re-melt the surface of the joint and fill

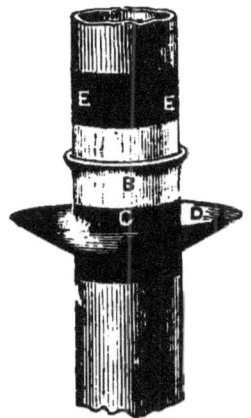

Fig. 42.—VIEW OF UPRIGHT JOINT-
ING, READY FOR MAKING.

Fig. 43.—VIEW OF AN
OVERCAST JOINT.

up the cellulose solder, caused by the coldness of the wiping;
and (*b*) to remove superfluities, and fill up deficiencies; but
no good joint-maker, in this advanced age of plumbing,
needs any such aid to make his joint either sound or true.
Directly the joint is wiped, and while the solder is still hot,
the neck-part (or, in some cases, the point) of a hot iron is
drawn up and down, or forwards and backwards, over its
surface, forming it into a ribbed joint, or giving it a large
number of facets, as shown at *b b b*, fig. 43. Any form of
wiped joint can be overcast with the iron, upright, underhand, block, or branch; but overcasting is rarely done

now, except to joints upon service-pipes under very great pressure, and to joints on copper pipes, and in brewery work, where great strains are put upon them.

CHAPTER XVII.

JOINT-MAKING (*continued*).

Block Joints, Flange Joints, and Branch Joints.

1.

A **BLOCK JOINT** is a wiped soldered joint, both uniting and supporting pipes fixed vertically in a chase; and when such joints are properly made there is no better way of fixing soil-pipes and ventilating-pipes inside a house. The other day, on examining some very tall stacks of 6 in. 7 lb. lead soil-pipe fixed on this method more than a quarter of a century ago, they showed no signs of age, and on testing them they were found to be perfectly sound.

2. **A wood block** of the thickness of a brick is placed over the top end of the lower pipe and built into the wall, as shown at Q, fig. 44. Around the hole on its upper surface a dishing is made, for opening out the end of the pipe, and for wiping a greater depth of solder upon the ends of the pipes.

3. A lead flange, F, is put over the end of the pipe and dressed down into the dishing of the wood block to solder upon, and to prevent the solder running through between the block and the pipe in making the joint. The hole in the flange must only be cut just large enough to admit the end of the pipe through it; and then when the latter is opened out, the inner edge of the flange will be made to fit

tightly to the pipe all round. The flange should be shaved and tinned before it is fixed, and it should have a margin on the outer edge of the shaving of about ½ in., which should be well soiled, as should also be its edges and underside, that there may be no difficulty in removing the surplus solder after the wiping.

4. The **end** of the **pipe** should be **opened** with a tanpin and rounded back with a mallet for its edge to stand up about ½ in. from the face of the tinned edge of the

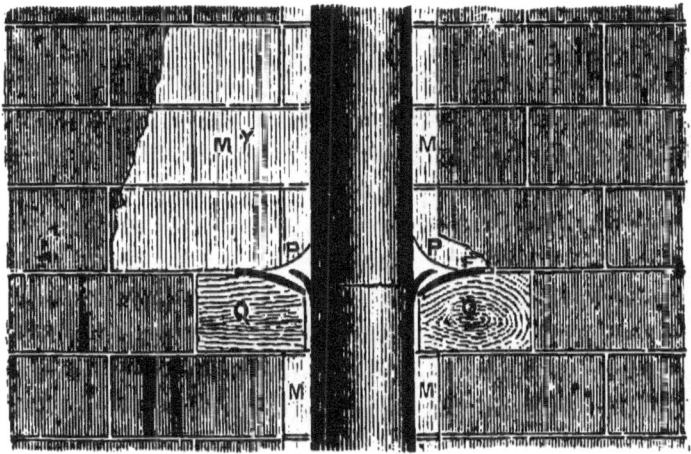

Fig. 44.—SECTION OF A BLOCK JOINT.

flange, so that the solder may unite both to its outer and inner surfaces for a depth of about 1¼ in., as shown at P, fig. 44.

5. In opening and turning back the end of the outer pipe upon the block be very careful not to turn any part of it back at **right angles** with the pipe, *i.e.*, for the inner edge of the taft to have a square edge, as in such cases the lower pipe is only united to the upper pipe by the thickness and strength of the soldering upon the *edge* of the pipe, in 7 lb. pipe only equal to about ⅛ in.; as no matter

how wide the taft may be, the only part in contact with the upper pipe, and soldered to it, is just the thickness of the pipe at the turned edge, and this may have been much weakened on its underside by the way it was tafted. This right-angled taft joint is one of the weakest that can be made, whereas the block-joint, as shown in fig. 44, is one of the very strongest.

6. To insure a **close-fitting jointing**, to prevent the solder running through to the inside in making the joint, tap the tan-pin into the end of each pipe at the moment of fixing them together.

7. The **joint** is easily **wiped** when there is room to get the ladle round the pipe in front and its right-hand and left-hand sides, the brickwork being cut away, as shown at M^Y, fig. 44, for the purpose. Splash on the solder well upon the end of the upper pipe, and work it well into its place with the splash-stick as you go on; and then, when it is ready for wiping, rub the iron right round on the edge of the upper pipe, letting it at the same time touch the outer edge, and wipe one-half or two-thirds of the joint with one wipe; change hands with the cloth and iron and complete the joint, leaving it without a mark of beginning or ending.

8. A **flange joint**, as shown in fig. 45, is made in a similar way to the block joint just described. It is chiefly made on waste-pipes, and small pipes where they pass through a floor.

In fixing the pipe, working from the bottom upwards, the top **end of the pipe** is made to stand an inch or two above the level of the floor. A lead flange (R, fig. 45), as described in the block joint, is then put over the end of the pipe, and a piece of board, about $\frac{3}{4}$ in. thick, is placed on the flange for the blade part of the saw to rest upon, as a guide in cutting the pipe off to the requisite length for tafting. When the pipe is cut off, the board is removed, and a turn-pin is driven down into the pipe with one or two sharp strokes of the mallet, and the end of the pipe is then tafted back upon the flange.

Great care should be taken to see that the end of the pipe stands up high enough to be well beaded back upon the flange. Sometimes when the pipe is brought through the floor, or bath-safe, or closet-safe, in an oblique direction, the pipe is cut off too short on its inner side to allow for a proper taft, and then no matter how well wiped the joint

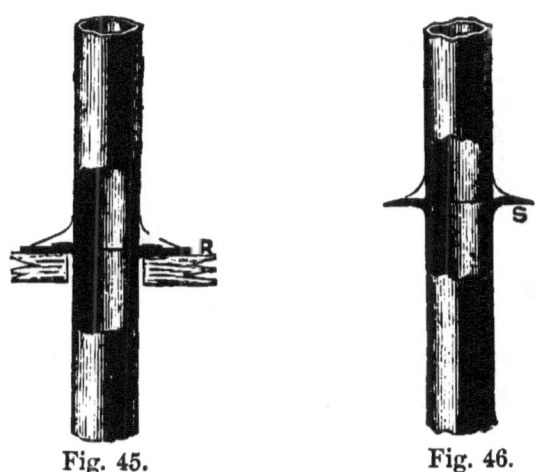

Fig. 45.   Fig. 46.

may *look* on the surface, a *defect* may soon be found in it and much evil caused. The connection of the upper pipe with the lower, and the soldering of the joint, need not be described.

9. There is no form of wiped soldered joints so easy to make as a **taft joint**, and wherever it is found, except to connect certain pipes together on floor surfaces, it is a mark of the incompetence of the joint-maker. The end of a pipe is tafted back from an inch to an inch-and-a-half to form a base for the solder to rest upon. The end of the pipe to be connected to it is shaved for a length of about 1¼ in. and

inserted into the end of the tafted pipe, as shown at s, fig. 46. The solder is then splashed or poured on, and the joint wiped. A feat that hardly an "X Y Z" plumber would crow over.

10. **A branch joint** is a joint uniting the end of one pipe to the side of another at any angle; but no branch, be it waste-pipe, soil-pipe, or drain, should enter a main pipe at right angles, as shown at B, fig. 47, though this is often done, especially to overcome some obstacle, as an iron joist or girder. In lead pipes, however slight the fall may be, the pipe can always be nosed over, or nosed downwards,

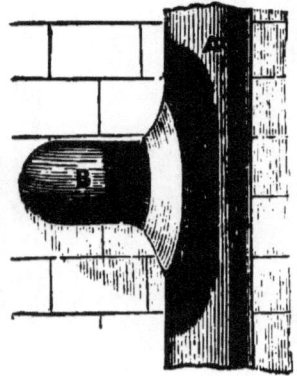

Fig. 47.

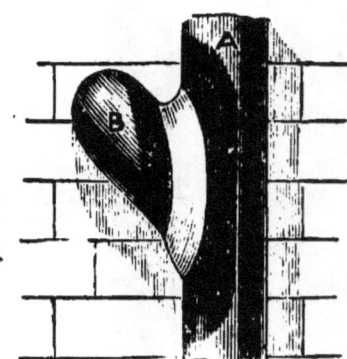

Fig. 48.

and made to enter the main pipe in the way of the current, as shown at B, fig. 48. And where a girder stands in the way, and compels a bend being made in the branch, as shown in fig. 49, instead of bending the pipe and entering the main soil-pipe at right angles, it can as readily be bent to enter it obliquely, as shown in fig. 48. Sometimes a knuckle-bend is all that is necessary to accomplish this.

11. In forming an **opening** in a lead soil or main waste-pipe to **receive a branch pipe**, cut an elongated hole in the main pipe, about half the size of the end of the branch pipe to be connected with it, and then work up the sides

with a bolt or hand-dummy, to form a *socket* upon the pipe, as shown at G, fig. 51, so that the branch pipe may enter it,

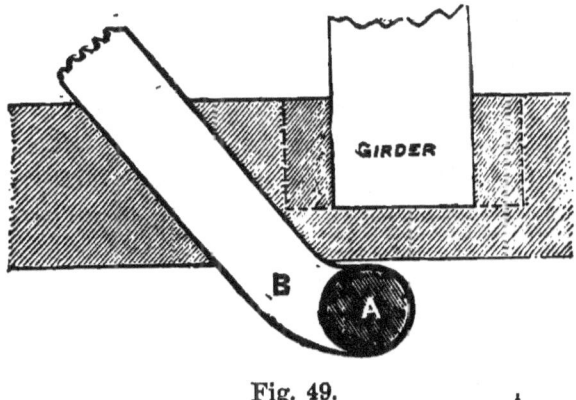

Fig. 49.

about three-eighths of an inch, without coming into the bore of the main pipe to form any kind of obstruction or collecting place there for filth.

Great care should be taken that the end of the branch pipe fits well against the sides of the socket all round, to prevent any solder running through to the inside when the joint is being made.

12. The pipes having been prepared, as shown in fig. 51, it only remains for them to be put together, and well secured, to make the joint. A man who can make an underhand joint and an upright joint ought to have no difficulty in wiping a branch joint; but there are two

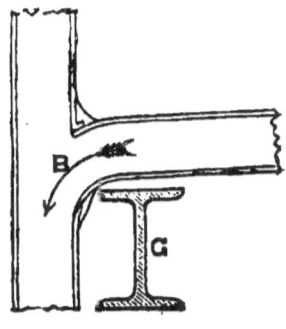

Fig. 50.

points the learner will do well to remember: (1) When the branch pipe is of smaller size than the main pipe the solder will stay well enough upon the jointing; but when the pipes are of equal sizes, the solder will have a tendency to fall off at the two opposite sides. In jointing such pipes keep the catch-board, or whatever the solder is caught upon, close to the underside of the main pipe; for the fallen solder will then not only help to keep the pipe hot, but it will also enable the plumber to dip his splash-stick into it, to supply the place of the fallen solder from the sides. (2) As the lower part of the jointing will be kept well heated by the solder upon it, splash the solder well upon the end of the branch pipe, and when sufficient solder has

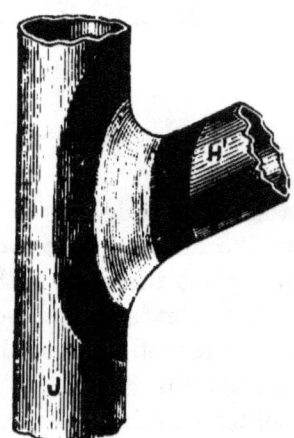

Fig. 51. Fig. 52.

been splashed on, and the joint has been roughly formed with the splash-stick as the splashing proceeded, take the iron, and after re-heating up the solder round about upon the jointing, quickly draw it round the upper edge (the edge of the shaving) on the off-side, and wipe the upper part of the joint; do the same with the lower part of the joint, and with the middle part; then change hands with the cloth and iron, and treat the near side in a similar way, and never rest satisfied with your branch-joint wiping until you can wipe a branch joint, not only strong but symmetrical, perfect in size, shape, and strength.

13. Fig. 51 shows a **socket**, G, formed upon the main pipe, and shaved ready to receive the branch, H, the end of which is also shaved ready for the connection to be made; and fig. 52 shows the pipes put together, and the joint wiped, leaving the bore in the main pipe, J, perfectly clear, and free from everything that would obstruct, or upon which matters could collect while passing through the pipe.

14. The old way of connecting branch pipes with main pipes by a **mitre joint** cannot be too severely condemned. If plumbers were also joiners, one could understand how the mitre joint, as shown in fig. 53, got introduced; but it is difficult to understand why plumbers should make such a connection, especially on waste water or sewage-carrying pipes. Probably one reason is because they have never considered the matter. They know that it is the best form of jointing in soldering lead nozzles to pump-barrels, for a socket, as shown at G, fig. 51, could not be properly formed on a stout lead pump-barrel, and as this form of joint had been in use in pump-making long before waste-pipes or soil-pipes were ever fixed, custom has given it a place in waste water and sewage-carrying pipes which it ought never to have. Such a joint takes more time, more solder, and is more difficult to make than the branch joint shown in figs. 51 and 52. It is also wrong in principle; for however careful the plumber may be, he cannot leave the main pipe perfectly smooth at K, and the waste discharges from branches fixed on the upper part of the main pipe would

Fig. 53.—MITRE JOINTING.

have to travel through this badly-fitted branch connection. The edges of the branch pipe, L, or of the main pipe, K, fig. 53, must form in some degree a collecting place for filth, and the solder in making such a joint would be more liable to work through the jointing to the inside of the pipe than it would in the other form of branch connection, fig. 51.

15. Though the branch mitre joint is now rarely made, an equally bad form of branch jointing is often made, and that, too, by student plumbers, who, with teachers at their backs, however badly they might perform their work, should not execute it on wrong principles. Even if nothing had ever been said or written upon the subject, it ought to be evident to the maker of such a joint that to allow the end of a branch pipe to protrude into the main pipe, as shown in fig. 54, he was doing his best to form an obstruction, if nothing worse. And yet many such joints, with the end of the branch pipe standing nearly an inch inside the main pipe, were sent to the Institute this year (1891) for my examination. And, as might be expected, the evil in nearly every case was much aggravated by the solder which had run through into the main pipe in making the joint. In some cases the solder inside the pipe was nearly as much as that upon the joint—it had fallen in tears, in ribands, in solder-spurs and droppings—a fantastic conglomeration of hidden treasure. Without a socket on the main pipe, as shown at G, fig. 51, it is almost impossible to keep the solder from running through when making the joint. When the hole in the main pipe is cut the full size of the branch pipe no lead is left to close in upon the connection to make it solder-tight.

16. There is another form of branch connection well known to many a young plumber, but which must be condemned. A socket is formed rightly enough upon the main pipe; but the end of the branch, instead of being inserted *inside* it, as shown in fig. 54, is fixed *over* it, as

shown in fig. 55, an error which no thoughtful student ought to commit. The end of the socket standing inside the branch not only forms an obstruction, but it also affords a place for filth to collect in.

17. In wiping a joint soil is sometimes rubbed off from the pipes, and left upon the joint, giving it a dirty appearance; or the cloth with which the joint has been wiped has been knocked about on the floor, as well as in the plumber's bag, and the marks of such carelessness show themselves upon the joint. All such discolourations can readily be re-

 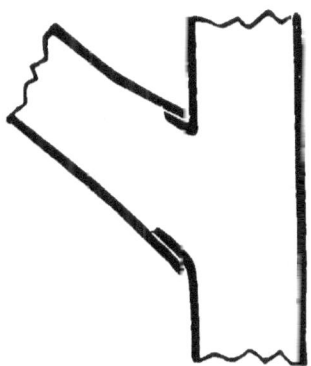

Fig. 54.—SHOWING BAD BRANCHING.   Fig. 55.—SHOWING BAD BRANCH CONNECTION.

moved by cleaning the solder with melted fat; and this is quickly supplied by rubbing the end of a tallow candle over the joint whilst it is still hot, and wiping it with somebody's silk pocket-handkerchief.

18. The plumber who desires to shine as a good wiper of solder should pay particular attention to his solder-cloths, and always keep a good assortment in a little bag to select from.

I have dwelt at length upon *wiped* soldered joints, because there is a sanitary way of joining pipes and an unsanitary way, and because good joint-wiping is a mark of a plumber's skill. It costs no more for a skilful joint-maker to make a perfect joint, than for an unskilful man to make an imperfect one. Nay, the imperfect joint is generally the costlier, for the excrescence of solder upon it is wasted, and its ugliness is a proof of want of dexterity. Unskilled labour (when skill is wanted) is always more expensive, as it consumes more time than skilled labour.

CHAPTER XVIII.

JOINT-MAKING (*continued*).

Copper-bit Joints, Blow-pipe Joints, and Astragal Joints.

1.

TO acquire the necessary skill to make a wiped soldered joint has cost the skilful joint-wiper so much time, so much pain—for has he not often burned his fingers, and poured the solder into his hand, instead of upon the cloth?—so much patience and perseverence, that now he is master of the cloth he scorns to use the copper-bit; but there is weakness rather than wisdom in the boycotting of copper-bit joints.

2. When a copper-bit joint or blow-pipe joint would reflect no want of ability in the joint-maker, when it would be better suited for its work, being neater and much less costly to make than a wiped soldered joint, it is difficult to understand the wisdom of a plumber spending several hours over the wiping of a plumbers' joint, which is often the case, when what he is pleased to call a "tinkers' joint" would be the stronger of the two; and would afterwards allow more room for the nut to travel up and down over

JOINT-MAKING.

the brass lining, as is the case where such joints are adopted in connection with lavatory fittings, etc.

The following description of copper-bit joints, blow-pipe joints, and astragal joints, is taken from my "Lectures."

3. I would not, however, allow a copper-bit joint to be made on a soil-pipe, funnel-pipe, or thin lead waste or ventilating-pipe, especially the usual form of copper-bit jointing, as shown at T, fig. 56, for though the union of the two pipes may be perfect, the jointing would not strengthen the piping like a wiped soldered joint, as shown in fig. 38. The band of solder round the pipe in a plumbers' joint strengthens it, like a belt round the waist of a navvy; moreover, instead of the solder being united only to very short edges of the pipes, it has a *grip* of fully 1½ in. on each pipe, and the body of strong soldering round such pipes keeps them in good rotundity.

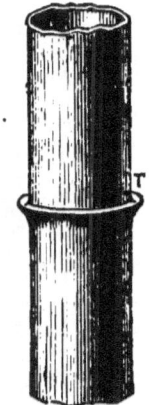

Fig. 56.—COPPER-BIT JOINT.

4. In soldering brasswork to lead, well tin the brass before making the joint — the plumber's mate should do such tinnings at odd times. The hatchet form of copper-bit is the best. It should be kept well tinned, and the soldering edges well feathered. The copper-bit float or flow joint, as shown at U, fig. 57, is easy to make. When the copper-bit is well heated, so that you can feel a genial warmth from it by holding it within a foot of the face, place one of the tinned edges against the tinned part of the brasswork, keeping the head of the bit as near the brass as practicable to assist in heating it; then push a strip of *fine* solder against the other tinned edge of the copper-bit, and the solder will flow round the pipe-base, U, fig. 57. When sufficient solder is formed on the top of the pipe, pull the copper-bit slowly round the jointing, allowing the tinned feathered part of the bit to

rest upon the pipe, and keeping the thin edge against the brasswork.

5. **A ribbon joint**, as shown at w, fig. 58, is also made with a copper-bit and fine solder. This joint is more difficult to make, but it is a better joint than the flow joint. A band of fine solder, about an inch wide and $\frac{1}{16}$ in. thick, is formed round the jointing, and this is so dexterously done by some plumbers, that it is difficult to see where the silver-coloured ring commences and where it ends, *i.e.*, there is no mark of the copper-bit left upon the soldering.

6. **An overcast ribbon joint** is simply a copper-bit jointing made as just described, and overcast with the

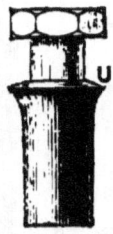

Fig. 57.—Flow Joint.

Fig. 58.—Ribbon Joint.

Fig. 59.—Overcast Copper-Bit Joint.

copper-bit, giving it several facets; fig. 59 shows a view of this form of joint. When joint-makers fail in putting a true ring, band, or ribbon of solder round the connection, they generally overcast it with a copper-bit to make good any unevenness, and when this is skilfully done the jointing looks very neat, and is at the same time very strong.

7. **A blow-pipe joint** looks precisely like a copper-bit joint (u, fig. 57); the difference being in the mode of making. One joint is made from the heat of a copper-bit, the other from the heat of a flame—from a handful of rushes tied together, or of a flame from a spirit-lamp—by the aid of a mouth blow-pipe. I need hardly describe a blow-pipe. It is a small trumpet-shaped copper tube,

about 9 in. or a foot long, with the thin end bent round, and an air-way of about one-eighth of an inch diameter through its smallest part. The larger end, which is about half an inch in diameter, is held in the mouth, and the smaller end is kept near the flame, so as to blow the heat upon the jointing just where it is wanted.

8. Though I condemned copper-bit jointing, as shown in

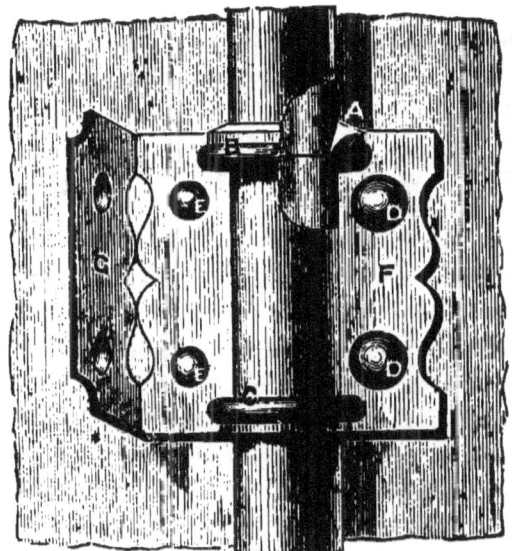

Fig. 60.—VIEW OF A SOLDERED JOINT WITH ASTRAGALS AND TACKS.

the woodcut at T, fig. 56, I am in favour of strong *fine solder joints* for *outside* soil-pipes, as shown at A, fig. 60, but there is a great difference in the two joints. There is three times the strength of soldering on this jointing, as will readily be seen by a glance at the illustrations, figs. 56 and 60, though the soldering in the latter is not shown quite bold enough. The astragals, B and C, can be cut out of ½ in. or ¾ in. strong lead pipe, and bent round and soldered to the funnel pipe; but I prefer them cast in moulds, in strips of a size to suit the size of the soil-pipe. They are very easily bent round on the pipe where they are to be fixed, and soldered to it with a copper-bit. The astragals are reversed, as shown at B and C, and the neck part of the upper astragal moulding is opened out a little, and rasped off on the inner edge, as shown in section, at A, to give space for a good body of fine solder for making a strong joint. The tacks are soldered to the pipe in the usual way, and to make them ornamental a device is cut out of the centre part, and dots are raised over the nail-heads, as shown at D. Roundheaded nails are fixed as shown at E, and that part of the tack which is to cover them is domed back by a tap or two from the small end of the mallet, as shown by the tack G, which is left unfolded for the purpose. The astragals round the |pipe help to strengthen it, combining thus the useful with the ornamental. Bacon noticed in his day the neatness of astragal jointings, for he speaks of leaden pipes " bound with leaden bands."

Some plumbers prefer to cast the socket and astragals in a mould, and burning or soldering the socket-ends upon the lead pipe to save time and labour. (Chap. XXVI., Art. 13.)

CHAPTER XIX.

ELBOW JOINTS AND PIPE-BENDING.

1.

IN my lectures to plumbers ten years ago, I expressed my sorrow that any man calling himself a plumber should be obliged to resort to solder—to an **elbow joint**—when circumstances compelled him to alter the course of a soil-pipe, ventilating-pipe, or rain-water-pipe. Judging from their written papers and their practical tests, the student plumbers in connection with the City Guilds Technological Examinations are determined that no such reproach shall fall upon them, when they have arrived at the stature of men in the plumbing world; but the knowledge of pipe-bending has still to be learnt by many men here and there about the country, who, if not well advanced in the art of bending pipes, are well advanced in age.

2. A man who would turn his back upon the plumber who made a copper-bit joint to the union of a lavatory plug-and-washer, and then go away and make an elbow **mitre joint**, as shown in fig. 61, would give a practical

   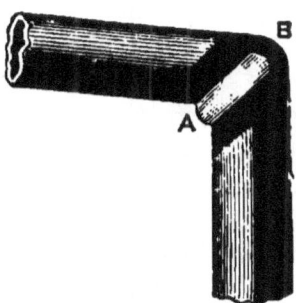

Fig. 61.—ELBOW MITRE JOINT.   Fig. 62.—ELBOW JOINT.

proof, not only of his want of knowledge of pipe-bending, but also of his want of comprehension in the fitness of things.

3. An **elbow joint**, however well made it may be, does not afford so good a passage for matters passing through a pipe as a bend, even though the later form of elbow joint, as shown in fig. 62, be adopted. Apart from any action the solder may have upon the lead, and the risk of solder running through at the mitreing during the soldering, there is the danger of fixing the underlap against the current, as shown at A, fig. 61. In fact this was a very frequent occurrence, as scores of old elbow joints have proved when

they have been cut out; and, as might be expected, such pipes showed most offensively where filth had collected in them.

4. As an elbow joint is inconsistent with good sanitary plumbing, and as it reflects a want of ability in the maker of it—elbowing the pipe because he cannot bend it—there is no necessity to describe how to make it.

5. It is about half-a-century ago that the more skilful plumbers began to bend soil-pipes, and gave up the bad practice of cutting and elbowing them with solder. And to-day so clever are the skilled in **pipe-bending**, that they can bend a lead pipe, of any size from $\frac{1}{2}$ in. to 6 in. diameter, into any shape that the most awkward of circumstances can call for. In my lectures I exhibited some specimens of 2 in. and $3\frac{1}{2}$ in. seamless lead pipe, bent into the shape of the well known S and half-S lead traps. Pieces of such strong lead pipe were also shown bent into the shape of capital letters, and when put side by side formed the word PLUMBING.

The following description of pipe-bending is largely taken from my "Lectures."

6. There is an **art in bending lead pipes**. Many try it, but miserably fail. In bending the pipe they considerably **reduce the strength of the lead**, especially at the *heel* of the bend, as shown by the illustration in fig. 63, at E and F. If the strength of a chain is only equal to its weakest link, the strength, and therefore the *safety*, of a stack of soil-pipe, or a stack of waste-pipe, is only equal to its weakest parts; so that when a 10 lb. or a 12 lb. lead waste-pipe, or an 8 lb. or a 7 lb. lead soil-pipe, is reduced at the bends to half its original strength, the whole length of the piping is depreciated accordingly.

7. There is not only the evil of *weakening* the pipe at the bend by men who are not skilled in pipe-bending, but there is also the further evil of **contracting the bore** of the

pipe, especially in the neck of the bend. The pipe at such parts is often contracted to quite half its original size, as shown at C and D. I often notice this as I travel about. Pipes of 4 in. diameter are reduced to 3 in. and less, and when this takes place in soil-pipes, waste-pipes, and ventilating-pipes, where the tubing should be *quite* of full bore at the bending, the value of such piping for its work is considerably reduced. If a stack of 4 in. pipe is reduced to 3 in. at its bends, the whole of the stack may as well have been 3 in., and the difference in the cost saved to the householder. I have seen, in bad workmanship, 5 in. piping re-

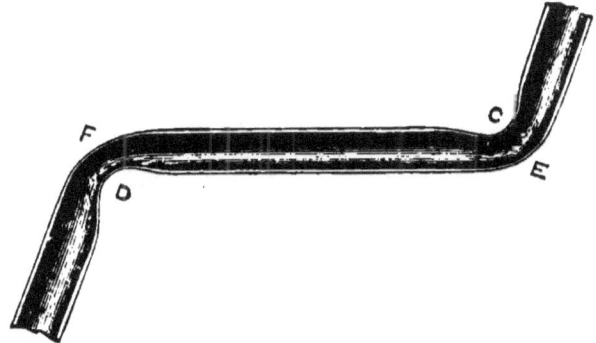

Fig. 63.—SECTION OF BADLY BENT PIPE.

duced to 4 in. at the bendings, 4 in. to 3 in., 3 in. to 2 in., 2 in. to $1\frac{1}{2}$ in., $1\frac{1}{2}$ in. to $1\frac{1}{4}$ in., $1\frac{1}{4}$ in. to 1 in. Now no sanitarian, with a fair knowledge of plumbing, would allow such pipe-bending on any of his works. All these pipes, if they had been bent by men skilled in their trade, would have been of *full bore* throughout.

8. In making an *elbow joint*, as fig. 62, you have to cut out and get rid of a V-shaped piece of piping, but in making a **bend** you are in want of a V-shaped piece of piping, as shown at G and H, fig. 64. The skilful plumber will provide for this, and knowing that he is working a pliable material he will, in bending the pipe, dress the lead round

from the neck (c, fig. 63), where there is a surplus, to the heel (G, fig. 64), where there is a deficiency.

9. In **making a bend** in a 3 in. or 4 in. lead soil or ventilating-pipe (or any size from 3 in. and upwards), well heat the pipe by a flame from a gas-jet, or from wood shavings put inside the pipe, or by pouring some hot lead or solder upon the part to be bent. In the part which is to form the neck of the bend where you are going to kink the pipe in pulling it up, heat the lead up to the point when water dropped upon it would hiss, but do not heat it beyond

Fig. 64.—SHOWING WHERE LEAD IS WANTED IN BENDING (G, H).

that point, for though it would not melt, the lead would become brittle and break in the bending. When water dropped upon the pipe assumes a spheroidal form, it is a proof that the lead is too hot. Why water assumes such a form when dropped upon metals very hot, red-hot, is that the " sphere of water does not come into contact[1] with the hot metal, but rests on an elastic surface or cushion of

[1] Prof. Dewar, in his juvenile lectures at the Royal Institution this last winter, on "Fire and Frost," "threw some molten lead out of a ladle with a bare wet hand, the steam formed upon the hand by the heat of the lead preventing actual contact between the metal and the skin."

ELBOW JOINTS AND PIPE-BENDING. 107

steam. As the metal cools, the heat is not sufficient to maintain this condition, and the water thus comes in contact with the metal, hisses, boils, and evaporates."

The pipe being properly heated, stride over it with your face towards the end (N, fig. 65) to be pulled up, and press your hand (with a felt or a thick cloth under it, to prevent the hand from being burnt) upon the pipe where it is to be bent, and get your mate to pull up the end of the pipe, humouring the bending part as much as possible to keep it in a circular form to prevent it from crippling. Lay the pipe down on one side quickly, and, with two or three sharp driving strokes of the dresser, jerk and dress the bulged part (K, fig. 65) of the piping from the *side* facing you, round towards the *heel*, L, of the bend. Turn the pipe over, while it is still hot, and dress

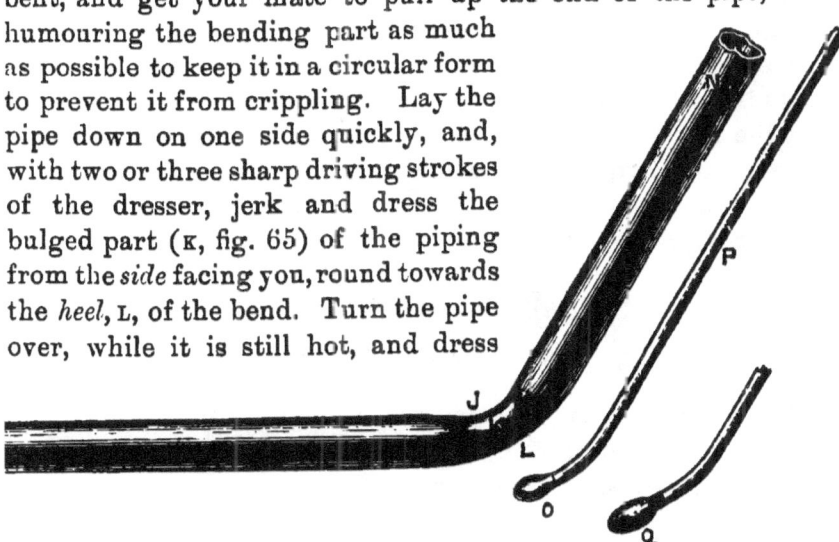

Fig. 65.—VIEW OF AN UNFINISHED BEND IN A LENGTH OF SOIL-PIPE, AND OF TWO LONG DUMMIES.

the bulged part of the opposite side round to the heel, in a similar way to that just described. By this means you will thicken the lead where it had been weakened in bending it, and you will at the same time be giving room for the dummy to work inside the pipe. Take the dummy (P, fig. 65) and put inside the pipe, N, and get your mate to knock up the *neck* part of the bend with the bulb of solder, O, on the end of the dummy, P, while you are dressing out the irregularities—dressing the lead ever towards the heel, L, to thicken the lead there. Do not attempt too much at a time, for to make a good bend, and to make it quickly, several such heats must be given it as just described. Watch the blows of the dummy, and see that they are rightly delivered, so that not a blow may be wasted.

10. A hand **dummy**, as illustrated in fig. 66, is a most useful tool for the plumber for many purposes, but in no piece of work is it more useful to him than in pipe-bending, when he can well reach the throttled pipe with it. The handle is generally made of cane, and the dummy, the bulb at the end, of solder. The *long* dummy, as shown at P, or Q, fig. 65, is wanted in various lengths, but a 5 ft. dummy is a very useful length. Some plumbers make their dummies with pieces of ⅝ in. iron rod, but the general

Fig. 66.—HAND DUMMY.

plumber uses ½ in. or ¾ in. gas-tubing, according to the length of the dummy.

11. Some young plumbers, to show that they have mastered the art of pipe-bending, **over-bend** their pipes. Wherever a bend is wanted in a pipe, they make it as sharp as possible. Now no pipe should be bent at a greater angle than necessity requires, and great care should be taken to keep the bend *rounding*, for plumbing is not gas-fitting, and no square elbow bends are required. It has this great advantage over cast-iron pipe, that lead pipe, by the skilled plumber, can be bent on the *spot exactly* as it is wanted.

12. No bend is properly made in a lead pipe where the lead is in any part reduced in strength below its original substance.

13. It is the practice now with some plumbers in bend-

ing pipes to use what are called **bobbins and followers**, for opening out the pipes, to make them of full bore. The funnel-pipe is partly bent, and then a bobbin, as shown at B, fig. 67, is put into the pipe with one or two followers, which are made of box-wood, in various lengths, as shown in the illustration, fig. 67, at F F F. When the pipe is bent to the required angle the bobbins and followers are put into the pipe, and driven through it by the driving-rod, B; but it will be seen at once by the careful observer that unless this is done with great care, there will be danger of damaging the pipe by driving the follower, F, athwart into

Fig. 67.—SECTION OF A BENT PIPE, SHOWING THE EVILS OF BOBBINS (B) AND FOLLOWERS (F).

the heel of the bend, as shown by the arrow in the woodcut.

14. Driving a bobbin through a bent pipe insures a full bore through it; but the inpingement of the bobbin or follower upon an indentation in the pipe may often weaken the lead in places unnoticed by the plumber. All the tools a man wants to make a **perfect bend** in a lead soil-pipe or ventilating-pipe, as illustrated in fig. 68, is a dummy and a dresser or two, though a strip or two of lead of various widths—dependent upon the radius of the bend—is an advantage for removing tool-marks and planishing the pipe. Fig. 68 illustrates a double bend made in a 10 ft. length of

3½ in. 8 lb. lead soil-pipe, made simply with a dummy and a dresser or two, with, of course, the slight assistance of an intelligent plumber.

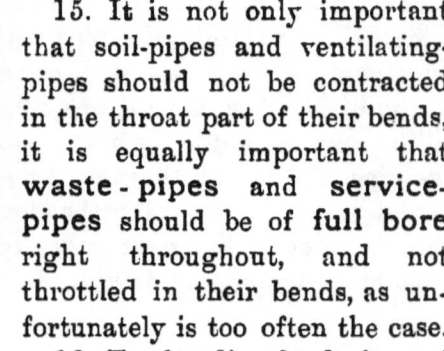

Fig. 68.—View of a Double Bend.

15. It is not only important that soil-pipes and ventilating-pipes should not be contracted in the throat part of their bends, it is equally important that **waste-pipes** and **service-pipes** should be of **full bore** right throughout, and not throttled in their bends, as unfortunately is too often the case.

16. For bending lead pipes of a size too small for the hand dummy or long dummy to be of any service, a piece of bent gas-pipe, or **iron bolts**, as shown at A and B, fig. 69, will serve the plumber's need. The bolts are better when made of steel.

17. A skilful pipe-bender can generally manage to **bend** strong lead **service-pipes** by giving them an easy radius, without contracting them to any noticeable extent. To do this, heat the pipe where it is to be bent up to hissing-point when spat upon. Then lay the pipe down on its side, placing a thick piece of soft leather or felt, or two or three thicknesses of carpet, under one of the bulged sides of the bend, and then, with your old cap or ladle-felt placed upon the other side—the part facing you— to act as a buffer to break the sharpness of the blows, drive the bulged part of the side round to the heel of the bend. Turn the pipe over, and do the same to the other side.

18. Although the method of bending service-pipes is also

very helpful in **bending light lead pipes**—as waste-pipes—the iron bolts must be resorted to, to work out the parts contracted in the bending; and this is readily done where the bend is near the end of a pipe; and for this reason pipes have often to be cut, but it is better to cut a pipe to a shorter length to make the bend in it full bore rather than fix a long pipe with a restricted bend in it.

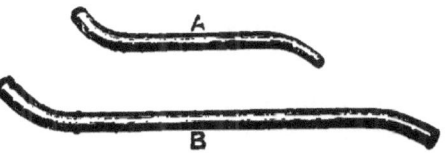

Fig. 69.—VIEW OF IRON BOLTS.

19. Lead funnel-pipes are also **bent by filling them with sand**; but in this method the substance of the lead at the heel—the back of the bend—gets much reduced, and there is no surplus or bulged parts for working round to thicken it again, as in a kink for dummying out (Art. 9).

CHAPTER XX.

NON-CLEANSING PLUMBERS' TRAPS.

1.

THE young plumber having in the days of his apprenticeship or mateship and improvership acquired the knowledge of joint-making and pipe-bending, is then in a position to assist in the execution of the internal plumbers' work of a building; but as the first thing generally to be done is to fix the soil-pipes, the **traps for the closets** must first be determined upon.

2. In the evil days, when **traps for the closets, sinks, baths, urinals, and lavatories were made up by hand,**

according to the sweet will of the plumber, he generally so willed it that they should be of the most accumulative kind; and so to every appliance, sanitary or otherwise, requiring a trap, he fixed an unsanitary D-trap.

3. In limiting the size of a trap to 9 in. or 10 in. the maker of the trap was not so much governed by the depth of his wisdom as by the depth of the joists—the space between the closet floor and the ceiling; as in scores of cases on ground floors, where there was no such limit, 13 in. and even 16 in. traps have been found fixed under pan-closets, the nature of which would tend to increase rather than to diminish the evil of so large and so foul a trap. I have seen a lead trap of the D-trap kind with two dip-pipes into it, and *two* pan-closets fixed upon it. The size chiefly used for fixing under a wash-hand basin was 6 in., no matter how small the basin or little its waste-plug; and it is not at all an infrequent thing, in making an examination of the sanitary appliances of a house, to come across 7 in. and even 8 in. D-traps fixed under small lead-lined sinks, with a round-hole waste-grating only equal to the flushing-out of a $1\frac{1}{4}$ in. round-pipe trap.

4. From the many old D-traps which have been cut out in the last twenty years, it may fairly be said that the greater the **capacity** of the **trap** the **smaller** must have been the capacity of the man who made it.; for whilst a man here and there did his utmost to improve it by contracting it, notwithstanding the size of the dip-pipe, $4\frac{1}{2}$ in., and the size of the soil-pipe from it, $4\frac{1}{2}$ in. and 5 in., the generality of men, when they found they could not make a trap of the *depth* they preferred, increased its *width* to make up for it, whence traps with 7 in., and in some cases even 9 in. bands. A pailful of filth has been taken out of many such a trap.

5. It may seem curious to search for any reason in the maker of a large **D-trap**, yet he had reasons for making

his traps **deep and wide**. In the larger size for **closets**—the 10 in. instead of the 9 in.—he could not only put the dip-pipe further down into the trap, to give it a greater depth of seal, but he could also increase the size of the hole to the outgo, making it round instead of ⌐-shape. And the wider band—7 in. and 9 in., instead of 6 in.—gave him a wider base upon which he could the better solder the end of the soil-pipe, which was often 5 in. bore.

6. In the case of **D-traps under sinks and lavatories**, experience taught the plumber that such traps soon stopped up; but rather than abandon that type of trap for one of a "self-cleansing" kind, he preferred to increase the size of the trap, so he made it large enough to solder a 4 in. or a $4\frac{1}{2}$ in., and in some cases even a 6 in. brass cap-and-screw in one of its cheeks, for a man's hand to be put into the trap, to remove any obstruction, and to clean out the accumulated filth. In examining a Fire Insurance Office in the city of London only a few months ago, it was found that a 12 in. D-trap with a 9 in. band, a 6 in. outgo, and a 5 in. brass cap-and-screw, had been fixed, within the last few years, under a lead-lined sink, the discharges from which would only be equal to filling a pipe $1\frac{1}{4}$ in. bore.

7. The D-trap has had a long reign in England, from the days of the privy, a century ago, to the dawn of house sanitary science, within the last two decades, when it was dethroned; although to this day it is not without its advocates, and a benighted man here and there about the country, and especially in London, still goes on fixing them, disgracing the craft with his evil practices. A few technological students, unlike Cæsar's wife, are not without suspicion; but judging from their written papers a very large majority of the students have a good knowledge of traps, which must be very gratifying to their teachers. If what has been said already and what follows does not convince the sceptic—the maker of D-traps—of the error of his

ways, neither would he be convinced though one of his victims returned to upbraid him.

8. About the **first form of trap** used for fixing under water-closets was the **syphon trap**, *i.e.*, a pipe bent and recurved in the shape of the letter ∽; but as the water in such a trap was easily syphoned or momentumed out, and the means of preventing such a loss of zeal little understood, the D-trap was invented. That the syphon or round-pipe trap was in use more than a century ago is proved by the date of Cumming's patent, where, in 1775, he shows a syphon-trap under a valve-closet, fig. 121, Chap. XXVIII.

9. There is proof in the records of the Patent Office that the D-trap was in use in 1790. Fig. 70 represents perhaps

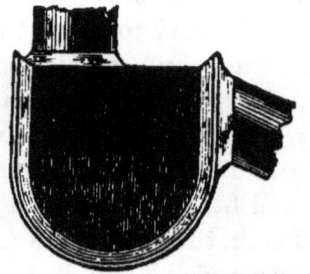 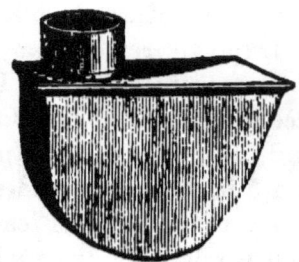

Fig. 70.—View of a D-Trap, Early Shape.   Fig. 71.—View of a D-Trap, Modern Shape.

the oldest form of it, with its cheeks soldered *outside* to the band; by this method the cheeks could be kept closer together than when the cheeks were soldered to the band inside the trap, and still give a wider base for soldering the outgo—the soil-pipe—to the trap.

10. The **internal surface** of a 9 in. **D-trap**, fig. 71, is nearly double that of a 4 in. round-pipe trap, fig. 83; and even the improved D-trap—the 4 in. band trap—is twice that of my "Anti-D," fig. 81, though a body of water can be discharged in less time through the "Anti-D" than through the D-trap. The internal surface of a 9 in. D-trap

NON-CLEANSING PLUMBERS' TRAPS. 115

with a 6 in. band is about 3 ft. 6 in. sup.; in the "improved" or narrow-band D-trap it is about 3 ft. In a 4 in. round-pipe trap, as fig. 83, it is under 2 ft.; in my closet "Anti-D-trap," fig. 81, it is only about 15 or 16 in. The outgo is not considered in the measurements of any of these traps.

In fig. 72 an illustration is given showing the internal surfaces drawn to scale of a closet D-trap, omitting the soldered angle, but showing where the surfaces would become coated over with filth. There are the inner sides of the two cheeks, A and B, the inner side of the band, C, the under side of the top, D, the outer side of the dip-pipe, E—which stands inside the trap—and its inner side, F. All these surfaces, A, B, C, D, E, are exposed to any matter sent into the trap from the water-closet upon it.

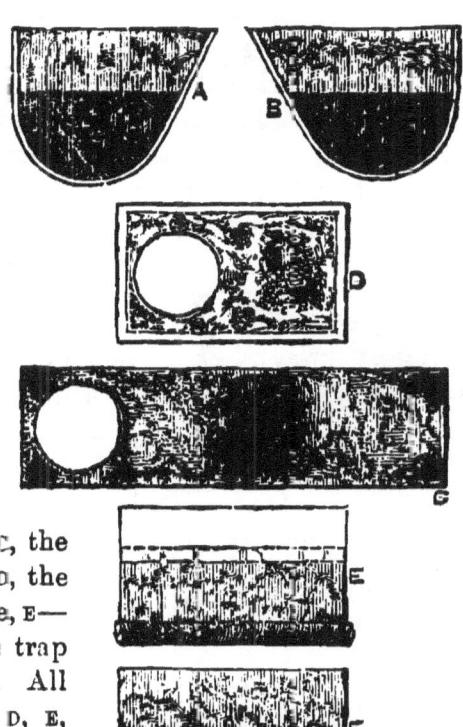

Fig. 72.—SHOWING INNER SURFACES OF A 9 IN. D-TRAP.

The misfortune is that when the large exposed surface became coated over with fæcal matter, from splashings and accumulations, it could not be thoroughly cleansed again, even by several flushes of water; for no scouring flush could be sent round upon the exterior of the dip-pipe, nor upon the upper part of the cheeks and the band at the back of the dip-pipe, nor over the under side of the top.

The matter sent into the trap may have come from a patient suffering from a most infectious disease; and, instead of trying to wash it out of the trap by several pulls of the closet-handle, only one flush of water may be given, and the larger portion of the **infectious discharge be left in the trap** to generate noxious gases to be sent up through the closet into the house by the next usage of the apparatus, to be added to by further secretions. The gases generated, as well as the stench given forth from such a storage of filth, would not only find their way out at the ventilating-pipe of the soil-pipe, to pollute the atmosphere surrounding the house, but often at a more serious place still, viz., at the disconnection at the foot of the soil-pipe. With an unventilated valve-box, and with the closet at rest, gases would also collect in the dip-pipe, as in an inverted jar, to be displaced by the next discharge of the closet, and sent up into the face of the person pulling the closet-handle.

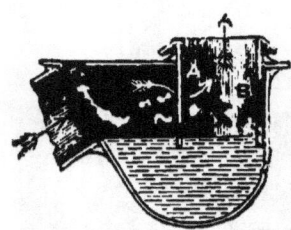

Fig. 73.—Internal view of an old D-trap, showing the evil of a Dip-Pipe being inside a Trap.

11. Apart from the evil of fixing a trap which can never be properly cleansed, as the D-trap, there is great **risk in fixing a trap with its dip-pipe, or part of its dip-pipe, standing inside the trap.** There is always a danger of the dip-pipe, or that part of it which partitions off the air in the soil-pipe from the house side of the water-seal of the trap, becoming defective, and that, too, in a part where a defect would never be disclosed, except to the olfactory nerves; for no matter how large such a defect might be, there would be no leakage of water from it to indicate any defect, as would at once be the case with a defect in the

dip of a round-pipe trap, as fig. 83, or in the "Anti-D," fig. 81.

Although no water-leakage would be indicated by any number of defects in that part of a dip-pipe which stands within a trap, the **bad air in the soil-pipe** would find an **easy passage** to the house side of the water-seal of the trap through only a small defect, as shown by the arrows in fig. 73.

12. At the discussion which followed my lectures ten years ago, an "improved" D-trap was talked about, a trap which had no existence prior to my criticism of the D-trap in general use. But, as I have explained elsewhere, this

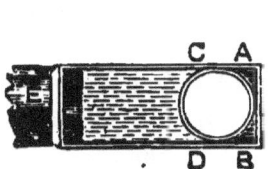

Fig. 74.—PLAN OF TRAP, FIG. 75.

Fig. 75.—VIEW OF THE "NARROW-BAND" D-TRAP, WITH SQUARE PIPE OUTLET (J).

trap possesses all the great evils of the old trap. The improvement consists in bringing the two cheeks (the sides) of the trap closer together, so as to leave as little space as possible between the dip-pipe and the inner sides of the cheeks, as shown on plan, fig. 74, i.e., in the *full-sized* D-trap, the *band*, c, fig. 72, is 6 in. wide, but in this trap, figs. 74 and 75, it is only $4\frac{1}{4}$ in. wide, so that the cheeks of the trap stand closer together by $1\frac{3}{4}$ in., making the trap more compact, and less difficult to flush out. But to call this trap *self-cleansing* would be misleading, for the *inner* surfaces of the trap are just the same as in the full-sized D-trap, minus about 5 in. sup., for the narrower band and narrower top, i.e., the internal surface of this "narrow-band" D-trap would be equal to about 3 ft. sup. No scouring flush could be sent up the two vertical angles, A and B, fig. 74, nor at D and C, so that these parts would become lodgments for filth; and the dip-pipe, though it would often get splashed over with excremental matter, would rarely, if ever, get thoroughly cleansed, for no frictional force could be brought to bear upon it, from F G H, and upwards. Then there is the evil of the *dip-pipe* being *inside* the walls of the trap (Art. 11).

13. The criticisms on the usual form of D-trap brought the "**Helmet**" D-trap into notice, but a moment's examination of the trap, illustrated in fig. 76, will suffice to show, that whilst the lower part of the trap is improved, all the bad principles of its elder brother are retained. As a matter of fact, nearly a quarter of a century ago I had our D-traps made up in a similar fashion, except that instead of burning the edges of the lead together, they were soldered. The lower part of the trap, the body, was *bossed* up on a hardwood block, in shape as shown in fig. 76.

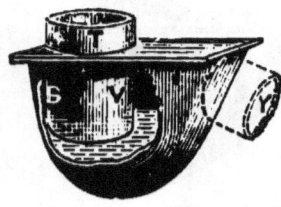

Fig. 76.—VIEW OF THE "HELMET" TRAP.

14. In Table No. 1, in the following chapter, the results of several **tests** made with both "non-cleansing" and self-cleansing **closet-traps** are given, to show at a glance the difference in the number of clean-water flushes required to rid the various traps of certain matters put into them. And as a practical proof was given to the audience, in one of my lectures in the rooms of the Society of Arts, of the difficulty of freeing even a small-size D-trap from filth, when once it had become fouled, an illustration of the trap used is given on the next page; and an extract from the "Lectures" is also made, as the result of the experiments may not be without interest to the student plumber.

"I will not say any more on the D-trap for water-closets; and instead of occupying your time with a lengthy criticism on the smaller sizes for trapping off what are called 'dirty water' wastes (to distinguish them from sewage wastes, soil-pipes, drains, etc.), we will give a few practical experiments to show their unfitness for such purposes. In doing this, we will not aggravate the case by using the trap unfairly, for instead of using such adhesive matter as greasy water from saucepans, etc., we will use a little soapy water, and after that some plain water with a little stone-blue put into it to colour it.

"I have had a small-size D-trap made with glass cheeks to it, for you to see the working inside, and this trap is connected to a small wash-hand-basin with 1 in. brass plug-and-washer, the usual size being only ¾ in. This trap is made *much smaller* than the usual 'small-size' hand-made D-trap, or than the small-size cast-lead D-trap, so that any experiment made upon it will be more favourable for cleansing it than would be the case with the D-traps as generally used in practice." Fig. 77 illustrates this trap, B, with a small wash-hand-basin, A, fixed upon it. The depth from the top to the band is 4 in., the width of the band, between the cheeks, 3 in., and the length along the top 6 in. The dip-pipe first used was 1 in., and the distance from the bottom of the basin to the standing water of the trap is 8 in. The short length of waste-pipe, C, consisted

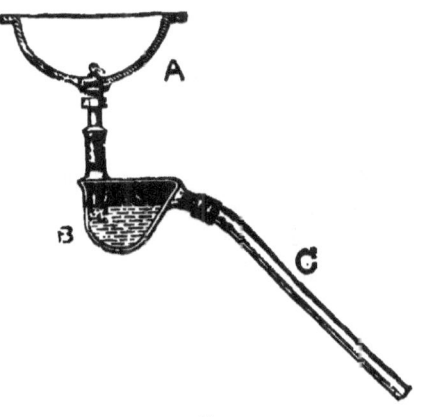

SCALE ¾ IN = 1 FT

Fig. 77.—SMALL-SIZE D-TRAP, WITH GLASS CHEEKS.

of a piece of glass tubing. [In some subsequent experiments the dip-pipe was increased in size to 1½ in., with a similar result, a non-cleansing of the trap.]

"Two or three experiments were then made with this model, to show the non-cleansing nature of D-traps. Some blue water, *i.e.*, water coloured with stone-blue, was put into the trap, and though two or three charges of clean water from the basin were sent into it, the whole of the blue water was not removed. The trap was then charged with soapy water, as in practice when fixed under lavatories would be the case, but though several flushes of clean water from the basin were sent into the trap, every vestige of soapy water was not removed, and with one flush the suds remained strongly in the trap, floating about and around the dip-pipe.

Fig. 78.—SECTION OF A BELL-TRAP.

"The experiments showed clearly enough how such traps become *cesspools*, or *filth-collecting* boxes. And yet there are thousands of such traps in use in England to-day, under baths, sinks, urinals, safes, lavatories, and water-closets."

15. The **bell-trap** is only introduced here to show the student plumber how poor a trap sufficed to satisfy the ideas of plumbers of a past generation; for to-day no plumber with any sanitary notions would venture to palm off so inadequate an appliance for preventing the passage of bad air into a house.

Its depth of water-seal is so small that the banging to of the door of the room where it is fixed, with the windows shut, would almost suffice to break the seal; but apart from the effect of any concussion of air upon the seal, it would soon be diminished by evaporation, or by capillary attraction from a piece of rag, hair, cotton, or worsted hanging over the weir of the trap, at *c*. Nor is its aptitude to lose its water-seal the only grievance caused by it; for to the cook, housemaid, and scullery-maid the great grievance is that they have to waste so much time in getting their slops through it.

16. As all mechanical appliances get out of order sooner or later, and as **traps** with **mechanical seals, or check valves**, have such devices fixed inside them where they cannot be seen, it is better not to trust to them, but to fix traps which have no parts or appliances to get out of order—traps which, with an anti-syphoning pipe, may be trusted to last as long as the fixture under which they are fixed, so that the failure first of that part which is visible shall lead to an examination of that part which, in the case of certain fixtures, is always out of sight. I have treated this subject more fully in " Dulce Domum."

CHAPTER XXI.

SELF-CLEANSING PLUMBERS' TRAPS.

1.

TO examine and criticise the various traps fixed by plumbers throughout the United Kingdom would need more space than is contained between the covers of this book; but having in the previous chapter discussed at some length the non-cleansing class, the traps which, like ponds, are filth-accumulators; and the traps which, when defective in certain of their parts, to the eye, even on close examination, would show no defect; as well as that most illusory of traps, the bell-trap; it will not occupy much space to discuss the **self-cleansing** class, the **traps** through which matters pass, when properly flushed, like jets of water through the air, leaving no trace behind.

2. Before discussing certain self-cleansing traps in use, it may be better to lay down the **principles on which traps** for plumbers' work and drainage work should be constructed, and the conditions on which they should be fixed. In doing this I extract largely from my "Lectures."

(*a*) The trap should be free from all angles, corners, and places where filth could accumulate.

(*b*) A free way should be made for the discharges to pass through the trap without breaking their form, *i.e.*, the traps should be like a round pipe, so made or bent as to form a water-seal of about $1\frac{1}{2}$ or 2 in. deep.

(*c*) The body of the trap should be smaller than its inlet, so as to hold as small a quantity of water as possible, consistent with the position in which it will be placed and the work it will have to do, to admit of easy changing every time a flush of water is sent through it.

(*d*) The minimum-sized trap should be used consistent with circumstances, but governed to some extent by the size of the waste-pipe or drain on which it is fixed, and the flush of water likely to be sent into it. A trap, though of a self-cleansing form, may become a little cesspool if the size is greater that can be cleansed by an ordinary flush of water from the "fitting," or "fixture"—wash-hand-basin, sink, or water-closet—on which it is fixed.

(*e*) The water-way into a trap for fixing to flat-bottomed vessels with a grating over its mouth, should be larger than its body part, or than the waste-pipe with which its outlet may be connected, so as to be able to send efficient water-flushes through the trap to cleanse it and its waste-pipe. When the trap is smaller than the waste-pipe, no good flushes can be sent through the pipe to cleanse it. (See figs. 79 and 80, showing such traps; or the plumber can easily cone a piece of lead pipe for receiving a larger

SELF-CLEANSING PLUMBERS' TRAPS. 123

grating or plug, or washer, and solder this to the inlet of a syphon-trap.)

(*f*) The inlet, or mouth of the trap, should be so arranged that the water-flushes shall fall upon the "standing water" of the trap with a vertical pressure, so as to drive everything foreign out of the trap, and to entirely change its previous contents.

(*g*) The *inlet* side of all traps fixed upon drains outside the house should be *open to the atmosphere*, so that any bad air rising from foul matter decomposing in the trap, or

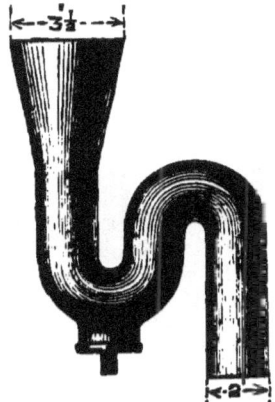
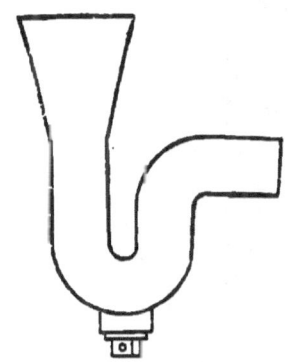

Fig. 79.—2 IN. S-TRAP, WITH ENLARGED MOUTH.

Fig. 80.—2 IN. HALF-S-TRAP, WITH ENLARGED MOUTH.

coming through it from the drain or sewer, may readily pass into the open air, or be largely diluted with fresh air before passing into any waste-pipe, soil-pipe, or drain emptying into such traps.

In cold countries, where the water standing in such open traps would be liable to freeze in severe frosts, the mouth of the trap should be sealed over, and the "foot-ventilation," or fresh air-induct, should be taken into the waste-pipe, soil-pipe, or drain some little distance up or away from the water-seal of the trap, to prevent the cold air-currents playing upon it and freezing it. In this country, in sheltered places, there is little or no risk; and if the trap (for disconnecting waste-pipes, soil-pipes, or drains) is kept well down into the ground in exposed places, there is no danger from frosts, though in very severe frosts it is well to throw a little straw upon the surface-gratings of such traps.

Another advantage is gained by keeping the fresh air-induct pipe some little distance up (say 15 ins.) from the bottom of a trapped soil or waste-pipe, for when a full and rapid discharge of water is sent into a soil or waste-pipe it

Fig. 81.—View of "Anti-D-Trap," for Closets.

Fig. 82.—Section.

does not get away as fast as it enters, but accumulates in the bottom of the pipe, and, rising up in the pipe, would readily flow into the foot-ventilating or air-induct pipe if kept too low down, and perhaps stop it up with foreign matter.

3. Of all the traps that are made there is none so easy to cleanse as the round-pipe trap commonly called the syphon-trap, when its body or lower part is contracted. With its lower part the same size as its inlet, *i.e.*, when it is of equal bore right throughout, for closets and sinks the "Anti-D-trap" is the more self-cleansing of the two. Nor is this difficult to understand. In the "Anti-D-trap," as

SELF-CLEANSING PLUMBERS' TRAPS.

shown in figs. 81 and 82, the lower part of the trap is purposely much reduced in size for the flushes to pass through it in the form of a water-plug, to scour out the whole of the interior of the trap. But in the round-pipe trap, fig. 83, whether Beard and Dent's cast-lead trap, or the "Du Bois" hydraulic drawn-lead trap, the lower part of the trap being of equal bore with the inlet, no frictional force is brought to bear upon the lower part of the trap, by an ordinary flush of water, to wash out any sediment.

4. **The quantity of water for closets** graciously allowed by the Water Companies of the Metropolis is two gallons. How can so small a quantity be discharged quickly enough through a waste-preventing apparatus to pass through a 4 in. trap in a volume large enough to fill the bore of so large a trap? And so, though the form of the round-pipe trap is even easier to wash out than the Anti-D-trap, in practice the latter is the most self-cleansing of the two, and this is also proved by certain tests (see Table on next page).

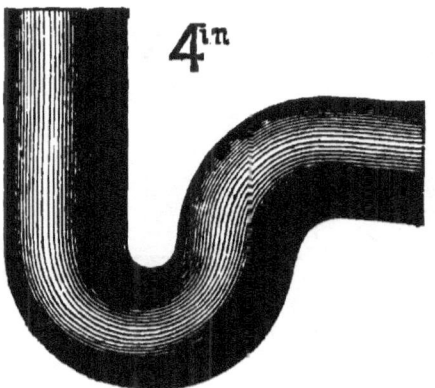

Fig. 83.—VIEW OF "HALF-S" ROUND-PIPE TRAP.

An Anti-D-trap has been in use under the closet shown at L, fig. 95A, for ten years, and it is still clean and wholesome. In making some tests with it just after it was fixed, it was found to be so self-cleansing, that with the supply of water to the closet by a 1¼ in. valve and bellows regulator apparatus, the following matters were readily washed out of the trap:

(a) Twelve pieces of water-closet paper, put into the

TABLE (No. 1) SHOWING THE NUMBER OF WATER-FLUSHES REQUIRED TO CLEANSE VARIOUS TRAPS OF CERTAIN MATTERS PUT INTO THEM.

NOTE.—The traps were each fixed in turn under the valve closet, A, and connected to the 4 in. soil-pipe at B, as shown in the woodcut, Fig. 86. The basin was filled up to the overflow-arm in each flush (about one gallon of water), and no water was allowed to come into the closet during the time of the discharge.

Quantity of Water held in Trap.	Depth of Water-seal.	Traps Tested.	RESULTS. Matter put into Traps, with number of Flushes to clean same out.				
			Twelve pieces of w.C. Paper, 6½ in. × 5 in.	Six pieces of Paper, and six pieces of short India-rubber Tubing.	Ten pieces of India-rubber Tubing.	Two teaspoonfuls of Ink.
2½ Pints	1⅝ in., f.	"Anti-D-Trap," *for closets*, fig. 81 . . .	One flush	One flush	One flush	One flush
4½ Pints	2 in.	"Round-pipe" Trap, "U-shaped," fig. 83	One flush	One flush cleared all, except one piece of paper.	One flush cleared all, except one piece of I. R.	One flush
6½ Pints	1¼ in.	D-Trap (Pullen's *cast lead*) .	Two flushes	Three flushes	Four flushes	Three flushes
5 Pints	1¼ in.	,, "*Narrow-band*," fig. 75	Three flushes	Three flushes	Three flushes	Three flushes
4¾ Pints	1¼ in.	,, "*Helmet*," fig. 76 . .	Three flushes	Two flushes	Three flushes	Three flushes

N.B.—With the same matters put into the closet-basin, A, instead of into the traps, it took an *extra* flush in the "self-cleansing" traps, and in the "non-cleansing" traps two extra flushes, to pass the same matters out of the basin and through the trap. With a proper service of water laid on to the closet, and the matters put into the basin instead of into the trap, the results were about the same as (in Table 1) with the matters put into the trap and no water laid on to the basin. The tabulated tests were made without any water laid on to the closet at the time of the discharge, to prevent one trap getting a greater flush than another.

SELF-CLEANSING PLUMBERS' TRAPS.

valve-closet basin, L, were easily sent out of the basin and through the Anti-D-trap, M, under it, with one pull of the closet-handle—*i.e.*, with the closet-handle pulled up as far as it would go, and held there for two seconds, or with the handle slowly pulled up and closed, giving only a fair flush of water.

(*b*) Ten pieces of india-rubber (5 ps. 1¼ in. dia. 1¾ in. long, and 5 ps. 1 in. dia. 1½ in. long) were easily sent out of the closet-basin, and through the trap, with one fair flush of water.

(*c*) With the water in the basin well coloured with plumbers' soil, one pull of the handle washed it out of the basin and trap, leaving not a vestige behind.

(*d*) After the closet had been used for the purpose of nature, one fair flush of water, by pulling up the closet-handle and slowly closing it, washed the matter both out of the basin and trap.

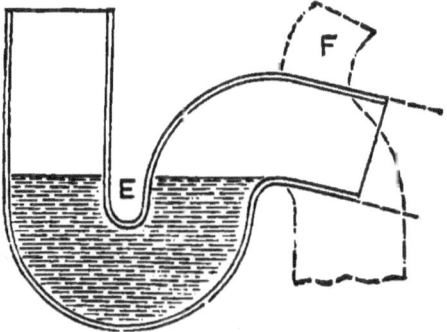

Fig. 84.—SECTION.

5. The body or lower part of the Anti-D-trap for closets is fully one-fourth smaller in diameter than at the inlet. It measures 4¼ in. at its mouth, and 3 in. under the tongue at B; that is, the **area of the water-way into the trap** is 14·18, and 7·06 in the lower part, against 12·56 in the 4 in. round-pipe trap; so that a body of water one-third less in volume would suffice to fill the bore of the former under the dip, than would be necessary to fill the bore of the latter at the same point.

In Table No. 1 the results are given of some experiments made with various traps fixed under a valve-closet, and in

128   PLUMBING.

fig. 85 an illustration is given of the apparatus experimented with.

6. In fixing round-pipe traps, as figs. 86 and 87, to flat-

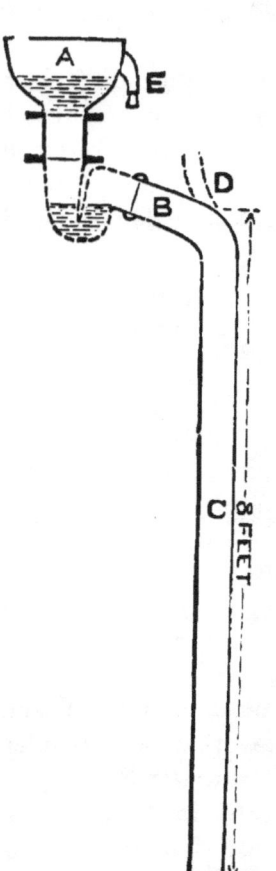

Fig. 85.—Showing Arrangement for Testing Traps.

Fig. 86.—"Half-S" Round-Pipe Trap.

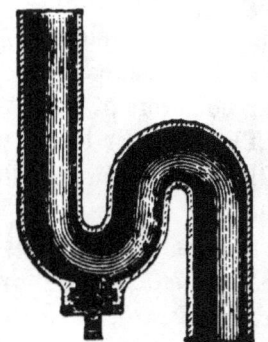

Fig. 87.—"S" Round-Pipe Trap, Section.

bottomed vessels, as sinks, trays, etc., it is difficult to **open the mouth of the trap** large enough to receive a brass grating, or plug-and-washer, which would give a water-way through them equal in area to the bore of the lower part of the trap. When a plumber is directed to fix a round-pipe trap to a sink, he should solder a cone or trumpet-pipe to the trap to increase the size of its mouth, as shown in figs. 79 and 80.

7. For the purpose of fixing a large brass plug-and-washer over the **sink-trap**, to insure a thorough cleansing of the trap every time a sink is emptied, the Anti-D-trap, fig. 88, is made with a tapering inlet; the mouth of the trap being two-thirds larger in area than in the body of the trap, as shown by the figured dimensions in the illustra-

Fig. 88.—View of Anti-D-Trap for Sinks, etc.   Fig. 89.—View of 1¼ in. Anti-D-Trap, with 2½ in. Inlet.   Fig. 90.—View of 1¼ in. Anti-D-Trap.

tion, the former being 3½ in., and the latter 2 in. For butlers' sinks, where a 1¼ in. or 1½ in. waste-pipe is a better size, being more easily cleansed than a 2 in. pipe, a 1¼ in. Anti-D-trap, with a 2½ in. inlet, as fig. 89, is large enough, as, possessing a large mouth, there is no difficulty in fixing a 2 in. brass plug-and-washer into it, and soldering them to the bottom of the sink.

8. In the lectures several tests (Art. 14, previous chap.) were made with a very small D-trap, to show how difficult it is to cleanse such a form of trap when fixed under sinks and lavatories, as well as when fixed under closets; and as

some **tests** were also made with a **round-pipe trap** to show the difference in the cleansing effect of small flushes of water on the two classes of traps, the result of the tests then made are quoted here. The trap experimented with is illustrated at D, fig. 91. It is a glass tube, 1 in. bore, bent into the shape of the "Half-S" round-pipe trap, and to enable the audience to see what took place inside it a strong light was thrown upon the trap from a bull's-eye lantern.

(*a*) "The glass 'round-pipe' trap (D, fig. 91) was charged with blue water, and a small flush of clean water was then sent into the trap from the wash-basin (B), washing out the blue water and leaving the trap perfectly clean.

(*b*) "The trap was then filled nearly up to the level of its 'standing water' to the top of the water-seal with india-rubber cut into small pieces, and this was completely washed out of the trap by a flush of about three pints of water sent into it from the basin.

(*c*) "The water in the trap was then well coloured with plumbers' soil, and a handful of gravel was also put into the trap; and the whole of it washed out, and the trap left clean, by a small flush of water from the basin.

(*d*) "The trap was also tested with strong soapy water with a like result, *i.e.*, the soapy water was washed out and the trap cleansed by a small flush of clean water from the basin."

CHAPTER XXII.

THE LOSS OF WATER-SEAL IN TRAPS.

1.

THE sole purpose for which a trap is employed is to prevent any passage of air into a house through a pipe which has been fouled by dirty water, soapy water, or by excrementitious discharges; and he who fixes a trap which does not comply with this essential acquirement incurs a responsibility which, in this enlightened age of anti-syphoning knowledge, no pleadings of ignorance should free him from.

2. The **water-seal** of a trap may be **lost in several ways.** It (a) may be forced out by back-pressure; or (b) be syphoned out; or (c) be momentumed out, or momentumed and syphoned out; or (d) it may be lost by evaporation; or (e) it may be blown out, or waved out. But as I have dwelt at great length on the subject of syphonage in my work "Dulce Domum," I need not go into the matter at great length here; and this is to be rejoiced in, for however much I might wish to extend the subject here, there is no space for me to do so.

3. In fig. 91 an illustration is given of a model bath and lavatory, fixed one over the other, which was fitted up for my experiments at the lectures, among other purposes to show how in practice a discharge from one fixture **syphoned out the water-seal** of a trap fixed under another fixture, when branched into the same stack-pipe, without an anti-syphoning pipe; and after briefly describing the apparatus I will give the results of several tests made in the presence of my audience.

132　　　　　　　　　PLUMBING.

The illustration nearly explains itself. The bath, A, is supposed to be fixed on the 1st floor, and the lavatory, B, on the ground floor, as so often occurs in practice. The traps

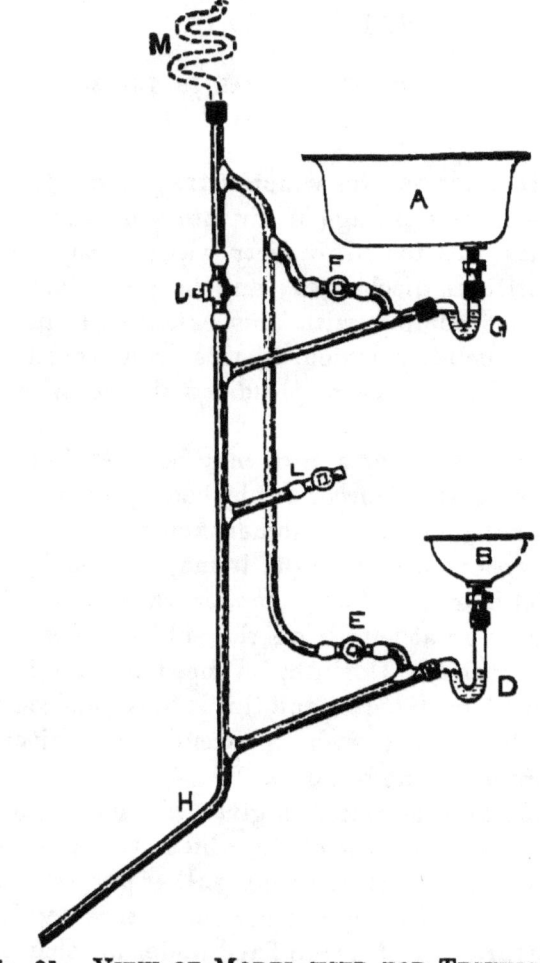

Fig. 91.—VIEW OF MODEL USED FOR TESTING TRAPS.

under the bath and lavatory are each 1 in., made of glass, in the shape exactly, or as near as may be, of the "Half-S" round-pipe trap. From each trap a lead branch pipe, 1 in.

bore, is branched into a stack of 1 in. lead waste-pipe. An anti-syphoning pipe, 1 in. bore, is fixed to each trap, under the control of clear-way stop-cocks, E and F, for putting it out of use when not required, and the pipe is branched into the main waste-pipe above the highest discharge into it. A stop-cock, J, is fixed in the main pipe just above the highest branch to shut off the ventilation-pipe for certain experiments. A branch pipe, L, with a stop-cock on its end, is also fixed upon the main pipe without an anti-syphoning pipe, for attaching traps to it when so wanted. The bent spiral pipe, M, was only occasionally used, its purpose being to prove that a bent ventilation-pipe on the top of a soil-pipe or waste-pipe, when kept full bore, had but slight influence upon the egress or ingress of air.

"Among other experiments, the following were made, the stop-cocks (E, F, and J) being shut to stop the ventilation.

(1a.) "By discharging a small quantity of water from the bath, A, the lavatory trap, D, was unsealed.

(2a.) "By discharging a basinful of water from the lavatory, B, the bath trap, G, above, was similarly unsealed.

(3a.) "By discharging a small quantity of water out of the bath, and suddenly shutting off the waste-valve, both traps, D and G, were unsealed.

(4a.) "By discharging a basinful of water from the lavatory, B, both the upper trap G, and lower trap, D, were unsealed.

(5a.) "The main waste-pipe was then ventilated full bore by opening the stop-cock J; and, though this prevented the bath-trap, G, from being syphoned by a discharge from the lavatory, it did not prevent the seal of its own trap, D, from being momentumed out.

(6a.) "With the main waste-pipe open at top and bottom, and the anti-syphoning pipe closed by the stop-cocks E and F, the emptying of the bath unsealed the lavatory trap and momentumed the water out of its own trap.

"Some experiments were then made with the D-trap, B, fig. 77, the Bower trap, fig. 92, and the "Eclipse" trap, to show that, though these traps were not syphoned with the ease with which round-pipe traps were, they were by no means proof against the action of discharges sent through them, or through the main pipes into which they may be branched.

(7a.) "The small D-trap, B, fig. 77, was fixed on the unventilated branch, L, and the stop-cocks, E, F, J, shut. The bath was then emptied. During the whole time of the discharge the water in the trap, as was readily seen through the cheeks, which were of glass, was kept in a very agitated state, and by the time seven or eight gallons of water had passed through the main pipe the D-trap had lost nearly half its seal.

Fig. 92.—"Bower" Trap.

(8a.) "The Bower trap, $1\frac{1}{2}$ in., fig. 92, was then fixed on the unventilated branch, at L, in lieu of the small D-trap, but before half-a-dozen gallons of water had been discharged from the bath it had lost more than three-fourths of its seal; and after a further discharge of a few gallons more the trap was practically syphoned to the edge of the dip-pipe, which only required the smallest vibration to break the seal."

4. The foregoing experiments proved that two traps fixed on one pipe, like two negatives in a sentence, destroy each other. And they also further proved that those who depend upon the ventilation of the main pipe only, be it a soil or waste-pipe, depend upon means inadequate for the protection of a house from bad air; for, as clearly shown, an air pipe on the main pipe, though of the same size, is insufficient to prevent round-pipe traps, and self-cleansing traps from being syphoned, when large bodies of water are sent through the main piping.

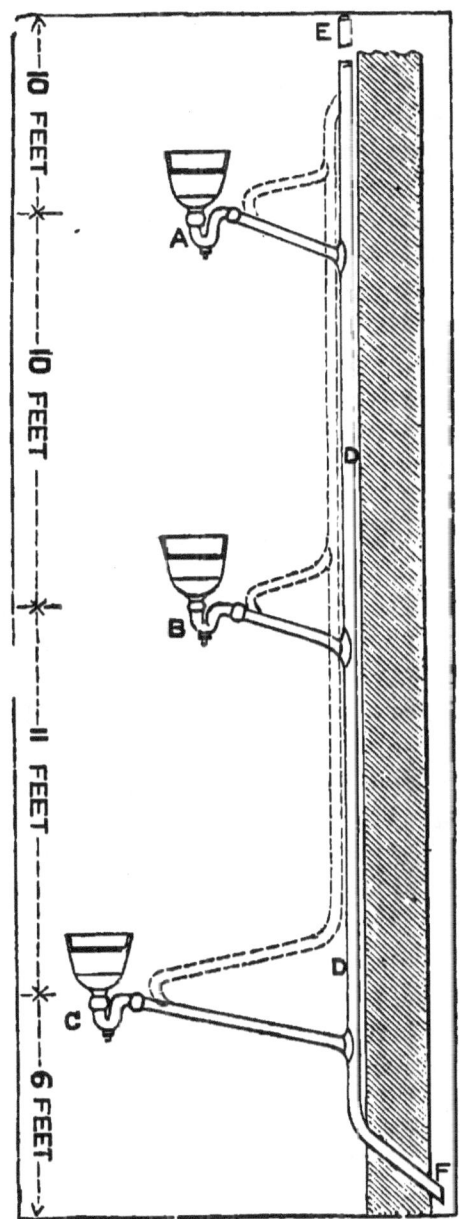

Fig. 93.—Showing a Stack of Waste-Pipe, with Three Slop-Sinks upon it, as used for Testing Syphonage of Round-Pipe Traps.

5. I have made a few extracts from the "Lectures," which will be found on the following two or three pages, giving the results of some further tests with traps, and which, like the results of certain tests already given, clearly prove that a main stack of pipe, waste-pipe or soil-pipe, with branches entering it in various levels, is insufficiently ventilated, though open full bore at top and bottom, to prevent loss of seal in the traps fixed upon it.

Fig. 93 represents a stack of 2 in. waste-pipe fixed inside a house to take the discharges from three slop-sinks—one each on the 1st floor, 2nd floor, and 3rd floor; 2 in. round pipe-traps—with pieces of glass fixed in their sides, to see into them—were fixed under the sinks at A, B, and C.

(1b.) Without the anti-syphoning pipe, shown in dotted lines, a pailful of water thrown down sink A syphoned more than half the water-seal out of traps B and C, and the emptying of the next pail practically unsealed them.

(2b.) With the top of the main waste-pipe, E, sealed over, and a pailful of water thrown down sink B, the water-seal of traps A and C was lowered each about an inch. Another pailful robbed these traps of their seals.

(3b.) With a 2 in. anti-syphoning pipe, as shown in dotted lines, the emptying of several pailfuls of water into sinks A and B produced no appreciable effect upon the other traps; but the trap under the sink into which the water was emptied lost part of its seal by momentum, or momentum and syphonage combined.

6. In fig. 94 another arrangement is shown for testing traps, and the results of some of the tests made with it follow the description of the apparatus. The main waste-pipe is 2 in., with 2 in. branches into it. A 2 in. round-pipe trap is fixed at O and P; $1\frac{1}{2}$ in. at Q and V; 4 in. at T; and $1\frac{1}{4}$ in. at U. A 2 in. anti-syphoning pipe is fixed, as shown in dotted lines, for certain experiments, and which was easily thrown out of use by shutting the stop-cocks, R,

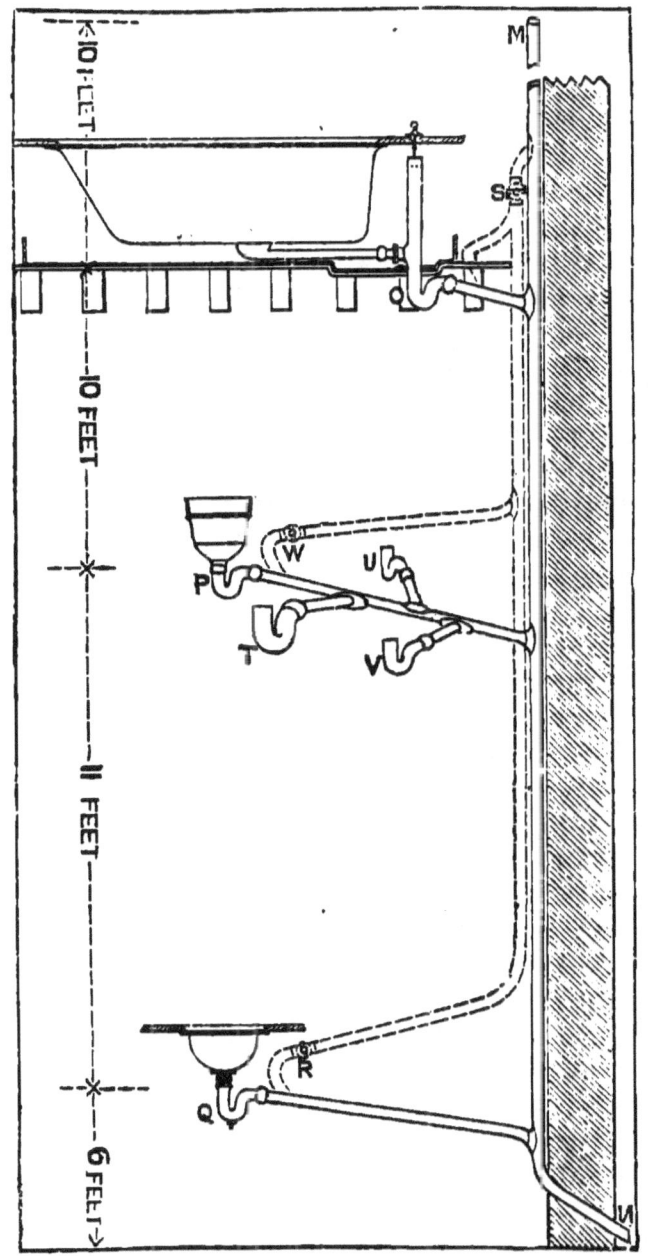

Fig. 94.—SHOWING A STACK OF WASTE-PIPE, WITH SEVERAL TRAPS UPON IT, AS USED FOR TESTING TRAP-SYPHONAGE.

w, s. Each trap had a piece of glass fixed in one of its sides for making observations.

(1c.) Without the use of the anti-syphoning pipe, the bath was discharged by opening the quick waste-valve, but before one-fourth of the water had passed through the waste-pipe, traps P, Q, U, and V were unsealed, and trap T had lost fully one-half of its seal, but air being then admitted into the branch through the syphoned traps, the action upon this trap (T) ceased.

(2c.) The same experiment was repeated, but with the anti-syphoning pipe in proper use, and though 60 gallons of water was sent out by the bath in $2\frac{1}{4}$ minutes, not one of the traps lost its seal. During the greater part of the time the bath was emptying, the water stood up from an inch to two inches in the dip, or inlet, of each trap—P, T, U, V, and Q; but directly the bath was empty the water returned to its normal level. There was no oscillation of the water in any of the traps, and on measurement it was found that trap U was the only one that had lost any water, and this trap had only lost $\frac{1}{8}$th of an inch, if quite so much.

(3c.) With a slop-sink fixed instead of the lavatory shown in the diagram, and a 2 in. trap under it, the stop-cocks, R, W, S, being shut to prevent trap-ventilation, two or three pailfuls of water thrown down this sink syphoned the water-seal out of trap P, and of several others fixed on the same branch, much reduced the seal of trap O, and its own trap, Q, was left nearly unsealed by the action of momentum, or momentum and syphonage combined.

(4c.) A pailful of water thrown down slop-sink P, without trap-ventilation, syphoned the water-seal out of the several traps fixed on the same branch, also out of trap Q, and considerably reduced the depth of the seal of trap O, and left its own trap, P, without any seal.

(5c.) With the anti-syphoning pipe in use, the stop-cocks R, W, S being open, several pailfuls of water thrown

THE LOSS OF WATER-SEAL IN TRAPS.   139

down the slop-sinks, similarly to the previous tests, failed to produce any serious effect upon the traps, except that in the trap through which the discharges were made the seal was often much reduced by momentum.

7. With the arrangement illustrated in fig. 94A, another series of testings with closet-traps was made. A stack of 3½ in. soil-pipe was fixed as shown, and a Narrow-band D-trap was fixed at B, a full-sized cast-lead D-trap at C, and an "Eclipse" trap at D. A trap was fixed at the foot of the soil-pipe, at E, as was the practice with many. In some of the testings the main pipe was opened to the air, both at top and bottom, but when this is done it is so stated. A Wedgwood ware valve-closet basin, A, was fixed directly over the upper trap, as shown, and the contents of the basin discharged by means of a basin-plug placed over its outlet.

(1e.) By discharging a basinful of water quickly (and sealing over the outlet of the closet-basin directly the discharge had completed its effect upon the trap under it, so that the further effect of the discharge through the main pipe might be thrown upon the other traps), the Narrow-band D-trap,

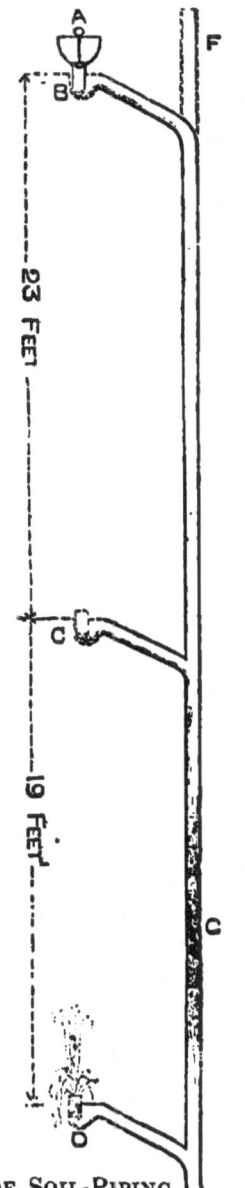

Fig. 94A.—SHOWING STACK OF SOIL-PIPING AS USED FOR TESTING SYPHONAGE AND BACK-PRESSURE.

at B, was syphoned, so much so that the water was left three-eighths of an inch below its dip-pipe; the cast-lead D-trap, at C, lost three-fourths of its seal by syphonage; and the "Eclipse" trap, at D, had some of its water blown out by back-pressure (to the height of three or four feet) on to the floor, causing it to lose more than one-third of its seal.

(2e.) With the Anti-D-trap fixed at B, instead of the Narrow-band D-trap, the result, in a similar trial, was just the same as in Test 1e, except that the water in this trap was left one-eighth of an inch lower.

(3e.) With a "full-sized" cast-lead D-trap fixed at B and the Narrow-band D-trap at C, a discharge from the closet-basin, A, as before, *forced* water out of the "Eclipse" trap at D, reducing its seal one-third; practically syphoned the seal out of the Narrow-band D-trap; and syphoned enough water out of the full-sized D-trap to leave it with only half the depth of its normal water-seal. But it is more than probable that this trap would have lost the whole of its seal had not the syphonic action upon it been broken by an accident. In one of the sides of the trap a piece of glass had been fixed for making observations, and upon the withdrawal of air from its interior by the motion of the piston-like discharge through the soil-pipe, the trap collapsed, which at once broke the glass and allowed the air to rush in to fill the partial vacuum, and to break the syphonic action upon the water-seal of the trap.

8. The positions of the various traps were changed, and it was found by a series of similar trials to those already given, that while the full-sized D-trap withstood the action of syphonage better than any other closet trap—which would be what most plumbers would expect—the seal of the Anti-D-trap was less easily *forced* out by back-pressure than any of the other traps fixed at D. It took ten discharges to drive or force out the seal of the Anti-D-trap,

fixed at D, by the back-pressure of air upon it from discharges sent through the main pipe, but some of the other traps had their seals forced out by only four discharges, the water playing up from them like a fountain, and partly falling back again into the trap, and partly falling outside, as shown in the illustration, fig. 94, A.

Another series of trials was made with the main soil-pipe open to the air *full bore*, at top and bottom, with the results as follows, viz. :—

(1*f*.) With the Anti-D-trap fixed at C, and the basin, A, filled with water and discharged *ten* times, the water was lowered about ¾ in., leaving the trap at the end of the ten discharges with 1 in. seal.

(2*f*.) With a Narrow-band D-trap fixed in the same position, at C, and a similar number of tests, it lost a little over ⅜ in., leaving it with ⅞ in. seal.

9. Another series of experiments were made with the small bath, A, fig. 91, instead of the closet-basin, and this bath was placed over a 4 in. round-pipe trap fixed at B. The bath was discharged by means of a basin-plug fixed over its outlet, and instead of a pipe full bore at F, a 2 in. air-pipe was fixed.

(1*g*.) In two discharges from this bath, the Narrow-band D-trap, fixed at C, lost *three-fourths* of its seal. During the whole of the time the discharge from the bath was passing through the main soil-pipe, the water in this trap was drawn away from its dip-pipe, and air passed through it to the soil-pipe very freely.

(2*g*.) The Anti-D-trap was then fixed instead of the Narrow-band D-trap, and subjected to the same test, and the result was that it was left with ⅛ in. less seal than the other trap.

(3*g*.) A 4 in. round-pipe trap was then fixed at C, and this trap was easily syphoned out by either a discharge from the c oset-basin or bath.

10. The foregoing experiments prove that soil-pipes, like waste-pipes, must have their branches ventilated to prevent loss of water-seal in the traps fixed upon them. They also prove that when more than one trap is fixed upon a vertical stack of pipe, it is not sufficient to fix an air-pipe from the top of the trap and carry it back into the soil-pipe, as shown at E and F, fig. 95. A way of escape must be made for the air driven down by discharges through the main pipe from fixtures on a higher level, or the water-seals of the traps fixed under the fixtures at a lower level will be liable to loss, not only by syphonage, but also by back-pressure, as demonstrated by the foregoing tests.

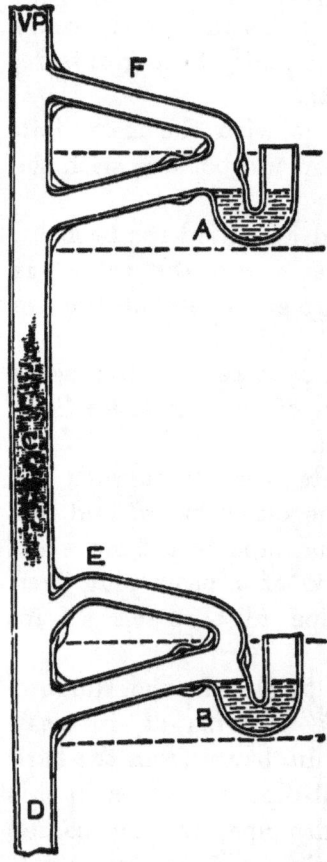

Fig. 95.—SHOWING BAD ARRANGEMENT OF TRAP-VENTS.

11. To ventilate the branches or traps, as shown in fig. 95, is not ventilating the traps according to their needs, though, unfortunately, in practice they are often so treated. With such a method, during the time a discharge is passing through the main pipe, *i.e.*, when the ventilation is most needed for the preservation of the seals of the traps, all ventilation is cut off from the traps below the place of the discharge; *e.g.*, a discharge sent through the upper trap, A, fig. 95, would often pass through the main pipe—waste-pipe or soil-pipe—in a volume large enough to fill the bore of the pipe, in

fact, like a water-plug, as shown at C, and which would for the time being leave the lower trap (or traps) without a vent, the evils of which we have just been considering.

12. As my space is limited, I must refrain from further quotations on traps, except to show how certain traps can be made to maintain their seals; and for this purpose I cannot do better than give the results of some tests made upon a stack of soil-pipes still in use in my factory, and which I extract from "Dulce Domum."

Fig. 95A represents a stack of 3 in. lead soil-pipe which was fixed in 1881, with three closets upon it (G, F, and L) for the use of the people in my factory. The pipe was fixed of this small size as I was satisfied that it was large enough for its purpose, and that it would at the same time afford severer tests to be made upon the seals of the traps fixed upon it when experimenting. I ought just to say, in passing, that this 3 in. pipe has never once stopped up or given the smallest trouble, though the closets have been used by between thirty and fifty people daily for the last ten years. An anti-syphoning pipe is fixed, as shown by the thin lines, under the control of stop-cocks, for experimenting purposes—that is, from the lowest branch upon the stack a 2 in. lead pipe is fixed, and continued up and connected to the stack a little above the highest branch, with a 2 in. branch into it from certain branches on the stack for the proper ventilation of the traps. And the following results, out of many more which might be quoted of a like nature, show clearly enough the value of fixing anti-syphoning pipes. In throwing large bodies of water down the stack through the upper closets, the greatest strain was brought to bear upon a trap fixed at M; and, as shown by the tests ($3h.$), an Anti-D-trap fixed at this crucial point, and when properly ventilated, stood a series of tests stronger than it is ever likely to sustain in practice, being left, after twelve discharges through the main pipe, with $1\frac{1}{2}$ in. seal.

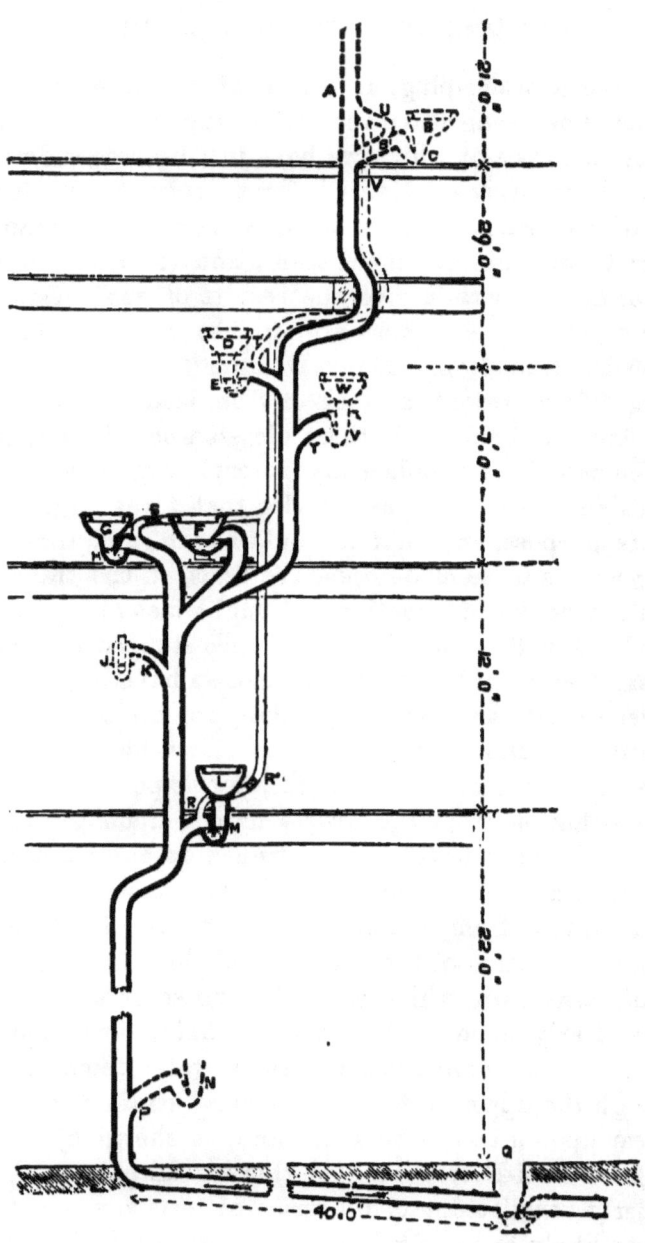

Fig. 95A.—SHOWING A STACK OF 3 IN. SOIL-PIPE, FOR TESTING THE CAPABILITIES OF A SMALL-SIZE PIPE, AND FOR EXPERIMENTING WITH TRAPS, reduced from my work, "Dulce Domum.

THE LOSS OF WATER-SEAL IN TRAPS. 145

(1*h*.) "With a pailful of water thrown down each of the 'hopper' class of closets, B F G, and with the valve-closet basin, D, filled to the brim and emptied sharply, and with the water from two small supply cisterns running into the two water-closets, F and G, as well, making in all about 15 gallons discharged into the main pipe at one time—the 2 in. trap-ventilation, R V, being in use—a 2 in. 'Bower' trap fixed at J, on the 2 in. branch, K, was syphoned; and a 9 in. 'Helmet' D-trap fixed on the 3 in. branch P, at N, had its water lowered $\frac{3}{4}$ in.

(2*h*.) "With another discharge of water as last, without refilling the traps, the india-rubber ball of the 'Bower' trap floated away from the dip-pipe, and the water was lowered enough in the trap to pass smoke through it into the room from the main pipe. The 'Helmet' trap lost $\frac{1}{8}$ in. more water by the second discharge, but it took ten further discharges to syphon this trap.

(3*h*.) "With the twelve foregoing discharges (15 gallons of water at a time) the ventilated 'Anti-D-trap' at M did not lose $\frac{1}{4}$ in. depth of water, *i.e.*, after the twelve discharges this trap had still $1\frac{1}{2}$ in. depth of seal.

(4*h*.) "With a $1\frac{1}{4}$ in. 'Bower' trap fixed at J, instead of a 2 in., a discharge of water through the main pipe as before completely syphoned it. After two such discharges smoke was sent through the trap into the room in volumes, by using an 'Asphyxiator,' and sending the smoke into the main pipe from the top, at A, above the roof.

(5*h*.) "With the 2 in. branch, K, lengthened, and the 'Bower' trap, either $1\frac{1}{4}$ in. or 2 in., standing 16 ft. away from the main pipe, there was little, if any, difference; for in similar trials to the last the trap lost its seal, both waterseal and 'mechanical' seal.

(6*h*.) "With a similar discharge as before, a $1\frac{1}{4}$ in. 'Du Bois' trap, a $1\frac{1}{2}$ in. and 2 in. round-pipe trap fixed at J, on the branch, K, were each syphoned in succession. A 4 in.

L

ditto lost $1\frac{1}{2}$ in. depth of seal in the first discharge, and after the second discharge the water stood $\frac{1}{2}$ in. below the dip.

(7h.) "With a similar discharge, a 2 in. 'Eclipse' trap, fixed in the same position as last, was syphoned in every trial. A 4 in. 'Eclipse' trap lost in the first discharge $\frac{1}{2}$ in., second $\frac{3}{8}$ in., and the third discharge syphoned it.

(8h.) "With a $1\frac{1}{4}$ in. 'Anti-D-trap' fixed in the same position, and with a similar discharge of water, this trap was also syphoned. A larger size 'Anti-D-trap' held its seal much better.

(9h.) "With a small 'Narrow-band' D-trap—$1\frac{1}{2}$ in. between the cheeks, and with $1\frac{1}{2}$ in. 'out-go'—fixed on the branch, K, a similar discharge of water as before lowered the water 1 in., another discharge lowered it $\frac{1}{8}$ in. more, the third discharge a little more, and the fourth discharge syphoned it. With a *full-size* 'Narrow-band' D-trap it took forty discharges to syphon it. The first discharge took out $\frac{3}{8}$ in., second $\frac{1}{8}$ in., and seven succeeding discharges took each $\frac{1}{16}$ in.

(10h.) "With a full-size 'Helmet' D-trap, fixed as last, the first discharge lowered the water in it $\frac{3}{4}$ in., second $\frac{1}{8}$ in., third $\frac{1}{8}$ in., and the five succeeding discharges took out by each discharge $\frac{1}{16}$ in."

CHAPTER XXIII.

LOSS OF WATER-SEAL IN TRAPS, AND TRAP-VENTILATION
(*continued*).

1.

IT may not be without some interest to theorize a little on the **cause of the loss of water-seals** in traps by **syphonage** and **back-pressure.** Trap-syphonage is chiefly caused by the removal of the atmospheric pressure from the pipe-side of the water-seal of a trap by the sucking action of a descending column of water through the pipe on which the trap is branched, or to which it is connected by a branch pipe; and this action is always at the side or rear of the column. Back-pressure is caused by a pressure of air upon the pipe-side of the seal of a trap greater than the atmospheric pressure upon it on the house-side; and this action is always in front of the column; but directly the column has passed the outlet of the trap, or the junction of the branch pipe on which the trap is fixed, the back-pressure is removed, and a sucking or syphonic action commences.

(A) In front of the discharge the air in the pipe is forced downwards with great velocity, as the air out of a pop-gun; and unless a way of escape is made for it by an anti-syphoning pipe, as shown in figs. 112 and 134, between the seal of the trap and the pipe through which the discharge is rushing—on every trapped branch upon the pipe—water will be forced out of the traps, as shown at D, fig. 94A. Where (*a*) there is no fixture upon the trap, the water forced out of it will partly fall on to the floor, and partly fall back again into the trap; or (b) where a closet-basin, urinal, or lavatory, or such-like fixture is fixed upon the trap, the water, foul or otherwise, will be forced up into the fixture to gravitate back again into the trap directly the back-pressure is removed; and if this were removed suddenly, as sometimes would be the case, then, with the energy gained by the fall, to partly flow out over the weir of the trap, and run away through the branch pipe, and partly to be syphoned out by the sucking action of the piston-like discharge; or (c), in the case of what is called a *running-trap*, the water would be forced up into the horizontal pipe, and leave the trap in some such cases without a seal. [For this reason I never allow running-traps to be fixed on any of my works.]

(B) The effect behind the discharge is equally disastrous upon the water-seals of traps when fixed upon a stack of pipe without an anti-syphoning pipe. For though the pipe be open to the atmosphere at top and bottom, the motion of a descending column of water through a pipe is so rapid that the air cannot enter the top of the pipe to reach the parts where it is wanted quickly enough to supply the demand, and to prevent a vacuum air rushes into the pipe through the trap or traps fixed upon it, frequently carrying with it enough water to leave the trap or traps without any seal. Or, in other words, the atmospheric pressure having been removed from the interior or outlet of the trap, by the withdrawal of air from the interior of the pipe, the atmospheric pressure upon the inlet of the pipe has pressed its way through the water-seal to fill the void.

2. **Trap-ventilation**, *i.e.*, an anti-syphoning pipe, not only prevents a disturbance of the seals of the traps in communication with a stack-pipe from back-pressure, by providing a way of escape for the air forced down in front of a column of water passing through the pipe, but it also prevents a disturbance of the seals of the traps at the rear

of the column, by giving air to each branch pipe, and freeing the traps from the action of syphonage.

The surplus of air in front of the column is forced up through each branch into the anti-syphoning pipe, to be sucked back again into the stack through the upper branches, to supply the great demand for air at the rear of the column; so that in many cases the supply almost equals the demand. This immediate supply of air from the pipe itself is of great value, for in such contests, especially in high pipes, the seals of many traps would be lost before air could come down through the top of the pipe to prevent a breach—a vacuum.

The air sucked down through the top of the pipe is of great value, though, like Blucher's army upon the field of Waterloo, it may arrive late.

3. The greater the distance between the ends of the stack-pipe—the top and bottom ends—that is, the **greater the height of a pipe** the greater will be the demand for air in its lower part by the passage through it of a plug-like discharge from some high point—from the fourth or fifth floor of a six or seven-storied house. Therefore when a soil-pipe (or waste-pipe) is of great height, with many branches upon it, it is a great advantage, even in the case where an anti-syphoning pipe is fixed, to increase the bore of the upper part of the pipe—the ventilation-pipe. Supposing a soil-pipe to be 4 in., the ventilation-pipe should be 5 in.; and where a waste-pipe is 3 in. in high buildings, its ventilation-pipe might with advantage be 4 in.; and traps fixed on a 2 in. stack would be benefited by a $2\frac{1}{2}$ in. ventilation-pipe fixed on the top of the 2 in. stack.

4. When the **bore of a pipe is only partially filled** by a body of water sent into it, the actions both of back-pressure and syphonage would be very much less than would be the case with a discharge which quite filled the pipe; for though there might be a great disturbance of the

air in the pipe, by the passage of the discharge through it, and though some of the air in the pipe would be entangled in the discharge and be forced downwards in front of it, enough air would escape between the discharge and the uncharged pipe, together with what had been sucked down through the top of the pipe, to prevent a vacuum; that is, sufficient air would be retained in the pipe, together with the current sucked down through the top, to about maintain the normal atmospheric pressure upon the seals of the traps. But even in such cases round-pipe traps with a rounded weir would often be subjected to a little loss of seal by the oscillation of the water in the traps.

5. How great the **current of air** may be in a 4 in. pipe of great height with a plug-like discharge of water into it on the ninth or tenth floor of a twelve-storied building, the men who have stood in a tunnel when an express train has gone through it at full speed may have some fair notion, but passengers who have only felt the current of air carried along by an express train when standing on the platform of a station can only have a bare idea.

In making some experiments a year or two ago, an anemometer fixed on the top of a stack of $4\frac{1}{2}$ in. soil-pipe, with 5 in. ventilation-pipe, in all 129 ft. long, registered 360 ft. lin. of air as having passed down into the pipe by a discharge from a valve-closet fixed on the seventh floor—the basin being filled up to its brim. A discharge from any of the lower closets did not suck down so much air; each floor made a difference.

6. When **several fixtures** are in communication with **one stack of pipe**, and their contents can be discharged at one and the same time into the pipe, the volume of water may be so increased as to endanger the seals of the traps by its passage through the pipe, though the discharge of any one of the fixtures alone may be too small to affect them. But a discharge simultaneously of a fixture on each

of several floors, when the bore of the pipe is not filled by any one of them, will not have so great an effect upon the seals of the traps fixed upon the stack as would a simultaneous discharge from several fixtures on a level, e.g., as a range of closets discharging into a stack of soil-pipe on an upper floor of a high building, or a range of baths or lavatories discharging into a waste-pipe on the fourth or fifth floor of a seven-storied house.

7. To prevent the water-seal of a trap being syphoned out by a body of water sent through the trap, or through a pipe on which the trap might be in communication, either directly or by means of a branch pipe, Dr. F. S. McClellan, of N. J., patented a few years ago what he has called an anti-syphon trap-vent for fixing on the pipe-side (sewer-side) of the seal of a trap, as shown at A, fig. 96.

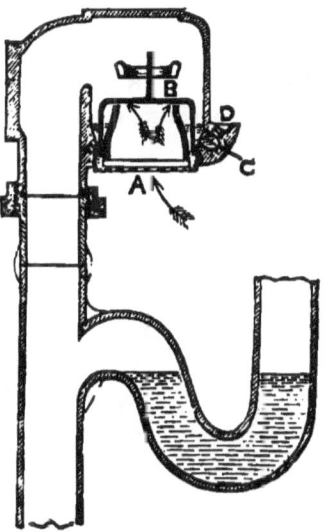

Fig. 96.—SECTION OF THE "ANTI-SYPHONING TRAP-VENT."

It is somewhat similar to an ordinary bell-trap, but for the admission of air instead of water, the entry being upwards instead of downwards, and that it has a mercury-seal instead of a water-seal.

Directly a body of water is sent through a trap on which it is in communication, the cup, B, is drawn up well above the seal by the suction of the discharge, and air is admitted freely through the grating, A.

In the many tests which I have made with this trap-vent I have found that even the water-seal of an ordinary round-pipe trap is well preserved against the action of syphonage. But it does not protect the seal of a trap from back-pressure, nor does it prevent the loss of the water-seal of a round-pipe trap by *momentum* (Art. 8).

The mercury is poured into the annular groove, C, through the screw-hole, D, after the trap-vent is fixed, to prevent any loss of the fluid in the fixing, for, mercury-like, it is soon gone; and also to prevent any loss of seal by a little lurching of the trap-vent, it should be well and securely fixed in its place. According to Dr. McClellan, the seal has " a gravity resistance on the sewer-side of more than four times that of the water-seal of a trap of usual

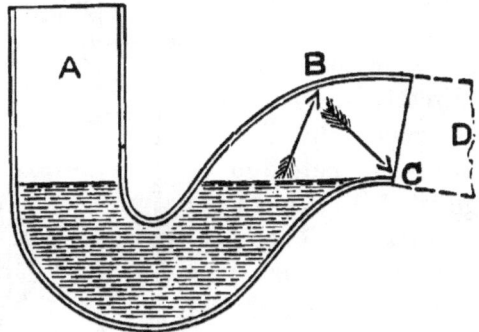

Fig. 97.—V-shaped Round-Pipe Trap.

depth." The trap-vent is made of cast iron, with a brass cap-and-lining for soldering to a lead pipe.

In all such devices there is some risk. These trap-vents would often be fixed where they would rarely be seen, and being "out of sight would be out of mind." The mercury seal might last a long time, but I should very much hesitate before allowing such an arrangement to be fixed in any important place inside a house, even in a position where it would be seen. In those that I have had fixed they are so placed that the air from a waste-pipe coming back through them from a broken seal would escape into the open air.

8. The nearer to an upright the ascending-pipe of a round-pipe trap is, and the sharper is its weir, the better will it maintain its seal against the action of **momentum**, whence U-shaped round-pipe traps maintain their seals better than V-shaped ones; but even a U-shaped trap does not retain its seal so strongly as an Anti-D-trap. With an easy slope in the ascending-pipe of the trap, and a rounded weir, as shown in fig. 97, it is almost impossible to send a discharge of water through it from a valve-closet or slop-sink without unsealing it. And the greater the fall into it, that is, the greater the distance between the water-seal of the trap and flap-valve of the closet-basin, or the bottom of the slop-closet (the longer the dip-pipe), the greater will be the loss of water in the trap by a quick discharge into it. In such a form of trap there is nothing to break the energy accumulated by the fall of a body of water into it, the consequence is, that the energy gained by the drop into the trap carries the water right through it, leaving insufficient behind to form any sort of seal.

9. In many experiments which I have made with such forms of traps, I have found it quite an easy matter to send a body of water through them, from a valve-closet or slop-closet, which left the trap with an air space, between the dip and the surface of the water, equal in area to half the bore of the trap. The water in passing through the trap impinges upon the arched top, and glancing off like a ball, falls down on the pipe-side of the weir, as shown by the arrows B C, fig. 97, and runs away. Nor is a U-shaped round-pipe trap proof against this action.

10. The "**Emptage**" trap has been specially designed to withstand the action of syphonage, and where an anti-syphoning pipe is fixed for this purpose, this trap is valuable, as it retains its seal tenaciously, but it is wrongly constructed to resist the action of momentum. In many experiments I have made with it, I have found it most easy,

with or without an anti-syphoning pipe, to unseal it when fixed under a valve-closet. With only a small quantity of water in the basin, a sharp pull of the closet-handle will leave the trap without a seal.

11. The **Anti-D-trap** is specially constructed, not only to be self-cleansing, but also to resist, as much as possible, the actions of syphonage and momentum; and no matter how great the body of water sent through it, the trap always retains a full seal, and that too without an anti-syphoning pipe. To stand against the action of *syphonage*,

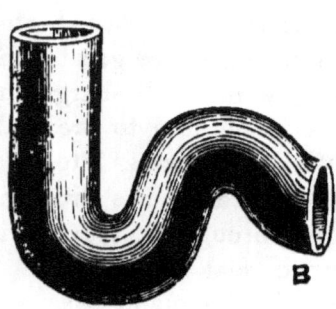

Fig. 98.—The "Emptage" Round-Pipe Trap.

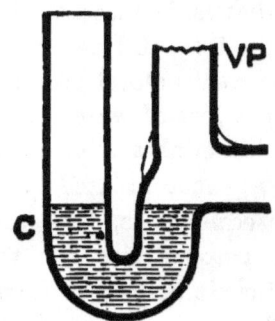

Fig. 99.—Showing Vent-Pipe for Water to Ascend up into it, to Recharge the Trap.

that is, to resist the syphonic action of plug-like discharges through the pipe on which it is fixed, or with which it communicates, it requires an anti-syphoning pipe, but such a pipe need not be fixed where it can become fouled—anywhere on the branch protects it, as shown in fig. 112.

12. In **round-pipe traps**, whether U-shaped or V-shaped, the **vent-pipe** must be so fixed that in the passage of a body of water through the trap part of the water shall go up into the vent-pipe to fall back again into the trap after the momentum action has ceased. There are at least two evils in such an arrangement: (*a*) The water carried up into the vent-pipe would not always be clean. In the

case of closet-traps and stop-sink traps, fæcal matters would be often washed up into the pipe, there to remain to contaminate the air passing through the ventilation pipe. (*b*) The vent-pipe being directly over the exposed surface of the water-seal of the trap, currents of air passing over it would take up some of the water and reduce the depth of the seal.

13. Traps lose their seals by **evaporation**. (*a*) When a current of air passes over an exposed surface of the water standing in a trap, as in the case where the trap-vent is fixed on the crown of the outlet of a trap, as shown at v p, fig. 99. (*b*) When hot water coils are fixed near them, and when pipes for the circulation of hot water are fixed close to them. (*c*) When an exposed surface of the water-seal of a trap is open to the dry air of a hot room. (*d*) When the rays of the sun can pass through the window of a closet and fall upon the exposed surface of the water-seal of a closet-trap; also traps fixed in exposed positions outside on the sunny side of a house.

14. In very exposed positions, and in gusty weather, where at times there is a great **blow-down** of air in a pipe, or where the atmospheric presence on the outlet of an open pipe may be suddenly removed, the seals of traps fixed upon the stack may be much reduced, especially in round-pipe traps with easy outlets.

CHAPTER XXIV.

LINING CISTERNS AND SINKS WITH LEAD.

1.

IN the days, not so long ago, when wood **cisterns** were **built** into very **confined places**, a plumber often showed more ingenuity in wriggling himself out of a cistern, after he had lined it with lead, than in getting into it; for not only would he be cramped in every limb from working many hours in attitudes which could hardly be described as kneeling, sitting, or standing, but he would have a narrower space to get through, by the thickness of the lead he had fixed upon the edge of the cistern. And when he had oozed out of such a place, through a trapdoor, hatch-door, or between joists and floors and ceilings, he would often be in such a plight as to be mistaken for a chimney-sweep (except that no sweep could ever have worked himself into such a position), for handling lead is not like handling linen, any more than working with soil and grease is like working with a needle and thread. But cisterns are not now so treated. They are brought out into larger places, where they can be seen and cleansed when so desired; and, instead of wood cisterns lined with lead, the cisterns chiefly used now are made of galvanized sheet iron. (See Chap. XXXVII., Art. 4.)

2. **Wood cisterns,** or tanks of any shape or size, can be **lined** in their places with **sheet lead** of any weight per superficial foot, for lasting a few years or for centuries, and for storing water, which does not act on lead (Chap. XXXVII., Art. 7), there is no other kind of cistern which can be so absolutely depended upon, or which is so

generally convenient. The strength of the bottom should be 1 lb. or 2 lbs. per sup. ft. stronger than the sides; but 7 lbs. bottom and 6 lbs. sides make a good cistern, though I prefer the bottom to be of 8 lbs. lead, and the sides and ends of 6 lbs.

3. For lining **tanks for chemical purposes,** the sheet lead should be manufactured from refined pig lead, and instead of soldering the angles, the edges of the lead should be burned. (Chap. V.)

4. In taking the **dimensions** of a cistern for **cutting out the lead**—when the angles are to be soldered—all the sizes wanted are the length, width, and depth of the wood cistern inside. The lead for the bottom should be cut out 1 in. larger each way—in length and width—than the cistern, to allow for squaring, straightening, and turning up at the edges—for wedging in at the angles of the four sides; *e.g.*, a cistern 6 ft. by 5 ft. and 3 ft. 6 in. deep would require a piece of lead for the *bottom* 6 ft. 1 in. by 5 ft. 1 in. These dimensions, added together, will give the *length* of the first side and end (though the first side and end to be put in is wanted $1\frac{1}{2}$ in. longer than the last, to allow for the return edges on to the wood, the two pieces are generally cut in equal lengths, to save time and trouble); thus, 6 ft. 1 in. by 5 ft. 1 in. = 11 ft. 2 in. This allows for squaring and straightening the ends, and for returning about three-quarters of an inch at each end on to the wood sides, for securing the lead in its position. The *width* is obtained by adding 3 in. to the depth of the cistern, to allow for straightening the edges, turning $\frac{3}{4}$ in. on the bottom (though many plumbers use an inch for this) and 2 in. to cover the top edge of the cistern.

5. Before lining a cistern, see that all the **holes** are cut in it for the various pipes, especially the hole in the bottom for the waste-pipe, taking care that the hole for the latter is made of sufficient size to allow the end of the

pipe to be well opened out to receive the brass washer-and-waste, the hole being counter-sunk for making the soldered joint flush with the lead bottom, so that the cistern may be quite emptied.

6. I will follow the order of lining a wood cistern, and speak of the sides first. Unroll the lead upon the floor adjoining the cistern to be lined, or if the cistern is in a roof and there is no floor, then upon some boards, and dress out any irregularities in its surface, and, before chalk-lining out the sizes, see that the cistern is perfectly square; for carpenters, like other people, do not always work on the "square." When a side and end are in one piece, such as we have been considering, and as is the practice, except in very large cisterns, when a separate piece is used for each side and end, line out the sizes with a chalk-line upon the lead, allowing a margin of about $\frac{3}{4}$ in. to stand on the bottom, and also for the returns at the two ends. The line for turning up the end, for forming the upright unsoldered angle, should be marked with a chalk-line, and never scratched with a sharp tool.

Having marked out the side and end, take a piece of quartering, or "straightedge," and turn up the edge for standing on the bottom. This is easily done by kneeling on the piece of quartering, to keep it stiff, and turning up the edge with the aid of a chipping-knife and dresser. Then break up the end by placing the piece of quartering upon the line for the upright angle (the angle which is not to be soldered) and boss up the bottom corner a little, for fitting tightly into the angle of the wood cistern. Some plumbers stupidly cut this corner, and in such a way as to leave a hole just where the solder can run in, and so get themselves into difficulties when soldering the cistern. In putting this piece of lead into its place in the cistern, bulge the centre part of the side and end inwards a little towards you, as you stand in the cistern, so as to be able to drive the angles of the lead tightly home. Be very careful with the *turned-up* angle, the *unsoldered* angle, and see that it fits *tightly into the angle of the cistern, before securing the lead at the ends;* for if the lead is not *well home* in such angles, when the side and end are fixed, and the dresser is used for driving it home, as is often done by unskilled men, the lead is very much weakened. I have known 6 lbs. lead reduced to 4 lbs. in such angles, and even for the edge of the dresser to be driven right through the lead, and the angle to require soldering. A nail in the *return* edge of the underlap, about 3 in. down from the top, is all that is wanted to secure the lead in its place. The edge of the lead is readily turned over the top of the cistern with a few sharp strokes of the dresser and fastened (the inner edge of the wood being rounded off a little before lining the cistern), and the stand-up part of the angle is easily bossed back. When forming this angle, the part to be bossed over the edge of the cistern should never be cut in, with the edge of the dresser or any other tool, or it will not boss over freely.

The other side and end are put in, in a similar way to that just described. The edges or overlaps returning upon the side and end already lined, should be carefully cut off with a chipping-knife when the lead is in its place, leaving about $\frac{1}{8}$th of an inch for driving into the angle, for keying the jointing and preventing the solder running through.

The sides and ends being lined, the bottom follows. Turn up the edges of the bottom in a rounding form, so as to allow the lead to stand up a little at each of the four sides, and boss up the corners of the bottom, so as to have a reserve of lead at such points for dressing into the corners of the cistern angles; then put the bottom in its place, and dress the lead well into each angle with the aid of the dresser and chase-wedge. Cut off the edge of the turn-up against the sides, so as to leave about $\frac{1}{8}$th of an inch stand-up, for well keying the lead into the angle.

Having lined the cistern, **soil** a margin of 4 in. or 5 in. on each side of the angles to be soldered, and, when dry, shave the angles. The **shaving** on the bottom, F, fig. 101, should be about ¼ inch wider than on the sides, G; the upright angles, fig. 100, should be of equal width each side. The shaving should not extend beyond the solder, for the lead is weakened with wide shaving, especially when the solder is wiped off from it again. In shaving the lead be very careful *not* to *dig* the point of the shave-hook into

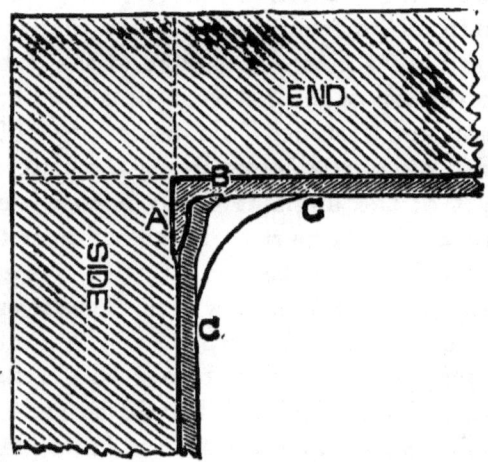

Fig. 100.—SECTION OF CISTERN SOLDERING. UPRIGHT ANGLE.

the lead and so reduce its substance; simply shave the lead to brighten it, that the solder may readily *tin* upon it. Pull the point of the shave-hook along on the edge of the lead at the joining the edge of the overlap, so as to *close up* any space between the two leads, to prevent the solder running in between them when soldering the cistern. Having shaved the angles, and greased them, to prevent tarnishing, punch in the edges, about every 9 in., with a *bright* punch, with, say, ¼ in. face, or other bright instrument, for securing the lead in its place, but do not put a single nail into the angles, or you will have some trouble in soldering over the heads, for they are sure to "blow."

The upright **angles** must be **soldered** first. If you cannot pour the metal upon a cloth or stick, and guide it into the angle in that way, you can splash the solder into the angle from the ladle with a splash-stick. Splash the solder very rapidly up and down the angle, and pull it

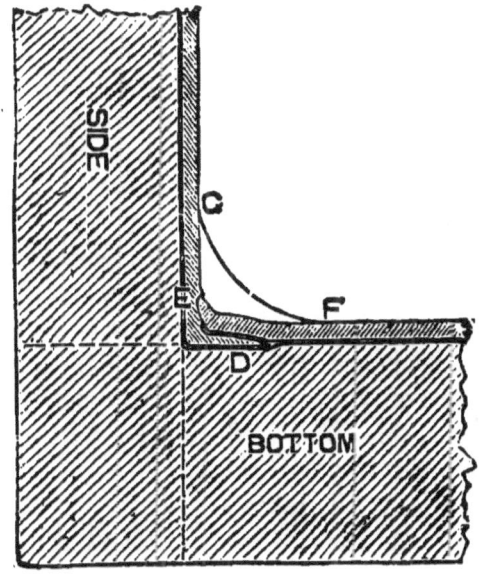

Fig. 101.—Transverse Vertical Section of Horizontal Angle.

up now and then with the splash-stick, and keep it in its place; and when you have a good body of solder in the angle, from the bottom to the top, take a well-heated and well-cleaned iron, and draw it up and down the angle, "patting" the solder into its place, then wipe down the angle *quickly*, pressing the cloth *hard upon each edge* of the soldering with the points of the fingers, so as to get clean wiping. In finishing off the upright angle at the bottom, pull away all the fallen solder, and well under-cut the angle with the shave-hook, for easy joining when wiping in the bottom. Having wiped the two upright angles, the bottom comes next, and with plenty of solder, and two or three irons, this is soon done. Rub a little chalk upon the soldering of the upright angles first to prevent the solder adhering to the angles above the wiping. Some men take many more irons to solder a cistern than others, but a skilled man ought to wipe out the cistern mentioned above with 6 irons—2 for the angles, and 4 for the bottom; such a cistern *ought* to be lined and soldered in about 10 hours.

Some plumbers make the **return edges**, the underlap, too wide or too narrow. When such is the case it is impossible to get nice clean edges of soldering, for the edge of the lead is sure to make the face of the lead covering it irregular, however much it may be feathered off with the shave-hook. When the edge of the lead stands as shown in fig. 100, the shaving-line is well outside the line of the edge, and is therefore free from any irregularities—*i.e.*, the return edge on to the wood should be less than $\frac{3}{4}$ in. or more than $1\frac{1}{2}$ in. Fig. 100 shows a section of the upright angle (half-full-size), and fig. 101 a section through the bottom angle, to the same scale.

7. Having fully described the method of lining a wood cistern with lead, it is not neceessary to describe how to **line a wood sink**. Where a sink is not likely to be much used, it may be lined in one piece of lead, soldering the vertical angles only, somewhat as a cesspool (Chap. VIII.). But sinks generally receive much wear and tear. Where this is the case the bottoms should be cut out of sheet lead, weighing 10 lbs. or 12 lbs. to the sup. ft., and the sides and ends out of 7 lbs. or 8 lbs., and the angles strongly wiped. The lead returned upon the top edges of the sink, where they are exposed and likely to receive rough usage, should be protected by oak cappings, secured with strong brass cap and screws. (Chap. XXXIII., Art. 12.)

CHAPTER XXV.

PIPE-FIXING.

1.

BEFORE preparing the ends of lead pipes for soldering, the pipes should be carefully **rounded and straightened up** on the bench, and all bruises and indentations taken out of them. To accomplish this it may be necessary in many cases to drive a mandrel through the pipe.

2. Sometimes, either from carelessness or from an accident, **a pipe receives a blow** after it is fixed, and in a place where no dummy can reach its interior, for the indentation to be dummied out again; in such cases a dent in a pipe can generally be drawn out by soldering the return end of a piece of copper to it, and pulling the other end with the strength equal to the purpose.

3. A vertical **pipe** which is **not fixed quite perpendicular** reflects want of care as well as the want of a true eye in the man who fixed it; for however incorrect his eyesight might be, he ought to find no difficulty in fixing a pipe quite upright with the aid of a plumb-line.

4. Lead soil-pipes, ventilation-pipes, waste-pipes, and light service-pipes should be secured to their places by **lead tacks** soldered to the pipes, and fastened by pipe-nails, wall-hooks, or screws. And in many cases it is also better that the service-pipes, whether strong or light, should also be secured by soldered lead tacks, *i.e.*, instead of bruising the pipe and contracting its water-way by driving in a wall-hook to grip the pipe, as shown at B, fig. 102, a narrow piece of stout lead should be soldered to the

side of the pipe, as shown at A. Such tacks are called face-tacks.

5. It is the bad custom with many plumbers to secure lead soil-pipes, ventilation-pipes, and rain-water-pipes with ears or lugs soldered, or burnt, to the lead pipe; but it surely wants no plumbing experience to know that a **lead tack** or a pair of lead tacks gives a much greater support to a pipe than a pair of ears. In the case of a lead tack, 10 in. by 9 in., or 9 in. by 9 in., the length of soldering upon the pipe is at least *three times greater* than the length of the

Fig. 102.

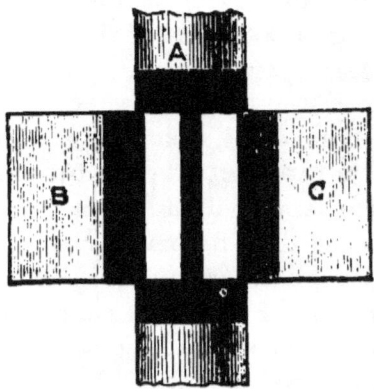

Fig. 103.—Showing a Pair of Tacks, Back View.

soldering upon a pipe when a lead ear is used; and with the tack these wall-hooks can generally be fixed as shown at F, fig. 104, whereas with a lead ear only one pipe-nail or one screw can be fixed. The ear is generally soldered to a pipe to match the lug of a cast-iron rain-water-pipe; but when a lead pipe—soil-pipe, waste-pipe, or ventilation-pipe—is to be fixed where it will be much in sight, tacks can still be soldered to the pipe, and the astragal kept further apart, as shown in fig. 60, Chap. XVIII.

A double tack, as shown at D, fig. 105, does not afford the strength of a pair of tacks; for, as will readily be seen by a glance at the two kinds, figs. 103 and 105, the solder in the former has a larger surface-holding upon the pipe than that of the latter.

6. The strength of a lead tack, whether cut from a piece of sheet lead or cast in a mould, should be of greater strength than the pipe, *e.g.*, pipes equal in substance to sheet lead weighing 6 lbs. to the sup. foot should have tacks of 7 lbs. lead, and pipes 1 lb. heavier should have tacks of 8 lbs. lead. Stronger pipes than 7 lbs. lead would be well secured by tacks of the same strength as the pipe,—8 lbs. soil-pipes,

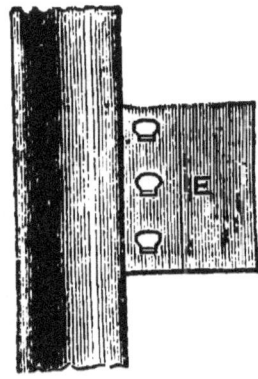

Fig. 104.—SHOWING A SINGLE TACK, BACK VIEW.

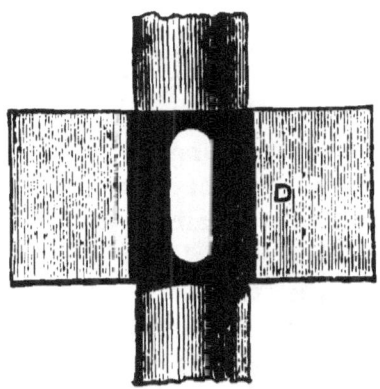

Fig. 105.—SHOWING A DOUBLE TACK, FRONT VIEW.

8 lbs. tacks; 10 lbs. soil-pipe, 10 lbs. tacks. The wall-hooks should be driven in close to the pipe, as shown in fig. 104.

7. Two pairs of tacks to a 10 ft. length of 4 in., 4½ in., or 5 in. pipe give great security; and even three tacks, fixed alternately one on one side of the pipe and one on the other, give good support to pipes of 4 in. diameter and under. For smaller pipes—3 in., 2½ in., 2 in.—tacks of a smaller size than those shown in figs. 103 and 104 should be used, and when fixed to woodwork face-tacks would be

preferable to folded-tacks. When the pipes stand in conspicuous places it is better to fix them with astragals and tacks—a pair of tacks and a pair of astragals every 6 ft.

8. Whether sheet-lead **tacks** or cast-lead tacks are soldered to a pipe, they should all be of **uniform size**. The whole of the tacks for a stack of soil-pipe, ventilation-pipe, or rain-water-pipe should be cut out together, so as to insure their being of one size, and also for quickness; and after feathering one of the edges with a rasp, for fitting against the side of the pipe, each tack should be soiled about 3 inches on the soldering face, and an inch on the opposite face. The tacks should then be shaved for soldering. The shaving should be about an inch wide, and a corresponding length and width should be shaved on the pipe, after soiling it. The tacks should all be fitted on the pipe, so that they may be soldered on in one heat. In soldering on a pair of tacks, as shown on fig. 103, pour the solder on each alternately, and then wipe them quickly one after the other. Your mate should be ready with his knife to cut off the ragged edges of the soldering, and to square it with the edges of the tacks—or the plumber can do this himself. Some plumbers manage to solder on tacks very well without an iron, but others prefer an iron.

9. I have seen ventilation-pipes 3 in. and 4 in. diameter, and 23 ft., and in some cases even 30 ft. long, resting on the edges of tiles on a high-pitched roof, with only the support gained by the joint where the pipe has passed up through the roof. Such pipes should be supported every 5 or 6 ft. by a wood block covered with lead, to which the pipe should be soldered. The block should be kept narrow, so as not to look conspicuous or unsightly; and to prevent leaves, etc., accumulating round it, the top end should be arrow-pointed.

10. To prevent the sun expanding and drawing a lead pipe with soldered joints out of its true line, and, in time,

breaking it, lead soil-pipes and ventilation-pipes on south fronts should be fixed in an angle where they will be screened from the sun, or where they will get some shade. Where there are no windows near such pipes, and where they are exposed to the rays of the sun, it is a good plan to fix them with telescope joints, to allow the pipes to expand and contract.

11. The plumber generally arrives upon the scene too late to ask for proper chases where he may so fix his pipes that each and all of them shall be readily accessible. But a good wide chase is very convenient for future examinations and other purposes. Each pipe should also be labelled.

12. Instead of securing "**horizontal**" **pipes** inside a house with lead tacks or wall-hooks, no matter what the size of the pipe may be, or what its purpose, it is better to support them on wood ledges or on boards hollowed out to receive them, to prevent the pipe sagging in any part. Plumbers rarely forget to give a soil-pipe or waste-pipe a fall, but they often forget to give service-pipes a fall, the consequence is, that when it is required to empty a service-pipe for repairs, or to prevent the water in it from freezing, it cannot be done.

13. This last severe winter (1890-91) [1] ought to stimulate plumbers to mend their ways in fixing service-pipes. The following extract on **pipe-freezing** is taken from my "Lectures." "No service-pipe should be fixed on the external nor on the internal face of an external wall, especially a wall facing the north or east, without being cased in and thoroughly protected. When possible, service-pipes should be fixed on the cross walls inside the house, and never on the main walls; for the cold penetrates through the external

---

[1] In my own house there was not the slightest inconvenience from frost, owing to the care that was taken in fixing the service-pipes and cisterns ten years ago.

walls and, reaching any pipe fixed on its face, though inside the house, freezes the water in it. If a pipe *must* come down on the internal face of a main wall, then an inch board should be put between the pipe and the wall, and the pipe cased up, and the casing filled with cocoa-nut fibre or silicated cotton. All service-pipes in roofs should be boxed in, and the boxes filled with this fibre. I do not like sawdust, for that decays; nor hair-felt, for that becomes full of moth, and rots; and besides, to cover pipes with such material where bad air could reach it would be to harbour smells, for the effluvia coming from persons using the water-closets would hang about such stuff and cause it to become 'stuffy.' Where the service-pipe could not be boxed or cased in, and where the cold air could reach it—as, *e.g.*, under water-closet seats, where the pipe has to leave the casing to reach the supply-valve of the water-closet—the pipe should be bound round with two or three thicknesses of gaskin, and then be covered over with canvas, to protect it from frost. The cold air coming in through the overflow-pipe of the safe, and blowing upon an unprotected pipe, would soon freeze it.

"If the positions of service-pipes are carefully considered, and the parts of questionable security protected in the manner described, no service-pipe in English houses need get frozen."

As a strong frost in very severe weather, and when continued for many days, often penetrates into the ground for a depth of two feet or more, even in sheltered parts, all mains and services should be laid at least two feet under the surface of the ground.

No service-pipe, whether it be the communication-pipe from a water company's main, or from a cistern, should be laid in any trench in which there is also a drain. The trenches for drains and service-pipes should be kept as far apart as possible.

CHAPTER XXVI.

RAIN-WATER AND RAIN-WATER-PIPES.

1.

WHERE sewage is utilized for irrigation, and also where liquid sewage is discharged into soakage-cesspools, the **rain-water** and the surface-water should be **kept out of the soil-drain**; except that in some cases, to save the expense of laying down what would be a costly piece of drain, and also where a rain-pipe has not much duty to perform, the rain-water may be turned into the soil-drain, as shown in fig. 107.

2. The **disconnecting trap** which should be selected for such a purpose should be one into which some fixture discharges, such as a bath, sink, or lavatory, to prevent the water-seal evaporating, which would at once set up air communication between the soil-drain and the rain-water drain.

3. In **country houses** there is generally little or no difficulty in separating the rain-water-drain from the soil-drain. When the rain-water is not collected into a storage tank for any purpose, it can be kept quite separate from soil-drains and dirty-water-drains, and conducted to some place where it can gravitate away without inconvenience to anybody or damage to anything.

4. Where the water supplied to a house from a company's main, or spring, or well is hard, the **rain-water** from the roofs should be **stored** in an underground tank, for laundry and lavatory purposes, if for no other. The capacity of the storage tank should be equal to a month's consumption, or more; and where a house would be entirely depen-

dent upon rain-water for all purposes, the storage should be equal to the supply of from between twenty and thirty gallons of water per head per diem for forty or fifty days; and where a house is wisely provided with hot-water circulation and a bath, the maximum quantity should be arranged for.

5. **Rain-water** should be **filtered** before it is allowed to enter the storage tank, not for the purpose of purifying it, but for clarifying it.

In fig. 106 a section of a fairly good filter is shown. A bed of well-washed fine gravel, to a depth of 6 in. or 9 in.,

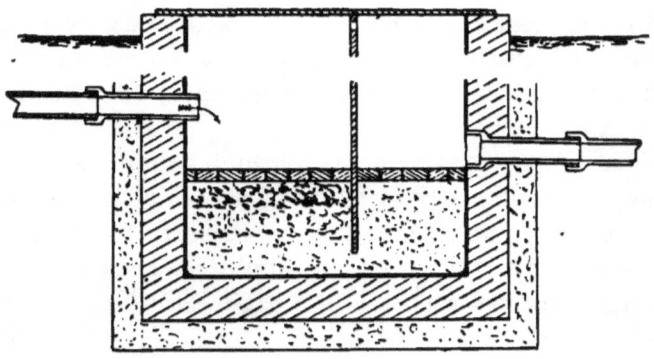

Fig. 106.—Rain-Water Filter.

is laid over the whole of the floor of a cement-lined and brick-built chamber, of a capacity equal to passing the water through it without overflowing. In the receiving compartment a stratum of coarse gravel, about 6 in. deep, is laid upon the bed of fine gravel, and over this is placed a layer of shingle or broken flint, and then over the whole a floor of bricks or tiles is laid, to form a better surface for removing leaves and other foreign matter which may get washed into the filtering chamber. The outlet compartment is filled up with fine gravel, so that when a covering of bricks is placed over the gravel—to prevent a rush of water carrying it away—the upper surface of the floor shall stand an inch or two below the outlet or pipe which is to convey the filtered water to the storage tank.

6. Roberts's Patent **Rain-Water Separator** is a clever arrangement for preventing the first portion of the rainfall passing into the storing tank, and where we have fixed them we have found them of good benefit.

7. The **soft water** from the storage tank can be **pumped** up into cisterns fixed high enough to supply draw-offs to sinks on the bedroom floors for toilet purposes; and a branch pipe from the service main can be carried to a slate cistern on a lower level, for supplying the water for boiling vegetables, and for filling tea-kettles, etc.

8. Rain-water pipes are often fixed of larger size than necessary. An occasional **stoppage** in **rain-water-pipes** is caused by a defective grating, or by a grating with too large a mesh, or by a badly-fitted grating over the cesspool socket or entrance to the pipe, rather than by the smallness of the pipe. This is often the case in country houses, where leaves are blown on to the roof and washed down into the cesspool.

There is not only the *débris* from the roof—the bits of mortar, the broken tiles or slates, the fallen leaves—there is the rust from the interior of the pipe, for this is the age of iron, and rain-water-pipes are generally made of cast iron. In times of little or no rain such things accumulate at the bottom of a stack of pipe and block it up; for it is seldom that any means are provided for the removal of such accumulations. Many years ago I invented and patented an access-shoe (as illustrated in fig. 107), which not only affords a ready access to the foot of a rain-water-pipe for cleaning it out, but gives it ventilation. Where a grating would suggest an improper use of the shoe, a movable cover can be substituted.

Where the mouth of a rain-water-pipe is under or near a

window, and it has not much rain-water to carry off, as when fixed to a small verandah or flat, to a porch or bay-window, it may be made to deliver over a surface channel.

9. Whatever kind of pipe may be used outside the walls of a house, all **rain-water-pipes fixed inside a house** should be of lead, with wiped soldered joints, so that there may be no doubt as to the soundness of the pipes or their joints. And then if any bad air got into such pipes through some bad trapping, or some defective arrangement of the drain connections, there would be no risk of the air entering the house through defective joints, as would be the case were cast-iron rain-water-pipes fixed.

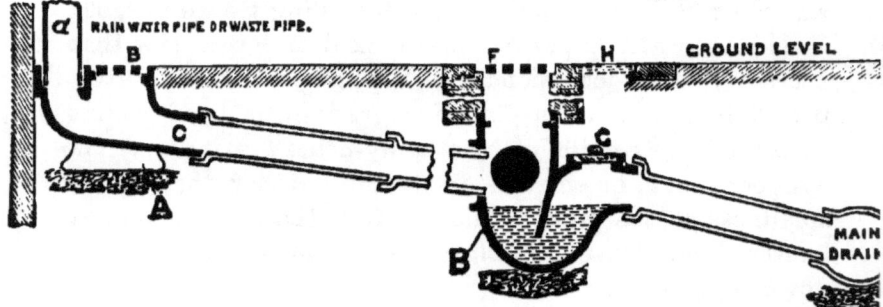

Fig. 107.—SHOWING DISCONNECTION AND ACCESS TO FOOT OF RAIN-WATER PIPE, ETC.

10. I know it is easy to lay down a rule that "all rain-water-pipes shall have their discharging ends opened up to the atmosphere before connection with either a dirty-water or soil-drain." But **where there are no areas**, where the external walls of a house or building stand upon the boundaries of the property, as is often found in cities, how is this to be done? Well, with care in the planning, even in such cases the pipes can be carried along on the face of basement walls, or suspended from the floor joists; or they can be collected into a drain and carried along under the basement floor, quite independent of the soil-drain, to one place of discharge.

If practicable, in such cases, the rain-water-pipe or rain-water-drain should be carried to the head of the soil-drain for the rain-water to be discharged into it through an automatic flushing tank, twenty, thirty, or forty gallons at a time. In any case only one opening should be made in the soil-drain, and the rain-water-pipe or drain should be carefully trapped off from it to exclude the drain air, and fresh air should be brought into the rain-water-pipe or rain-water-drain, on the house side of the trap, from some convenient place above the pavement, a grating being fixed in the wall over the mouth of such induct pipe.

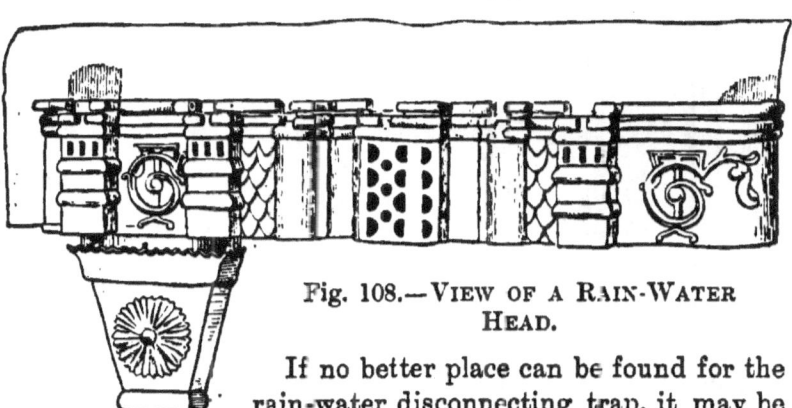

Fig. 108.—VIEW OF A RAIN-WATER HEAD.

If no better place can be found for the rain-water disconnecting trap, it may be fixed in the disconnecting chamber of the house-drain to the sewer, and this can be so done that no air shall be able to pass from the chamber into the rain-water-pipe.

11. In the rain-water-heads and rain-water-pipes of an artistic building, the skilful plumber has often a grand opportunity afforded him, not only for displaying what skill he possesses in the art of manipulating lead and working it up into noble, well-proportioned heads, but for showing his ability in ornamental tacking and graceful bending of the pipes.

12. Where two cesspools, or two gutter-shoes, stand near

each other, instead of fixing two stacks of rain-water-pipes or carrying one of the socket-pipes along the face of a wall horizontally, to deliver into a small rain-water-head, it is better to extend the head for one gutter or socket-pipe to empty into it at one end, and the other socket-pipe at the other end. The stack-pipe can go down from the middle, or from one end, as shown in fig. 108, which is illustrated

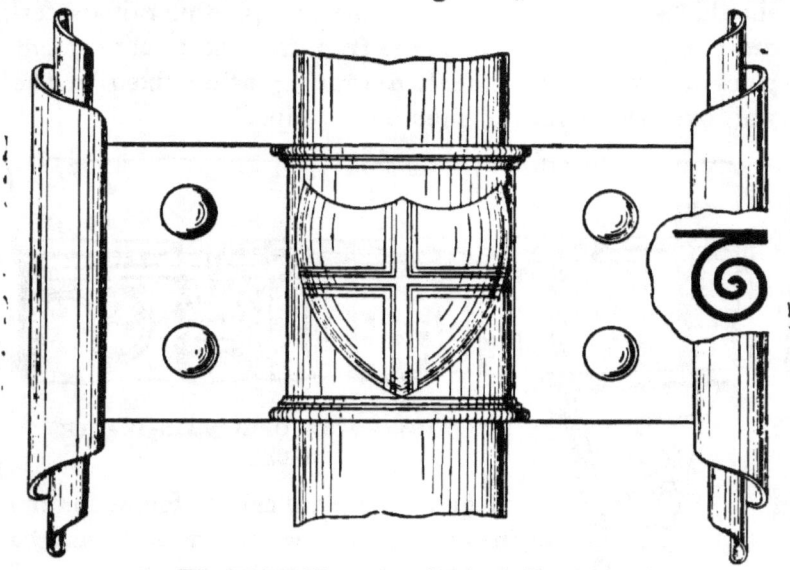

Fig. 109.—View of Socket-Tacks.

from a photograph of a head made at my works about eighteen years ago.

13. Instead of reducing the bottom end of a 6 ft. length of pipe, and thereby restricting the water-way, the top end of the lower pipe should be opened out, and a deep socket formed upon it for the end of the upper pipe to enter it freely. Almost any device can be formed on the socket, or planted upon it. Or the socket and astragals can be cast all in one, with or without the tacks. (Chap. XXV., Art 5.) The edges of the tacks can be curled, as shown in fig. 109, or treated in a great variety of ways.

CHAPTER XXVII.

SOIL-PIPES AND THEIR DISCONNECTION AND VENTILATION.

1.

IN **seamless lead pipe** for soil-pipe, rain-water-pipe, cold water wastes, and services—where the water would not act on them, or acting would not hurt anybody—the plumber rejoices in the use of a pipe, which, for soundness, wholesomeness, durability, compactness, appearance, and the reliability of its wiped solder joints, as well as for the ease with which it can be made to follow any course, not only compares favourably with any other known pipe, but is, in fact, as proved by experience, superior to earthenware, stoneware, zinc, copper, cast-iron, or wrought-iron pipe.

2. It is peculiarly the plumber's duty to see that the **lead pipe** he fixes—soil-pipe, waste-pipe, ventilation-pipe, or service-pipe—is of an **even thickness** all over, for if one pipe manufacturer does not so make it another does. It may cause some extra trouble and expense to get such pipe, but now that it is so manufactured it would be manifestly unfair to the owner of a property to fix a pipe which, while equal to lasting a century on one side, could not be relied upon for a quarter of a century on the other. Where there is no anxiety on the plumber's part to seek out good soil-pipe manufacturers, and where the pipe he uses inside a house is of an uneven thickness, the strength of the pipe should be increased say from 8 lbs. lead to 10 lbs. lead, so that the pipe in its weakest part may be equal in thickness to sheet lead weighing 8 lbs. to the superficial foot. (Chap. II.)

3. A **lead soil-pipe** ⅛ in. thick—*i.e.*, equal to sheet lead weighing 8 lbs. to the superficial foot, and of a true and even thickness all over—can be so fixed that it shall last a century and more; and during the whole of that period it need not cost its owner, or rather its successive owners, one farthing. And when the time comes for its renewal it will fetch, as old lead, one-third of its original cost, unless past history is no guide for the future.

4. When **soil-pipes** are of **lead** the work of fixing them can be carried on with less forethought and more expeditiously than with either cast-iron or wrought-iron pipe. In the case of either of the latter, however carefully the work may have been set out at first, a deviation from the original plan in some of the fixtures, or a deviation in the course of a pipe—which in a building of some magnitude, where growing minds are at work upon it, will be sure to occur—would probably call for a bend, or a junction, or a special pipe, which would lead to waste of time until such parts were furnished. In the case of the former, plenty of lead pipe being on the job, or within ready reach, no deviation in the course of a pipe need delay operations for a minute, for the plumbers could bend or branch it, to suit the altered circumstances, as they progressed with their work.

5. The **duration** of a stack of **iron pipe** exposed to the influences of the atmosphere, even if it be of the water-main strength, is much shorter than that of a lead pipe, though in many cases it would be cheaper to fix the latter than the former. No matter what means may be adopted for protecting iron pipe from rusting, I know of none that will prevent iron pipe from oxidizing in some of its parts after a time, and when exposed to the London atmosphere. But where iron pipe is used, whether for soil-pipe, rain-water-pipe, waste-pipe, or drains, it should have a protective coating inside and out; for in iron pipes there is

not only a corrosive action going on outside, but there is also a corrosive action going on inside, *i.e.*, such pipes deteriorate from within as well as from without.

6. For fixing cast-iron soil-pipe **outside a** house on the faces of external walls, I prefer the pipe to be *galvanized*, and afterwards coated with Dr. Angus Smith's solution, and then painted outside to suit the colours of the adjacent iron rain-water-pipes. The joints in such cases are stronger if made with Spence's metal than with most of the "cements" used; but where not exposed to the heat of the sun, in the longest and shortest hours of the day, they can be well and soundly made by caulking in a ring or two of spun yarn, and filling up the remainder of the socket with marine glue by the aid of a blow-pipe or blowing lamp.

7. For fixing **inside** a house the pipe should be of greater strength, with stronger, wider, and deeper sockets, so that the joints may be made with blue metal, *i.e.*, that two or three rings of spun yarn may be caulked into the socket, and the

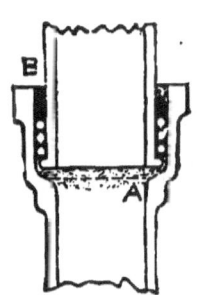

Fig. 110.—SECTION OF A CAULKED LEAD JOINT.

socket filled in with molten lead, and caulked, as shown at B, fig. 110. As such a pipe would be too expensive to galvanize, it should be *properly* coated inside and out with "Dr. Angus Smith's solution," though there is a difference of opinion as to which of several methods is the best one. As far as my experience goes, no known or tried method can be absolutely depended upon to prevent oxidation when iron pipe is exposed to the atmosphere.

8. **Cast-iron soil-pipes** and waste-pipes for fixing **inside a house** should be very carefully examined before they are coated, to see that they are free from all defects, from flaws and fractures, as the coating would cover over

small defects and screen them from sight. The pipes both inside and outside should also be cleaned before they are dipped into the cauldron; and immediately before fixing a pipe in its place it should be sounded and well tested, to see that it is free from fracture. Captain de Place, of Paris, has invented a mechanical contrivance called a "sciséophone," to detect the presence of flaws in metals.

The pipes should also be well examined, to see that they are of an even thickness all over, except of course in the hub or socket, and for an inch or two below the socket, which should be of much greater thickness; but in no part of the pipe should the thickness be less than $\frac{1}{4}$ in. before it is coated.

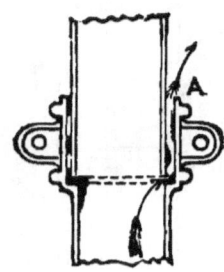

Fig. 111.—DEFECTIVE CEMENT JOINT.

In my works, when **cast-iron soil-pipe** is insisted upon, for inside work I require that the pipe shall be that known as underground water-main, the **thickness** being nowhere less than $\frac{3}{8}$ in. For outside soil-pipes I prefer that the pipe shall be not less than $\frac{3}{16}$ in. thick in its thinnest parts, and that there shall be a space of at least $\frac{1}{4}$ in. all round between the external face of the spigot and the internal face of the socket, for filling in a fair thickness of cement, whether Spence's metal, as preferred, or marine glue, or any other kind.

9. Cast-iron pipes much too thin to be durable, and with thin **sockets too small to have dependable joints** made to them, are very frequently fixed even in houses of some pretension; but the plumber should have nothing to do with iron pipes for soil-pipes and waste-pipes which will not admit of a fairly reliable joint being made to them. When the spigot end of a pipe occupies the entire space of a socket, how is it possible to work down into the socket, between the faces of the two pipes fitting so closely,

a thickness of any kind of cement which shall be durable? The consequence is that such joints are soon made faulty by the sucking actions of the discharges sent through the pipe, even supposing they are not broken by the expansion and contraction of the pipes.

Where pipes are simply painted, the unprotected faces of the socket and the spigot oxidize rapidly. And this rust or oxide which forms upon the iron goes on increasing in bulk, taking up oxygen from the air, until its force is sufficient to break the socket of thin iron pipes. Also such sockets are at times charged with water, from the condensation which runs down the pipe, and in severe frosts this water becomes frozen and bursts the socket.

10. Then, as I have explained elsewhere, the jointing of iron pipes is never so wholesome as the jointing of lead pipes. With lead pipe, as shown in section, fig. 36, the connection is so close that there is no space or ledge for filth to accumulate in or upon; but in iron pipes, whether cast or wrought, thick or thin, there is always an annular space, or a ledge, or uneven faces where filth more or less can accumulate in or upon. And this evil is aggravated, for in order to keep the molten metal, or fluidal "cement" from running into the interior of the piping, the sockets are first partly filled with a ring or two of spun yarn, and this absorbent material, when there is a stoppage, or when the pipe is charged, soaks up liquid matters, whether infectious or otherwise. It may not be much in quantity, but if multiplied by every joint in a stack, and by every stack in London, the air of the metropolis would not be so pure as it might be, or as it would be, were lead soil-pipes, with wiped soldered joints, fixed everywhere.

11. As the mouth or top of a rain-water-pipe is generally so situated that any air emitted from it would enter the house through some window, skylight, or lantern light,

180 PLUMBING.

or between the slates or tiles, or in some other way, no

Fig. 112.—SHOWING A STACK OF SOIL-PIPE, WITH MAIN AND MINOR BRANCHES, AND WITH LEAD TRAPS SOLDERED TO SAME, FOR RECEIVING A RANGE OF VALVE-CLOSETS ON EACH OF TWO FLOORS, WITH ANTI-SYPHONING PIPE COMPLETE.

soil-pipe or dirty-water-waste should be fixed in communication with a rain-water-pipe.

SOIL-PIPES AND THEIR DISCONNECTION.

12. I was much criticised when giving my lectures a decade ago for advocating the use of **small soil-pipes**, but more especially for recommending **outside soil-pipes**. Since that time thousands of stacks of 3 in., and 3½ in., and 4 in. soil-pipes have been fixed on the external faces of external walls, where they have stood trials from within as well as without with perfect success. But as I said at the time, "I would not pull down a house in order to fix the soil-pipe outside"; nor would I do what is often done, viz., in order to keep the main soil-pipe outside the house, fix long branches from it to the closets, the united length of which would make the total length of soil-pipe inside the house—calculating the parts which pass through the internal wall — greater than would have been the case had the main stack been fixed in a chase inside the house.

(a) Where a lead soil-pipe, if fixed outside, would be exposed to the full power of the sun for many hours in the middle part of the day, to prevent the pipe being contorted, and, perhaps, broken by expansion and contraction, I should prefer it fixed inside.

(b) I should also prefer the pipe

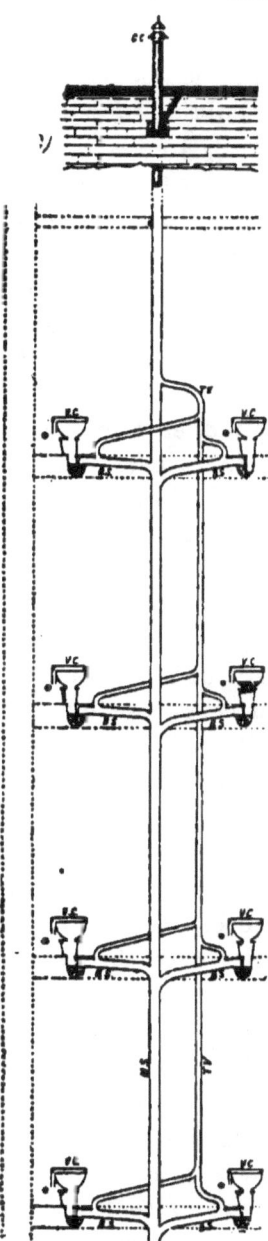

Fig. 112A.

fixed inside where a closet on each of many floors branched into it, as shown in fig. 112A, and where the trap-vents would in such case have to be carried through the external wall, to reach the anti-syphoning pipe, as would be the case with round-pipe traps where the main soil-pipe and trap-ventilation pipes were fixed outside.

(c) I should greatly prefer the soil-pipes to be fixed outside if they had to be of cast iron, as their joints could not be relied upon for any very great length of time.

(d) I should also prefer the soil-pipes to be fixed outside, even though the pipes were of lead, $\frac{3}{16}$ in. thick, if the plumber who was to fix them were not a good and sound joint-wiper. (See Joints, figs. 32 and 34, Chap. XV.)

13. The **size** that a **soil-pipe** should be, like many another thing in plumbers' work, depends much upon circumstances.

(a) In a building of great height, with closets on the upper and lower floors entering a stack, to prevent syphonage of the closet traps the pipe should be of larger size than in the case of a two, three, or four-storied house. (See Chap. XXIII., Art. 3.)

(b) The size should also depend upon the treatment it is likely to receive. In a private house a $2\frac{1}{2}$ in. pipe would be less liable to chokage than a $3\frac{1}{2}$ in. in an hotel. All sorts of things are thrown into hotel closets, and if there is to be no blockage of the soil-pipe it is obvious that whatever can be passed through a closet, where it is often assisted by the prodding of some instrument, must be able to pass still more freely through the soil-pipe.

(c) Where valve-closets are fixed, and the face-plates of their basin-valves are of earthenware, the pipe should be large enough for the broken parts to pass through it, or the face-plates should be made of unbreakable material.

14. **Branches** into minor branches, or into main pipes, should always be made to enter a pipe in the direction of

the current by Y-shaped connections, as shown in figs. 112 and 112A, and never at right angles, or T-shaped, as shown in fig. 47, Chap. XVII.

A diagrammatic section of a range of closet traps is given in fig. 113, to show the errors of bad branching and bad ventilation. An excrementitious discharge through any of the traps, C, D, E, would wash up into the branch pipe, and foul it; and any matters in this way back-washed up into the branch would remain there until a closet higher up was used; but anything which got washed back beyond the furthest closet, E, would remain in the pipe, to send off bad

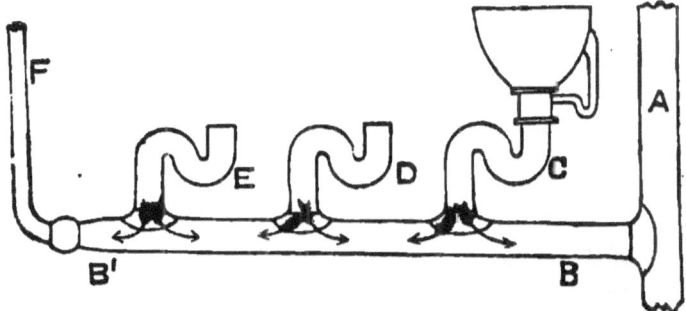

Fig. 113.—SHOWING BAD BRANCHING.

air through the badly arranged ventilation-pipe, F, even if in time this pipe did not get completely blocked up in the bend, or between the bend and the branch, B¹.

15. Where a stack of **soil-pipe** would be in **communication with a foul drain**, or an old brick drain which the householder or owner will not remove, instead of allowing the air from such a drain to pass into the soil-pipe, it should be excluded by a disconnecting trap, as shown at S (fig. 112), or as shown in fig. 114, or in some such way. Fresh air can be taken into the foot of the soil-pipe from any convenient point. When it stands close to the soil-pipe, where any air driven out of it—by a discharge sent

through the soil-pipe—would enter the house through an adjacent door or window, the mouth of the pipe should be provided with a mica-valve to prevent egress of soil-pipe air.

16. Where a proper system of drainage exists, or is to be laid down, the **soil-pipe can be branched directly into the drain,** or fixed in continuation of it, as shown in fig.

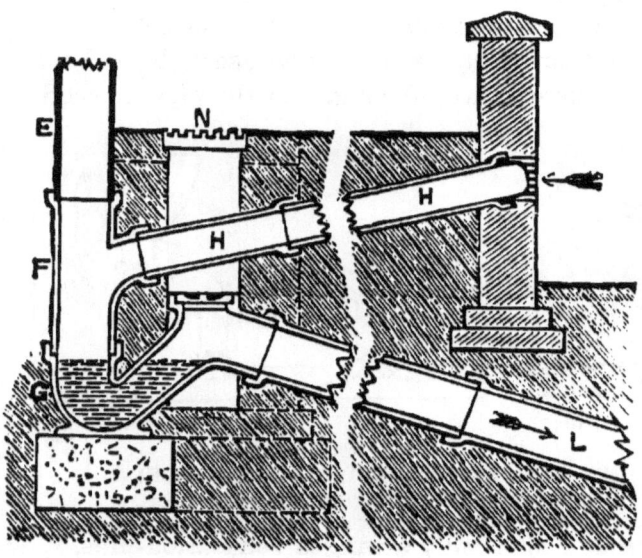

Fig. 114.—SOIL-PIPE TRAP, WITH FOOT-VENTILATION.

115; and, where it can be afforded, a man-hole should be built, something like that shown in the illustration, and fresh air brought into it from some near point, where no offence would be given to anybody should there be a reaction in the air-current for a minute or two. In some cases it may be desirable to fix a mica-valve over the mouth of the pipe. In some cases a grating can be fixed directly over the man-hole; but more often than not a grating would allow all sorts of surface washings or dirt to pass

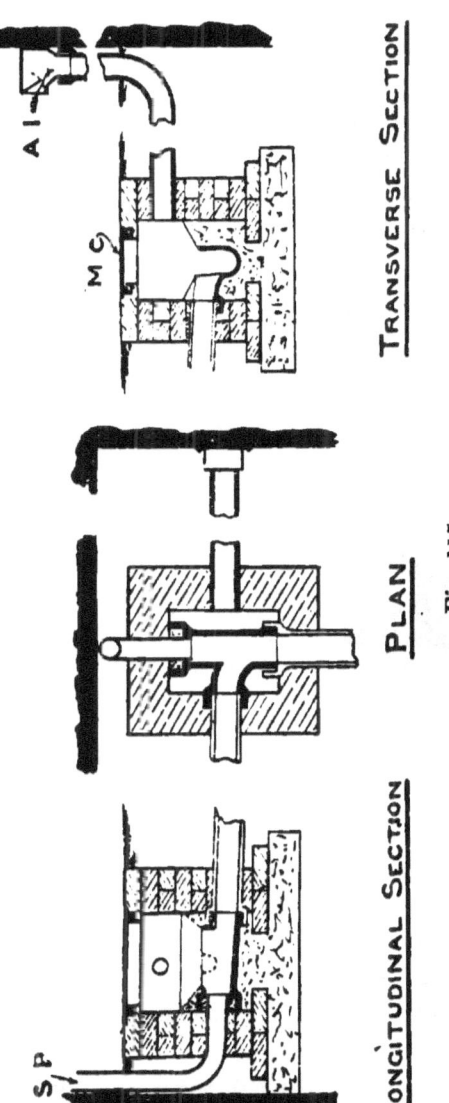

Fig. 115.

into the man-hole to foul it. Where the mouth of a fresh-air induct-pipe would stand in a flower bed or place where earth would be liable to fall into it, or gravel or other foreign matter, a standard inlet, as shown in fig. 117, could be fixed on the pipe.

17. For efficient ventilation it is better to continue the soil-pipe up full bore, or of a larger size where a building is of great height (Chap. XXXIX.), to some point well above the roof, where the air emitted from it would not enter the house through a broken skylight, lantern, trap-

Fig. 116.—View of a Mica-Valve.

Fig. 117.—"Mushroom" Air-Inlet.

door, chimney, or window, and where it would not contaminate any cistern water.

18. The question of cowls—which has been dealt with pretty fully in my work "The Plumber and Sanitary Houses"—is too large to discuss here; but a good kind of cowl, which would assist rather than retard the up-current in a pipe, and which would also prevent or reduce the down-draught, could not fail to be of great advantage in many instances. Especially would this be the case where the mouth of a fresh-air induct-pipe stood near an opening to a house, or near the traffic of foot passengers.

19. Much care is often taken to prevent the passage of soil-pipe air into the room of a closet, but very little care to

SOIL-PIPES AND THEIR DISCONNECTION.   187

exclude it from a bedroom (fig. 118). In thousands of instances throughout the United Kingdom the air emitted from the ventilation-pipe of a soil-pipe or drain is as near to a window or opening into a house as the smoke which escapes from the bowl of a churchwarden tobacco-pipe is to the face of the man who smokes it.

Fig. 118.—SOIL-PIPE TERMINAL. BAD POSITION.

20. A lead soil-pipe can be soundly connected to a cast-iron pipe or drain by soldering a brass, gun-metal, or copper ferrule or sheath to the lower part of the pipe, as shown in fig. 119, and running the joint in with molten lead, and caulking it.

As copper is acted upon by fæcal matters, as proved by the destruction of copper pans in pan-closets, it is better to carry the lead soil-pipe right down into the socket, where it should be tafted back and soldered to the flanged end of the copper ferrule, to prevent matters back-washing up between the lead pipe and the copper sleeve.

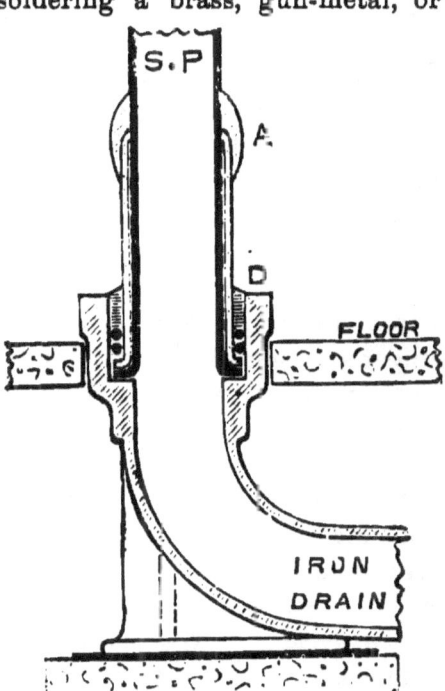

Fig. 119.—CONNECTION OF LEAD SOIL-PIPE TO AN IRON DRAIN.

The copper ferrule must be stout enough to stand the caulking.

21. As shown in the woodcut, fig. 119, a thick flange or base, with a strong web, is cast on the underside of the bend for the purpose of standing it upon a piece of stone laid on a bed of concrete or brickwork, to give a solid support to the vertical pipe. It is known by the name of "duck's-foot" bend.

CHAPTER XXVIII.

HISTORY OF WATER-CLOSETS.

I HESITATE to burden this work with matters which the reader may consider better left outside, but as a brief history of the first use of "places of convenience" inside a house may not be without interest to the sanitary student, I give here some extracts *in extenso* from my "Lectures":—

"**Privies** served their purpose well enough when every man had a garden or piece of ground, but when men congregated together in cities and towns, remote places for putting such conveniences could not be found, and drains and sewers had to be made, into which the general slops of the house were thrown.

"Instead of building water-closets as we do now, the rich ancients used close-stools, or pans which were frequently made of gold, besides the water-closets which were made in vaulted recesses in their kitchens.

"In writing of the discoveries made by antiquarians in Pompeii, Fosbroke says, in his 'Encyclopædia of Antiquities' (p. 78), 'The kitchen is descended by stairs, on the left hand of which is an arched stone dresser, used as the hearth for cooking. On the right hand is a vaulted recess for a privy, three feet deep, formerly provided with a door and seat, an ancient appendage to a kitchen, still retained in modern Italy.'

"The Romans placed vases, called *gastra*, upon the edges of roads and streets, just as we now fix urinals.

"In Sir William Hamilton's account of 'Discoveries at Pompeii,' he says, in a paper [1] read before the Society of Antiquaries, in 1775, 'Close to the Temple of Isis is a theatre, no more of which has been cleared than the scene, and the corridor that leads to the seats. In this corridor was a retiring-place for necessary occasions, where the pipe to convey the water, and the basin, like that of our water-closets (A.D. 1775), still remain, the wood of the seat only having mouldered away by time.' As Pompeii was destroyed by an eruption of Mount Vesuvius in the year A.D. 79, this W.C., which Sir William Hamilton saw, must have been 1,700 years old at the least.

"Fosbroke, in his 'Encyclopædia of Antiquities' (p. 397), says, 'The water-closet in the Palace of the Cæsars is adorned with marble arabesques and mosaics; at the back of one is a cistern, the water of which is distributed by cocks to different seats.'

"Olympiodorus says that 'in the Thermæ of Antoninus' (which were baths and gymnasium combined) 'there were 1,600 seats of marble pierced like *chaisés-percées* for the convenience of those who bathed.' [2]

"The fall of the Roman Empire led to the disuse of *water*-closets, and to a return to the customs of earlier ages.

"Beckman says that in Paris, so late as the fourteenth century, the people had the liberty of throwing anything from their windows whenever they chose, provided they gave notice three times before by crying out, '*Gare l'eau !*'

[1] "Archæologia," vol. iv. p. 168.
[2] Fosbroke's "Encyclopædia of Antiquities," p. 67.

This practice was, we learn, forbidden in 1395.[1] A like practice seems to have continued much later in Edinburgh; for in A.D. 1750, when people went out into the streets at night, it was necessary, in order to avoid disagreeable accidents from the windows, that they should take with them a guide, who, as he went along, called out with a loud voice, 'Haud your han!' This must have been a good time for hatters and tailors. At that period, when the luxury of water-closets was unknown, it was the custom for men to perambulate the streets of Edinburgh carrying conveniences (pails) suspended from a yoke on their shoulders, and enveloped by cloaks sufficiently large to cover both their apparatus and customers, crying, 'Wha wants me for a bawbee?'[2] It has since been used against the Edinburgh people as a joke or satire upon an ancient custom. By way of set-off, however, it may be observed, that in 1846 almost every house in Edinburgh had a water-closet.

"In a Parisian code of laws, which was improved in 1513, it was expressly ordered that every house should have a *privy;* but in the year 1700 they had not this 'luxury' in every house, for at that time, only 180 years ago, the police had instructions to see that each house had a privy, or to lock the house up if the occupants did not make one within a month.

"If we turn to Spain, matters were worse, for we are told that 'the residence of the King of Spain was destitute of this improvement, at the very time that the English circumnavigators found privies constructed, in the European manner, near the habitations of the cannibals of New Zealand.'[3]

"*Privies* seem to have been common in the large and

---

[1] Beckman's "Inventions," vol. i. pp. 277-281 (1846).
[2] "Letters from Scotland" (1760).
[3] Footnote, "Cook's First Voyage," vol. ii. p. 281.

flourishing towns of Germany much earlier than in Paris. In the annals of Frankfort-on-the-Maine, we are told that an order was issued, in 1496, by the Council, forbidding the proprietors of houses, situated in a certain place planted with trees, to erect privies towards the side where the trees were growing. In 1498, George Pfeffer von Hell, I.U.D., Chancellor of the Electorate at Mentz, fell by accident into a privy, and there perished—a privy chancellor! Beckman, speaking of Berlin, in 1846, does not say much in favour of the sanitary arrangements there at that time—forty-five years ago. He says: 'In most of the houses small closets are located on the landings of the stairs, which require to be emptied every other night, to the no great satisfaction of the olfactory nerves. Nor are the streets kept in a very proper state, large puddles of filth being allowed to collect before the doors even of the best houses, and which, especially in the hot summer months, diffuse a most horrible stench.'

"But let us return to our own country. Stow tells that, ' In 1290, the monks of White Friars complained to the King and Parliament, that the *putrid exhalations* arising from the Fleet river were so powerful as to overcome all the frankincense burnt at their altars during divine service, and even occasioned the deaths of many brethren. Many attempts were made to cleanse this river and restore it to its ancient condition of utility as a navigable stream; but they proved unavailing, and the stream which formerly conducted vessels with merchandise as far as Fleet Bridge and Old Bourne (now Holborn) Bridge, if not farther, became, in the language of Pope,

> "The king of dykes! than whom no sluice of mud
> With deeper sable blots the silver flood." '

" Sir John Harrington is credited by Nares with the invention of the English water-closet, or *latrine*, in Queen Elizabeth's time; but Fosbroke says that this is a mistake, though probably Sir John made them known in England. Portable close-stools (the regal one was made of silver) were used in the reign of Queen Elizabeth, and placed in garrets, and were called 'ajaxes.'[1]

"Aubrey, writing in 1718, describes a water-closet he had seen. He says: 'Here [at Sir Francis Carew's, Beddington, Surrey] I saw a pretty machine to cleanse an "House of Office," viz., by a small stream of water no bigger than one's finger, which ran into an engine made like a bit of a fire-shovel, which hung upon its centre of gravity, so that when it was full a considerable quantity of water fell down with some force and washed away the filth.'[2]

"I have been looking through a very interesting old book, entitled 'The London Art of Building,' published in 1734, and though 'the Plumber' occupies a place of honour in the book, and a schedule of plumber's works is given, there is nothing in the whole book to warrant one in supposing that *traps* were used in those days.

"Nor is there the smallest reference to *water-closets* in the 'plumber,' or 'joiner'—for making the seats, or 'mason'—for shaping the closet-pan just referred to; but many references are made to the drainage of a house. I have culled a few extracts, and will leave you to determine whether there is enough in them to warrant one in saying that soil-pipes or water-closets wastes were fixed in those days—I mean soil-pipes from water-closets fixed 'upstairs.' There can be no doubt about water-closets being at that time fixed in yards, and places where they could be connected with the drain direct. Here is one of the Rules:—

"'That convenient Drains, to carry away Soil, &c., be well contrived, and secretly placed, with Vents to dis-

---

[1] "American Mechanical Dictionary," vol. iii. p. 2763.
[2] Aubrey's "Surrey," vol. ii. p. 160.

charge the noisome Vapours that usually arise from them.'[1]

"'*Conduits.* Sewers or Gutters to convey away the Suillage of a House.'

"'*Sewers*, in Architecture, are Conduits, or Conveyances, for the Soilage and Filth of a House.'[2]

"'That convenient Cisterns be well placed, plentifully to furnish every Office with Water; and that proper Machines be made to raise the same therein.'

"Campbell in his book, 'A Compendious View of all Trades practised in the Cities of London and Westminster,' published thirteen years after this (in 1747), in speaking of the plumber's duties, does not say a word about *traps, soil-pipes*, or *water-closets*, except that the plumber must lay on water to the 'Office Houses.' Under the head of 'Plumbers' Business,' he says: 'He must furnish us with a cistern for water, he must fix a sink with lead, he covers a house with lead when it requires it, and makes gutters to carry off the rain-water, he makes pipes to convey water into our kitchens and Office Houses.'

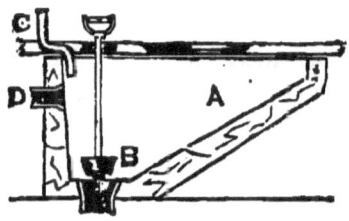

Fig. 120.

"As far as I can make out, fig. 120 represents the best form of water-closet used in England about a century or a century and a half ago. These water-closets were made of marble—A the pan; B the waste-plug; C the service-pipe; D the overflow. We have one (an old one) in our warehouse to-day. In examining the sanitary arrangements of Osterley House, about twelve years ago, I found two such water-closets. A niche in a fair-sized room was formed to receive the marble closet-pan, and a door, shut-

---

[1] "The London Art of Building" (1734).   [2] *Ibid.*

ting up close to the seat, hid the whole arrangement from sight. A lead soil-pipe was connected with the outlet plug-waste of the pan, and continued from it to the drain, which was brought into the house to receive it. The soil-pipes had no ventilation.

"Patents of privilege, or monopoly, have been granted for several hundred years. The annals of some in very many instances have gone into oblivion. No. 1, standing first in supplementary numerical order, was a patent of privilege, or monopoly for thirty-one years, granted to Simon Sturtevant, on the 29th of February, A.D. 1611, 'for "Metallica," a treatise to *neale, melt,* and work all kinds of metal *ores, irons,* and *steeles,* with sea coale, pit coale, earth coale, and brush fewell.'

"The first patent in this country under Laws of Patents for Inventions, as far as I can glean, was granted by James I. in 1617; but according to the Records of the Patent Office, not a single **patent** was taken out for a **water-closet** until the year 1775, or 158 years after special licenses were granted for protecting inventions. The presumption is, therefore, that no water-closet other than that of a simple nature (as fig. 120) had been in use up to this date, 1775. But the specification of the first patented water-closet clearly establishes the fact that water-closets were in use at that time, for the inventor calls his invention a 'Water-closet upon a New Construction'; and the drawing annexed to the specification clearly proves that soil-pipes at that time were well known, and that water-closets were fixed 'upstairs,' *i.e.*, in various parts of the house.

"In the year 1775 Alexander Cumming, a watchmaker in Bond Street, took out the first patent for a water-closet —and many closets in use to-day are more unsanitary than this one. Fig. 121 is a faithful representation of the drawing annexed to the inventor's specification. The water is brought into the basin, very low down, at E, and is kept in the basin by what the patentee calls the 'slider,' *e*. The details are all carefully engraved, and explain themselves. I will give two or three extracts from Cumming's specification, as it will show us that traps were used under closets at this period, and that they were offensive; also that soil-pipes were fixed without ventilation, and that such pipes

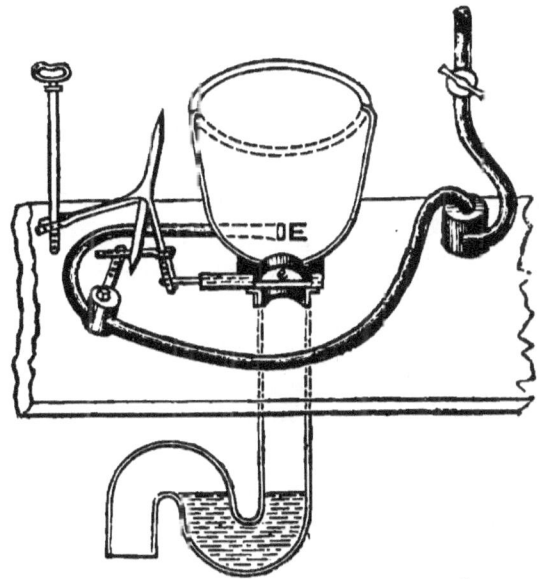

Fig. 121.—CUMMING'S CLOSET.

emptied themselves into drains, and the drains into cess-pools:—

"'The advantages of the said water-closet depend upon the shape of the pan or bason, the manner of admitting water into it, and on having the stink-trap so constructed that its contents shall, or may, be totally emptied every time the closet is used. . . . .'

"'The stink-trap hitherto used for water-closets is too well known to require a description here; and although it may serve effectually to cut off all communication of smell from the drains, pipe, and cesspool, it becomes in itself a magazine of fœtid matter, which emits an offensive smell every time that it is disturbed by using the water-closet. In this water-closet, the pipe which carries off the soil and water is recurved about twelve or eighteen inches below the pan or bason, so as constantly to retain a quantity of water sufficient to cut off all communication of smell from below, and this stagnated water in the recurved part of the pipe is totally emptied, and succeeded by fresh every time the pan or bason is emptied.'

"As shown in the illustration, the trap under Cumming's closet is a *round-pipe*, or syphon-trap. And as he includes it in his patent I take it that this was the first time it was used in England (1775). [But it does not follow that syphon-traps had not been used before; for the ancients knew the working of *syphons*, and may have used syphon-traps. Syphons are shown in Egyptian tombs of the date of 1450 B.C. The syphon was a favourite contrivance with Hero of Alexandria (150 B.C.) in his various toys and automata, of which the Cup of Tantalus is a favourite instance.]

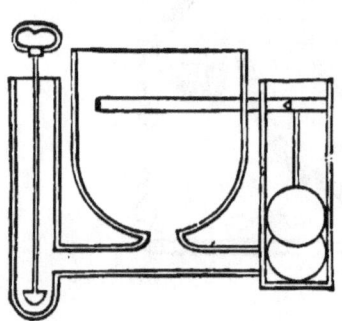

Fig. 122.—PROSSER'S WATER-CLOSET.

"About two years later (*i.e.*, in 1777), Samuel Prosser, a plumber, living in the parish of St. Martin-in-the-Fields, took out a patent for what he describes in his specification as 'A Water-closet upon an entirely New Construction, which will always remain free from any Offensive Smell.' A very desirable closet for everybody to have to-day if such were the case. But I should say it was about as bad as the pan-closet, *i.e.*, a water-closet which would *never* ' be free' from an 'offensive smell.' Fig. 122 shows this closet as copied from the drawing annexed to the inventor's specification. Two pages suffice to include his specification, preamble, claims, and license. It will be seen by the woodcut that excremental matter has free access to places where it could never get properly cleansed.

"In 1778, Joseph Bramah, of Cross Court, Carnaby Market, Middlesex, cabinet-maker, took out a patent for his invention of the now well-known valve-closet. I give

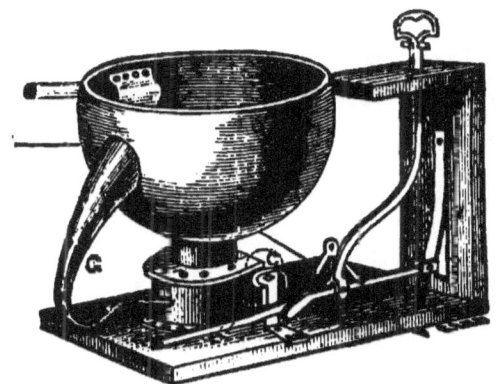

Fig. 123.—BRAMAH'S CLOSET.

an illustration of this water-closet in fig. 123, as taken from the drawing attached to the inventor's specification.

"As you will see, by looking at the woodcut, the shape of the basin is very similar to Alexander Cumming's closet, referred to just now. The great advantage of Bramah's closet over Cumming's is that the former is made with a valve which *seats* itself against the bottom of the basin by a *cranking* arrangement, whereas the latter *slides* under the bottom of the basin, as shown at *e*, fig. 121. In his specification, Bramah says, 'The valve is placed under the bottom of the basin, and when closed retains any water that may be therein, thus cutting off all smell.'

"The difficulty in getting the 'slider' (e, fig. 121) of Cumming's closet, and the *cranked* metal-valve of Bramah's, to always seat themselves, so as to keep the basin always charged with water, and to stand rough usage, led to the introduction of the **pan-closet**.

"William Law, a founder in Soho, made certain improvements in **pan-closets** in 1796. But the pan-closet was not much used, though other improvements were made in it before the early part of this century. In 1826 William Downe, sen., of Exeter, also a founder, made further improvements in the pan-closet, 'reducing the size of the *container*,' etc. You see they gave this excrement-holder the right name, for it is not simply a receiver, it is a 'container' too.

CHAPTER XXIX.

WATER-CLOSETS (*continued*).

1.

ABOUT a century ago a founder in Soho sought to improve the **pan-closet**, but notwithstanding his improvement, and the many other improvements made in it since that time, it is still the most unsanitary closet made—a thing to "point a moral and adorn a tale."

2. Among some of the **improvements** made in **pan-closets** during the last century are the following, viz.: (*a*) reducing the size of the container, N, fig. 124; (*b*) porcelain enamelling the interior of the container; (*c*) increasing the depth of the pan, O, to hold more water, and for it to stand higher in the basin; (*d*) making the pan of copper, and tinning its interior; (*e*) improving the shape of the fan or basin-spreader, and making it of copper, with

its exposed surface tinned; (*f*) making the basin, M, with a flushing-rim; (*g*) fixing a vent-pipe to the top of the container, S, and continuing it out to the open air, instead of allowing the bad smells and the gases generated in the closet (and in the D-trap) to escape under the closet-seat into the room, to "hurry up" its daily visitors.

In fixing this vent-pipe, S, to the container of the closet

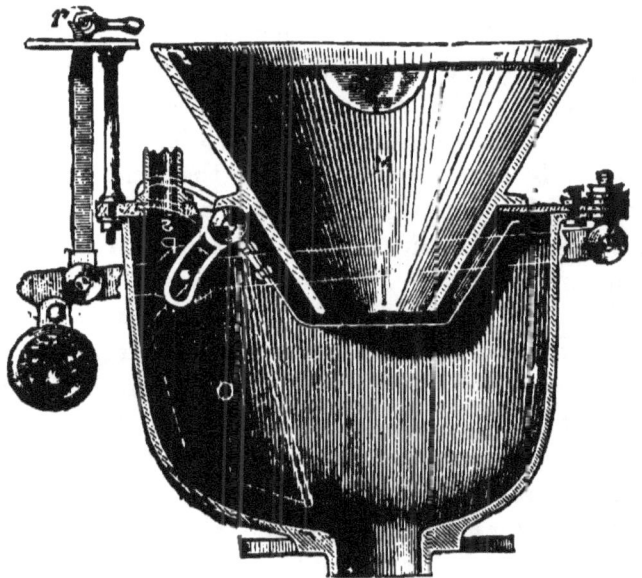

Fig. 124.—Transverse Vertical Section of a Pan-Closet.

some plumbers showed gross ignorance of sanitary knowledge, for they often connected the other end of the vent-pipe to the soil-pipe, or to the ventilation-pipe of the soil-pipe, making "the remedy worse than the disease."

3. I can think of three reasons why the pan-closet should have been more extensively used during the past century than any other closet: (*a*) its price, being much cheaper in its common form than the valve-closet; (*b*) its capability to stand rough usage, and, having no basin-valve, being less

likely to get out of order than a valve-closet; and (c) want of sanitary knowledge, the general belief being that all closets, like polecats, must have a distinguishing characteristic of their own. The amount of dried excrement which can be cleaned out of the container of an old pan-closet, when it is "taken up to be sweetened," is about 2 lbs., as an average.

4. The **exposed surfaces** of a pan-closet, leaving out the inner side of the basin, which can and which, in use, does get fouled, is equal to about 5 ft. sup., or more than four times greater than that of a good valve-closet. And this evil is much aggravated, for whilst a scouring flush can readily be brought to bear upon the exposed surface of the valve-closet for keeping it clean, no frictional flush can be sent over the interior surfaces of the pan-closet.

In my work "Dulce Domum," I have given a graphic view of the interior of an old pan-closet; and after what was said about it there, and at the lectures, and its exposure and condemnation by all authorities, as well as its inhibition by the Local Government Board, one would have thought, at any rate, that not a pan-closet would be *made* now, in this last decade of the nineteenth century. And yet, after making inquiries, I find that hundreds are still being made. Probably I should not have referred at all to pan-closets here, but for this reason; and, also, because that one or two students seemed by their answers to have been tainted with the pan-closet fever. Fortunately, now that colours can be photographed, we shall be able to show the interior of an old closet in its true colours, if it does not very soon become quite extinct.

4. The light of a candle does not die down all at once. Often in its last flickering moments it extends its flame with so much vigour that a stranger to its ways may be pardoned for thinking that it had recovered its lost energy, and was coming back to life and light again. And so it is

with the pan-closet; practically extinguished some years ago, it is coming back to use again, but only to give the registered plumber and the technological student the job of pulling them out again.

5. It has been well said that there can be no true progress without pain of some kind. The pan-closet having advanced Great Britain a stage in the knowledge of water-closets, is now about to do the same for Russia, where, as I am informed, thousands have been sent in the last year or two. But the pan-closet is not the only unsanitary closet made.

6. It would occupy too much space to examine into the merits and demerits of the very **great variety** of **closets** which have been springing up like mushrooms, here, there, and everywhere, in the last ten or fifteen years; but as the new kinds can all be more or less discussed under two classes, viz., the "wash-out" and the "wash-down"—whether of the pedestal kind, the basin and trap being in one piece; or the separate kind, the basin and trap being in two pieces—it need not occupy much space to compare the two classes.

Then, as to the closets with a mechanical contrivance for keeping water in the basins, the pan-closet being already placed *hors de combat*, it will need but few words to dispose of that impostor, the plunger-closet, under whatever name or guise it may come up for examination; and so leave the valve-closet, where Bramah stood it more than a century ago, the chief of closets.

7. I am quite able to discuss and compare the merits and demerits of the "wash-out" and "wash-down" classes of closets impartially, possessing as I do patent rights for both kinds.

My "water-battery" wash-out closet, though it has a greater depth of water in the basin than most of that class, and is so constructed that the basin and trap are more easily flushed out and freed from foreign matters than the majority of that kind, I do not consider it a perfectly sanitary closet, for, in common with all closets of this kind, it possesses the following demerits:—

(*a*) The water in the basin being too shallow to submerge a costive stool, the fumes from the upper part of pyramidal *excreta* pass into the room so freely that with a long seat-holder the state of the atmosphere becomes and remains unbearable for some minutes to any other visitor.

Fig. 125.—"Water-Battery" Wash-out Closet: Basin and Trap in Two Pieces.

In many cases, especially where the atmosphere of the house is warmer than that of the closet, the polluted air of the closet-room would pass freely into the house.

(*b*) The excrement, no matter in what state it has come from the body, is driven with such force against the upper side of the closet-basin by the inrush of water, that, though it may get washed off again, or nearly so, where there is a good continuous flush, it will leave its marks behind, and such fouling will be added to by each usage of the closet, till after only a very short while it will but need an inspection of the entrance way to the closet-trap to wish one had looked out of window instead.

(c) The energy of the flush, which is as much needed for cleaning and scouring out the trap as for washing out the basin, is chiefly spent in forcing the stool out of the basin, and in its impingement upon the side of the closet, the consequence generally is that an ordinary flush of water

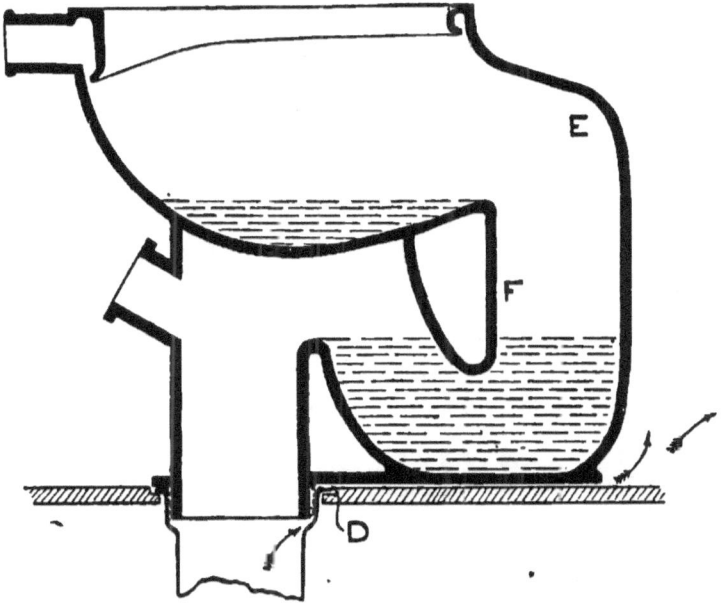

Fig. 126.—" Wash-out " Closet: Basin and Trap in one piece.

rarely washes every vestige of filth out of both the basin and trap.

(d) The large exposed surface between the weir of the closet-basin and the water-seal of the trap. As already explained, this part of the closet in time becomes much corroded with fæcal matter, and the bad air thrown off from it generally passes readily enough into the house.

(*e*) That where the closet becomes most fouled it is least seen.

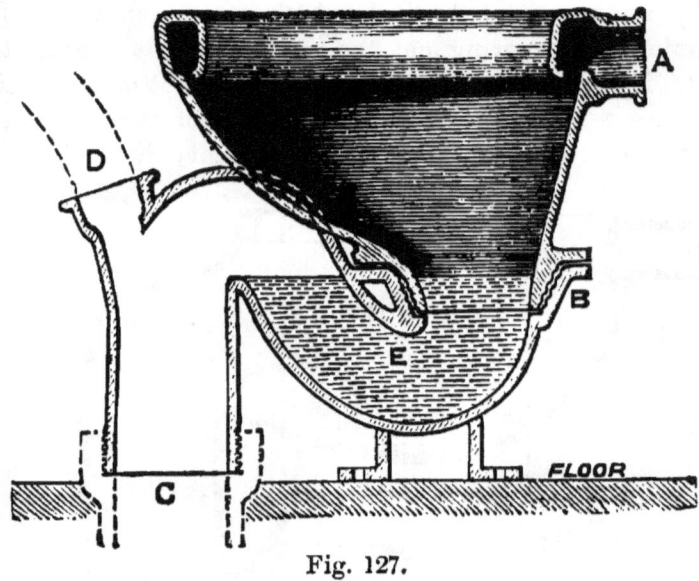

Fig. 127.

7. In the **wash-down** class of closets, whether its basin

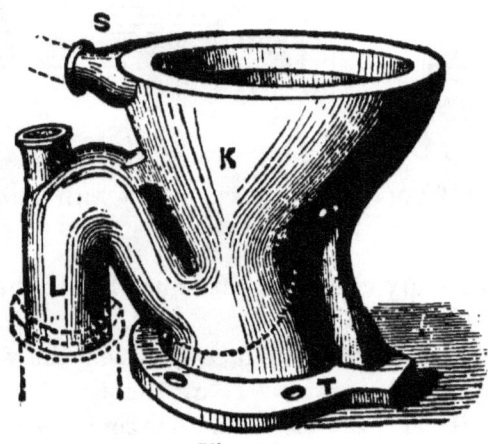

Fig. 128.

and trap are in two pieces, as shown in fig. 127, or in one

piece, as shown in fig. 128, the exposed surface which in usage can become fouled is much smaller than that of the wash-out class of closets. Then the force of the flush, instead of spending itself upon the basin as in the wash-out, passes through the trap with a scouring action, washing out the whole of its interior.

8. In all closets where the exposed **surface of the water standing in the basin** has a much smaller area than that of the seat-hole, the excretions are liable to fall upon the sloping sides either of the back or front, and which the flush does not always remove. But when this happens it would be in such a conspicuous part of the closet that the fæces would at once be seen and another flush given, by all cleanly people; or the housemaid's or attendant's attention being called to the state of the basin, it could be very easily cleaned.

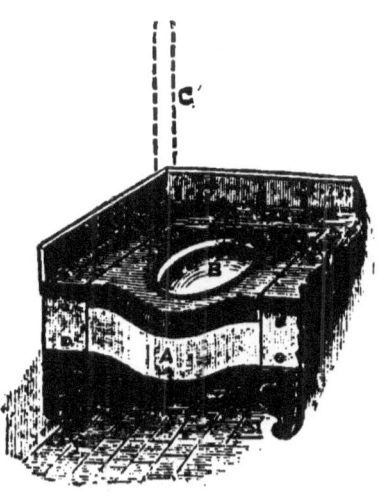

Fig. 129.—SEAT-ACTION CLOSET.

Before using such a closet, I prefer to pull the flushing handle so as to wet the basin, for the better removal of anything which might fall upon it. With a seat-action flushing arrangement, as shown in fig. 129, on sitting down upon the seat a small flush of water is sent into the closet, just enough to wet the basin, and on rising from the seat a full flush follows.

9. The tapering **hopper**, whether long or short, with its side or bent inlet arm, as shown in fig. 130, is so difficult to keep clean that its use should be entirely prohibited.

Instead of destroying the thousands already made, they

might be used by market gardeners for protecting certain things from frost, as rhubarb, etc.

The water enters the closet with such a twirling motion, that by the time it has twirled itself down to the trap it has no energy left to carry anything with it; and so it just gravitates through the drain to the sewer, leaving matters in the closet pretty much as it had found them.

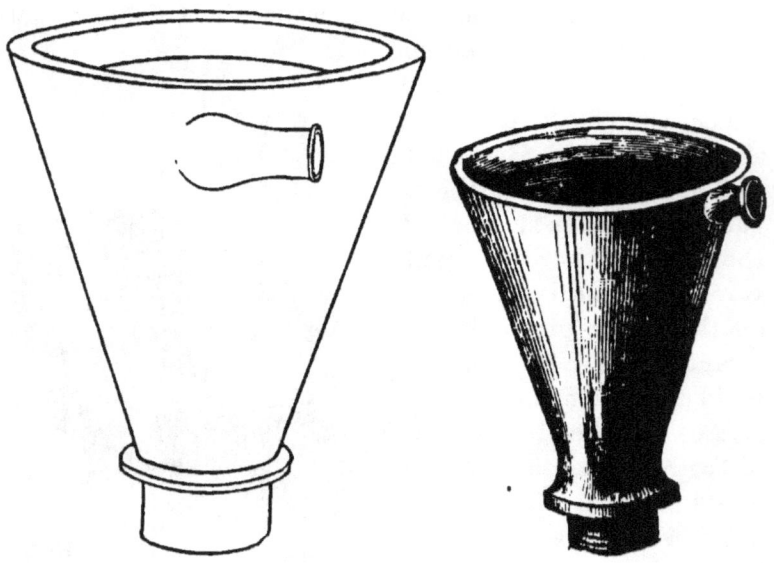

Fig. 130.—Hopper with Side-Inlet.   Fig. 131.

10. Though the flushing-rim hopper, as shown in fig. 131, with a straight inlet arm, is an improvement on the hopper, fig. 130, it is not a wholesome closet. The long tapering sides of the interior of these closets afford such a field for fæces to fall upon, that it is difficult to pass a body of water over the surface of the basin with sufficient frictional force to free it of foreign matters, and so the fæces remain largely upon the exterior parts of the basin after the flush has gone to indicate the whereabouts of the closet.

11. A plug or **plunger-closet** is a simple device for keeping water in a basin. It has been much used in connection with trapless closets. I have discussed this class of

Fig. 132.—SHOWING TRAPLESS CLOSETS. BAD ARRANGEMENT.

closet at length in another work; and as no sanitarian of authority would allow such a closet to be fixed on any of his works, it is not necessary to enlarge upon it here. The illustration, fig. 132, which I have extracted from my

" Lectures," speaks for itself. Apart from the great risk of bad air entering a house through a trapless closet-basin, which had lost its water through a defective basin-plug, B, fig. 132, there would be the continuous contamination of the water in the basin, or the air in the room, by the filth which would accumulate upon the exposed surface of the plug, A, or plunger, G.

CHAPTER XXX.

WATER-CLOSETS (*continued*).

1.

IN public buildings and for general purposes, where the closets would be in constant use—to prevent evaporation of the water-seal of the trap—I should be content to fix self-cleansing wash-down closets, though I should want the traps of lead when they were fixed upstairs, for connection to the soil-pipes, as shown in fig. 138, by wiped soldered joints.

2. For private closets, and where the closets would not be used for weeks together, I should greatly prefer **valve-closets**, of the best description; and I should consider that I had gained the following advantages by adopting this class of closet, viz. :—

(1) A large exposed surface of water in the closet, greater in area than the seat-hole, to prevent the fæces falling upon any part of the basin, and adhering to it.

(2) A large body of water to receive fæcal matters, (*a*) to dilute the liquid portion, and (*b*) to convey the solids away through the closet-trap and soil-pipe in a sort of water envelope.

(3) A great depth of water, for a costive motion to (*a*)

be well and completely submerged under water; and (*b*) to prevent fumes rising from it into the closet-room.

(4) The thorough emptying of the basin, together with the flush of water coming into it, simultaneously, to free the closet from every vestige of matter passed into it.

(5) Supposing the closet to be out of use long enough for the water to evaporate out of the basin, there would still be the basin-valve to exclude the soil-pipe air; or if the basin-

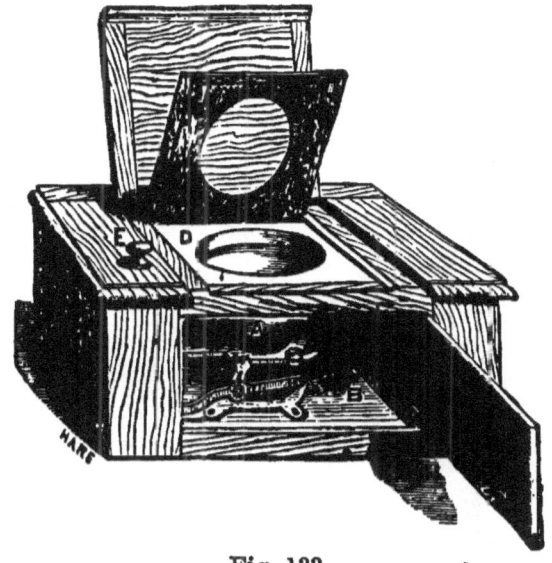

Fig. 133.

valve were defective, the water-seal of the trap would remain as an air-barrier to the soil-pipe. I have made many trials, and have found that after several months, when the water has evaporated out of the basin, the *trap* has still retained a seal, though after a few months the seal gets much reduced. A trap ventilated on the crown of its outgo would not maintain its seal anything like so long as a trap ventilated some little distance away, as shown in fig. 112 and fig. 112A. (Chap. XXIII., Art. 13.)

P

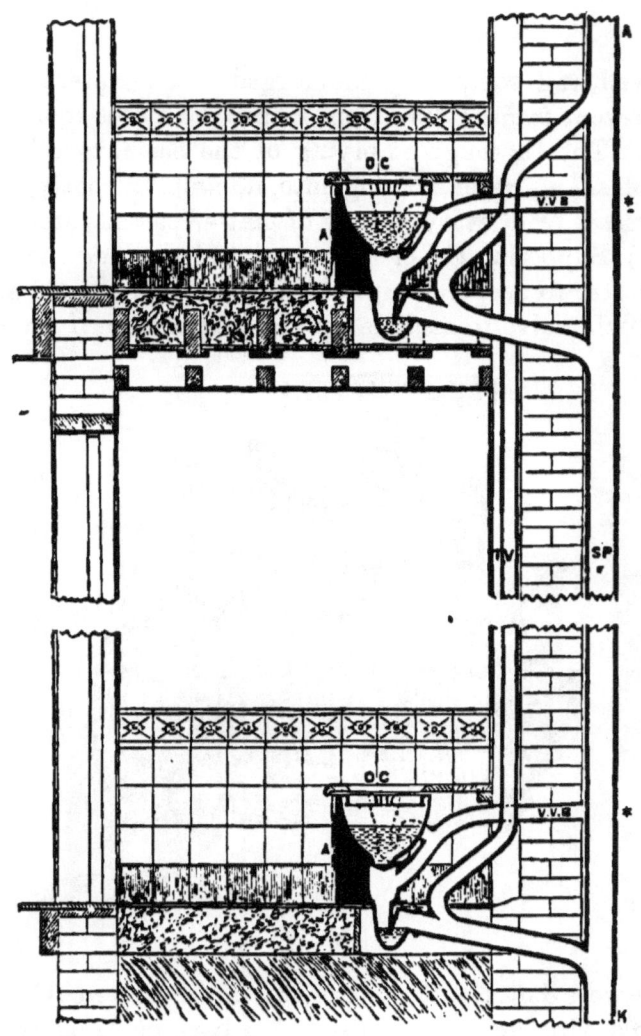

Fig. 134.—Section showing two Valve-Closets, with Traps, Soil-Pipes, and Trap-Ventilation.[1]

[1] Vents from valve-boxes carried out to the open air.

(6) The trap being independent of the closet, a removal of the latter for repairs, or in case of breakage, leaves the trap still standing, to keep the soil-pipe air out of the house.

(7) The trap being of lead, its connection with the soil-pipe by a wiped soldered joint is permanent and reliable—a most important consideration. (Chap. XXXI., Art. 1.)

3. In using a valve-closet strangers often pull up the handle such a little way that there is no room for the paper to pass out of the basin, the consequence is that pieces of paper are often caught between the outlet of the basin and the basin-valve, and then when the next visitor comes to the closet he finds no water in it, and condemns the closet, instead of condemning the person who so badly treated it. [A printed notice put up in a conspicuous place in the closet-room, telling strangers how to pull up the closet-handle, generally corrects such an error.]

4. There is another **drawback to valve-closets.** Where there are no slop-sinks, a servant wishing to empty a pailful of slops into the closet finds herself for the moment in the want of *three* hands, one to pull up the closet-handle, whilst with the other two she empties the pail. I have provided for this in my patent "Optimus" closet with downright overflow, etc., fig. 133. A pailful of water can be emptied into the closet, and then when the handle is pulled, a flush of water will pass into it, to cleanse the closet and charge the basin with clean water.

5. Many valve-closets are made with most **defective overflow** arrangements. An overflow-pipe is often carried from the basin into the valve-box without a water-seal, or with a seal so small that for the purpose of preventing a passage of air from the valve-box into the closet apartment it is practically of no value, and is worse than useless. The evil of an inefficient seal (fig. 135) is further aggra-

vated by the fact that very often in such cases the overflow-trap is only charged when a pailful of slops is emptied into the closet.

6. In fig. 134 I show two of my patent "Optimus" closets, fixed with lead "Anti-D-traps" under same, and branching into a stack of 3½ in. 8 lbs. lead soil-pipe, with 2 in. lead anti-syphoning pipe, all complete, and 2 in. lead puff-pipes or vents to valve-boxes, the ends of which are left open to the atmosphere.

7. In **fixing traps** for **valve-closets** be careful to leave a wide margin for the seat-rail at the back, for clothes. Where it can be allowed, 16 in. or 17 in. from the centre of the dip of trap to the face of the plastered wall at the back of the closet answers very well. In fixing traps care must always be taken to so fix them that they shall have their full seal. Where there are no safes the mouth of the dip should be rounded over and soldered to a lead flange, or be very carefully tafted back and rebated into the floor.

Fig. 135.—Overflow-Trap, Inefficient Seal.

8. Where the closets are open to view and the floors are of marble or tiles, an **overflow-pipe** fixed to the floor and carried through the wall is all that is necessary to prevent a ceiling from being washed down, in case of a breakdown of the service-pipe or supply-valve, from frost or any other cause. In such cases it is well to give the floor a fall all ways towards the overflow.

9. Where the closets are inclosed it is better to fix a **lead safe** (or tray) under them, with a stand-up 4 in. high on each side, and large enough to catch any water which may flow over from the closet-basin at any and all points. It is the custom with some plumbers to dog's-ear the corners, but the corners are better either bossed or

soldered; for in case any filth washed over the closet at any time the matter might find its way between the corner lappings, and remain there.

The safe should be soldered to the closet trap, as shown in fig. 16, Chap. VIII.

The mouth of the overflow-pipe can be opened out a little with a turn-pin, and soldered to the safe, as shown at A, fig. 136. But in all cases the end of the pipe must be made to discharge into the open air.

It is usual to fix a brass or **copper-hinged flap** on the

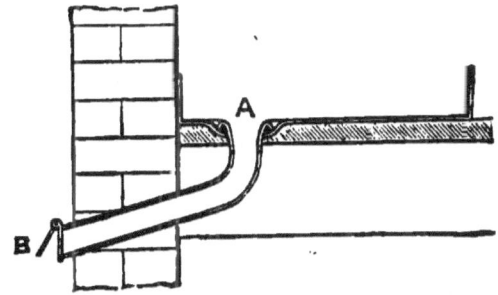

Fig. 136.—SAFE AND ITS OVERFLOW-PIPE.

end of the overflow-pipe, D, fig. 136, for the double purpose of excluding draught and preventing birds building in the pipe. But where it is desirable to utilize such a pipe for the purpose of admitting air into the closet-room, and where there would be no risk from such a treatment—from pipe freezing, etc.—a copper bird-guard can be fixed on the end of the pipe (instead of the flap) for keeping out birds. But where the end of an overflow-pipe faces the north or north-east, and the mouth of the pipe, A, inside the closet-room stands also inside the closet inclosure, there would be danger of the service-pipe freezing, and also of the supply-valve, as well as the water in the closet-basin.

CHAPTER XXXI.

WATER-CLOSETS (*continued*).

1.

TO make a reliable connection of an earthenware closet or an earthenware closet-trap to a lead soil-pipe is generally a work of great difficulty; and if the thousands of such connections which have been made in the last ten years were tested to-day, a large number would be found defective.

The difficulty is increased when the closet and trap are made in one piece, and the outlet of the trap is formed upon the underside of the closet base, as shown by the arrows in fig. 126. In fact such a connection cannot be relied upon even for a year. In the many examinations I have made, out of hundreds of such connections, I have only found a few that could be considered both air-tight and water-tight; and even of those it would have been impossible to have said how long they would have remained sound. If earthenware closets or earthenware traps are to be connected to *soil-pipes*, whether of lead or iron, the connection should be so made that it may be readily seen and examined, without any disturbance of the surroundings, to see that it is sound and good.

2. On referring to the first edition of my work "Dulce Domum," published fourteen years ago, I find that I called special attention to the connection of earthenware closets to soil-pipes, and what is there said is so important, that I think it well to make some extracts.

"All traps fixed inside a house should be separate and independent of the 'fitting,' be that what it may, which

CONNECTIONS TO WATER-CLOSETS. 215

is to be fixed upon them, and be made 'fixtures' in a very complete way with the soil or waste-pipe to which they are to be attached.

"And then when the 'fitting' gets out of order, whether water-closet, urinal, slop-sink, or whatever the fitting may be, it can be removed for repairs without interfering with the trap or exposing the house to the waste-pipe, soil-pipe, or drain.

"But when the trap forms a part of the 'fitting,' and is in one piece with it, it cannot be removed for repairs (or for renewal in case of breakage) without exposing the soil-pipe, and perhaps drain as well, to the house, leaving it, in fact, in free and open communication with the soil or waste-pipe on which the 'fitting' was fixed.

"But there is another and stronger reason why the trap should be independent of the fitting. The connection of

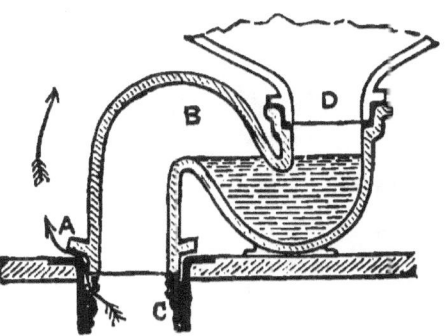

Fig. 137.—SHOWING DEFECTIVE JOINT OF EARTHENWARE TRAP TO SOIL-PIPE.

the appliance with the trap—whether closet, slop-sink, bath, urinal, sink, or lavatory basin—is not so important as the connection of the trap with the soil-pipe or waste-pipe; for the latter being on the drain side (sewer side) of the water-seal of the trap would allow any bad air or noxious gases in the soil-pipe or waste-pipe to escape through a defective joint into the house, as shown by the arrows at A, fig. 137, whereas the former—the connection of the closet with the trap—being on the house side of the trap (D, fig. 137), would still, in case of a defect, leave the house protected by the water-seal of its trap. The jointing of a trap with a soil-pipe or waste-pipe is therefore of the utmost importance."

3. I am still of the opinion which I gave fourteen years ago, that a connection of earthenware to lead or iron is inferior to that of lead to lead, for—apart from the risk of exposing the house to the soil-pipe, during the time a broken trap, or a fractured part of an earthenware closet, was being changed for a new one, a not infrequent occurrence—I know of no means of connecting earthenware to lead, or earthenware to iron, so absolutely reliable as the union of a lead trap to a lead soil-pipe by a wiped soldered joint, as shown at s, fig. 138.

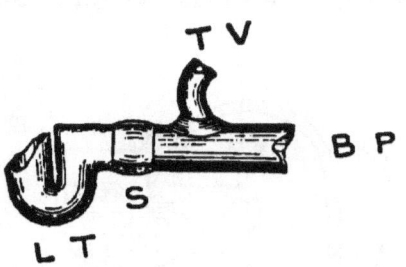

Fig. 138.—Showing Connection of Lead Trap to Lead Soil-Pipe.

4. Where the **closets** are to be **connected** to a stoneware or a cast-iron **drain**, where they would have a very solid base, and the surroundings would be very rigid, there is no stronger way of making the connection than by a Portland cement joint; but the joint should be kept above the floor, as shown in fig. 128, where it can be readily seen, and the cement should be of the best kind. I have tested such joints many years after they have been made, and found them quite sound and good. In some trial tests with such connections, I have found a Portland cement joint to stand 30 lbs. to the square inch.

5. But where earthenware closets or earthenware traps are fixed "upstairs," for connection to a lead or cast-iron soil-pipe, the conditions are different; for in the latter case there is not only the vibration of the floors, which in some buildings is very great, and the sinking of the walls,

which in newly-built houses of good height is often sufficient to cause a fracture in the earthenware closet (where it is connected to an iron pipe by a Portland cement joint), or to break the connection, but there is also the unequal expansion and contraction of the different materials. And though a brass socket soldered to a lead soil-pipe would enable a more rigid joint being made to an earthenware closet, viz., by a Portland cement joint, it would increase the numbers of the different materials to be incorporated

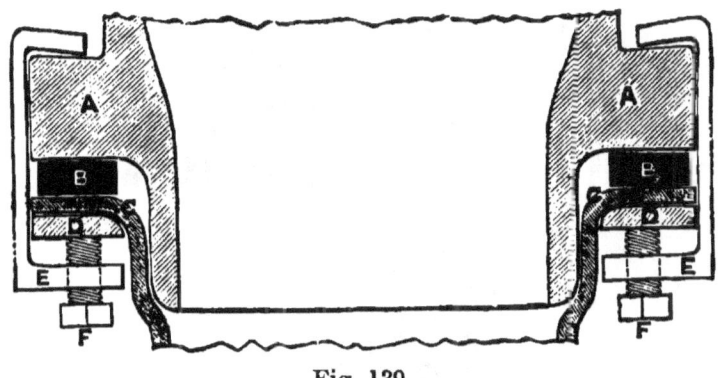

Fig. 139.

in the connection—earthenware, Portland cement, brass, solder, and lead.

6. For connecting earthenware traps ·or earthenware closets to lead **horizontal branches**, for years past I have had strong flanges formed upon the outlets of my closets, as shown at A, fig. 139, for bolting to the soil-pipe, where the joint can at all times readily be got at, as shown at F, fig. 140; using a flange (B, fig. 139) made of the best india-rubber between the two faces. There is also another advantage gained by such an arrangement, viz., that the anti-syphoning pipe can be soldered to the lead soil-pipe, as shown in fig. 140.

I have had such joints tested up to 25 ft. head of water,

and found them to stand that pressure without leaking. To prevent the india-rubber from deteriorating and losing

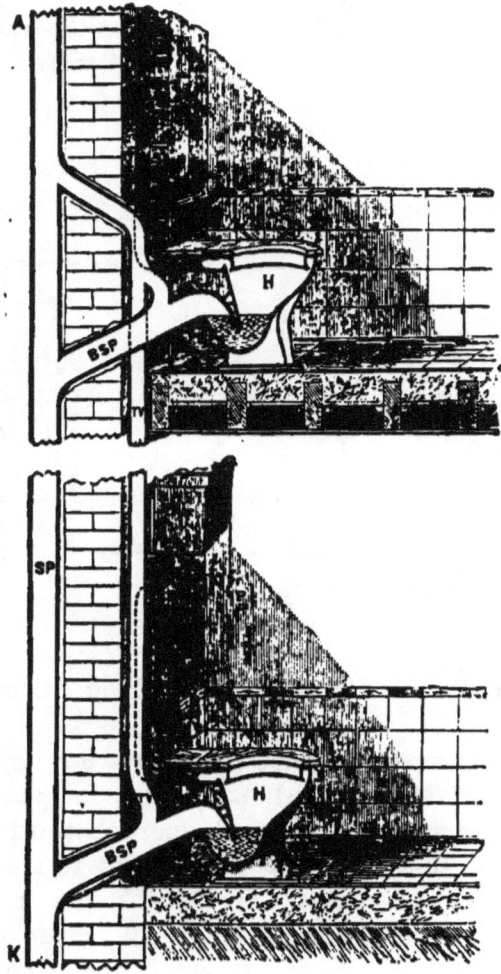

Fig. 140.—SHOWING CONNECTIONS OF EARTHENWARE CLOSETS WITH A LEAD SOIL-PIPE.

its elasticity, I have had some rings of the best india-rubber covered with asbestos, and I have found that a connection

CONNECTIONS TO WATER-CLOSETS. 219

made with such a packing, as shown in fig. 139, to stand a pressure of 7 lbs. to the square inch without leaking. The surface of the asbestos covering being rougher than that of the plain india-rubber, the connection requires to be screwed up tighter, and as I can see an element of danger in this, the asbestos india-rubber packing is abandoned for the present.

Although I have never come across a defective connection made as shown in figs. 139 and 140, I have heard of two cases where some plumbers in the country showed poor skill in tafting back the end of the lead soil-pipe to fit to and correspond with the face of the earthenware flange, and then endeavoured to correct their errors by screwing up the clips (E, fig. 139) and breaking the flanges.

7. As a **spigot-and-socket connection** admits of a little adjustment, and when the socket stands upright, a good filling in can be made with an elastic cement which is fluidal when heated. I have had many kinds of such "cement" tested, and have found that some compositions, which had been considered good for such joints, would not stand 3 ft. head of water.

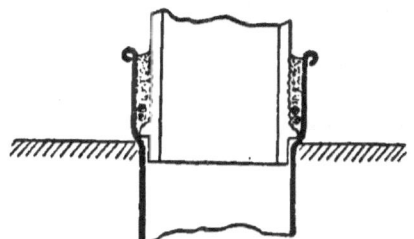

Fig. 141.—SHOWING JOINT MADE WITH ELASTIC CLOSET CEMENT.

Some joints, similar to that shown in fig. 141, made with a strong adhesive cement, and which I have named the "Elastic Closet Cement," stood a pressure equal to 30 ft. head of water without leaking. To prevent the cement, when in a hot fluidal state, running through the connection into the interior of the pipe, a ring or two of spun yarn is caulked into the socket, and the composition is melted into the socket by the aid of a lamp (fig. 3 or 4), great care being taken to well warm both the socket and spigot before melting in the cement.

CHAPTER XXXII.

WATER-CLOSETS (*continued*).

1.

ELSEWHERE I have enlarged upon the advantages gained by exposing closets to view, as in the now much-used pedestal kind—whether of the wash-out or wash-down pattern—but though an **open closet** possesses the great advantage of showing its surroundings at a glance, it does not prevent servants indifferent to their duties from sweeping the dirt out of a closet-room round into any little place behind the closet-trap. And as it has now become the bad practice with many men to treat such closets as if they were urinals, it will generally be found that there is more filth outside such closets than inside. At any rate, closets so treated are not so wholesome as closets so inclosed that no sweepings can be swept round behind them, and no urine allowed to run down outside them.

2. During the last year or two hundreds of **closets** have been fixed in **exposed positions** without inclosures, and the consequence has been that when such closets have not been broken by frost they have often been rendered useless by the water in their traps becoming frozen. (Chap. XXIII., Art. 13.) An inclosure to a closet not only deadens the sound of the incoming water, but it forms a great protection to closets from frost; and one great advantage of a lid to a closet-seat is that—when it is put down—it

shuts out the cold air and helps to keep the water in the closet from freezing.

3. **Water supply to closets.**—It would hardly be possible to over-estimate the value of good water flushes to a closet for keeping it clean and wholesome; and though the quantity is unwisely limited to two gallons by many companies, it is no reason why the plumber should weaken the power of such a flush, either by using poor flushing appliances, or by badly bending the service-pipe.

No water-waste-preventer, or flushing-cistern, should be used which will not allow the full flush to pass into the closet by one pull of the flushing-handle. And the supply of water to the waste-preventer, or flushing-cistern, should be so arranged that a second flush may be given to a closet, when so needed, in quick succession to the first; the very outside limit that a flushing-cistern should take to recharge itself should be two minutes, though half that time with a good arrangement is ample for the purpose. In hundreds of cases, where inefficient flushing-cisterns have been fixed, and incompetent plumbers have executed the work, a second flush of water could not be given—even though the first failed to free the closet from filth—without waiting at least five minutes for the little flusher to fill, and I have counted eight minutes while so wasting my time.

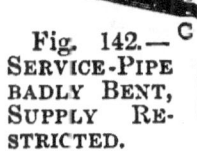

Fig. 142.—SERVICE-PIPE BADLY BENT, SUPPLY RESTRICTED.

4. Where there are no restrictions, it is better to fix *three*-gallon **flushing-cisterns**, as shown at c, fig. 140, and in some cases four-gallon ones, or even larger. For instance, when a closet discharges into a soil-pipe which empties into a branch drain, with its receiving end remote

from the main drain, a larger quantity of water is required to cleanse the closet, soil-pipe, and long length of branch drain, than would be the case with a closet fixed upon the main drain, or within a very short distance of it.

As the flushing-pipe to the closet (s, fig. 140) would only be charged with water during the time of the flushing it needs no protection from frost; but where the flushing-cistern would be likely to freeze, it should be inclosed, and the service-pipe to it protected from frost (Chap. XXV., Art. 13) and cased in. When the back of the flushing-cistern would stand upon the internal face of an external wall of the house, especially a north wall, it should have a piece of board fixed behind it to break the contact.

To deaden the noise of flushing to anyone in a room at the back of a closet flushing-cistern, a board fixed behind the cistern (c, fig. 140) and the flushing-pipe is very valuable, especially with a sheeting of india-rubber between the board and the wall. A silence-pipe should be fixed on the nose of the ball-valve, and the flusher should be fitted with a cover.

5. When there is no water company to interfere with the supply of water to closets, there is no better way of **supplying a valve-closet** than by a valve-and-regulator apparatus attached to the closet, as directly the closet-handle is pulled, and even before the contents of the basin have passed out, water is made to enter the closet to dilute fæcal matters and cleanse the basin before the bottom valve is closed again. And no matter how carelessly the handle may be returned to its place, how suddenly it may be dropped, sufficient water will be retained in the basin, or will come into it after the flap-valve has been closed, to recharge the basin.

6. The service-pipe should be of such a size, that a flush of about three gallons of water can be sent into the closet

in about five seconds. Where the head of water upon the supply-valve is under 3 ft., the service-pipe should be 2½ in., and the supply-valve 2 in. With a foot or two more head of water, 2 in. pipe and 1½ in. valve will give a good flush. With 8 or 10 ft. head of water, 1½ in. pipe, and 1½ in. or 1¼ in. valve. From about 10 ft. to 15 ft., 1¼ in. pipe and 1¼ in. valve. Above 20 ft., 1 in. pipe and 1 in. valve. Instead of supplying a valve-closet from a service-pipe with a greater head of water than 30 ft., it is better to fix a small cistern over the closet—a cistern holding not less than six gallons of water; and, for the sake of appearance, the cistern could be of wood, panelled, and lined with lead. The cistern could be painted to match the surroundings, or it could be inclosed in polished mahogany.

7. Where water companies insist upon a water-waste-preventing arrangement to a valve-closet, instead of fixing an ugly water-waste-preventer over the closet, it is better to fix an "under-the-seat" waste-preventing supply-valve for flush and after-flush, such as those made by Messrs. J. Tyler and Sons, or Messrs. T. Lambert and Sons, or any good waste-preventing valve of which the company may approve.

8. All **apartments** in which water-closets or slop-sinks are fixed should be so **ventilated** that the air in the room may readily be changed by proper inlet and outlet tubes or shafts. And the ventilation should be so planned and arranged, that no effluvia from the closet apartment—or only after such offensive air had been much diluted—should enter the house; and that should chiefly be from what had hung about the clothes of the person using it. Especially should this be the case in all public water-closets, and, indeed, in every closet likely to receive several visitors in quick succession, or its last visitor would be likely to beat a hasty retreat, under the impression that he

had found out a secret way to the lower regions. This subject is too large to go into here, but it may be worth while to caution the zinc-worker—for *he* is the man (not the plumber) who does this kind of work in London—to be careful with the jointings of such ventilation tubes, and see that they are all air-tight, to prevent the effluvia escaping through them into any other apartment, or in fact into any part of the house.

Fresh air should be made to enter the closet apartment as near its doorway as possible, so that whatever air was sucked into the house through the closet apartment should be diluted with the fresh air brought into the room through the Tobin—the fresh-air inlet.

The outlet should be from the ceiling, from the highest part of the room, and preferably over the closet-seat. And the shaft from it should be carried up above the roof, with a cowl fixed over it to prevent down-draught. Or it may be taken into some general W.C. air-shaft, when fixed in large buildings, with some artificial means for inducing an up-draught.

CHAPTER XXXIII.

SLOP-SINKS AND DRAW-OFF SINKS.

1.

A SLOP-SINK should be fixed on every alternate floor, if not on every floor of a dwelling-house, on which there are many bedrooms, and where they are likely to be much occupied. Where there is no such convenience, despite all warnings to the contrary, the slops will be emptied down the nearest closet, which will most likely be found out in a disagreeable sort of way by the next person using the closet; for it is not every chambermaid who is thoughtful enough to wipe up any spillings upon the seat.

2. In a small house, where the mistress has more control, and to save expense, the closet on the chamber floor might be constructed to answer the double purpose of **water-closet** and **slop-closet combined**; but where this is done, and for certain reasons the pedestal or open closet is objected to, the closet-basin should be constructed with a table-top, and so fitted up that not a drop of slops or a particle of foul matter shall be able to find its way inside the inclosure.

3. In my works I prefer to separate slop-sink waste-pipes from soil-pipes, and to " disconnect " them from the soil-drain, either by a disconnecting-trap, such as shown at G, fig. 143, or by a similar trap, but with a mica-valve fixed on the mouth of the fresh-air induct, as circumstances may require. See fig. 114.

In cases where such traps would stand under a window, or near the entrance to the house, and especially so in the case of hospitals, I should seal over the top of the trap and bring fresh air into it from some convenient place, and if circumstances called for it I should fix a mica-valve over the mouth of the induct-pipe, to prevent foul air escaping through it in times of down-draught, etc.

4. I prefer the separation of slop-sink waste-pipes from soil-pipes, and also their " disconnection " from soil-drains, because a slop-sink has only *one* seal—the water-seal of its trap between the house and its conduit, and which may be broken either by evaporation, or by a cleansing of the sink. Servants have admitted that they have dipped their flannels into the water held in the trap when cleansing such sinks. In testing the drains of a house a year or two ago (which had been previously tested by more than one engineer and found to be sound, but where there were continued com-

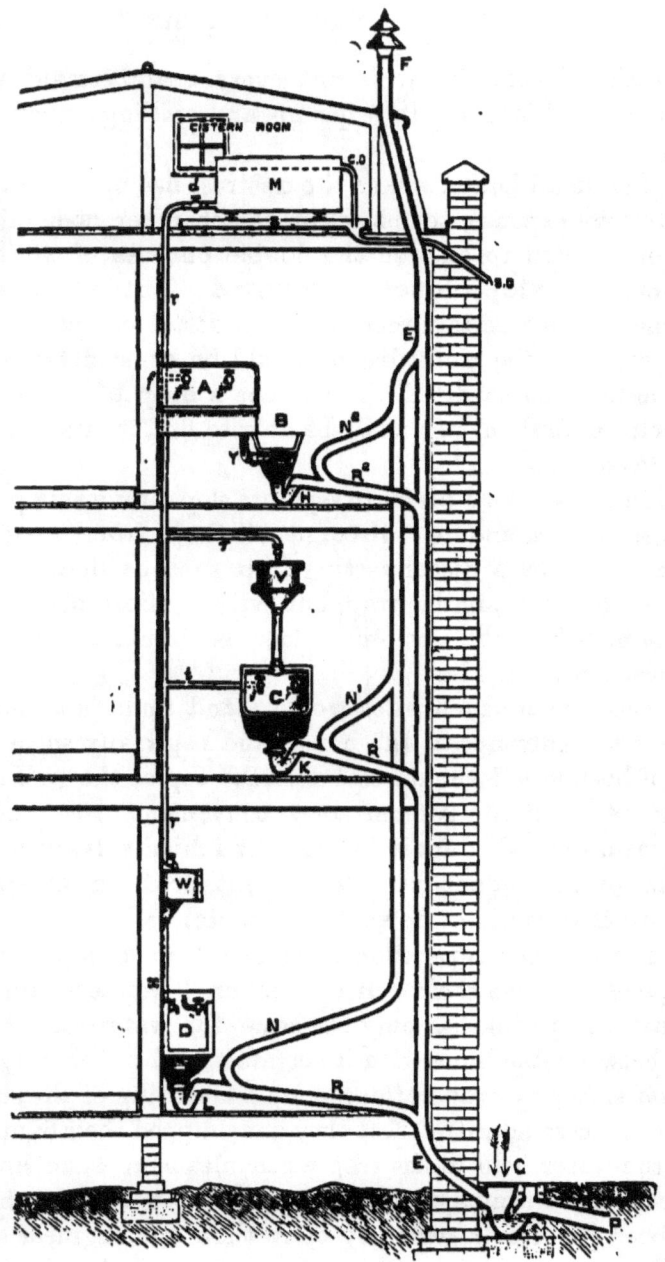

Fig. 143.

plaints of bad smells), smoke poured into the house through a slop-closet so robbed of its water-seal; and the housemaid confessed to me that she had often dipped her flannel into the closet-trap, when cleansing the basin, and robbed it of its seal, doing it in ignorance.

But the connection of the waste-pipe from a slop-sink with that of a soil-pipe is rather a question of the class of closet fixed upon the soil-pipe—leaving out of consideration the question of hot water. For if *one* seal between the house and the soil-pipe is considered sufficient—as in the "wash-out" and "wash-down" closets—the matters sent through a slop-sink and water-closet being of the same character, or nearly so, there can be no reason why *one* pipe should not be made to answer the double purpose of slop-sink waste and soil-pipe combined.

5. But where valve-closets are fixed on a soil-pipe, as they are provided with more than one seal (Chap. XXX., Art. 2), there would be good reason for keeping the waste-pipe from a slop-sink out of it, and carrying it down independently of the soil-pipe and disconnecting it from the soil-drain.

Or in the case of a private house, the waste-pipe from the slop-sink and wash-up sink combined might be branched into the waste-pipe from the general sinks, or into the waste-pipe from a bath, as shown in fig. 153; but the bathroom in such cases should have no communication with a bedroom, and the waste-pipe in every such case should discharge with an open end into a disconnecting-trap.

6. In private houses, where hardly anything but liquid slops—from chamber utensils and toilet basins—would be emptied into the slop-sinks, a 2 in. waste-pipe, as shown in fig. 143, would be found to be large enough. And where so required, a wash-up sink of white-ware or fire-clay, for scalding out the chamber utensils, could be fixed, in combination with the slop-sink, as shown at A. Or a slop-sink with a flushing-rim could be fixed, as shown at C, with

a syphon flushing-cistern, as shown at v, for flushing out the sink-waste when so required.

7. For **hospitals**, where excreta, poultices, etc., etc., would be emptied into the slop-sinks, the waste-pipes should be treated as soil-pipes—fixing 3 in., 3½ in., or even 4 in. pipes, as circumstances might require; though a 3½ in. pipe (with trap-ventilation) is large enough for a tier of two or three slop-sinks.

The "McHardy" patent hospital slop-sink is specially

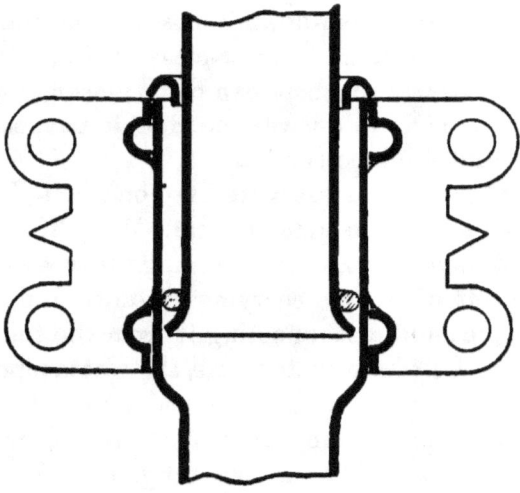

Fig. 144.—Expansion or Telescope Joint.

constructed for cleansing bed-pans and bottles. The bed-pan is put into the sink, which is specially constructed to receive it, when a powerful flush of water is sent up into its interior from the bottom of the sink, and the pan thoroughly cleansed and flushed out; which greatly reduces the risk of the nurse inhaling infected air.

8. Where **hot water** draw-off sinks are fixed in combination with the slop-sinks, or hot water is laid on in any way to the sinks, and the waste-pipes are of lead and fixed *out-*

side—as should be the case where possible—telescope joints, or expansion joints, as shown in fig. 144, should be made upon the pipes, to allow them to expand and contract without breaking. Some joints which I had made upon 2 in. bath-wastes and 3 in slop-sink waste-pipes eight or nine years ago, were found to be sound and good when last tested, and water at a very high temperature has often been sent through the pipes.

To make the joint, open the end of the under and outer pipes by driving a mandril (or a gradation of sizes) into it for a depth of about 7 in., taking care to keep the mandril true all the while; and to prevent one part of the socket stretching more than another, well heat the pipe first. Round up the end of the inner pipe upon a mandril. A little grease rubbed over the mandril will enable it the better to be withdrawn after it has done its work; but where india-rubber is to be fixed between the pipes, the grease—which acts injuriously upon india-rubber—should be carefully removed from the pipes again. An india-rubber ring should be drawn over the end of the inner pipe, and the outer pipe opened just enough to allow the pipe and ring to enter, so that the end of the inner pipe, when put together, stands about an inch above the shoulder of the socket of the outer pipe. A sliding cap should be fixed on the top, as shown in fig. 144, to keep dirt, etc., out of the socket.

9. Where the waste-pipe from a tier of slop-sinks, or from a tier of wash-up and slop-sinks combined, or from a tier of general draw-off sinks, would be subject to expansion and contraction from hot and cold water discharges, and the pipe could not be fixed outside, instead of fixing the pipe of *lead* inside the house it would be better to fix coated cast-iron pipe with india-rubber expansion joints, as shown in fig. 146; or the pipe could be of wrought iron—galvanized inside and out—with screwed joints.

10. Traps should be fixed under the slop-sinks as circum-

stances require, a larger size being fixed in hospitals; in fact in such places the traps, waste-pipes, and ventilation-pipes should be of the sizes as used for the water-closets. (Art. 7.)

11. No slop-sink or slop-closet should be fixed without a means of flushing it out. Flushing-cisterns, similar to those described for flushing out closets (Chap. XXXII., Arts. 3 and 4), should be fixed where possible, as shown at v and w, fig. 143.

12. It seems a waste of words to say that a **sink** made of a **non-absorbent** material is more wholesome than one made of an absorbent kind, such as wood or sandstone; and yet the latter kinds are often fixed in places where there would have been no difficulty in fixing sinks of fire-clay, stoneware, earthenware, or copper, supposing the man who provided the sandstone sink had some objection to lead-lined sinks.

13. For washing up glass or china, wood sinks lined with tinned copper are preferable to either earthenware or fire-clay—where money and tempers are valued; for whilst there would be no elasticity in the latter (fire-clay), there would be just enough in the former (copper sink) to prevent many breakages of glass, china, and temper.

14. Round about the top of a sink there should be no opening, crevice, or place where filth could fall into, and by accumulating become offensive.

15. The bottoms of sinks should fall towards their outlets, and the outlets or apertures ought always to be large enough to receive gratings, or plugs-and-washers, which should have a water-way through them equal in area to fully charge the bore of the trap and waste-pipe to be fixed to them, as shown at A, fig. 145. (Chap. XXIV., Art. 7.)

The brass cobweb-grating, which was introduced and named by me many years ago, whether fitted to a brass rim or not, whether soldered over the mouth of the trap or fitted to the washer of a brass plug-and-washer, allows a sink to be emptied so much quicker than a round-hole grating, that one wonders why this kind of screener has not become universal; but its use is becoming more extensive every year.

16. All sinks which could have their apertures—their outlets—sealed up with fitted plugs should have overflow-pipes fixed to them; and this overflow-pipe, where it could not be carried out to the open air, should be connected to the sink in such a way that it could readily be flushed out and cleaned. (Chap. XXXV., Art. 4.)

17. For **pantry sinks,** a 2 in. brass plug-and-washer, a

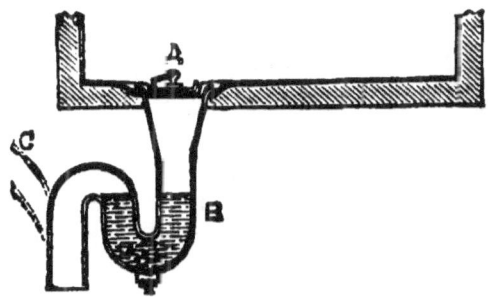

Fig. 145.

1¼ in. anti-D-trap, as fig. 89, and 1½ in. lead waste-pipe discharging under the grating of an aerial disconnecting-trap fixed outside the house, make a wholesome arrangement. But in all cases, whether this kind of trap or a round-pipe trap be fixed, where the discharging end of the waste-pipe is more than four or five feet below the trap, it is necessary that the trap or waste-pipe should be vented, to prevent syphonage.

18. A 2 in. waste-pipe is quite large enough to take the branches of two or three sinks fixed on the several floors of a four-storied building. As previously explained, where hot water is laid on to a tier of sinks, and the waste-pipe is

of lead, the pipe should be fixed outside, with expansion joints, as illustrated in fig. 144. Or if the elevation of the building will not admit of any such pipe being fixed outside, and the pipe is required to be carried down inside, galvanized wrought-iron pipe should be fixed with screwed joints and Y-junctions. Or instead of galvanized wrought-iron pipe, strong cast-iron pipe could be fixed, coated inside and out with solution, and with India-rubber expansion joints, as shown at A, fig. 146. The lead trap and lead branch waste being connected to the iron pipe by a gun-metal coupling union, as shown at B.

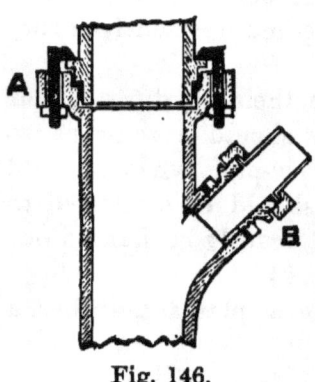

Fig. 146.

19. As the **anti-syphoning pipe** would only be slightly affected by the hot water sent down the waste-pipe, that could be fixed in lead in the usual way, connected by lead branches to the lead branch wastes by wiped soldered joints.

CHAPTER XXXIV.

SCULLERY SINKS.

1.

THE general **sink** in the scullery, into which all kinds of liquids and matter are emptied, from green-water to greasy matters, should be made of a non-absorbent material, such as stoneware or fire-clay. Or if the sink is to answer the double purpose of receiver and washer, *i.e.*, if instead of washing the dinner-plates, etc., in a tub placed within the sink, the sink itself is to be used for the purpose, then instead of fixing a sink of non-elastic material, as stoneware or fire-clay, a wood sink lined with tinned copper should be fixed, copper being sufficiently elastic to prevent the breakage of crockery ware, and its surface being smoother and therefore cleaner than lead. In such cases the depth of the sink should not be less than about 11 or 12 in., with its front well sloped back towards the bottom; and where the sink would be much used, and the usage would be rough, the copper sides should not be less than $2\frac{1}{4}$ lbs. to the superficial foot, and the bottom about $3\frac{1}{4}$ lbs., but a greater strength still would be preferable. The top edges should be protected from the wear and tear of utensils over them by oak cappings secured to the sink by brass cups and screws.

2. There should be no openings, spaces, or crevices round about the tops of the sinks where filth could fall into and become a nuisance. The draining-board should sail over the edge of the sink, with a water-groove on its underside, to prevent the drainings running back over the top edges of the sink and dropping on to the floor, or to keep them from soaking into the woodwork.

3. Where the wash-up sinks are lined with tinned copper, the **draining-board** should also be covered with tinned copper, with draining-channels properly formed in same. Or the draining-board could be covered with lead, as the latter could easily be dressed into the grooves or channels, for carrying off the drainings from the plate-rack. Or milled lead, with a corrugated upper surface, could be fixed on the draining-board.

4. For **washing vegetables**—where it could be well afforded—a separate sink with two compartments should be fixed, made either of slate or fire-clay, one compartment being used for washing the vegetables in, and one for

rinsing. The sink should be about 1 ft. deep, and the front should slope well back towards the bottom, to give room for the knees and clothes.

Next the division, in the back corner of the bottom of the compartment for holding water, should be fixed a 2½ in. (or 3 in. or 2 in.) brass washer, with a cobweb-grating, fly-nut and union, fitted with a ground-in brass hollow plug, to which should be soldered or brazed a tinned copper trumpet-pipe to form the overflow. And this standard overflow should be protected by a tinned copper movable perforated guard, to prevent damage from potatoes, turnips, and such like vegetables.

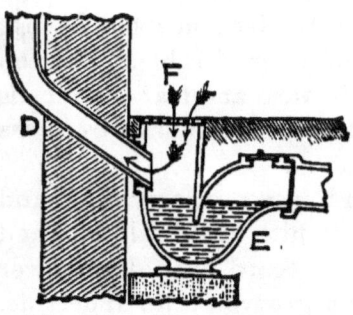

Fig. 147.—SECTION OF A STONEWARE "DRAIN-INTERCEPTOR."

A similar arrangement could also be fixed in the rinsing compartment; but where this compartment is not required to hold water, a simple brass cobweb-grating of good strength, or a rim and grate, soldered to the trap, is all that is necessary.

A lead trap can be fixed under such compartment, and the waste-pipes branched into one pipe and carried through the wall; but as the discharges from such sinks would not be of a foul character, there is no reason why one trap should not take the wastes from the two sinks; and then where the waste-pipe, to reach the disconnecting-trap outside, would not be of a long length, and would not have more than 2 or 3 ft. fall, there would be no necessity to vent it to prevent syphonage.

5. There is no difficulty in disposing of the **waste-pipe** from the **vegetable washers**; that, in all cases, should discharge with an *open end*, into a self-cleansing stoneware drain-interceptor fixed outside the house.

6. But there is often great difficulty in determining the best method of treating the **waste-pipe** from the **general sink**; for it is impossible to pass bodies of greasy water through a drain, and for the drain at all times to keep as wholesome as would have been the case had the grease been intercepted by a grease-intercepting trap, as shown in fig.

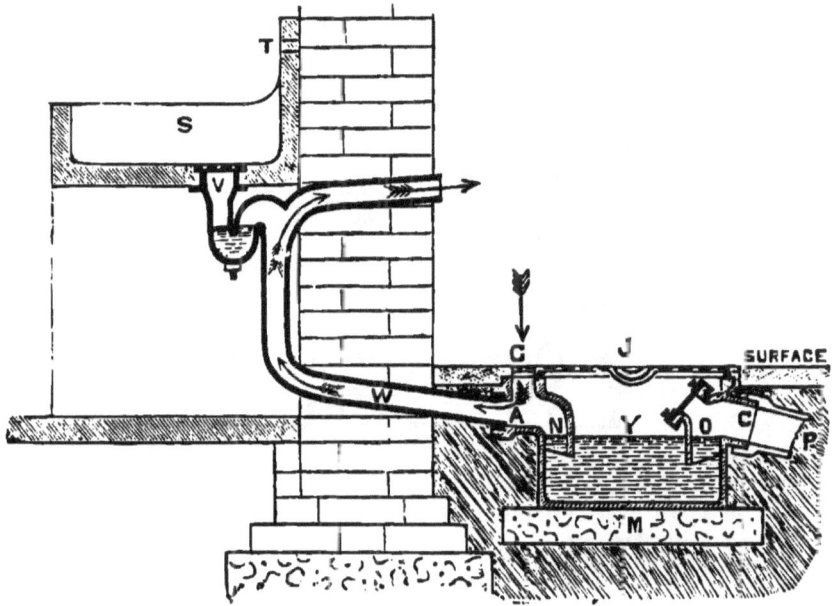

Fig. 148.—Section of "Grease-Intercepting Trap" in Stoneware.

148 or fig. 149. But where the grease is caught in such a fashion it must be carried away. There is no difficulty about this in country houses, or in houses with gardens to them, for then the gardener, or some odd man or boy about the place, can clean out the trap once a week and bury the grease; but a better use should be found for it. In some cases that I know of, it is boiled down, clarified, and used for greasing cart wheels, etc. [I have only recently ex-

amined the drains of several houses that have been treated in this way for several years, and one for ten years, and I found the drain in each case beautifully clean and free from grease. And in no case was there a flushing-tank for flushing out the drain.]

7. But though there is no difficulty in getting rid of the grease and filth from grease-traps in the country, there is great difficulty in getting rid of it in towns and cities where dustmen refuse to carry it away. And for householders to employ labour periodically—about once a month

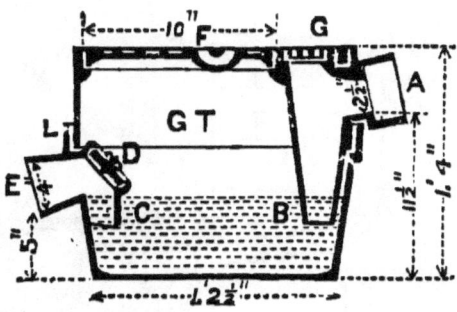

Fig. 149.—Section of "Grease-Intercepting Trap" in Cast Iron, in two pieces, for Inlet, A, to be turned round to suit Drain.

—to clean out the grease-trap, and then to have to pay for the removal of the grease and filth, means a yearly expense of a few pounds that can ill be afforded in these hard times and heavy expenses. And this is not all, for in the case of most terrace houses the grease would have to be carried right through the house, and where such matters are not deodorized this would become a nuisance.

8. It has often been a wonder to me that the authorities should allow grease to enter a sewer, but as there is no objection to this, the best way of getting rid of grease in towns and cities is to intercept it by the use of some such

trap as shown in fig. 150, and to flush it through the drain to the sewer, in congealed pieces, once or *twice* a day, according to circumstances.

The stoneware flushing-rim "Flush-out" grease trap, fig. 150, has been designed and patented by me. It is

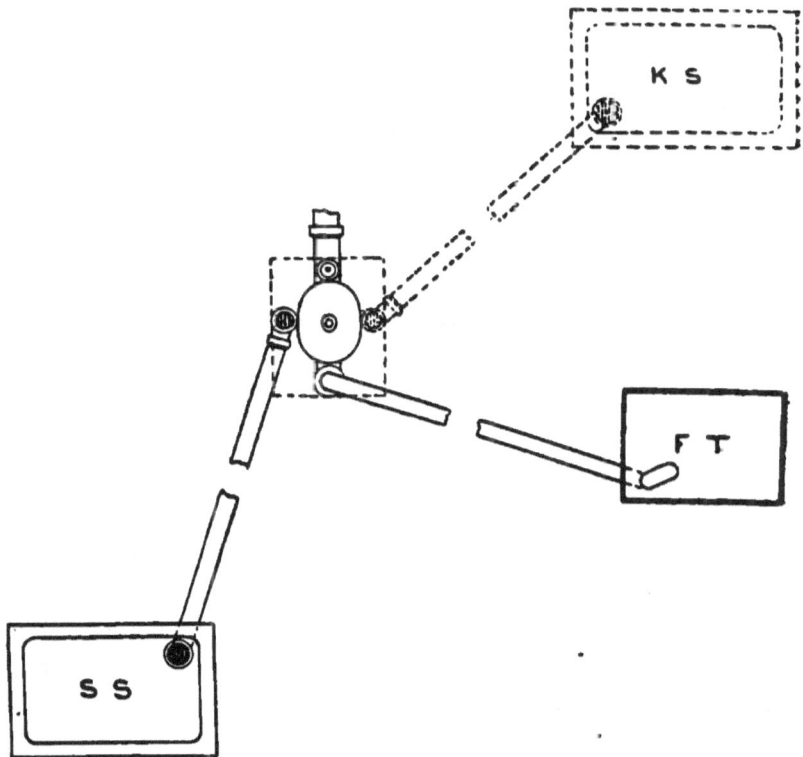

Fig. 150.—"Flush-out" Grease-Trap.

provided with single or double inlet arms on one or both sides of the trap, for receiving the waste-pipe or waste-pipes, from one or more sinks, as may be required.

9. Where the general sink in the scullery is also used for washing dinner-plates and greasy things in, and it is

made to hold a *large body of water*, a grease-trap is generally found to be quite unnecessary. Several houses have been treated in this way by my firm during the last six or seven years with great success. In some small houses, however, where the usual grease-trap was dispensed with, and the sinks were small and shallow, and where a good table was generally kept, the sewer disconnecting-trap became clogged at times with grease, and all sorts of evil things followed; but a twenty-gallon flushing-tank for washing the grease through the drain once or twice a day remedied the evil.

CHAPTER XXXV.

BATHS AND LAVATORIES.

1.

IN discussing the many things which the sanitary plumber requires to know before he can properly sanitate a house, it is most refreshing to be able to turn to a branch of the subject which in itself is inviting,—to the subject of baths and lavatories; for I suppose no one would care to dwell for ever upon certain branches of a subject, which, though so closely connected with the purifying elements,—air, light, and water,—is not the sweetest in the world.

2. It is passing strange that a bath or lavatory, wherein we may " wash and be clean," should be so constructed that any of its parts should ever become foul. And yet scores of baths and wash-hand-basins, if they were examined in their overflow arrangements, would be found to be most repulsive. A secret overflow, where much soap is used, soon becomes corroded with decaying soapsuds; for

with every desire to keep the bath and lavatory clean and wholesome, the housemaid could only wash out such pipes by allowing the bath and basin to overflow, *i.e.*, the bath or lavatory would have to be filled up to within about two inches of the brim before the water would flow over from the secret stand-pipe into the combined overflow-pipe; and as it would still be necessary to leave the supply-cocks running for a time to cleanse such pipes, it would appear to the servant a waste of water, together with some risk of washing down a ceiling or doing some other kind of damage.

Nor would the servant have any clear idea of the necessity of such a duty, for the secret-pipes, however filthy they may have become, would be out of sight, and therefore out of mind, if not quite out of the sense of smell. The fact is, the water would not be allowed to flow through the secret overflow except by accident, and often when this occurred it would be at a time when the pipe had become so corroded with soap that it would not allow the water to flow away fast enough, and an overflow from the bath would then bring the plumber upon the scene, to disclose this soap-corroded secret-pipe in about as filthy a state as it could well be.

The bad air which would be thrown off from such pipes would pass freely enough into the room in which the bath or lavatory was fixed. A look into the interior of a secret overflow arrangement of a lavatory, and even of a bath where much scented soap had been used, would suffice to dispense with the sense of smell.

3. No matter what kind of bath may be fixed, whether copper, tinned iron, enamelled cast iron, zinc, or earthenware, both its waste-pipe and its overflow-pipe should be so arranged that no part belonging to them or to the bath itself should be able to get foul.

4. Whilst it is important that the overflow-pipe to a

bath or lavatory should be equal in carrying capacity to the supply of water from both the hot and cold supply-cocks, in case they were left running by accident, the mouth of the pipe should be kept at such a height that in the ordinary use of the bath or lavatory no water or scum should flow into it, to foul it. The overflow-pipe can be so fixed to a bath that it may readily be disconnected and scalded out and cleansed when necessary. And in the case of a lavatory, the overflow can be so formed in the side of the basin, as shown in fig. 151, that it may readily be

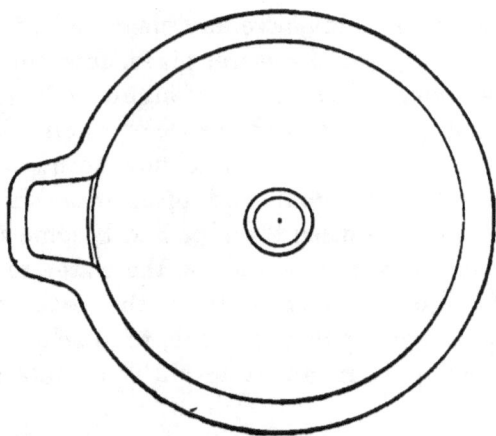

Fig. 151.—LAVATORY WITH ACCESSIBLE OVERFLOW.

cleansed by the housemaid, either by pouring water into it or by the use of a little mop.

5. In order that the **bath water might be utilized for washing out the drain**, a 5 ft. 6 in. bath should be made to empty itself in two minutes, and a 2 in. waste-pipe will do this well enough, provided that the trap, waste-valve, and grated outlet of the bath are all made equal in area to the fully charging bore of a 2 in. pipe, as shown at R F J, fig. 153.

6. Instead of connecting the trap to the safe in a way for

the latter to drain into it, in case of an overflow from the bath, or for the bath-waste to be turned down into its dip-pipe, as shown at M, fig. 152, the inlet of the trap should be connected directly with the bath-waste or waste-valve, as shown at R, fig. 153, or by a continuous pipe-connection, so that, in the discharge of the bath, no water, clean or otherwise, should be able to well up into the safe, or to escape outside the bath-pipe, waste-valve, trap, or waste-pipe to foul any part which could not readily be cleansed again by a flush from the bath; *i.e.*, the bath-pipe, waste-valve, trap, and waste-pipe should all be self-cleansing.

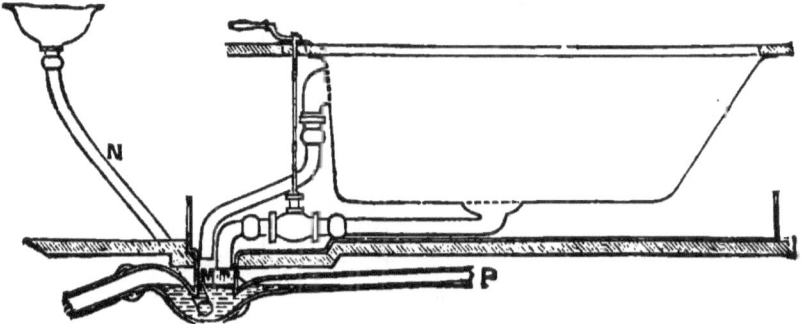

Fig. 152.—SHOWING ONE TRAP RECEIVING WASTE-PIPES FROM MORE THAN ONE FIXTURE. BAD ARRANGEMENT.

7. Where a bath is inclosed, it should have a **lead safe** fixed under it, the full size of the inclosure, inside; and the stand-up on each side should not be less than 4 in. The floor under the safe should be made to fall all ways towards the mouth of the overflow-pipe.

8. The **overflow-pipe** from the safe, going out preferably from one end of it, should never be connected with the bath-trap or bath-waste, but should be carried out through an external wall to discharge into the open air, as shown at Y, fig. 153. Where such a pipe would empty into a street, the overflow-pipe from the bath should not discharge into

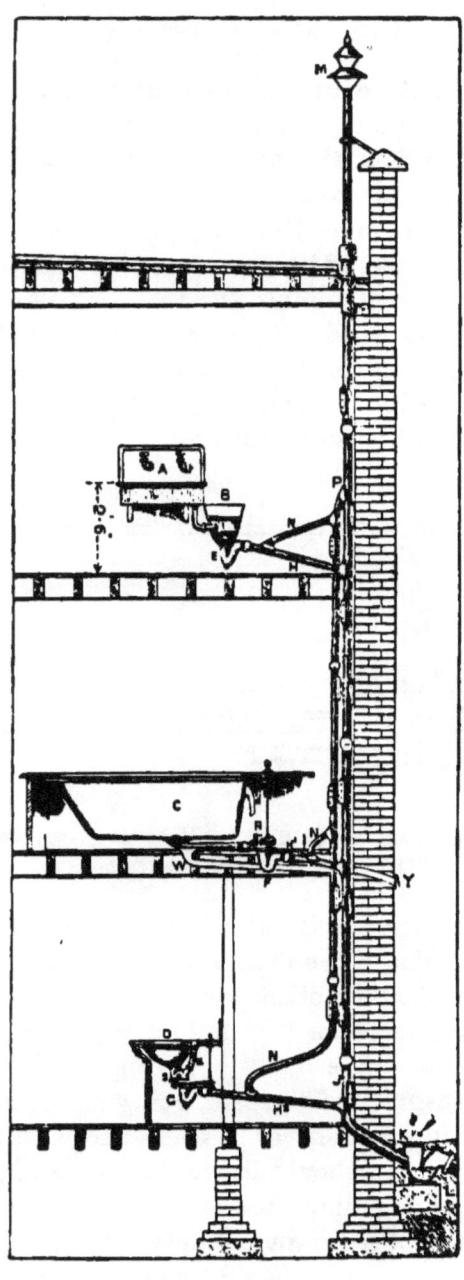

Fig. 153.—Showing Bath, Lavatory, and Draw-Off Sink discharging into one Waste-Pipe, aerially disconnected from the Drain, K, with Anti-Syphoning Pipe, N, and Ventilation-Pipe, P, incomplete. The slop-sink, B, is only intended for the reception of the contents from slop-pails, from floor-washings, and toilet-basins.

BATHS AND LAVATORIES. 243

the safe, but should be connected to the outlet side of the waste-valve, in a way not to become fouled.

9. Notwithstanding all that has been said about the evils of **small plug-holes** in wash-hand-basins, basin manufacturers still go on making lavatories which will only receive ½ in. or ¾ in. brass plugs-and-washers, as shown in fig. 154; though some of the more enlightened manufacturers make the holes and countersinkings large enough to take an *inch* clear-way plug-and-washer; but for a basin to receive a 1¼ in. plug-and-washer, as shown in fig. 156, it would

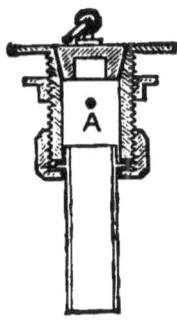

Fig. 154.

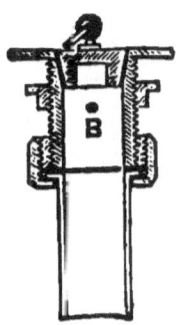

Fig. 155.

require to be specially made, or to be obtained from a special house.

10. With such a **small plug-and-washer** as shown in fig. 154, it is impossible to empty a basin fast enough to satisfy the person using it, or in a way to be of any value for cleansing either the trap or waste-pipe. Where such plug-basins are fixed, the traps under them should only be 1 in., and this size trap is only large enough for basins with 1 in. plugs, as fig. 155; but for 1¼ in. plugs, as fig. 156, or 1¼ in. and 1½ in. waste-valves, as shown at s, fig. 153, the traps should be 1¼ in. with 1¼ in. or 1½ in. waste-pipes from them.

11. The evil attending the use of a brass plug-and-washer

244   PLUMBING.

is the handling of the **chain**, and although many people have no objection to a chain, for many years past in my works we have fixed a special waste-valve, which is actuated by a pull-up knob arrangement fixed to the lavatory top, as shown in fig. 153.

12. The great advantage of a **tip-up basin** is that you can turn the contents of the basin out into a receiver instantaneously; but, as a general rule, the under side of a tip-up basin and the interior of the receiver soon become foul and filthy; I mean when they are fixed in private houses. In places where there is a lavatory attendant, it would be his special duty to look after them; and if lift-out (as well as lift-up) basins, as improved by the Messrs. Jennings, were fixed, the attendant would have no difficulty in keeping them clean.

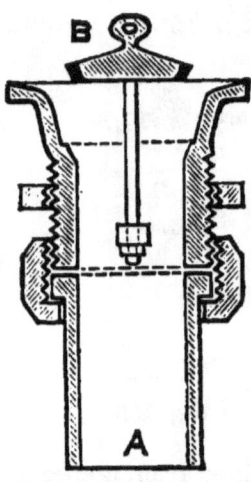

Fig. 156.—1¼ IN. CLEAR-WAY PLUG-AND-WASHER.

13. In my works I prefer a **trap under each basin**, as shown in fig. 157, especially when such a range of basins would be fixed near a bedroom or living-room.

14. How often one comes across, not **two or three basins emptying into one trap**, but ten, fifteen, and even more than twenty, and that too adjoining a dormitory, if not actually in direct communication with it. In such an arrangement the waste-pipes from the basins are generally branched into the "horizontal" waste-pipe at right angles, as shown at B and C, fig. 158. In such cases a discharge from the basin, B, would flow back towards E^1, as well as towards the natural outlet, E. At the lectures I gave an ocular demonstration of this, using a small wash-hand-basin and a *glass* waste-pipe. A little soapy water was put

BATHS AND LAVATORIES. 245

into the basin—similar to the basin, B, in the diagram (fig. 158),—and on pulling up the plug the water flowed both ways in the "horizontal" pipe; and though the water

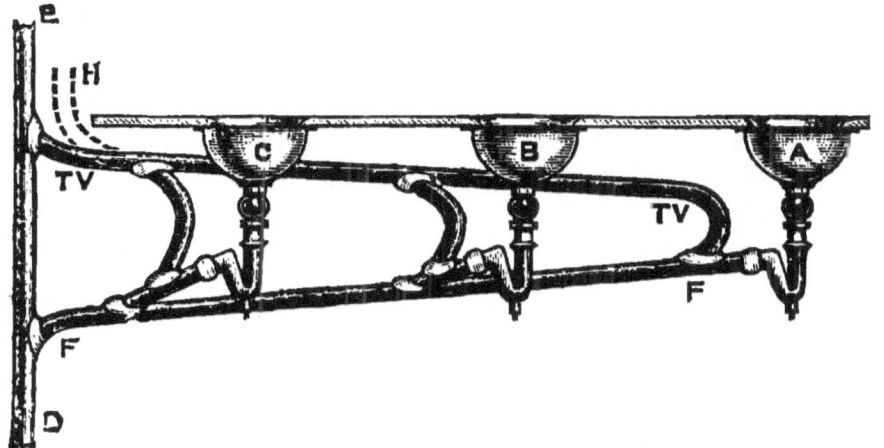

Fig. 157.—SHOWING A RANGE OF BASINS PROPERLY TRAPPED.

naturally gravitated out of the pipe again, the suds remained behind, where in practice they would decompose and throw off bad air.

There is another evil attending such an arrangement.

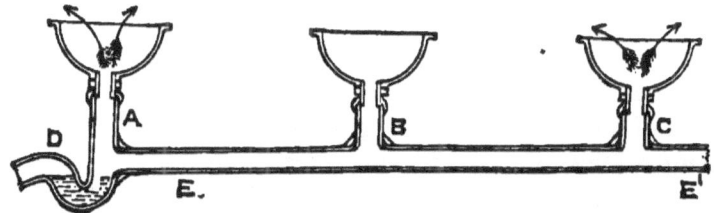

Fig. 158.

A discharge from the basin, C, would drive the foul air out through the basin, A, as shown by the arrows, and this would be aggravated in a longer range. The foul air thus sent out of the basin, or its overflow, would often be

246　PLUMBING.

breathed by the person bending over it to wash his face or his hands.

For *general* and well-ventilated lavatories, remote from bedrooms and living-rooms, I should have no very great objection to the arrangement shown in fig. 158; but I should want a greater fall in the " horizontal " waste-pipe, which should only be of a size which could readily be flushed out, and I should require the branches from the basins to be connected by bent pipes or Y-junctions, to prevent backwash. And, further, I should not care to extend the horizontal waste-pipe beyond the third basin. I should also

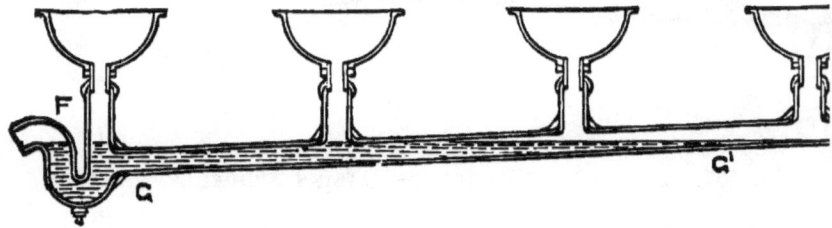

Fig. 159.—Diagrammatic Section of a Range of Basins, showing Bad Arrangement.

require the basins to be supplied with hot water, so that the pipe should be scalded out occasionally.

15. A still greater error is often made in the arrangement of lavatory wastes, where a range of basins is discharged into *one* trap. The main branch is taken into the heel of the trap in such a way that about two-thirds of its length always stands full of water, as shown in the diagrammatic section, fig. 159. When this is the case, how is it possible to change the water standing in the waste-pipe, G G¹, and trap, F, with a flush of water sent through either of the basins? The body of water standing in the trap and piping might become very offensive from the use of scented soap and the washings-down of the lavatory top, and it would prevent the waste-pipe from being cleansed; for

no flush of water could be sent through the pipe with any cleansing force in such an arrangement.

16. All **waste-pipes** from baths and lavatories should be made to discharge with an **open end** into self-cleansing disconnecting-traps fixed outside the external walls of the house; 3 in. stoneware traps are quite large enough in most cases. Or where there is a stack of lavatories, or of bath and lavatories, the pipe can discharge into a drain-interceptor, similar to that shown at K, fig. 153. The ventilation-pipe, P, should be continued up full bore, or if a larger size, to some high point, well above all windows.

The **anti-syphoning pipe** should be of equal bore, or it should not be smaller than the bore of the traps, as shown at N N N, fig. 153, which is 2 in., the main waste-pipe being also 2 in.

17. The **waste-pipe** from the **draw-off and slop-sink** combined is shown in the illustration (fig. 153) to be in communication with the bath and lavatory waste-pipe, but this slop-sink is only meant to receive the general slops from bedroom pails, which would be much diluted by the water from the toilet basins, and into which a great deal of slop water—from the draw-off sink—would be constantly running, to keep the pipe clean. But I would not allow a general slop-closet to be connected to a bath-waste, especially a slop-closet fixed in hospitals, into which excreta and all sorts of filth are emptied. (Chap. XXXIII., Art. 7.)

18. It sometimes happens that though a **bath** is fixed in a **dressing-room**, in direct communication with a bedroom, it is but rarely used, the owner of the bedroom having little or no liking for water. In such cases the waste-pipe should have no connection with any other waste-pipe, not even a waste-pipe from a lavatory, and the pipe in such cases, instead of discharging under the grating of a disconnecting-trap, should empty into an open channel-pipe leading into a trap; and if it is of any great length,

it should have aerial disconnection again before entering the bath-room, so that, in case of evaporation of the water-seal of the bath-trap, the risk of bad air entering the house through the lost seal of the bath-trap would be reduced to a minimum.

19. **Combination baths,** combining what many consider to be nothing more than fads, such as spray, sitz, douche, and shower baths, can be fitted up to suit the sweet wills and long purses of the rich; but it is not necessary here to go into the great variety now in use. Wherever any such bath is fixed, and whatever form it may take, great care should be bestowed upon its trapping and its ventilation, so that whilst no part of a bath may become an inlet for bad air to enter a house, so no part of a bath or its traps, or its waste-pipe or overflow-pipe, shall become a collecting place for soapsuds to decompose in.

CHAPTER XXXVI.

URINALS.

1.

URINE is difficult to treat, as it cannot be caught like grease and made to float, for it settles down upon everything it touches or comes into contact with. It can only be got rid of by copious flushes of water, and that too before it has time to settle down upon the urinal, trap, waste-pipe, or drainage. Therefore, when this corrosive matter is passed into a vessel and its belongings, plenty of water should go with it to carry it right away.

It would be very valuable if the contents of chamber utensils and urinal basins could be passed directly into the running water of the sewer without having to pass through any waste-piping or drainage. As this cannot very well be done, an arrangement should be adopted, where water is plentiful, for keeping a small body of water in the urinal basin or basins, with a constant supply of water laid on, to

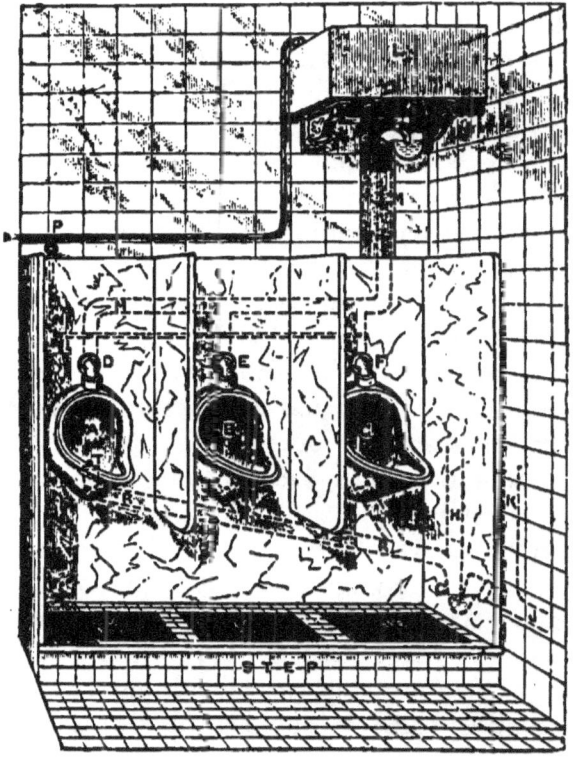

Fig. 160.—Showing a Range of Urinal Basins.

largely dilute the urine before it passes into the wastepipe.

2. An automatic flushing-cistern (L, fig. 160), discharging a gallon of water into each urinal basin once every quarter of an hour, or oftener where the urinals are much used, is

most valuable; but, unfortunately, many water companies will not allow such a convenient and wholesome method of flushing, and insist upon water-waste preventers, which only give a gallon of water to each basin when actuated by some cranking or labour movement—something which requires attention, and which in this automatic age is not always given.

3. It has become the bad custom of treating pedestal closets as if they were urinal basins, the consequence is, that though the interior of such closets may be kept clean enough, their exteriors, and the floor round about them, often become foul and filthy; for a man—especially if advanced in years—would require to be an expert to pass the whole of his water into so remote a vessel without mishaps. It is not every shot that hits the target.

4. Where there are pedestal closets in a private house, instead of treating them as urinal basins for one of the purposes of nature, the persons using them should sit right down upon the seat, just opening the fly-front, and this could be so done that not a drop of urine should fall down outside the closet-basin.

5. As explained elsewhere, a lip-urinal does not afford a sufficient area for receiving the urine. I prefer basins with wider fronts. And where very old people are not likely to use a urinal—in public urinals, in private hotels, clubhouses, etc.—I prefer a step, as shown in fig. 160, to compel the persons using them to stand up nearer to the basins. The illustration, fig. 160, speaks for itself. In more public urinals it would be necessary to fix a water channel on the floor next the back of the urinals, and to dispense with the step. In such cases the channel should be kept well flushed out by an automatic arrangement in connection with the general supply to the urinal basins.

CHAPTER XXXVII.

WATER AND ITS STORAGE.

1.

PLUMBERS are so partial to water, that however deficient they may be in other branches of plumbing knowledge, they ought not to be deficient in the knowledge of water and its storage. As I have said in "Dulce Domum," I believe "many illnesses which are now put down solely to bad drainage would, if it were possible to ascertain the actual facts, be attributable to the bad state of the water." Although analysts, like doctors, disagree, the plumber should not trust to his own opinion of a water; but, in all doubtful waters, he should throw the responsibility of determining the wholesomeness—the fitness or unfitness—of a water upon a public or duly qualified analyst, to whom samples should be sent (in Winchester quarts) for analyzing.

2. As a supply of water cannot at all times be relied upon, even where there is a "constant supply" from the water company's main, a sufficient storage should be provided to meet the requirements of the household during the longest time the water would be likely to be turned off. This inconstancy would generally depend upon circumstances—upon the source of the supply, the state of the mains, and the resources of the authorities, and also upon the locality and the altitude of the storage cisterns. In some cases it might not be more than an hour or two, in others it may continue over many hours, especially where the mains are under repairs or alterations. As far as my

experience goes, it would hardly be safe to provide for less than a day's (twenty-four hours) consumption.

The magnitude of the water supply in London is appalling: "London is said to require a daily supply of more than 150 [1] million gallons of water. Of this about 15 million gallons come from deep wells in the chalk, the rest from other sources, principally from the Rivers, Thames and Lea."

3. It seems a pity that lead-battened cisterns should have gone out of use, for they showed a nice piece of workman-

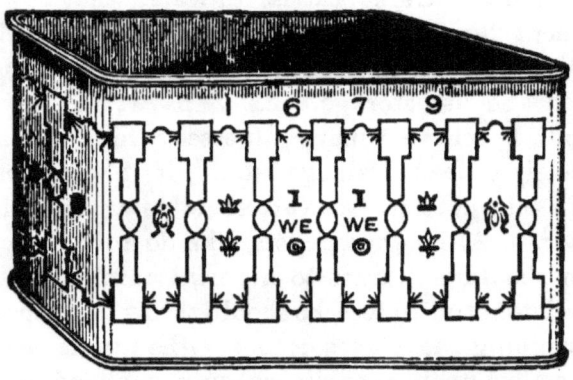

Fig. 161.—VIEW OF AN OLD LEAD-BATTENED CISTERN.

ship, and they generally lasted longer than any other handmade thing in or about a house. The one illustrated in fig. 161 has been in constant use for more than two centuries in the old and new buildings of the oldest bankinghouse in London; and it is still doing duty, and will perhaps last another century or two.

4. Though lead-lined cisterns are very suitable for storing water for supplying water-closets, slop-sinks, and urinals, water for dietetic purposes, especially if it is of a character to act on lead (Chap. II., pp. 8, 9), should be stored in **slate cisterns**, or in white enamelled **earthenware cisterns**; or, where a storage of 200 or 300 gallons is

[1] The Official Return for June, 1891, gives 190 millions.

required, in cisterns made of fire-clay and salt-glazed. But most people are content to store the water in **galvanized wrought-iron cisterns**, chiefly, I believe, because they are so readily made to suit almost any position, and also because they are not so liable to damage as slate cisterns. But though the action of water on galvanized iron is not so great as on lead, such cisterns are by no means free from action, especially when charged with water which would act on lead. In such cases where large tanks are necessary, and the water would act on lead and therefore on galvanized iron, the tanks should be made of cast-iron plates or wrought-iron, and be bolted together and strongly limewhited inside.

Messrs. T. and W. Farmiloe's titancrete cistern or tank is made of almost any capacity, varying from 10,000 gallons to 20 gallons. Above a certain size it is better built on the spot. It is composed of an iron and wire frame, entirely embedded in a special concrete, which, it is alleged, does not affect water. I have had no experience of these tanks.

5. I have seen **lead-lined cisterns** which have been in use for more than half-a-century, if not absolutely free from any action of water on them, so good and perfect that their surfaces, except perhaps in a few places in the soldered angles, have shown no signs of any action. But, on the other hand, I have seen lead-lined cisterns which have only been in use a year or two so acted upon, that in places they have lost half their original substance. (Chap. II., pp. 8, 9.)

6. In new lead-lined cisterns, with some waters, a film is formed over the face of the lead, which is most valuable, as it prevents, to a very great extent, any further action of the water upon it. And in cleaning out such cisterns, great care should be taken not to scratch off any part of this film.

7. In my "Lectures" I gave some extracts, by permission

of Dr. Sedgwick Saunders, from his translation of M. Belgrand's essay on "The Action of Water upon Lead Pipes," and which I reproduce here.

"Lead has been employed in the manufacture of conduit pipes ever since the distribution of water in towns was first established by the Romans, the first aqueduct, the Appian, according to Varro,[1] being constructed in the year of Rome 442.

"From that period leaden pipes have been in constant use; all the water services in the interior of ancient towns being made of that metal.

"In Paris the leaden *branch-pipes* connecting dwelling-houses with the main supply number about 39,500, and their average length may be put at 40 mètres,[2] and their total length at 1,580,000 mètres.

"In the case of houses that are occupied, the longest period for the water to remain in the leaden pipes can be estimated thus:—

Houses having unlimited supply . . . } 9 hours during the night.
 from 5 to 10 min. during day.
Gauged supply . . from 3 to 6 hours at the most.

"As will be seen further on, the time the water is in contact with the interior surface of the pipe is too short for the lead to be attacked.

"I have already stated that in the net-work of main pipes there are about three kilomètres[3] of lead piping. These are from time to time removed, and on examination their interior surfaces are invariably found to be perfectly smooth and without any trace of corrosion.

"I now exhibit two pieces to the Academy: one comes

---

[1] Varro, "Marcus Terentius," a learned writer at Rome, B.C. 116.—W. S. S.

[2] A mètre is 39·263 inches English.—W. S. S.

[3] A kilomètre is 1,000 mètres.—W. S. S.

from the service-pipe of the Faubourg Saint-Antoine, laid down in 1670, at the time when the pump of the Bridge of Notre Dame was erected; it is therefore more than 200 years old, and in the interior the impression of grains of sand is still to be seen. The other was taken up from a side street of Saint-Germain Market; it is somewhat less old, but equally unblemished.

"It may be added that the leaden pipes become firmly and rapidly coated with a thin crust [1] which prevents the water coming in contact with the lead.

"The harmlessness of leaden pipes appears to me proved by these facts, which explain why they are in use in all the towns of France, and in most European cities, without ever having given cause for complaint.

"M. Le Blanc has undertaken other experiments, by leaving the lead in water for a much longer period (than nine or ten hours). I quote his own words:—

"'ON THE ACTION OF WATERS UPON LEAD.

"'Chemists have long known with what facility lead becomes oxidized when immersed in distilled water in contact with air. Very small white shiny crystals of the hydrated oxide of lead are very rapidly formed, their quantity augmenting until a copious sediment at the bottom of the vessel has formed; the same obtains with pure rain water.

"'On the contrary, water containing a given quantity of salts, principally from selenitic wells, does not attack the lead under the same conditions at all.

"'Such are the results of experiments made by Professors of Chemistry during the last forty years in public lectures, and M. Dumas never omitted to place them before his class at the Sorbonne.

"'Chemists have often remarked upon the harmlessness

---

[1] Carbonate of lime.—W. S. S.

of lead with regard to potable waters, circulating in pipes of this metal, because of the *saline* matters which preserve the metal from oxidation.

"'No doubt it would be difficult to give an explanation of these facts, but they seem of the same kind as those which have been established with regard to iron, which can be preserved without oxidation in distilled water, even when aërated, if only a few drops of an alkali be added to it, whilst it is oxidised rapidly in pure aërated water. But it is curious to observe that by augmenting to a certain extent the proportion of alkali, oxidation can be facilitated.

"'Which salts are the most efficacious, when present in minute quantities, in preventing oxidation of lead in contact with water? Salts of lime alone are unquestionably so, even in the smallest proportions; in the absence of lime other salts are capable of protecting lead, in quantities of 0·1 gramme per litre. Nevertheless, after from twenty-four to thirty hours the water becomes faintly coloured by sulphuretted hydrogen; but this oxidation soon ceases. The following experiments were made to ascertain the particular influence of different salts.

"'Solutions were made with sulphate of soda, chloride of sodium, chloride of potassium, sulphate of magnesia, the strength of each solution being 0·1 gramme per litre. The lead was immersed in these for twenty-four hours, when the water became coloured by sulphuretted hydrogen, but the solvent action did not continue, and it may be said that the solutions in question are without notable action upon lead, for, at the end of ten days, the re-agent did not produce any real precipitate.'

"Upon the whole there is absolutely no danger of poisoning from the use of water flowing through leaden pipes.

"Furthermore, in the "Journal des Savants" (October, 1871, p. 488), one reads:—

"'It may not be inopportune to draw attention to a fact not sufficiently known to the public—namely, that rain waters alter leaden and zinc vessels more than waters containing salts in solution, well waters for example. The result of this is that *these latter waters may remain in a leaden vessel without attacking it, and without becoming poisonous, while rain waters, free from saline matters, dissolve oxide of lead and thus become poisonous*. This observation, quoted from Guyton de Morveau, is perfectly true. I have verified it at the time of my investigation on the waters of the Bièvre.'"

8. In this advanced age of sanitary knowledge (in the year 1891) it ought not to be necessary to lay any great stress upon the **positions of cisterns**, or upon the wastepipes for cleaning them out. But even to-day cisterns are often so fixed that only an expert can get into them; and certainly no maid-servant or member of the family could get at them to clean them out without risk of drowning, or some other dreadful catastrophe, as falling down a staircase, or through a skylight. But though such cisterns may be inaccessible for ready cleansing, they are often accessible enough to bad air; for although they are not now fixed inside water-closet apartments, or only rarely so, they are often fixed at the top of staircases into which doors from several closets open. And they are still fixed in scullerys, and places where the vitiated atmosphere of the house can be absorbed by the water in them.

9. As, at all times to insure a ready supply of water, it is essential to have a storage (Art. 2), it should be stored in a proper **cistern-room**, where the cisterns could be readily got at, and where no vitiated air could reach them, and the cisterns should be covered over to keep out dust, etc. (M, fig. 143).

In most cases where slate or iron cisterns are fixed in cistern-rooms over important parts of the house, it will be found advisable to fix **lead safes** under them, not only as a wise precaution against breakage and leakage, but also to protect the floor, when of wood, from condensation droppings. The overflow-pipe from the safe must discharge into the open air, standing out 2 or 3 ins. clear of the wall, as shown at s o, fig. 143. And if this overflow-pipe is also made to answer the purpose of taking away the overflow from the cistern, as shown at c o, the size of the pipe should be about twice the size of the ball-valve.

10. Although there is no risk of any **closet air** passing back through a **service-pipe** to a cistern 20 or 30 ft. away, where a self-closing supply-valve is attached to the closet, and the branch supply-pipe is trapped (*i.e.*, so bent that a seal of water should remain in the pipe in case the main service-pipe and cistern should ever get empty), for the sake of sentiment it is better to entirely separate the closet supply from the cisterns and services which supply the general draw-off, etc., for potable purposes, etc.—*i.e.*, no closet, slop-sink, or urinal should be supplied direct from a service-pipe or cistern which supplied a draw-off cock for any other purpose. Where flushing-cisterns are employed for flushing closets, slop-sinks, and urinals, this is simple enough, as shown at v w, fig. 143, and L, fig. 160. (Chap. XXXII., Art. 3.)

11. As most waters form a sediment, and as all waters take up impurities, proper provision must always be made for **cleaning out cisterns**; but this cannot be done through the ordinary overflow-pipe. It is necessary, therefore, to fix a waste-pipe from the bottom of the cistern, and to continue it to some place of discharge where it would do no damage, and where no bad air could enter it. All plumbers do not remember this, nor are they always reminded of their errors by architects; and even the sanitarian sometimes overlooks such a treatment of cistern-waste as could not be considered but unsanitary. I have

only recently come across two or three instances of bad treatment. In one case the bath-waste delivered into a small cistern-head, into which also emptied the cistern-waste, and the bad air driven out by the discharges from the bath passed readily enough up the cistern-waste to contaminate the water in the cistern. In another case the waste-pipe from a tier of sinks delivered into a channel, and close beside it stood the open end of the cistern-waste, and the foul air which was driven out by every discharge of any one of the sinks upon the stacks passed readily enough up the cistern-waste. The mouth of the overflow-pipe or standing-waste should be so placed and so arranged that any cold air which might find its way through it should not impinge upon the ball-valve, service-pipe, or water, to freeze them. And where several cisterns are connected together, the overflow should be taken from the cistern in which the ball-valve is fixed.

12. In fig. 162 an illustration is given of the way waste-pipes from cisterns were often treated some ten or fifteen years ago; and even now this bad practice is followed where men are non-observant, or are slow in learning the right principles of sanitation.

13. All **waste-pipes**, as well as overflow-pipes from cisterns, whether storing water for closet purposes or dietetic purposes, should discharge into the *open air*, well away from all places where foul or contaminated air could enter them. Where such pipes can be made to discharge into a roof-gutter or on to a flat, there would be nothing to trouble about—except frost; but to take them into a rain-pipe head, into which also emptied either a sink-waste, lavatory-waste, or even a bath-waste, would be to run great risk of getting foul air into the cistern-room, as shown by the arrows in fig. 162. But though the evil would be reduced by taking the cistern-waste into a pipe-channel or stone-channel in communication with a self-cleansing dis-

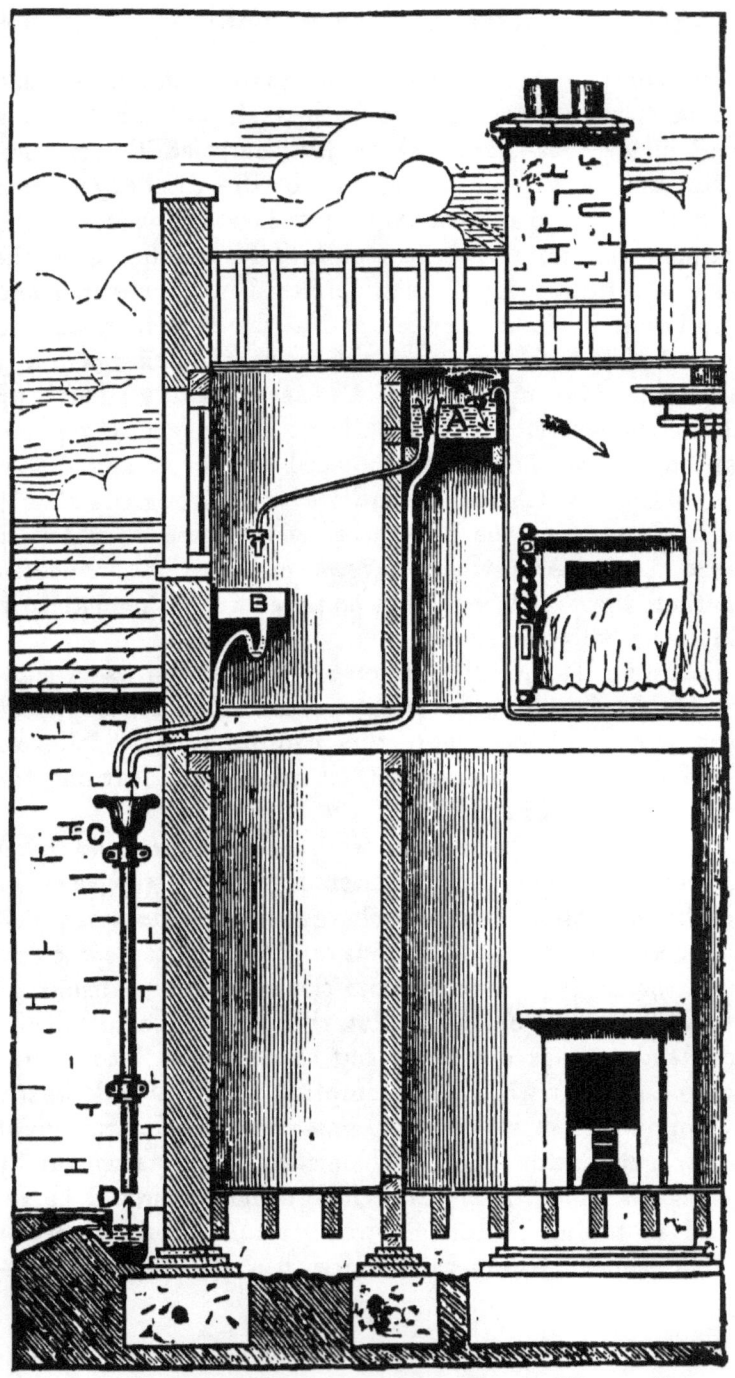

Fig. 162.—SECTION OF A CISTERN AND ITS WASTE-PIPE. FAULTY ARRANGEMENT.

connecting-trap, the arrangement would not be perfect, especially if dirty water waste-pipes also discharged into the same channel. Where the stone-channel or channel-pipe lead into a large gully-trap, the evil would be aggravated, for the discharges into it would stir up any foul decomposing matter in the gully, and the bad air thrown off from such agitation would pass freely enough into the cistern-waste.

14. With a brass **plug-and-washer** fixed to the bottom of the cistern, and soldered to the under waste-pipe, the air communication is cut off, except during the time the cistern is being cleaned out; but a chain affords no control over the plug in case it is desired to replace it during the time the cistern is being emptied; but with a standard-plug, as in the case of a trumpet-waste, the plug could be replaced instantly, and at pleasure. But even with a solid plug the discharging end of the cistern-waste should be carried to a place where no bad air would enter it.

15. Where the water does not require to be filtered, it is a good plan to lay on a service to some convenient place of draw-off *direct from the communication-pipe from the water company's main.*

16. I have no space here to go into the question of filters, and having dealt with it somewhat at length in another work, I simply remind the reader that filters may, and often do, become contaminators from want of proper attention.

CHAPTER XXXVIII.

HOUSE-DRAINS.

1.

THE plumber, to be fully equipped with the knowledge of sanitary plumbing, and to be up to date, must ever continue a learner, for though he has not now, as in the days that are gone, or are vanishing, to embellish his knowledge of the plumber's craft with that of the painter, glazier, paper-hanger, gas and hot-water fitter, he is required to know a great deal more than the old three-branched hand; and though sewage disposal can hardly be considered to come within the domain of his ken, his drainage knowledge should extend up to the sewer or cesspool.

In fact, in the case of iron drains, he would generally be called upon to lay them down, and even where they are of stoneware it would still be to his interest, where the drains are laid inside a house, as well as for the general safety of those who inhabit the house, not only to see that the drains were properly disconnected and ventilated, but that they were also sound, or his own good and sound work might get the discredit of some defect or defects in the drains.

2. It is curious—or, as Artemus Ward would put it, "cussed contrariness"—that telegraph wires, which would be better underground, better out of sight as well as out of reach, should be fixed overhead, where they are so much in sight that they often obstruct the vision, and that drains which, when inside a house, would be better fixed above the ground, where they could be seen and examined, should be laid underground, where they can only be inspected after

a good deal of opening out, and where only rats are acquainted with their ramifications.

3. In **planning the drainage of a house** it will often be found that an alteration in the position of some water-closet—sometimes by simply moving it from one side of an apartment to another—will suffice to shorten considerably the length of a drain inside a house; or if the drain may not be reduced in its length by any such alteration, the alteration may enable the drain to be fixed above the floor, where it can readily be seen and examined, even if in some cases it does not wholly dispense with the necessity of bringing a drain inside the house.

In reconstructing the drainage of old houses I have often found it possible to do away with every foot of drain under the ground by carrying some soil-pipe, waste-pipe, or rain-water-pipe on the face of the basement walls, or by laying the pipes on piers in sub-basements. Only the other day, on coming across a defective drain which ran under the floor of the basement from one end of the house to the other, I found that by carrying a lead soil-pipe, waste-pipe, and rain-water-pipe across a room on the face of the wall to the outside, the whole of the underground drain could be dispensed with.

4. With good arrangement of the sanitary appliances it ought never to be necessary to fix a soil-drain inside the external walls of a **detached or semi-detached house.** Where a soil-pipe from some special reason is fixed inside a house, it should always be continued through the external wall, for connection with the drain outside, some few feet away from the foundations. And where the pipe is of lead, to prevent contact with lime and mortar where it passes through the wall, it should be encased with stoneware pipe, and the space between the two pipes should be filled up with dry sand. Where the soil-pipe is of cast iron a stone lintel should be fixed over it, where it passes through the wall, or

a relieving-arch should be turned over it, clear of the pipe, to prevent damage to the soil-pipe or drain, in case of a settlement.

5. In **terrace houses** it is generally absolutely necessary to bring the soil-drain into the house, sometimes to carry it from the front vaults—from the sewer—to the back of the house, where the closets and sanitary fixtures are generally situated. But even in such cases it is not always necessary to bury a drain; for where there is a sub-basement it could be carried upon brick piers, or it could be carried under the floor in a brick-built tunnel, for ready access at any time.

6. It seems a great oversight on the part of architects not to build or form a **subway** to every terrace house, in which could be fixed, not only the drains—waste-drain, soil-drain, and rain-water-drain—but the gas-main or electric-lighting main, telephone wire, communication-pipe from the water company's main, etc., etc.; but our authorities—our City Commissioners or County Councils, our Vestry Boards—are so little alive to the value of subways, to underground thoroughfares, that rather than have an underground London, where the many alterations and repairs to water-mains, gas-mains, electric-lighting mains, telephone wires, etc., etc., could be carried on without interference with traffic in the streets, they are content to allow the streets and pavements to be ever in the hands of workmen.

7. The **essential features of a good drain** are as follows, viz., that (*a*) it shall be sound, both air-tight and water-tight, under greater pressure than it is ever likely to receive in practice; that (*b*) it shall be permanently sound, *i.e.*, that it shall not only be sound on completion, but that it shall be so constructed that it shall continue so for a lengthy period; that (*c*) it shall be aerially disconnected from the sewer (or cesspool), and ventilated; that (*d*) it shall be self-cleansing, *i.e.*, it shall be laid at a proper

gradient, and shall have no dips or places in it for harbouring filth; that (e) it shall be laid in straight lines, with inspection-chambers (where cost is no great object) at every change of direction, so that a light may be flashed through it from chamber to chamber, for easy and ready examination.

8. In my works I do not like to trust to **stoneware pipes** for soil-drains inside a house. Thousands of pipes have been rejected by my people during the last ten years because of one or more of the following faults in them, viz.: fire-flaws or fractures; pinholes or blisters; or from want of hardness, or because they had been insufficiently glazed; or because of their crookedness—want of straightness and truth; or, because of the lopsidedness of their sockets, the sockets having dropped down on one side before they were burnt or in the burning, no good and reliable joint could be made to them, except where a drain deviated from a true line.

Although manufacturers are now making their stoneware pipes with more care, it is still extremely difficult to get perfect pipes, especially country-made pipes. At the very time I am writing this, in one of my drainage works at a country house we have had to throw on one side more than twenty per cent. of country-made stoneware pipes, which had been guaranteed, and which in an unfortunate moment I had been prevailed upon to purchase.

In my works I chiefly use the town-made pipes of Messrs. Doulton and Co.'s manufacture, their *picked and tested pipes*, distinguished with the mark T upon each pipe.

9. With stoneware pipes there is not only the difficulty of getting pipes which would stand the water-test without sweating, etc., but there is the further difficulty of making **sound and reliable joints**, and the greater number that such pipes require over iron pipes. It is true that bricklayers are getting much more skilful in laying drains, but

my experience is that if a man has not had some good practice in building manholes and in making cement joints he will come to grief, if not in the manhole, in the joints. And there is not only the special skill which is necessary to make a water-tight joint, but there is also the necessity for the right kind of cement, for Portland cement varies much in quality, as many a bricklayer has found to his sorrow, after he has laid in his drain and found it leaking freely at every joint.

Some men prefer the joints to be made with hemp and cement. A length of spun yarn—long enough to form two (or three) rings—is steeped in cement grout and caulked or rammed into the joint, the remaining space being filled up with stiff cement. Others rely entirely upon cement.

Some authorities prefer drain-pipes with Stanford's or Doulton's joints, or with a combined joint. I confess that I have never been able to satisfy my mind on the use of drain-pipes with such joints unless the joints are also cemented. I prefer a Portland cement joint.

10. In laying down a drain, the first important thing is to arrrange the **falls**, and then to excavate to the necessary depths for the drain, great care being taken not to dig out more ground than necessary, so that the concrete may rest upon virgin ground. Where any ground has been disturbed in error, the **bottom of the trench** should be well rammed before the concrete is put in, and where the ground has been much loosened, notwithstanding the ramming, the concrete should be put in deeper at such points.

11. Every pipe should rest on a solid **bed of concrete** [Blue Lias lime concrete, properly made in the proportion of 1 of lime to 6 of ballast]. In the bottom of all trenches which are to receive stoneware-pipe drains inside or round about a house, lay a bed of concrete 6 in., 9 in., or even 12 in. deep, according to the nature of the ground, and about 8 in. wider than the outside diameter of the pipes to

be bedded thereon, and dished out for the hand to pass round under the joints of the drain-pipes. Stakes could be driven down in the bottom of the trench at intervals of 6 or 12 ft. to mark the height at which the concrete is to be filled up, and wood templets employed for forming the dishings for the joints.

12. The drain from point to point—manhole to manhole—should be laid true in line and section, and the joints of the drain-pipes should be carefully and soundly made with Portland cement, so that the joint is of equal thickness all round, the underneath portion being well tucked into the socket with the fingers, care being taken that none of the jointing material is left projecting inside the pipes. The cement should be highly faced off round the joint at about an angle of 45°.

13. After the drain has been laid it should be allowed to stand for about 24 hours, when it should be filled with water and tested. A little of the water will be absorbed by the cement and also by the drain-pipes, but this can readily be allowed for. Practically the drain should be required to hold water like a bottle. The drain having been thus tested and found to be sound, flaunch off the sides of the drain with Portland cement concrete; or, if preferred, cover over the upper part of the drain, and encase it with concrete to the depth of 3, 4, or 6 in., as circumstance may dictate. And if the drain is inside the house, test it again.

14. No right-angled junctions, bends, or elbows should be used, and where inspection-chambers are not built so that channel-pipes could be fixed and adjusted to suit the requirements, the junctions should be tilted a little, to prevent back-wash up the branches. Special channel-pipes and junctions are now made by most pipe manufacturers.

15. I confess that I often come across a lot of money sunk in building **manholes** which I think could be better employed than in affording means of access to a drain which

may never be used. For the drainage of my own house, provided I knew the work would be well and efficiently carried out, I should be quite content to have just one or two inspection-chambers in the whole system. But for examining and for testing drains manholes are of great value.

16. **For soil-drains inside a house,** and for all places where any leakage from a drain would soak into or under a house, I prefer cast-iron pipe, of the heavy underground water-main strength, *i.e.*, for a 5 in. drain, and under that size, the pipe in its thinnest part should be $\frac{5}{8}$ in. thick; and for 6 in. and 7 in. drains the pipe should not be less than $\frac{7}{8}$ in. The pipe should be coated with solution (Chap. XXVII., Art. 7), and each pipe should be tested before it is fixed by ringing it with a sounding blow from a hammer. (Chap. XXVII., Art. 8.)

The joints should be carefully caulked with a ring or two of spun yarn, and the remaining space filled up with molten lead (soft pig lead) and caulked in, the depth of the lead being not less than 2 in., but $2\frac{1}{2}$ in. is better (see fig. 110).

As already explained (Art. 6), I prefer iron drains to be carried upon brick piers, or strongly secured to the face of a basement wall, or the wall of a subway. At any rate, no iron drain should be allowed to come into contact with lime; and where an iron drain is laid in a trench, and it is not carried upon piers with a granolithic or stone bed hollowed out to receive the drain (two to a 9 ft. length), and is laid upon a concrete bed, the concrete should be made with Portland cement.

17. Although the **size of a drain** is now much more considered than was the case some years ago, the drain is often of much larger size than necessary. A 6 in. drain is large enough for ninety per cent. of the houses in London, and a 5 in. drain would be quite sufficient for scores of cases where even to-day 6 in. drains are being fixed.

18. I have a great objection to **access-chambers** to drains **inside a house**, either manholes to stoneware drains or sight-holes to iron drains, for in my examinations I have often found that the covers and means of access have not been made absolutely air-tight; that jobbing men, in their examination of a drain, have not always been careful enough to replace the manhole covers or sight-hole covers as they found them. But where no access is provided, some half-fledged sanitarian, when he happens to be called in, throws up his hands in wonderment, and frightens the poor householder into an order to fix sight-hole pipes or inspection chambers "immediately."

In fig. 163 is shown a heavy cast-iron sight-hole pipe, for

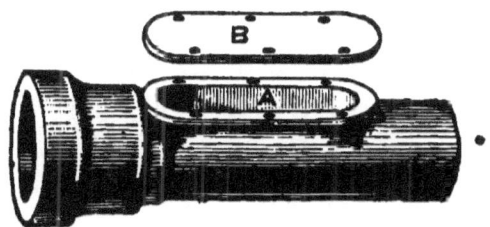

Fig. 163.—VIEW OF A SIGHT-HOLE PIPE.

fixing to an iron drain by caulked lead joints, and with strong gun-metal bolts for securing the cover, B, to the pipe.

DRAIN-FLUSHING.

19. It is now the good custom to fix at the head of the main drain (and in some cases at the head of every important branch drain) an **automatic flushing-tank** for cleansing the drain, by passing a scouring flush of water through it every 24 hours. Instead of fixing such tanks for discharging about 150 gallons of water at a time, as some authorities arrange, I prefer flushes of less than half that quantity, and in many cases I should prefer 40 or

50 gallons of water discharged every 12 hours, to 80, 150, or 200 gallons discharged once in every 24 hours. With the larger flushes there is often great danger of syphonage. I have known the water-seals of several drain-traps—intercepting-traps to sinks and lavatories, etc.—syphoned out by such discharges: and more than that; in one case, where a great engineer had been concerned in planning the drainage, the automatic flushing-tank discharged such an enormous body of water that fæces and other matters were back-washed up through many of the surface-traps, and the water-seals of closet-traps syphoned out.

CHAPTER XXXIX.

HOUSE-DRAINS (*continued*).

DISCONNECTION AND VENTILATION.

1.

THE value of disconnection is now so generally understood that it would be a waste of words to discuss the necessity of trapping off sewers and cesspools, and aerating the drains.

We are now so near to the closing cover of this little book, that there is no space left to discuss the many disconnecting-traps now in use.

2. Unfortunately several vestry boards still insist upon that obstructional appliance the **valve-flap**. This flap they require to be fixed upon the end of the drain inside the sewer. Where a flap-valve is insisted upon, the last length of drain-pipe into the sewer should have a sharp fall, even if it entailed less fall in the other part of the drain.

3. Although the manhole drain-syphon, fig. 164, has been superannuated for some years, it is still being used here and there where the light of sanitation has not yet dawned. When such traps are examined, after they have been in use only a short while, they are found to contain pailfuls of filth.

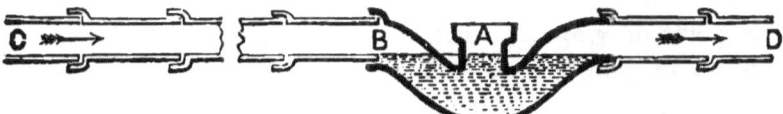

Fig. 164.—SECTION OF A MANHOLE DRAIN-SYPHON.

In measuring the quantity of water held by a 6 in. manhole drain-syphon, as fig. 164, I have found it to hold more than twice the quantity of water held by my patent disconnecting-traps, figs. 165, 167, 170, and 174. A 6 in. man-

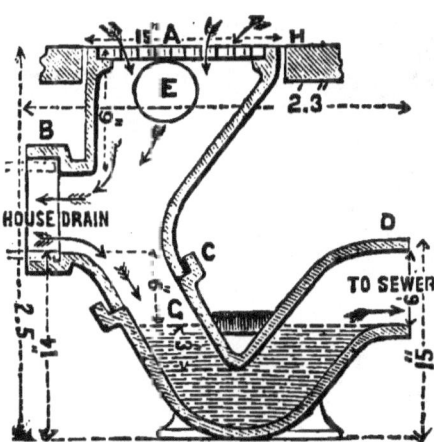

Fig. 165.—SECTION OF A 6 IN. VENTILATING DRAIN-SYPHON.

hole drain-syphon, as fig. 164, holds generally more than two gallons of water. How is it possible to change the contents of such a trap with the flush of water allowed for closets, viz., two gallons? The fact is, such traps are always foul and filthy, whereas such traps as shown in figs. 165, 166, 167, 168, 169, and 170 are readily cleansed.

4. Fig. 166 shows a Buchan's "Disconnecting-trap" with a water-drop, and which has been greatly used during the last ten or fifteen years, and with great success.

5. In laying in new drains the value of a **water-drop** in a disconnecting-trap is not always appreciated. From my point of view it would be better that the house-drain should be laid with a little less fall rather than a discon-

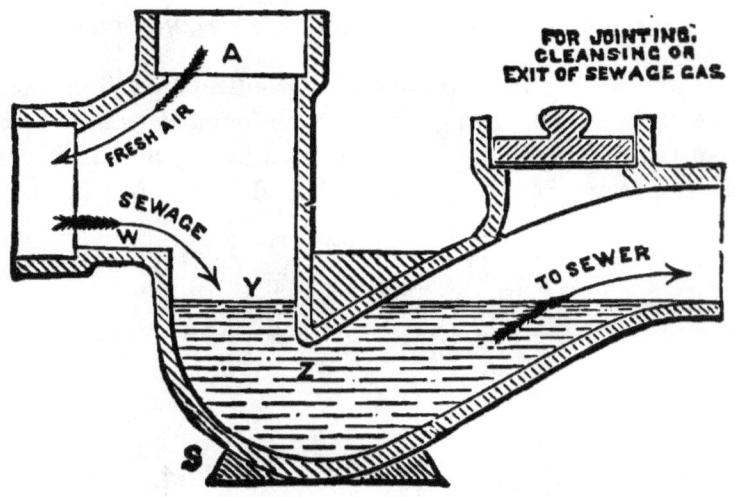

Fig. 166.

necting-trap should be fixed without a water-drop; for besides the advantage gained by a cascade action of water-flushes into a trap for keeping it clean and wholesome, there is the further value of insuring a plug-like seal of water in the mouth of the trap under the greatest back-pressure that is ever likely to be brought upon the trap from any barometric change in the sewer.

Where a trap has no water-drop, the smallest back-pressure from the sewer forces the water-seal down on the outlet side of the trap, whence, rising up on the inlet side, it flows up into the drain, and in times of great atmospheric pressure the sewer air would readily force its way through

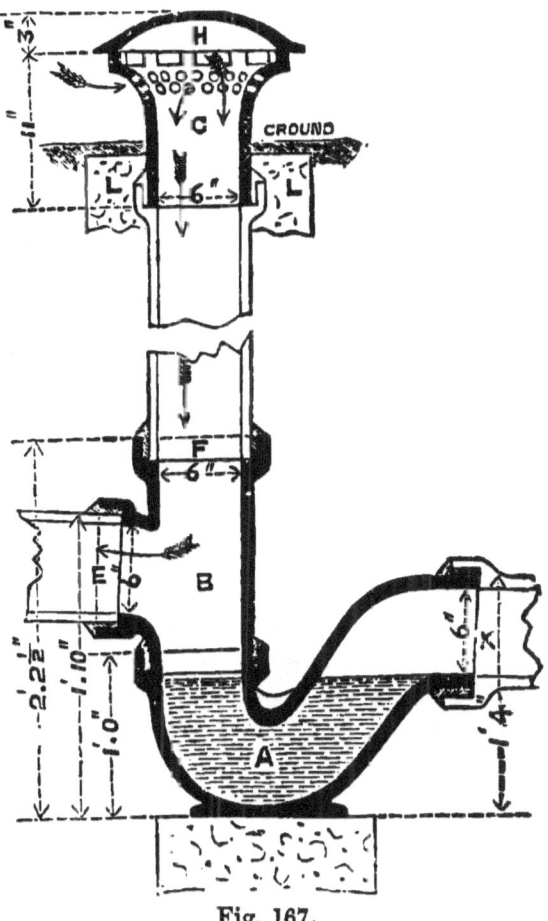

Fig. 167.

the lost or weakened seal of the trap into the house-drains.

In addition to the drop of about 6 in. in my trap (fig. 165), there is the extra depth of the water-seal (2½ in.), so that under no back-pressure which such a trap would ever be subjected to would it be left without a water-plug or seal in its dip-pipe to exclude sewer air from the house-drain.

6. Manholes for giving access to the disconnecting-traps cannot always be afforded, but this need occasion no great worry, for **pipe-shafts** can be fixed at very little expense, either as shown in fig. 167 or fig. 168, illustrations showing the methods I have employed for the disconnection of hundreds of drains with great success.

7. Where existing drains are larger than necessary, and they are not allowed to be replaced by others of smaller size, in fixing a disconnecting-trap it is better to fix the smallest trap suitable for the case, with diminishing pipes, as shown at H and K, fig. 169, the smaller traps being more readily cleared of their contents. In the woodcut, fig. 169, tapering pipes 9 in. to 6 in., and 6 in. to 9 in., are shown for interposing a 6 in. trap to an existing drain 9 in. bore; but supposing the drain to be 12 in., additional tapering pipes could be used, viz., 12 in. to 9 in., and 9 in. to 12 in., and the 6 in. trap still retained.

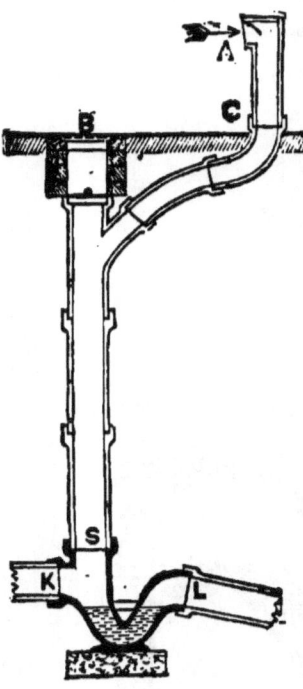

Fig. 168.

8. Some years ago I invented the "**Drain-sentinel**" trap, shown in figs. 170 and 171, for disconnecting drains from sewers, and for affording ready access to both sides of the seal of the trap; to the house-drain, as shown at N, fig.

171; and to the sewer, as shown at D C B, fig. 170; and also at T B, fig. 171. The U-shaped head of the trap

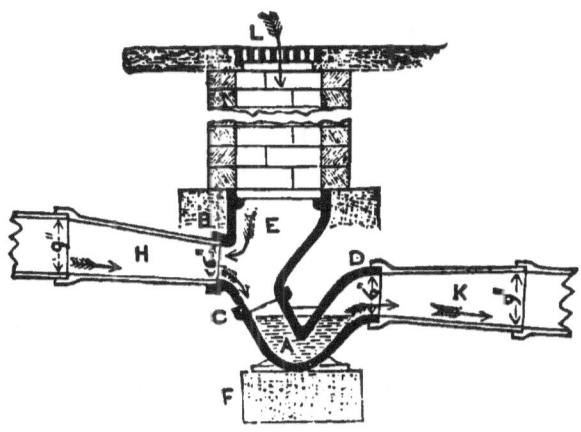

Fig. 169.—SECTION OF A 6 IN. VENTILATING DRAIN-SYPHON, WITH TAPERING PIPES, AND BRICK AIR-SHAFT.

affords a better means for connecting a channel-pipe to the trap, where a manhole is formed for giving access to the drain. The trap is made in four sizes, for 4 in., 6 in., 9 in., and 12 in. drains. Special channel-pipes, as shown in figs. 172 and 173, are made for receiving branch drains, and the side inlets, W and Y, are so formed that matters travelling through the main channel shall not flow up into the branches to foul them, and that the matters flowing out of the branches shall be turned into the channel-pipe in the way of the current.

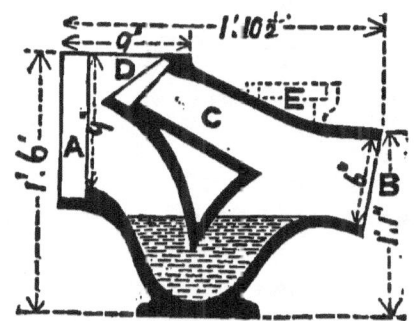

Fig. 170. — SECTION OF THE "DRAIN-SENTINEL" DISCONNECTING TRAP.

9. A manhole cover is shown at E, but a grating, where circumstances admit of it, can be fixed instead of an air-tight cover. The advantage of a solid cover, apart from other reasons, is that it prevents dirt and various other things from falling down upon the benches on the shelving sides of the manhole bottom, to become a nuisance.

There are many so-called air-tight covers now in the market, but in testing drains with smoke I have often found that, though they are designated "air-tight," they

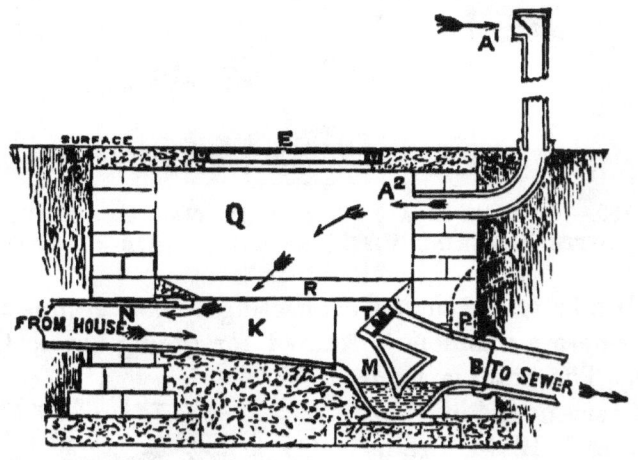

Fig. 171.—SECTION OF "DRAIN-SENTINEL" DISCONNECTING-CHAMBER.

are not smoke-tight. It is better to fix two sets of covers rather than rely upon a cover which is not absolutely air-tight.

10. Where a **manhole** is built over the disconnecting-trap **inside a house,** or in a cellar with its doorway opening into the basement, the manhole should be made both absolutely air-tight and water-tight. Its interior, though built of good bricks, should be well cemented on all sides, and highly faced with a trowel. The access cover should be absolutely reliable.

11. **Fresh air** should be admitted at the upper part of the manhole, as shown at A^2, and the mouth of the induct, A^1, fixed where it would be least likely to be offensive in case of any reaction in the air-current.

12. **A mica-valve** would often be necessary (fig. 116, Chap. XXVII.). Some authorities prefer the mica-flap to stand open a little, so that fresh air may pass into the induct-pipe without any effort. But I prefer, where it is necessary to fix a mica-valve at all, that the mica-flap should entirely seal over the

Fig. 172.—VIEW OF CHANNEL-PIPE, WITH A RIGHT-HAND INLET.

mouth of the induct-pipe when at rest. The current of air for fifty-five minutes out of sixty, where the ventilation-pipes are properly arranged, will find good ingress, and the tight-fitting flap prevents back-draught better than the open one.

I claim the credit of both designing and introducing the first mica-valve for fixing over the mouth of a fresh-air induct to soil-pipes and drains. I know that the late Mr. Eassie thought that he was the first to introduce this

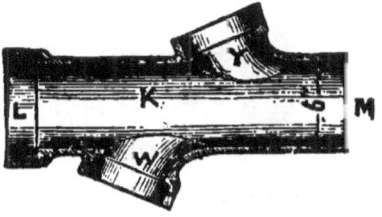

Fig. 173.—PLAN OF CHANNEL-PIPE, WITH INLET ON EACH SIDE.

most useful appliance; but I asked him to tell me where he had the first one made, and then we could soon settle the question, and this did settle it, not only to my own satisfaction, but to his as well. When it occurred to my mind that "foot-ventilation" to a soil-pipe would be a good thing, I had a small pipe, a 2 in. pipe, fixed for the purpose, and then it was that I found that some contrivance was necessary for preventing down-draught or back-draught, and though I sent to all the people in London who would be likely to have any knowledge of a mica-valve for such a purpose, had there ever been one made, I could find nothing, and had one made up specially, which I believe is still working, though the mica has had to be renewed.

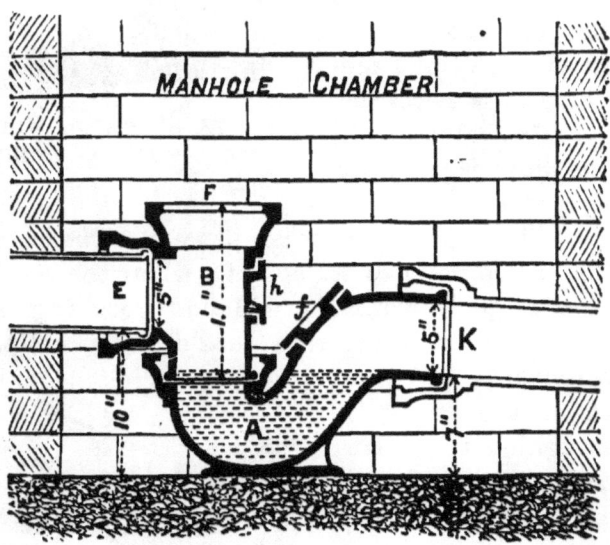

Fig. 174.—SECTION OF CAST-IRON TRAP, WITH TURN-ROUND INLET, AND HEAD FOR PIPE-SHAFT.

13. My patent " Combination " disconnecting-trap (fig. 174) is made in *cast-iron* of great strength for connection to cast-iron drain-pipes by caulked lead joints. The connecting-piece, B, can be turned round upon the trap to suit any angle, and the oval-shaped doorway, H, affords access to the trap for introducing a stopper into the end of the drain, at E, for charging the house-drain with water for testing purposes, etc. The connecting-piece, B, can be fixed

one upon another to allow several branch drains to discharge into one disconnecting-trap.

Fresh air may be admitted through a grating fixed over the pipe-shaft, as shown in figs. 167 and 169, or the top may be sealed down by a stopper, with a cover-plate over it, and fresh air brought into the pipe-shaft, as shown at A, fig. 168, from the most suitable place, with or without a mica-valve, as circumstances required.

14. By the use of a **cast-iron disconnecting-trap**, as shown in fig. 174, the trap could be made to stand in a

Fig. 175.—SCOTT-MONCRIEFF'S CAST-IRON TRAP.

brick-built manhole-chamber, and be inspected at any time without exposing the house to drain air; and, as all the joints to the trap with the drain-pipes would be made with metallic lead, there would be no risk of unsoundness in the connections.

15. Fig. 175 illustrates Mr. Scott-Moncrieff's patent lever-locked **cast-iron inspection-chamber and trap**, for receiving several drains, for connection by caulked lead joints. And fig. 176 shows another form, combined with trap, inspection-chamber, and surface cover and frame. The illustrations speak for themselves.

16. In figs. 177 and 178 illustrations are given of Messrs. John Smeaton, Son, and Co.'s **cast-iron manhole and**

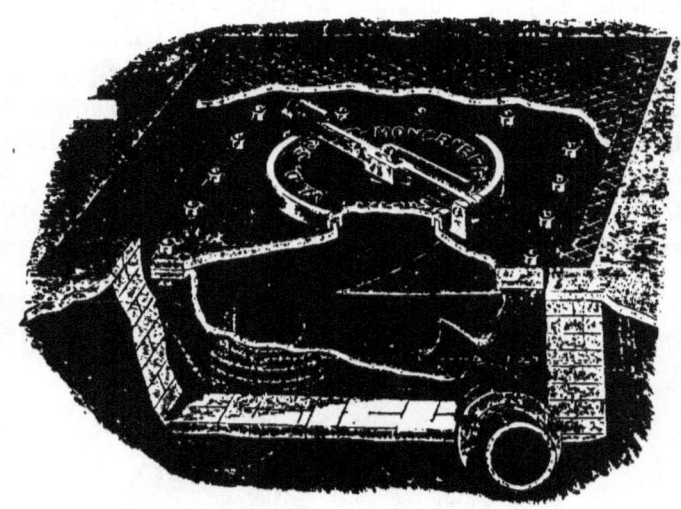

Fig. 176.—Scott-Moncrieff's Cast-Iron Drainage-Trap.

trap combined. The cover, as shown in fig. 177, is secured in its place by two cover-fasteners, and the packing between the cover and the manhole consists of india rubber.

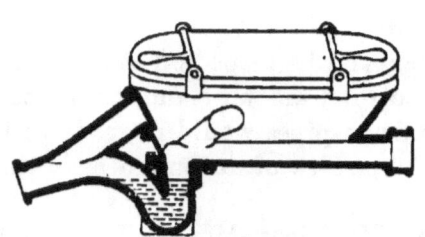

Fig. 177.—Section of Smeaton's Cast-Iron Manhole and Trap.

17. In **ventilating a drain** the inlets and outlets should be so arranged that the air in every part of the drain should be constantly changed. In one of my lectures about ten years ago I showed, by means of glass tubes and smoke, that a single pipe, no matter of what size, or in what part of a drain it was placed, acted only as a *vent* to a drain, or to a soil-pipe, and did not change the air in it.

18. **A model house-drain,** consisting of inch glass tubes and stoneware traps of corresponding size, was placed upon the table, practically as shown on plan, fig. 179. Inch glass tubes were fixed at $s\,p^1$ and $s\,p^2$, to represent vertical stacks of soil-pipe, and these were so arranged that either or both could be sealed over and put out of use at pleasure. Model traps, made of stoneware, were connected to the house-drain for disconnecting the bath, sink-wastes, and rain-water-pipe.

A trap for securing the grease from the drain was fixed as shown on plan, and provision made for fixing an automatic flushing-tank at the head of the drain.

The trap to aerially disconnect the drain from the sewer was fixed at D T, with a glass pipe-shaft carried up to the surface, for the admission of air to the drain directly over the head of the trap; but for the purpose of seeing from what distance air could be brought into a drain without materially affecting the ventilation, another air-inlet was attached to the pipe-shaft, as shown in dotted line $F\,A\,I^2$, both inlets being under control by the use of stoppers.

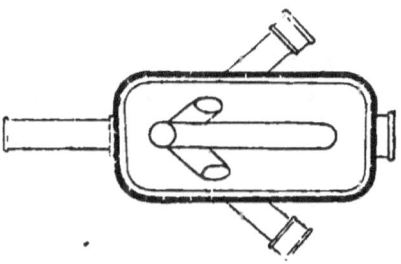

Fig. 178.—PLAN OF TRAP, FIG. 177.

19. The glass drain was filled with smoke and the stack-pipe, $s\,p^2$, opened full bore, all the air-inlets being sealed off, as was also the stack-pipe $s\,p^1$, but there was no perceptible movement of smoke in the drain, though a little smoke at times issued from the open stack-pipe, but only as the smoke and air in the drain and pipe expanded, from being more rarefied.

But even a partial opening of the air-inlet, either directly over the disconnecting-trap, at $F\,A\,I^1$, or of the more distant inlet at F A I², sufficed to rid the drain of every vestige of smoke. With both stack-pipes open for ventilation it was found that the current was generally greater in one stack-pipe than in the other; and this proved what had been stated in a previous lecture, viz., to insure perfect ventilation of a stack of soil-pipe, every stack-pipe should have its own inlet as well as outlet, or one stack upon a drain,

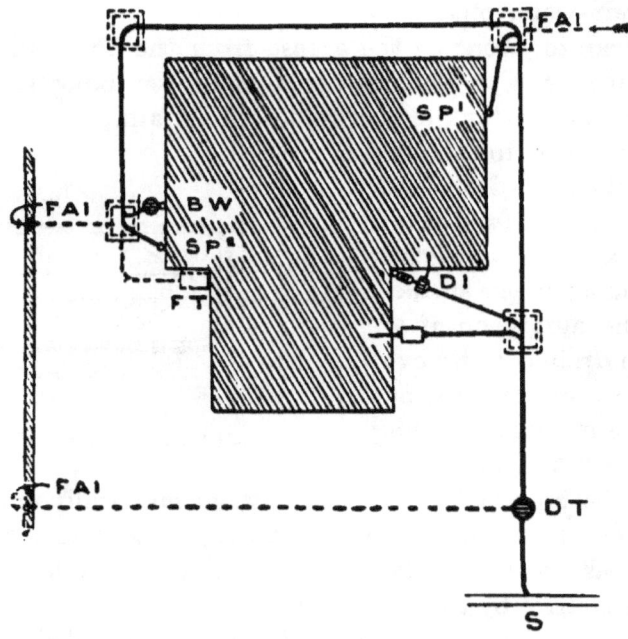

Fig. 179.

where there were several others, and the admission of air to the drain was from one point only, would get more than its fair share of fresh air,—as one sucking-pig, by vigorous sucking, generally manages to get more milk out of a trough than any other of a litter.

20. To set up an **air-current** in the drain, and to quickly clear it of smoke, it was only necessary to expose

both ends of the drain to the air in the room. Nor was it necessary for the complete clearance of smoke to open the ventilation-pipes full bore; *i.e.*, a ventilation-pipe at the head of a drain at s P^2, though only equal to one-fourth of that of the latter, with an induct-pipe at F A I^1, also of a size much smaller than that of the drain, would create a current right throughout the system, whilst a *single* pipe at s P^2, or at s P^1, or in any other part of the drain, though of larger bore, would only allow the air in the drain to come out of the pipe as it expanded in the stack-pipe from the heat of the sun, or became rarefied in the drain from hot water discharges through it, or from displacement, but there would be no ventilation either of the drain or the soil-pipe by one open pipe.

21. If there is to be ventilation in a drain, or soil-pipe, there must be both an **inlet** and **an outlet**, for the air to pass in in one place and out at another. From nothing you can take nothing. So, my reader-friend,—to turn for a moment from the house for the body to the house for the mind,—if you want to take any money out of the bank when you are too old to work for it, you must put it in now when you are young and able to make it, and when you do not stand so much in need of the comfort it brings, or there will be but poor currency for you should such an evil day ever come when the circulation ceases, for where no money comes into a pocket no money can go out of it.

22. When the drainage system is perfect, there is not the same necessity for **trapping off soil-pipes and disconnecting** them from the soil-drain as there is where the drains are foul and faulty. (Chap. XXVII., Art. 15.) In fact in many cases it would be better to make all the soil-pipes upcasts to the drains, and not to trap them off; though where they are so treated it is always advisable to aerate them—to provide each soil-pipe with a fresh-air inlet, *i.e.*, over the junction of the soil-pipe (the branch

drain) with the main drain there should be built a manhole, somewhat as shown in fig. 115, Chap. XXVII., and also as shown in dotted lines at F A I³ and F A I⁴, fig. 179. As explained in Chap. XXVII., Art. 16, where the mouth of such an inlet would stand inconveniently near an entrance to the house, near a window or door, or in a confined nook, etc., it should have a mica-valve fixed over its mouth.

23. Where cast-iron **ventilation-pipes** are fixed, and their *interiors* are not protected from rusting, proper pockets for catching rust should be fixed at the bottom of all long vertical lengths, to prevent blockage.

24. Whatever kind of pipe may be fixed, whether cast-iron (Chap. XXVII., Art. 5), or galvanized cast-iron (Chap. XXVII., Art. 6), or lead (Chap. XXVII., Arts. 1, 2, and 3), the **pipes** should be **carried up** to the very highest parts of the roof, full bore, where the wind coming from any direction could blow any foul air emitted from them away from the surroundings.

25. To terminate a ventilation-pipe from a drain or soil-pipe, as shown in fig. 118, or in fig. 180, in any of the following positions—which, alas! is often done—is only an ostrich-like way of "protecting" a house; viz., terminating a ventilation-pipe under the eaves of a roof, or close upon the sloping side of a roof, where the foul air would find an easy passage through the tiles or slates into the roof, and thence into the house; under or near a skylight, dormer, or other kind of window; near a void or well-hole; or in the vicinity of the cistern-room, or place of water-storage, where the bad air emitted from such pipes could enter the cisterns to contaminate the water; or at the top of some chimney-stack, where the ventilation-pipe could pour its contents almost undiluted down a chimney, as shown by the illustration, fig. 180, which, together with the explanation which follows, are taken from my "Lectures":—

"In 1881 I was staying at the Royal Castle Hotel, Lynton, which is built on the crest of a hill overlooking the Bristol Channel, and the valley of the East Lynn. Being anxious to get a good view from my bedroom window, I selected a bedroom at the top of the house, and lived to

Fig. 180.—SHOWING BAD POSITION OF THE TERMINAL OF A VENTILATION-PIPE FROM A DRAIN.

regret it; for though the morning's sun 'tipped the hills with gold,' I could not see them for the dense smoke which filled my room. I was not long in seeing where the smoke came from, so I jumped out of bed, and provided an exit for it by opening one of the windows, and then returned to bed again to watch the movements of the smoke. Down the chimney it came in clouds, filling the room from floor to ceiling, and went out of the window in a fitful sort of way, and as it gave every sign of continuing this course for some hours, I withdrew from the bedroom, feeling comforted that it was only smoke, for if a ventilation-pipe had been near such a chimney, it might have been drain air instead of smoke, and what a change of air that would have been, even though I had come from Cologne!"

I have quoted this explanation of the picture—where the arrows are crossing over the bed, like the rats in the well-known magic-lantern slide—as it may not be without some interest to any reader who may have honoured me by wading through this weary work to its weary end.

INDEX.

ACIDS and lead, 9; tin, 14.
Access-chambers to drains, 269.
Action of water on lead, 8, 254, 255; heat on lead, 8; water on iron, 256.
Advantages of valve-closets, 208.
Air-currents in drains, 282.
Air-inlets to manholes, 184-186, 277.
Air-tight covers to manholes, 276.
Airo-hydrogen blow-pipe, 21.
Alloys of tin, 13, 16.
Analysis of water, 251.
Angle soldering, 38.
Anti-D-traps, 114, 124, 125, 140, 146; for sinks, 129.
Anti-syphoning pipes, use of, 133, 143, 148; to baths and lavatories, 247.
Anti-syphon trap-vent, 151.
Apartments for water-closets, 223.
Apron curb, 69.
Apron-flashing, 29.
Astragals, 101; joints, 101.
Automatic flushing cistern for urinals, 249; tank for drains, 269.

Back-pressure in pipes, 147, 272.

Baths, 238, 248; and their wastes, 240, 247; overflow pipes, 240; safes, 240; in dressing-rooms, 247.
Bays, lead, 54, 62, 71.
Belgrand, M., on the action of water on lead pipes, 254.
Bell-traps, 120.
Bending pipes, 104.
Birds' eyes in lead, 27.
Bird-guards to end of safe overflow pipes, 213.
Blanc, M. le, experiments on the action of water on lead, 255.
Block joint, 88.
Blow-down of air in a pipe, 155.
Blowing-lamp, "self-acting," 17.
Blow-pipe, 100.
"Blow-pipe," lamp, 18.
Blow-pipe joint, 100; solder, 16.
Bobbins and followers, 109.
Bolts, iron, 110.
Bossing, care in lead roofing, 27.
Bower traps, 134, 145.
Bramah, Joseph, water-closet, 197.
Branch joints, 76, 92, 182; pipes, 182.
Breaks, bossing of, 29.
Brick piers for iron drains, 268.
Briggs' patent "Solderer" lamp, 18, 23, 220.

Buchan's "Disconnecting-trap," 272.
Burning, lead, 20.

Capillary attraction, 46, 54.
Castings, lead, manufacture of, 9, 11.
Cast-iron drain-pipes, 268; soil-pipes, 177; waste-pipes, 177.
Caulked lead-joints, 177, 187, 268.
Cement joints, 178, 216, 266.
Cerusite, 5.
Cesspools, roof, 37.
Chain to plug and washer, 244.
Channels, stone, 35.
Channel-pipes, 267, 275, 277.
Chases for pipes, 167.
Cisterns, 156, 251; lead-battened, 252; slate, 252; earthenware, 252; galvanized wrought-iron, 253; lead-lined, 253; Titancrete, Farmiloe's, 253; for closet flushing, 221; slop-sink flushing, 228; cleaning out, 258; lining with lead, 23, 156; dimensions for cutting out, 157; position of, 257; soldering, 160; and their wastes, 258.
Cistern rooms, 257.
Cleats, 38.
Closet inclosures, 220.
Cloths, solder, 97.
Coating iron pipes, 177, 268.
Cobweb-grating, 230, 234.
Collars, lead, 85.
Combination baths, 248.
"Combination" disconnecting-trap, 278.
Condensation channels, 54.
Concrete, 266.
Connection of earthenware to lead and iron by Portland cement, 216; a flange, 217; elastic closet cement, 219.
Copper-bit, 24; joint, 99.
Copper bird-guard, 213; ferrules, 187; flap to end of pipes, 213; tacks, 60.
Corners, bossing-up, 29, 33.
Cornices, lead covering to, 34.
Cotton and Johnson's patent "Torch" lamp, 17.
Counter sinking, 40.
Cover flashings, 29, 36, 43.
Cowls, 186.
Curbs, 29, 69.
Cumming, Alex., water-closet, 194.

D-trap, 112, 134; narrow-band, 117, 139, 146; Helmet, 118, 145, 146.
Disconnection and ventilation, 270.
Disconnection of slop-sink wastes from soil-drains, 225; soil-pipes from drains, 175, 183.
"Disconnecting-trap," Buchan's, 272; "Combination," 278; Scott-Moncrieff's, 279; Smeaton's, 280.
Domes, 61.
Dormers, 42.
Dormer cheeks, 29, 43; sills, 29, 44.
Double tacks, 165.
Doulton's stoneware drain-pipes, 265.
Dowels, dots, 37; lead, 36.
Drains, 262; arranging the falls, 266; access-chambers, 269; essential features of good, 264; channel-pipes, 267; cast-iron pipes, 268; inside a house, 263,

268; outside a house, 263; terrace-houses, 264; testing of, 267, 278; trenches, 266; stoneware pipes, 265; size of, 268; interceptors, 234; ventilation, 280.
Drainage, planning, 263.
"Drain-sentinel" trap, 274.
Draining-board for sinks, 233.
Draw-off sinks, 231; and slop-sink combined, 242.
Dressing-room, bath in, 247.
Drifting-plate, 5, 45.
Drips, 44.
Du Bois traps, 125, 145.
"Duck's-foot" bend, 188.
Dummy, hand, 108; long, 108.
Durability of lead, 25, 176.

Ears or lugs, 164.
Earthenware cisterns, 252; connection with lead, 216.
"Eclipse" traps, 139, 146.
Elastic closet cement, 219.
Elbow joints, 102; mitre joints, 103.
Emptage traps, 153.
Evaporation of water in closet basins, 209; traps, 155.
Expansion joints, 228.
Experiments with traps, 115, 145, 153.

Face tacks, 164.
Falls of a drain, 266.
Farmiloe's Titancrete cistern, 253.
Fillets, 35.
Filters, 261.
Fine solder, 15.
Fireplaces, 20.
Flange, lead, 88, 90; connection of earthenware to lead, 217; joint, 90.
Flaps on end of pipes, 213.
Flashings, 29, 63.
Flats, 29, 47.
Flow-joints, 99.
Flushing cisterns, 218, 221, 228, 230, 258; of closets, 221; urinals, 248.
Flushing-rim hopper closet, 206; slop-sink, 227.
"Flush-out" grease trap, 237.
Followers and bobbins, 109.
Foot ventilation, 184, 186.
Freezing, water in pipes, 167.
Funnel pipe, lead, 11.
Furnace, reverberatory, 6.

Galena, 5.
Galvanized cast-iron soil-pipe, 177; wrought-iron cisterns, 253.
Gargoyles, 42.
Grease, fouling drain, 235; intercepting trap, 235; trap, "flush-out," 237.
Gun-metal coupling unions, 232.
Gutters, deep, 49; long, 48; secret, 63, 65.

Half-S traps, 123, 132; experiments with, 130.
Heads of rain-water pipes, 173.
Helmet D-traps, 118, 145, 146.
Hips, 29, 50.
Hip rolls, 52.
Hopper water-closet, 205; flushing rim, 206.
Horizontal pipes, 167.
Hospital slop-sinks, 228, 247.
House-drains, 262; model, 281.

Inclosed closets compared with open closets, 220.
Interceptors for drains, 234.
Iron bolts, 110; rusting, 176; soil-pipes, 176; soil-pipes coated, 177; soil-pipes painted, 179.

Jennings' tip-up lavatory basin, 244.
Joint-making, 74.
Joints, Astragal, 101; block, 88; blow-pipe, 17, 100; branch, 76, 92, 182; caulked lead, 177; cement, 178, 216, 266; copper-bit, 99; earthenware to lead and iron, 214-219; elbow, 102; elbow mitre, 103; expansion, 228; flange, 90; flow, 99; marine glue, 177; mitre, 95; overcast, 87; Portland cement, 266, 267; ribbon, 100; ribbon overcast, 100; taft, 91; tinker's, 98; underhand, 76, 83; underhand lengths, 81; upright, 76, 82, 84; upright lengths, 81.

Lambert's under-the-seat water-waste preventing valve, 223.
Lamp, "blow-pipe," 18; "self-acting blowing lamp," 17; "solderer," 18, 23, 220; "torch," 17.
Laps, 53.
Lavatories, 238; and their wastes, 239, 247; and scented soap, 246; waste valves, 244.
Lavatory basins, "tip-up," 244; Jennings', 244; ranges, 245, 246.
Lead, 5; action of acids on, 9; action of heat on, 8; action of water on, 8; bays, 54, 62; birds' eyes in, 27; collars, 85; connected to earthenware, 216; dowels, 36; durability of, 25, 176, 255; flanges, 88, 90; funnel-pipe, by hand, 11; funnel-pipe, by hydraulic power, 11; milled, manufacture of, 10; mines, 5; old, 25; oxygen and, 8; pig, 8, 13; pipes and castings, manufacture of, 9; pipes, weights, 12; production and consumption of, 13; properties of, 8; safes to baths, 241; safes to water-closets, 212; soil-pipes, 176.

Lead burning, 20.
Lead laying, 25; care in bossing, 27; strengths for roofing, 29.
Lead-battened cisterns, 252.
Lead-lined cisterns, 253.
"Lectures on the Science and Art of Sanitary Plumbing," extracts and references, 20, 81, 99, 104, 167, 188, 208, 253, 284.
Lining cisterns and sinks, 23, 156; tanks, 24.
Lip-urinal, 250.
Lugs or ears, 164.

Manholes, 184, 267, 276.
Manhole drain-syphon, 271.
Mansard roofs, 53.
Marine glue joints, 177.
McClellan's patent anti-syphon trap-vent, 151.
"McHardy" slop-sink, 228.
Melting point of lead, 8; tin, 13.
Metropolis Water Act, 125, 221.
Mica valves, 184, 186, 225, 277.
Milled lead, 10; made in various towns, 12.
Mines, lead, 5.

Mitre-joint, 95 ; elbow, 103.
Momentum, loss of seals by, 153.
Morveau, Guyton de, on action of water on lead, 257.
"Mushroom" air-inlet, 186.

Ogee-shaped roofs, 61.
Old lead, 25.
Open closets compared with inclosed, 220.
Open end for bath and lavatory wastes, 247 ; for overflows from safes, 213, 241 ; for valve-box vents of valve-closets, 210.
"Optimus" valve-closet, 209, 210, 211.
Oscillation of water in traps, 150.
Outside soil-pipes, 181.
Overcast joints, 87 ; ribbon joints, 100.
Overflow pipes, 41 ; from baths and lavatories, 238 ; from bath safes, 241 ; from sinks, 231 ; from water-closet safes, 213.
Overflow-pipe-trap to valve-closets, 212.
Overlaps, 44.
Oxygen and lead, 8 ; and tin, 14.

Painting of iron pipes, 179.
Pan-closets, 198.
Pantry sinks, 231.
Passings, 53.
Pedestal closets, 220 ; as urinals, 251.
Pig-lead, 8, 13.
Pipes, filling and fixing, 81, 163 ; lead, manufacture of, 9.
Pipe bending, 104 ; freezing, 167 ; shafts, 273, 274.
Place, Captain de, patent for detecting flaws in metals, 178.

Planning the drainage of a house, 263.
Plug or plunger water-closets, 207.
Plug-holes, small, 243.
Plug and washers, 243, 261 ; chain, 244.
Plumber, always a learner, 262.
Plumber's bag of tools, 1 ; solder, 15 ; stove, 20.
"Plumber and Sanitary Houses" ("Dulce Domum"), extracts and references, 5. 186, 200, 214.
Portland cement, 216, 266 ; connecting earthenware to lead, 216.
Position of cisterns, 257.
Principles of self-cleansing traps, 122.
Privies, 188.
Properties of lead, 8.
Prosser's water-closet, 196.
Pull-up knob for lavatories, 244.

Rain-water, 169 ; filter, 170 ; heads, 173, 259 ; pipes, 171 ; separator, 171 ; shoe, 171 ; storage, 169, 257.
Reverberatory furnace, 6.
Ribbon joints, 100 ; overcast joints, 100.
Richemont, Count de, airo-hydrogen blow-pipe, 21.
Ridges, 29.
Roberts' patent rain-water separator, 171.
Rolls, 47, 50, 52, 55, 62.
Roof cesspools, 37 ; coverings, Mansard, 53.
Round pipe or syphon trap, 114, 124, 128 ; experiments with, 130.
Rubble-work, 64.

Running-trap, 148.
Rusting of iron, 176.

S-trap, 123, 128.
Safes to baths, 241; overflow pipes, 241; cisterns, 258; water-closets, 212.
Sal-ammoniac, used in tinning, 14.
Salts, in water, 257.
Sand, for bending pipes, 111.
Saunders, Dr. Sedgwick, on the action of water on lead pipes, 254.
Sciséophone, for detecting flaws in metals, 178.
Scott-Moncrieff's cast-iron disconnecting-trap, 279.
Scullery sinks, 232.
Seal, loss of, in a trap, 131.
Seam rolls, 55, 62.
Seamless lead pipe, 11, 175.
Secret overflows, 238.
"Self-acting blowing lamp," 17.
Service pipes to closets, 222, 223, weights of, 12.
Sheets, lead, 12.
Sight-holes to iron drains, 269.
Silence-pipe for flushing-cisterns, 222.
Single tacks, 165.
Sinks, lining with lead, 23, 156; for hospitals, 228, 247; materials for, 230, 232; pantry, 231; scullery, 232; slop and draw-off, 224; for washing vegetables with two divisions, 233.
Sinkings, shallow, 35.
Slate cisterns, 252.
Slop-sinks, 224-230; "McHardy," 228; wastes, disconnection from soil-pipe, 225.

Smeaton's cast-iron disconnecting-trap, 280.
Smith, Dr. Angus, solution, 177.
Snow-boards, 73.
Soakers, 29, 63, 66.
Socket-pipes, 39.
Socket-tacks, 174.
Soft water, 171.
Soil-pipes, 175; disconnection and ventilation, 175; lead, 176; cast-iron, 177; carried to roof, 186; outside, 181; sizes of, 182; traps for, 183.
Solder, blow-pipe, 16; cloths, 97; fine, for copper-bit, 15; plumbers', 15, 78, 79; soft, 16.
"Solderer," patent lamp, 18, 23, 220.
Soldering, angle, 38; cisterns, 160; tacks, 166.
Spence's metal, 177.
Spigot and socket connection of earthenware to lead, 219.
Splash stick, 86.
Splayed edges to drips, 45.
Spouts, 41.
Step-flashings, 29, 63.
Stoneware pipes for drains, 265.
Storage of water, 251; rain-water, 169.
Stove, plumbers', 20.
Standard overflows, 234.
Strength of lead, for roofing, 29.
Subways to terrace houses, 264.
Syphonage, 147; of drain traps, 270.
Syphon traps, 114, 124, 128.

Table-top, for use of closets for slops, 225.
Tacks, 29, 60, 68, 164; socket, 174; soldering, 166.

INDEX.

Taft joints, 91.
Tanks, lining of, 24, 157.
Telescope joints, 167, 228.
Terrace houses, drains, 264.
Tilts, wood, 49, 71.
Tip-up lavatory basin, 244; Jennings', 244.
Tin and its alloys, 13, 16, 78.
Tin, block, to incase lead pipes, 12; Cornish production of, 15; places brought from, 14.
Tinning, copper and iron, 14.
Tinstone, 14.
Titancrete cistern or tank, 253.
Tools, plumbers', 1.
"Torch," patent lamp, 17.
Torus, 29, 69.
Traps, Anti-D, 114, 124, 125, 140, 146; Bell, 120; Bower, 134, 145; Buchan's disconnecting, 272; D, 112, 134; drain sentinel, 274; Du Bois, 125, 145; experiments with, 115, 145, 153; eclipse, 139, 146; emptage, 153; for slop-sinks, 229; for valve-closets, 212; grease intercepting, 235; half-S, 123, 125, 128; half-S, experiments with, 130; Helmet D, 118, 145, 146; momentum in, 153; narrow-band D, 117, 139, 146; non-cleansing, 111; one to several fixtures, 241; principles on which they should be constructed, 122; round pipe, 114, 128, 132; S, 123, 128; self-cleansing, 121; compared with non-cleansing, 126; syphon, 114, 124; syphonage, 147; U-shaped and V-shaped, 153, 154; ventilation, 148; with mechanical seats or check-valves, 121.

Trapless closets, 207.
Trumpet pipe overflow, 234.
Tylor's "Waste-not" valve, 223.

U-shaped traps, 153, 154.
Underhand joints, 76.
Underlap, 44, 51.
Under-the-seat waste preventing valves, 223.
Upright joints, 76.
Urine, 248.
Urinals, 248; lip, 250; step to, 250; wide fronted, 250.

V-shaped traps, 153, 154.
Valleys, lead, 71.
Valves, waste, to lavatories, 243, 244; waste preventing, 223.
Valve and regulator supply to valve-closets, 222.
Valve-closets, advantages of, 208; overflow arrangements, 211.
Valve-flap to drains, 270.
Vents from valve-boxes, 210.
Ventilating drain-syphon, 271; tubes for water-closet apartments, 223.
Ventilation, 270; of drains, 280; of drains, inlet and outlet, 283; soil-pipes, 175, 186; traps, 148.

Wall-hooks, 163.
Warping of boards, flats, and gutters, 47.
Wash-out and wash-down closets, 201.
Waste-pipes from baths and lavatories, 239, 247; cisterns, 258; draw-off sinks, 229, 231; slop-sinks, 225, 227, 229, 247; one to several fittings, 242; weights of, 12.

Waste-valves to lavatories, 243, 244.
Water, action on iron, 256; action on lead, 8, 255; action on lead-pipes, 254; analysis, 251; storage, 251.
Water Company, weights of pipes, 12.
Water-drop in a disconnecting trap, 272.
Water seal, loss of, in traps, 131.
Water supply to closets, 221; in London, 252.
Water Battery water closet, 201.
Water channels to urinals, 250.
Water-closets, Bramah's, 197; Cumming's, 194; history of, 188; Hopper, 205; Hopper flushing-rim, 206; hygienic, 204; marble, 193; Optimus, 209, 210, 211; pan, 198; pedestal, 220, 251; primitive, 188; privies, 190; Prosser's, 196; plug or plunger, 207; safes, 212; valve, advantages, 208; wash-out and wash-down, 201; water battery, 201; without traps, 207; with seat-action, 205.
Water-closet apartments, ventilation of, 223.
Water test for drains, 267, 278.
Water waste preventers, 221, 250.
Well water, 257.
Welts, double, 72; single, 71.
Wide flashings, 29.
Wood blocks, 88, 166; rolls, 50, 55; tilts, 49.
Workman, British, 2 (note); judged by his tools, 1.
Wrought-iron cisterns, 253.

CHISWICK PRESS :—C. WHITTINGHAM AND CO., TOOKS COURT, CHANCERY LANE.

TECHNOLOGICAL HANDBOOKS.

"The excellent series of technical handbooks."—*Textile Manufacturer.*
"The admirable series of technological handbooks."—*British Journal of Commerce.*
"Messrs. Bell's excellent technical series."—*Manchester Guardian.*

Edited by SIR H. TRUEMAN WOOD.

A Series of Technical Manuals for the use of Workmen and others practically interested in the Industrial Arts, and specially adapted for Candidates in the Examinations of the City Guilds Institute.
Illustrated and uniformly printed in small post 8vo.

DYEING AND TISSUE-PRINTING. By WILLIAM CROOKES, F.R.S., V.P.C.S. 5s.

"Whether viewed in connection with the examination room or the dye-house, the volume is one which deserves a work of welcome."—*Academy.*
"The only previous qualification of which the student is assumed to be possessed is an elementary knowledge of chemistry such as may be acquired from almost any of the rudimentary treatises on that science. The author, building upon this foundation, seeks to explain the principles of the art from a practical rather than from a theoretical point of view. From the very outset he endeavours to explain everything with which the learner might be puzzled."—*Chemical News.*

GLASS MANUFACTURE. INTRODUCTORY ESSAY by H. J. POWELL, B.A. (Whitefriars Glass Works); CROWN AND SHEET GLASS, by HENRY CHANCE, M.A. (Chance Bros., Birmingham); PLATE GLASS, by H. G. HARRIS, Assoc. Memb. Inst. C.E. 3s. 6d.

COTTON SPINNING: Its Development, Principles, and Practice. With an Appendix on Steam Engines and Boilers. By R. MARSDEN, Editor of the "Textile Manufacturer," and Examiner for the City and Guilds of London Institute. Fourth Edition. 6s. 6d.

CONTENTS.—Introductory—Cotton—The Mill—Manipulation of the Material—Carding and Combing—Drawing, Stubbing, and Roving—Development of Spinning—The Modern System of Spinning—The Modern Mule—Throstle and Ring Spinning; Doubling—Miscellanea—Appendix.

"An admirable work on the subject."—*Manchester Examiner and Times.*
"Practical spinners, of whom Mr. Marsden is evidently one, will value this volume as a handbook, and learners will find the fullest information given with the greatest possible clearness."—*Manchester Courier.*

COTTON WEAVING. By R. MARSDEN, Examiner to the City and Guilds of London Institute, Author of "Cotton Spinning." With numerous illustrations. [*In preparation.*

COAL-TAR COLOURS, The Chemistry of. With special reference to their application to Dyeing, &c. By DR. R. BENEDIKT, Professor of Chemistry in the University of Vienna. Translated from the German by E. KNECHT, Ph.D., Head Master of the Chemistry and Dyeing Department in the Technical College, Bradford. 2nd Edition, Revised and Enlarged. 6s. 6d.

"The original work is popular in Germany, and the translation ought to be equally appreciated here, not only by students of organic chemistry, but by all who are practically concerned in the dyeing and printing of textile fabrics."—*The Athenæum.*
"The volume contains, in a little space, a vast amount of most useful information classified in such a manner as to show clearly and distinctly the chief characteristics of each colouring matter, and the relationship existing between one series of compounds and another."—*Journal of the Society of Dyers and Colourists.*

WOOLLEN AND WORSTED CLOTH MANUFACTURE. By Professor ROBERTS BEAUMONT, Textile Industries Department of the Yorkshire College, Leeds. Second Edition, Revised. 7s. 6d.

CONTENTS.—Materials—Woollen Thread Manufacture—Worsted Thread Construction—Yarns and Fancy Twist Threads—Loom-Mounting, or Preparation of the Yarns for the Loom—The Principles of Cloth Construction—Fundamental Weaves—Hand Looms—Power Looms—Weave-Combinations—Drafting—Pattern Design—Colour applied to Twilled and Fancy Weaves—Backed and Double Cloths—Analysis of Cloths and Calculations—Cloth Finishing.

"The book is a satisfactory and instructive addition to the Messieurs Bell's excellent technical series."—*Manchester Guardian.*

"It should be studied and inwardly digested by every student of the textile arts."—*Textile Recorder.*

"A valuable contribution to technological literature."—*Irish Textile Journal.*

"The latest addition to the admirable series of technological handbooks in course of publication by Messrs. Bell and Sons is a most valuable work, and will take at once a very high place among technical manuals."—*British Journal of Commerce.*

PRINTING. A Practical Treatise on the Art of Typography as applied more particularly to the Printing of Books. By C. T. JACOBI, Manager of the Chiswick Press; Examiner in Typography to the City and Guilds of London Institute. With upwards of 150 Illustrations, many useful Tables, and Glossarial Index of Technical Terms and Phrases. 5s.

"The work of a man who understands the subject on which he is writing, and is able to express his meaning clearly. Mr. Jacobi may further be complimented on having supplied an excellent index."—*Athenæum.*

"A practical treatise of more than common value. . . . This is a thorough, concise, and intelligible book, written with obvious mastery of all details of the subject."—*The Speaker.*

"Mr. Jacobi goes into the minutest particulars . . . contains a large amount of information which will prove interesting to anyone who has ever had occasion to look into a printed book or newspaper."—*Saturday Review.*

"It deals with the subject in an exhaustive and succinct manner. . . . We wish it all the success it deserves in its efforts on behalf of technological education."—*Printing Times and Lithographer.*

"There is much about it which pleases us. . . . It is well printed and well illustrated. . . . He has written tersely and to the point."—*Printers' Register.*

"'Printing' is a book that we can recommend to our readers. It is literally full of items which will be of importance to the printer in his daily toil."—*Effective Advertiser.*

BOOKBINDING. A Practical Treatise on the Art. By J. W. ZAEHNSDORF. With 8 coloured Plates and numerous diagrams. Second Edition, Revised. 5s.

"No more competent writer upon his art could have been found. . . . An excellent example of a technical text-book."—*Industries.*

"To professional as well as amateur binders it may confidently be recommended."—*Paper and Printing Trades Journal.*

"Its phraseology is simple, straightforward and clear, its arrangement systematic, and its completeness apparently without a flaw."—*Guardian.*

PLUMBING. Its Theory and Practice. By S. STEVENS HELLYER. With numerous illustrations. [*Immediately.*

SILK-FINISHING. By G. H. HURST, F.C.S. [*In the press.*

"THE SPECIALISTS' SERIES."

A New Series of Handbooks for Students and Practical Engineers.
Crown 8vo, cloth. With many Illustrations.

ELECTRIC TRANSMISSION OF ENERGY, and its Transformation, Subdivision, and Distribution. A Practical Handbook by GISBERT KAPP, C.E., Member of the Council of the Institution of Electrical Engineers, &c. With numerous Illustrations. Third Edition, thoroughly revised and enlarged. 7s. 6d.

"We have looked at this book more from the commercial than the scientific point of view, because the future of electrical transmission of energy depends upon the enterprise of commercial men and not so much upon men of science. The latter have carried their work to a point, as is admirably shown by Mr. Kapp in his work, where the former should take hold."—*Engineer.*

"The book is one of the most interesting and valuable that has appeared for some time."—*Saturday Review.*

"We cannot speak too highly of this admirable book, and we trust future editions will follow in rapid succession."—*Electrical Review.*

HYDRAULIC MOTORS: Turbines and Pressure Engines. For the use of Engineers, Manufacturers, and Students. By G. R. BODMER, A.M. Inst. C.E. With numerous Illustrations. 14s.

"A distinct acquisition to our technical literature."—*Engineering.*

"The best text-book we have seen on a little-known subject."—*The Marine Engineer.*

"Mr. Bodmer's work forms a very complete and clear treatise on the subject of hydraulic motors other than ordinary water-wheels, and is fully up to date."—*Industries.*

"A contribution of standard value to the library of the hydraulic engineer."—*Athenæum.*

THE TELEPHONE. By W. H. PREECE, F.R.S., and J. MAIER, Ph.D. With 290 Illustrations, Appendix, Tables, and full Index. 12s. 6d.

Mr. Rothen, Director of the Swiss Telegraphs, the greatest authority on Telephones on the Continent, writes:—"Your book is the most complete work on the subject which has as yet appeared; it is, and will be for a long time to come, *the* book of reference for the profession."

"Messrs. Preece and Maier's book is the most comprehensive of the kind, and it is certain to take its place as the standard work on the subject."—*Electrical Review.*

ON THE CONVERSION OF HEAT INTO WORK. A Practical Handbook on Heat-Engines. By WILLIAM ANDERSON, M. Inst. C.E. With 61 Illustrations. Second Edition, revised and enlarged. 6s.

"We have no hesitation in saying there are young engineers—and a good many old engineers too—who can read this book, not only with profit, but pleasure; and this is more than can be said of most works on heat."—*The Engineer.*

"The volume bristles from beginning to end with practical examples culled from every department of technology. In these days of rapid book-making it is quite refreshing to read through a work like this, having originality of treatment stamped on every page."—*Electrical Review.*

ALTERNATING CURRENTS OF ELECTRICITY. By THOMAS H. BLAKESLEY, M.A., M. Inst. C.E. Second Edition, enlarged. 4s. 6d.

"It is written with great clearness and compactness of statement, and well maintains the character of the series of books with which it is now associated."—*Electrician.*

"A valuable contribution to the literature of alternating currents."—*Electrical Engineer.*

BALLOONING: A Concise Sketch of its History and Principles. From the best sources, Continental and English. By G. MAY. With Illustrations. 2s. 6d.

"Mr. May gives a clear idea of all the experiments and improvements in aëro-navigation from its beginning, and the various useful purposes to which it has been applied."—*Contemporary Review.*

SEWAGE TREATMENT, PURIFICATION, AND UTILIZATION. A Practical Manual for the Use of Corporations, Local Boards, Medical Officers of Health, Inspectors of Nuisances, Chemists, Manufacturers, Riparian Owners, Engineers, and Ratepayers. By J. W. SLATER, F.E.S., Editor of "Journal of Science." With Illustrations. 6s.

"The writer in addition to a calm and dispassionate view of the situation, gives two chapters on 'Legislation' and 'Sewage Patents.'"—*Spectator.*

A TREATISE ON MANURES; or, the Philosophy of Manuring. A Practical Handbook for the Agriculturist, Manufacturer, and Student. By A. B. GRIFFITHS, Ph.D., F.R.S. (Edin.), F.C.S. 7s. 6d.

"We gladly welcome its appearance as supplying a want long felt in agricultural literature, and recommend every farmer and agricultural student to possess himself with a copy without delay."—*Farm and Home.*

COLOUR IN WOVEN DESIGN. By Professor ROBERTS BEAUMONT, of the Textile Industries Department, The Yorkshire College. With 32 Coloured Plates and numerous Illustrations. 21s.

"An excellent work on the application of colour to woven design."—*Textile Manufacturer.*

"The illustrations are the finest of the kind we have yet come across, and the publishers are to be congratulated on the general excellence of the work."—*Textile Mercury.*

Works in Preparation—

LIGHTNING CONDUCTORS AND LIGHTNING GUARDS. By Professor OLIVER J. LODGE, D.Sc., F.R.S., M.Inst.C.E. With numerous Illustrations. [*In the press.*

THE DYNAMO. By C. C. HAWKINS, A.M.I.C.E., and J. WALLIS. [*Preparing.*

CABLES AND CABLE LAYING. By STUART A. RUSSELL, A.M.Inst.C.E. [*Preparing.*

THE ALKALI-MAKERS' HANDBOOK. By Professor Dr. GEORGE LUNGE and Dr. FERDINAND HURTER. Second Edition, revised, and in great part rewritten. [*In the press.*

ARC AND GLOW LAMPS. New and Revised Edition. [*Preparing.*

THE DRAINAGE OF HABITABLE HOUSES. By W. LEE BEARDMORE, A.M.Inst.C.E., Hon. Sec. to the Civil and Mechanical Engineers' Society.

LONDON: GEORGE BELL & SONS, 4, YORK STREET,
COVENT GARDEN,
AND WHITTAKER & CO., PATERNOSTER SQUARE.

CATALOGUE OF
BOHN'S LIBRARIES.

740 Volumes, £158 14s.

The Publishers are now issuing the Libraries in a NEW AND MORE ATTRACTIVE STYLE OF BINDING. The original bindings endeared to many book-lovers by association will still be kept in stock, but henceforth all orders will be executed in the New binding, unless the contrary is expressly stated.

New Volumes of Standard Works in the various branches of Literature are constantly being added to this Series, which is already unsurpassed in respect to the number, variety, and cheapness of the Works contained in it. The Publishers beg to announce the following Volumes as recently issued or now in preparation:—

Goethe's Faust. Part I. The Original Text, with Hayward's Translation and Notes, carefully revised, with an Introduction and Bibliography, by C. A. Buchheim, Ph.D., Professor of German Language and Literature at King's College, London. *[Immediately.*

Arthur Young's Tour in Ireland. Edited by A. W. Hutton, Librarian, National Liberal Club. 2 vols. *[Preparing.*

Euripides. A New Literal Translation in Prose. y E. P. Coleridge. 2 vols. 5s. each.
  Vol. I.—Rhesus—Medea—Hippolytus—Alcestis—Heraclidæ—Supplices—Troades—Ion—Helena.
  II.—Andromache — Electra — Bacchae — Hecuba — Hercules Furens — Phœnissæ—Orestes—Iphigenia in Tauris—Iphigenia in Aulis—Cyclops. *[See p. 15.*

Voltaire's Tales. Translated by R. B. Boswell. Vol. I. 3s. 6d. *[See p. 8.*

Count Grammont's Memoirs of the Court of Charles II. With the Boscobel Tracts, &c. New Edition. 5s. *[See p. 9.*

Gray's Letters. New Edition. Edited by the Rev. D. C. Tovey, M.A. *[In the press.*

Schools and Masters of Fence. By C. Egerton Castle. New Edition. With numerous Illustrations. *[In the press.*

Montaigne's Essays. Cotton's Translation, revised by W. C. Hazlitt. New Edition. 3 Vols. *[In the press.*

Hartley Coleridge's Essays and Marginalia. Edited by the Lord Chief Justice. *[Preparing.*

Hoffmann's Works. Translated by Lieut.-Colonel Ewing. Vol. II. *[In the press.*

Bohn's Handbooks of Games. New enlarged edition. In 2 vols. *See p. 21.*
  Vol. I.—Table Games, by Major-General Drayson, R.A., R. F. Green, and 'Berkeley.'
  II.—Card Games, by Dr. W. Pole, F.R.S., R. F. Green, 'Berkeley, and Baxter-Wray.

Bohn's Handbooks of Athletic Sports. 8 Vols. *[See p. 21.*

For BOHN'S SELECT LIBRARY, see p. 23.

March, 1892.

BOHN'S LIBRARIES.

STANDARD LIBRARY.

338 *Vols. at* 3s. 6d. *each, excepting those marked otherwise.* (59*l*. 12s.)

ADDISON'S Works. Notes of Bishop Hurd. Short Memoir, Portrait, and 8 Plates of Medals. 6 vols.
This is the most complete edition of Addison's Works issued.

ALFIERI'S Tragedies. In English Verse. With Notes, Arguments, and Introduction, by E. A. Bowring, C.B. 2 vols.

AMERICAN POETRY. — *See Poetry of America.*

BACON'S Moral and Historical Works, including Essays, Apophthegms, Wisdom of the Ancients, New Atlantis, Henry VII., Henry VIII., Elizabeth, Henry Prince of Wales, History of Great Britain, Julius Cæsar, and Augustus Cæsar. With Critical and Biographical Introduction and Notes by J. Devey, M.A. Portrait.

—— *See also Philosophical Library.*

BALLADS AND SONGS of the Peasantry of England, from Oral Recitation, private MSS., Broadsides, &c. Edit. by R. Bell.

BEAUMONT AND FLETCHER. Selections. With Notes and Introduction by Leigh Hunt.

BECKMANN (J.) History of Inventions, Discoveries, and Origins. With Portraits of Beckmann and James Watt. 2 vols.

BELL (Robert).—*See Ballads, Chaucer, Green.*

BOSWELL'S Life of Johnson, with the TOUR in the HEBRIDES and JOHNSONIANA. New Edition, with Notes and Appendices, by the Rev. A. Napier, M.A., Trinity College, Cambridge, Vicar of Holkham, Editor of the Cambridge Edition of the 'Theological Works of Barrow.' With Frontispiece to each vol. 6 vols.

BREMER'S (Frederika) Works. Trans. by M. Howitt. Portrait. 4 vols.

BRINK (B. ten). Early English Literature (to Wiclif). By Bernhard ten Brink. Trans. by Prof. H. M. Kennedy.

BROWNE'S (Sir Thomas) Works. Edit. by S. Wilkin, with Dr. Johnson's Life of Browne. Portrait. 3 vols.

BURKE'S Works. 6 vols.

—— **Speeches on the Impeachment** of Warren Hastings; and Letters. 2 vols.

—— **Life.** By Sir J. Prior. Portrait.

BURNS (Robert). Life of. By J. G. Lockhart, D.C.L. A new and enlarged edition. With Notes and Appendices by W. Scott Douglas. Portrait.

BUTLER'S (Bp.) Analogy of Religion, Natural and Revealed, to the Constitution and Course of Nature; with Two Dissertations on Identity and Virtue, and Fifteen Sermons. With Introductions, Notes, and Memoir. Portrait.

CAMOËNS' Lusiad, or the Discovery of India. An Epic Poem. Trans. from the Portuguese, with Dissertation, Historical Sketch, and Life, by W. J. Mickle. 5th edition.

CARAFAS (The) of Maddaloni. Naples under Spanish Dominion. Trans. from the German of Alfred de Reumont. Portrait of Massaniello.

CARREL. The Counter-Revolution in England for the Re-establishment of Popery under Charles II. and James II., by Armand Carrel; with Fox's History of James II. and Lord Lonsdale's Memoir of James II. Portrait of Carrel.

CARRUTHERS. — *See Pope, in Illustrated Library.*

CARY'S Dante. The Vision of Hell, Purgatory, and Paradise. Trans. by Rev. H. F. Cary, M.A. With Life, Chronological View of his Age, Notes, and Index of Proper Names. Portrait.
This is the authentic edition, containing Mr. Cary's last corrections, with additional notes.

CELLINI (Benvenuto). Memoirs of, by himself. With Notes of G. P. Carpani. Trans. by T. Roscoe. Portrait.

CERVANTES' Galatea. A Pastoral Romance. Trans. by G. W. J. Gyll.

—— **Exemplary Novels.** Trans. by W. K. Kelly.

—— **Don Quixote de la Mancha.** Motteux's Translation revised. With Lockhart's Life and Notes. 2 vols.

CHAUCER'S Poetical Works. With Poems formerly attributed to him. With a Memoir, Introduction, Notes, and a Glossary, by R. Bell. Improved edition, with Preliminary Essay by Rev. W. W. Skeat, M.A. Portrait. 4 vols.

CLASSIC TALES, containing Rasselas, Vicar of Wakefield, Gulliver's Travels, and The Sentimental Journey.

COLERIDGE'S (S. T.) Friend. A Series of Essays on Morals, Politics, and Religion. Portrait.

—— **Aids to Reflection. Confessions** of an Inquiring Spirit; and Essays on Faith and the Common Prayer-book. New Edition, revised.

—— **Table-Talk and Omniana.** By T. Ashe, B.A.

—— **Lectures on Shakespeare and** other Poets. Edit. by T. Ashe, B.A.
Containing the lectures taken down in 1811-12 by J. P. Collier, and those delivered at Bristol in 1813.

—— **Biographia Literaria; or, Biographical Sketches of my Literary Life and Opinions; with Two Lay Sermons.

—— **Miscellanies, Æsthetic and** Literary; to which is added, THE THEORY OF LIFE. Collected and arranged by T. Ashe, B.A.

COMMINES.—*See Philip.*

CONDÉ'S History of the Dominion of the Arabs in Spain. Trans. by Mrs. Foster. Portrait of Abderahmen ben Moavia. 3 vols.

COWPER'S Complete Works, Poems, Correspondence, and Translations. Edit. with Memoir by R. Southey. 45 Engravings. 8 vols.

COXE'S Memoirs of the Duke of Marlborough. With his original Correspondence, from family records at Blenheim. Revised edition. Portraits. 3 vols.
*** An Atlas of the plans of Marlborough's campaigns, 4to. 10s. 6d.

COXE'S History of the House of Austria. From the Foundation of the Monarchy by Rhodolph of Hapsburgh to the Death of Leopold II., 1218-1792. By Archdn. Coxe. With Continuation from the Accession of Francis I. to the Revolution of 1848. 4 Portraits. 4 vols.

CUNNINGHAM'S Lives of the most Eminent British Painters. With Notes and 16 fresh Lives by Mrs. Heaton. 3 vols.

DEFOE'S Novels and Miscellaneous Works. With Prefaces and Notes, including those attributed to Sir W. Scott. Portrait. 7 vols.

**DE LOLME'S Constitution of England, in which it is compared both with the Republican form of Government and the other Monarchies of Europe. Edit., with Life and Notes, by J. Macgregor.

DUNLOP'S History of Fiction. New Edition, revised. By Henry Wilson. 2 vols., 5s. each.

EDGEWORTH'S Stories for Children. With 8 Illustrations by L. Speed.

ELZE'S Shakespeare.—*See Shakespeare*

EMERSON'S Works. 3 vols.
Vol. I.—Essays, Lectures, and Poems.
Vol. II.—English Traits, Nature, and Conduct of Life.
Vol. III.—Society and Solitude—Letters and Social Aims—Miscellaneous Papers (hitherto uncollected)—May-Day, &c.

FOSTER'S (John) Life and Correspondence. Edit. by J. E. Ryland. Portrait. 2 vols.

—— **Lectures at Broadmead Chapel.** Edit. by J. E. Ryland. 2 vols.

—— **Critical Essays contributed to** the 'Eclectic Review.' Edit. by J. E. Ryland. 2 vols.

—— **Essays: On Decision of Character;** on a Man's writing Memoirs of Himself; on the epithet Romantic; on one aversion of Men of Taste to Evangelical Religion.

—— **Essays on the Evils of Popular** Ignorance, and a Discourse on the Propagation of Christianity in India.

—— **Essay on the Improvement of** Time, with Notes of Sermons and other Pieces.

—— **Fosteriana:** selected from periodical papers, edit. by H. G. Bohn.

FOX (Rt. Hon. C. J.)—*See Carrel.*

GIBBON'S Decline and Fall of the Roman Empire. Complete and unabridged, with variorum Notes; including those of Guizot, Wenck, Niebuhr, Hugo, Neander, and others. 7 vols. 2 Maps and Portrait.

GOETHE'S Works. Trans. into English by E. A. Bowring, C.B., Anna Swanwick, Sir Walter Scott, &c. &c. 14 vols.
Vols. I. and II.—Autobiography and Annals. Portrait.
Vol. III.—Faust. Complete.
Vol. IV.—Novels and Tales: containing Elective Affinities, Sorrows of Werther, The German Emigrants, The Good Women, and a Nouvelette.
Vol. V.—Wilhelm Meister's Apprenticeship.
Vol. VI.—Conversations with Eckerman and Soret.
Vol. VII.—Poems and Ballads in the original Metres, including Hermann and Dorothea.
Vol. VIII.—Goetz von Berlichingen, Torquato Tasso, Egmont, Iphigenia, Clavigo, Wayward Lover, and Fellow Culprits.
Vol. IX.—Wilhelm Meister's Travels. Complete Edition.
Vol. X.—Tour in Italy. Two Parts. And Second Residence in Rome.
Vol. XI.—Miscellaneous Travels, Letters from Switzerland, Campaign in France, Siege of Mainz, and Rhine Tour.
Vol. XII.—Early and Miscellaneous Letters, including Letters to his Mother, with Biography and Notes.
Vol. XIII.—Correspondence with Zelter.
Vol. XIV.—Reineke Fox, West-Eastern Divan and Achilleid. Translated in original metres by A. Rogers.

—— **Correspondence with Schiller.** 2 vols.—*See Schiller.*

—— **Faust.**—*See Collegiate Series.*

GOLDSMITH'S Works. 5 vols.
Vol. I.—Life, Vicar of Wakefield, Essays, and Letters.
Vol. II.—Poems, Plays, Bee, Cock Lane Ghost.
Vol. III.—The Citizen of the World, Polite Learning in Europe.
Vol. IV.—Biographies, Criticisms, Later Essays.
Vol. V.—Prefaces, Natural History, Letters, Goody Two-Shoes, Index.

GREENE, MARLOWE, and BEN JONSON (Poems of). With Notes and Memoirs by R. Bell.

GREGORY'S (Dr.) The Evidences, Doctrines, and Duties of the Christian Religion.

GRIMM'S Household Tales. With the Original Notes. Trans. by Mrs. A. Hunt. Introduction by Andrew Lang, M.A. 2 vols.

GUIZOT'S History of Representative Government in Europe. Trans. by A. R. Scoble.

—— **English Revolution of 1640.** From the Accession of Charles I. to his Death. Trans. by W. Hazlitt. Portrait.

—— **History of Civilisation.** From the Roman Empire to the French Revolution. Trans. by W. Hazlitt. Portraits. 3 vols.

HALL'S (Rev. Robert) Works and Remains. Memoir by Dr. Gregory and Essay by J. Foster. Portrait.

HAUFF'S Tales. The Caravan—The Sheikh of Alexandria—The Inn in the Spessart. Translated by Prof. S. Mendel.

HAWTHORNE'S Tales. 3 vols.
Vol. I.—Twice-told Tales, and the Snow Image.
Vol. II.—Scarlet Letter, and the House with Seven Gables.
Vol. III.—Transformation, and Blithedale Romance.

HAZLITT'S (W.) Works. 7 vols.
—— **Table-Talk.**
—— **The Literature of the Age of Elizabeth and Characters of Shakespear's Plays.**
—— **English Poets and English Comic Writers.**
—— **The Plain Speaker.** Opinions on Books, Men, and Things.
—— **Round Table.** Conversations of James Northcote, R.A.; Characteristics.
—— **Sketches and Essays,** and Winterslow.
—— **Spirit of the Age;** or, Contemporary Portraits. New Edition, by W. Carew Hazlitt.

HEINE'S Poems. Translated in the original Metres, with Life by E. A. Bowring, C.B.

—— **Travel-Pictures.** The Tour in the Harz, Norderney, and Book of Ideas, together with the Romantic School. Trans. by F. Storr. With Maps and Appendices.

HOFFMANN'S Works. The Serapion Brethren. Vol. I. Trans. by Lt.-Col. Ewing. [*Vol. II. in the press.*]

HOOPER'S (G.) Waterloo: The Downfall of the First Napoleon: a History of the Campaign of 1815. By George Hooper. With Maps and Plans. New Edition, revised.

HUGO'S (Victor) Dramatic Works: Hernani—RuyBlas—The King's Diversion. Translated by Mrs. Newton Crosland and F. L. Slous.

—— **Poems**, chiefly Lyrical. Collected by H. L. Williams.

HUNGARY: its History and Revolution, with Memoir of Kossuth. Portrait.

HUTCHINSON (Colonel). Memoirs of. By his Widow, with her Autobiography, and the Siege of Lathom House. Portrait.

IRVING'S (Washington) Complete Works. 15 vols.

—— **Life and Letters.** By his Nephew, Pierre E. Irving. With Index and a Portrait. 2 vols.

JAMES'S (G. P. R.) Life of Richard Cœur de Lion. Portraits of Richard and Philip Augustus. 2 vols.

—— **Louis XIV.** Portraits. 2 vols.

JAMESON (Mrs.) Shakespeare's Heroines. Characteristics of Women. By Mrs. Jameson.

JEAN PAUL.—*See Richter.*

JOHNSON'S Lives of the Poets. Edited, with Notes, by Mrs. Alexander Napier. And an Introduction by Professor J. W. Hales, M.A. 3 vols.

JONSON (Ben). Poems of.—*See Greene.*

JOSEPHUS (Flavius), The Works of. Whiston's Translation. Revised by Rev. A. R. Shilleto, M.A. With Topographical and Geographical Notes by Colonel Sir C. W. Wilson, K.C.B. 5 vols.

JUNIUS'S Letters. With Woodfall's Notes. An Essay on the Authorship. Facsimiles of Handwriting. 2 vols.

LA FONTAINE'S Fables. In English Verse, with Essay on the Fabulists. By Elizur Wright.

LAMARTINE'S The Girondists, or Personal Memoirs of the Patriots of the French Revolution. Trans. by H. T. Ryde. Portraits of Robespierre, Madame Roland, and Charlotte Corday. 3 vols.

—— **The Restoration of Monarchy in France** (a Sequel to The Girondists). 5 Portraits. 4 vols.

—— **The French Revolution of 1848.** Portraits.

LAMB'S (Charles) Elia and Eliana. Complete Edition. Portrait.

LAMB'S (Charles) Specimens of English Dramatic Poets of the time of Elizabeth. With Notes and the Extracts from the Garrick Plays.

—— **Talfourd's Letters of Charles Lamb.** New Edition, by W. Carew Hazlitt. 2 vols.

LANZI'S History of Painting in Italy, from the Period of the Revival of the Fine Arts to the End of the 18th Century. With Memoir and Portraits. Trans. by T. Roscoe. 3 vols.

LAPPENBERG'S England under the Anglo-Saxon Kings. Trans. by B. Thorpe, F.S.A. 2 vols.

LESSING'S Dramatic Works. Complete. By E. Bell, M.A. With Memoir by H. Zimmern. Portrait. 2 vols.

—— **Laokoon, Dramatic Notes, and Representation of Death by the Ancients.** Trans. by E. C. Beasley and Helen Zimmern. Frontispiece.

LOCKE'S Philosophical Works, containing Human Understanding, Controversy with Bishop of Worcester, Malebranche's Opinions, Natural Philosophy, Reading and Study. With Introduction, Analysis, and Notes, by J. A. St. John. Portrait. 2 vols.

—— **Life and Letters,** with Extracts from his Common-place Books. By Lord King.

LOCKHART (J. G.)—*See Burns.*

LUTHER'S Table-Talk. Trans. by W. Hazlitt. With Life by A. Chalmers, and LUTHER'S CATECHISM. Portrait after Cranach.

—— **Autobiography.**—*See Michelet.*

MACHIAVELLI'S History of Florence, THE PRINCE, Savonarola, Historical Tracts, and Memoir. Portrait.

MARLOWE. Poems of.—*See Greene.*

MARTINEAU'S (Harriet) History of England (including History of the Peace) from 1800-1846. 5 vols.

MENZEL'S History of Germany, from the Earliest Period to 1842. Portraits. 3 vols.

MICHELET'S Autobiography of Luther. Trans. by W. Hazlitt. With Notes.

—— **The French Revolution** to the Flight of the King in 1791. Frontispiece.

MIGNET'S The French Revolution, from 1789 to 1814. Portrait of Napoleon.

MILTON'S Prose Works. With Preface, Preliminary Remarks by J. A. St. John, and Index. 5 vols. Portraits.

—— **Poetical Works.** With 120 Wood Engravings. 2 vols.

MITFORD'S (Miss) Our Village. Sketches of Rural Character and Scenery. 2 Engravings. 2 vols.

MOLIERE'S Dramatic Works. In English Prose, by C. H. Wall. With a Life and a Portrait. 3 vols.
'It is not too much to say that we have here probably as good a translation of Molière as can be given.'—*Academy.*

MONTAGU. Letters and Works of Lady Mary Wortley Montagu. Lord Wharncliffe's Third Edition. Edited by W. Moy Thomas. New and revised edition. With steel plates. 2 vols. 5s. each.

MONTESQUIEU'S Spirit of Laws. Revised Edition, with D'Alembert's Analysis, Notes, and Memoir. 2 vols.

NEANDER (Dr. A.) History of the Christian Religion and Church. Trans. by J. Torrey. With Short Memoir. 10 vols.

—— **Life of Jesus Christ, in its Historical Connexion and Development.**

—— **The Planting and Training of** the Christian Church by the Apostles. With the Antignosticus, or Spirit of Tertullian. Trans. by J. E. Ryland. 2 vols.

—— **Lectures on the History of** Christian Dogmas. Trans. by J. E. Ryland. 2 vols.

—— **Memorials of Christian Life in** the Early and Middle Ages; including Light in Dark Places. Trans. by J. E. Ryland

NORTH'S Lives of the Right Hon. Francis North, Baron Guildford, the Hon. Sir Dudley North, and the Hon. and Rev. Dr. John North. By the Hon. Roger North. Edited by A. Jessopp, D.D. With 3 Portraits. 3 vols. 3s. 6d. each.
'Lovers of good literature will rejoice at the appearance of a new, handy, and complete edition of so justly famous a book, and will congratulate themselves that it has found so competent and skilful an editor as Dr. Jessopp.'—*Times.*

OCKLEY (S.) History of the Saracens and their Conquests in Syria, Persia, and Egypt. Comprising the Lives of Mohammed and his Successors to the Death of Abdalmelik, the Eleventh Caliph. By Simon Ockley, B.D., Portrait of Mohammed.

PASCAL'S Thoughts. Translated from the Text of M. Auguste Molinier by C. Kegan Paul. 3rd edition.

PERCY'S Reliques of Ancient English Poetry, consisting of Ballads, Songs, and other Pieces of our earlier Poets, with some few of later date. With Essay on Ancient Minstrels, and Glossary. 2 vols.

PHILIP DE COMMINES. Memoirs of. Containing the Histories of Louis XI. and Charles VIII., and Charles the Bold, Duke of Burgundy. With the History of Louis XI., by Jean de Troyes. Translated, with a Life and Notes, by A. R. Scoble. Portraits. 2 vols.

PLUTARCH'S LIVES. Translated, with Notes and Life, by A. Stewart, M.A., late Fellow of Trinity College, Cambridge, and G. Long, M.A. 4 vols.

POETRY OF AMERICA. Selections from One Hundred Poets, from 1776 to 1876. With Introductory Review, and Specimens of Negro Melody, by W. J. Linton. Portrait of W. Whitman.

RACINE'S (Jean) Dramatic Works. A metrical English version, with Biographical notice. By R. Bruce Boswell, M.A. Oxon. 2 vols.

RANKE (L.) History of the Popes, their Church and State, and their Conflicts with Protestantism in the 16th and 17th Centuries. Trans. by E. Foster. Portraits 3 vols.

—— **History of Servia.** Trans. by Mrs. Kerr. To which is added, The Slave Provinces of Turkey, by Cyprien Robert.

—— **History of the Latin and Teutonic Nations.** 1494-1514. Trans. by P. A. Ashworth, translator of Dr. Gneist's 'History of the English Constitution.'

REUMONT (Alfred de).—*See Carafas.*

REYNOLDS' (Sir J.) Literary Works. With Memoir and Remarks by H. W. Beechy. 2 vols.

RICHTER (Jean Paul). Levana, a Treatise on Education; together with the Autobiography, and a short Memoir.

—— **Flower, Fruit, and Thorn Pieces,** or the Wedded Life, Death, and Marriage of Siebenkaes. Translated by Alex. Ewing. The only complete English translation.

ROSCOE'S (W.) Life of Leo X., with Notes, Historical Documents, and Dissertation on Lucretia Borgia. 3 Portraits. 2 vols.

—— **Lorenzo de' Medici,** called 'The Magnificent,' with Copyright Notes, Poems, Letters, &c. With Memoir of Roscoe and Portrait of Lorenzo.

RUSSIA, History of, from the earliest Period to the Crimean War. By W. K. Kelly. 3 Portraits. 2 vols.

SCHILLER'S Works. 7 vols.
Vol. I.—History of the Thirty Years' War. Rev. A. J. W. Morrison, M.A. Portrait.
Vol. II.—History of the Revolt in the Netherlands, the Trials of Counts Egmont and Horn, the Siege of Antwerp, and the Disturbance of France preceding the Reign of Henry IV. Translated by Rev. A. J. W. Morrison and L. Dora Schmitz.
Vol. III.—Don Carlos. R. D. Boylan—Mary Stuart. Mellish — Maid of Orleans. Anna Swanwick—Bride of Messina. A. Lodge, M.A. Together with the Use of the Chorus in Tragedy (a short Essay). Engravings.
These Dramas are all translated in metre.
Vol. IV.—Robbers—Fiesco—Love and Intrigue—Demetrius—Ghost Seer—Sport of Divinity.
The Dramas in this volume are in prose.
Vol. V.—Poems. E. A. Bowring, C.B.
Vol. VI.—Essays, Æsthetical and Philosophical, including the Dissertation on the Connexion between the Animal and Spiritual in Man.
Vol. VII. — Wallenstein's Camp. J. Churchill. — Piccolomini and Death of Wallenstein. S. T. Coleridge.—William Tell. Sir Theodore Martin, K.C.B., LL.D.

SCHILLER and GOETHE. Correspondence between, from A.D. 1794-1805. Trans. by L. Dora Schmitz. 2 vols.

SCHLEGEL (F.) Lectures on the Philosophy of Life and the Philosophy of Language. Trans. by A. J. W. Morrison.

—— **The History of Literature,** Ancient and Modern.

—— **The Philosophy of History.** With Memoir and Portrait. Trans. by J. B. Robertson.

—— **Modern History,** with the Lectures entitled Cæsar and Alexander, and The Beginning of our History. Translated by L. Purcell and R. H. Whitelock.

—— **Æsthetic and Miscellaneous Works,** containing Letters on Christian Art, Essay on Gothic Architecture, Remarks on the Romance Poetry of the Middle Ages, on Shakspeare, the Limits of the Beautiful, and on the Language and Wisdom of the Indians. By E. J. Millington.

SCHLEGEL (A. W.) Dramatic Art and Literature. By J. Black. With Memoir by Rev. A. J. W. Morrison. Portrait.

SCHUMANN (Robert), His Life and Works. By A. Reissmann. Trans. by A. L. Alger.

—— **Early Letters.** Translated by May Herbert. With Preface by Sir G. Grove.

SHAKESPEARE'S Dramatic Art. The History and Character of Shakspeare's Plays. By Dr. H. Ulrici. Trans. by L. Dora Schmitz. 2 vols.

SHAKESPEARE (William). A Literary Biography by Karl Elze, Ph.D., LL.D. Translated by L. Dora Schmitz. 5s.

SHERIDAN'S Dramatic Works. With Memoir. Portrait (after Reynolds).

SISMONDI'S History of the Literature of the South of Europe. Trans. by T. Roscoe. Portraits. 2 vols.

SMITH'S (Adam) Theory of Moral Sentiments; with Essay on the First Formation of Languages, and Critical Memoir by Dugald Stewart.

—— *See Economic Library.*

SMYTH'S (Professor) Lectures on Modern History; from the Irruption of the Northern Nations to the close of the American Revolution. 2 vols.

—— **Lectures on the French Revolution.** With Index. 2 vols.

SOUTHEY.—*See Cowper, Wesley, and (Illustrated Library) Nelson.*

STURM'S Morning Communings with God, or Devotional Meditations for Every Day. Trans. by W. Johnstone, M.A.

SULLY. Memoirs of the Duke of, Prime Minister to Henry the Great. With Notes and Historical Introduction. 4 Portraits. 4 vols.

TAYLOR'S (Bishop Jeremy) Holy Living and Dying, with Prayers, containing the Whole Duty of a Christian and the parts of Devotion fitted to all Occasions. Portrait.

TEN BRINK.—*See Brink.*

THIERRY'S Conquest of England by the Normans; its Causes, and its Consequences in England and the Continent. By W. Hazlitt. With short Memoir. 2 Portraits. 2 vols.

ULRICI (Dr.)—*See Shakespeare.*

VASARI. Lives of the most Eminent Painters, Sculptors, and Architects. By Mrs. J. Foster, with selected Notes. Portrait. 6 vols., Vol. VI. being an additional Volume of Notes by Dr. J. P. Richter.

VOLTAIRE'S Tales. Translated by R. B. Boswell. Vol. I., containing 'Babouc,' Memnon, Candide, L'Ingénu, and other Tales.

WERNER'S Templars in Cyprus. Trans. by E. A. M. Lewis.

WESLEY, the Life of, and the Rise and Progress of Methodism. By Robert Southey. Portrait. 5s.

WHEATLEY. A Rational Illustration of the Book of Common Prayer.

YOUNG (Arthur) Travels in France. Edited by Miss Betham Edwards. With a Portrait.

HISTORICAL LIBRARY.

23 Volumes at 5s. each. (5l. 15s. per set.)

EVELYN'S Diary and Correspondence, with the Private Correspondence of Charles I. and Sir Edward Nicholas, and between Sir Edward Hyde (Earl of Clarendon) and Sir Richard Browne. Edited from the Original MSS. by W. Bray, F.A.S. 4 vols. 45 Engravings (after Vandyke, Lely, Kneller, and Jamieson, &c.).
N.B.—This edition contains 130 letters from Evelyn and his wife, printed by permission, and contained in no other edition.

JESSE'S Memoirs of the Court of England under the Stuarts, including the Protectorate. 3 vols. With Index and 42 Portraits (after Vandyke, Lely, &c.).

—— **Memoirs of the Pretenders and their Adherents.** 6 Portraits.

GRAMMONT (Count). Memoirs of the Court of Charles II. Edited by Sir Walter Scott. Together with the 'Boscobel Tracts,' including two not before published, &c. New Edition, thoroughly revised. With Portrait of Nell Gwynne.

PEPYS' Diary and Correspondence. With Life and Notes, by Lord Braybrooke. With Appendix containing additional Letters and Index. 4 vols., with 31 Engravings (after Vandyke, Sir P. Lely, Holbein, Kneller, &c.).
N.B.—This is a reprint of Lord Braybrooke's fourth and last edition, containing all his latest notes and corrections, the copyright of the publishers.

NUGENT'S (Lord) Memorials of Hampden, his Party and Times. With Memoir. 12 Portraits (after Vandyke and others).

STRICKLAND'S (Agnes) Lives of the Queens of England from the Norman Conquest. From authentic Documents, public and private. 6 Portraits. 6 vols.

—— **Life of Mary Queen of Scots.** 2 Portraits. 2 vols.

—— **Lives of the Tudor and Stuart Princesses.** With 2 Portraits.

PHILOSOPHICAL LIBRARY.

17 Vols. at 5s. each, excepting those marked otherwise. (3l. 19s. per set.)

BACON'S Novum Organum and Advancement of Learning. With Notes by J. Devey, M.A.

BAX. A Handbook of the History of Philosophy, for the use of Students. By E. Belfort Bax, Editor of Kant's 'Prolegomena.'

COMTE'S Philosophy of the Sciences. An Exposition of the Principles of the *Cours de Philosophie Positive*. By G. H. Lewes, Author of 'The Life of Goethe.'

DRAPER (Dr. J. W.) A History of the Intellectual Development of Europe. 2 vols.

HEGEL'S Philosophy of History. By J. Sibree, M.A.

KANT'S Critique of Pure Reason. By J. M. D. Meiklejohn.
—— **Prolegomena and Metaphysical Foundations of Natural Science,** with Biography and Memoir by E. Belfort Bax. Portrait.

LOGIC, or the Science of Inference. A Popular Manual. By J. Devey.

MILLER (Professor). History Philosophically Illustrated, from the Fall of the Roman Empire to the French Revolution. With Memoir. 4 vols. 3s. 6d. each.

SCHOPENHAUER on the Fourfold Root of the Principle of Sufficient Reason, and on the Will in Nature. Trans. from the German.

—— **Essays.** Selected and Translated by E. Belfort Bax.

SPINOZA'S Chief Works. Trans. with Introduction by R. H. M. Elwes. 2 vols.
Vol. I.—Tractatus Theologico-Politicus—Political Treatise.
Vol. II.— Improvement of the Understanding—Ethics—Letters.

THEOLOGICAL LIBRARY.

15 *Vols. at* 5s. *each* (*except Chillingworth*, 3s. 6d.).   (3l. 13s. 6d. *per set.*)

BLEEK. Introduction to the Old Testament. By Friedrich Bleek. Trans. under the supervision of Rev. E. Venables, Residentiary Canon of Lincoln. 2 vols.

CHILLINGWORTH'S Religion of Protestants. 3s. 6d.

EUSEBIUS. Ecclesiastical History of Eusebius Pamphilus, Bishop of Cæsarea. Trans. by Rev. C. F. Cruse, M.A. With Notes, Life, and Chronological Tables.

EVAGRIUS. History of the Church. —*See Theodoret.*

HARDWICK. History of the Articles of Religion; to which is added a Series of Documents from A.D. 1536 to A.D. 1615. Ed. by Rev. F. Proctor.

HENRY'S (Matthew) Exposition of the Book of Psalms. Numerous Woodcuts.

PEARSON (John, D.D.) Exposition of the Creed. Edit. by E. Walford, M.A. With Notes, Analysis, and Indexes.

PHILO-JUDÆUS, Works of. The Contemporary of Josephus. Trans. by C. D. Yonge. 4 vols.

PHILOSTORGIUS. Ecclesiastical History of.—*See Sozomen.*

SOCRATES' Ecclesiastical History. Comprising a History of the Church from Constantine, A.D. 305, to the 38th year of Theodosius II. With Short Account of the Author, and selected Notes.

SOZOMEN'S Ecclesiastical History. A.D. 324-440. With Notes, Prefatory Remarks by Valesius, and Short Memoir. Together with the ECCLESIASTICAL HISTORY OF PHILOSTORGIUS, as epitomised by Photius. Trans. by Rev. E. Walford, M.A. With Notes and brief Life.

THEODORET and EVAGRIUS. Histories of the Church from A.D. 332 to the Death of Theodore of Mopsuestia, A.D. 427; and from A.D. 431 to A.D. 544. With Memoirs.

WIESELER'S (Karl) Chronological Synopsis of the Four Gospels. Trans. by Rev. Canon Venables.

ANTIQUARIAN LIBRARY.

35 *Vols. at* 5s. *each.*   (8l. 15s. *per set.*)

ANGLO-SAXON CHRONICLE. — *See Bede.*

ASSER'S Life of Alfred.—*See Six O. E. Chronicles.*

BEDE'S (Venerable) Ecclesiastical History of England. Together with the ANGLO-SAXON CHRONICLE. With Notes, Short Life, Analysis, and Map. Edit. by J. A. Giles, D.C.L.

BOETHIUS'S Consolation of Philosophy. King Alfred's Anglo-Saxon Version of. With an English Translation on opposite pages, Notes, Introduction, and Glossary, by Rev. S. Fox, M.A. To which is added the Anglo-Saxon Version of the METRES OF BOETHIUS, with a free Translation by Martin F. Tupper, D.C.L.

BRAND'S Popular Antiquities of England, Scotland, and Ireland. Illustrating the Origin of our Vulgar and Provincial Customs, Ceremonies, and Superstitions. By Sir Henry Ellis, K.H., F.R.S. Frontispiece. 3 vols.

CHRONICLES of the CRUSADES. Contemporary Narratives of Richard Cœur de Lion, by Richard of Devizes and Geoffrey de Vinsauf; and of the Crusade at Saint Louis, by Lord John de Joinville. With Short Notes. Illuminated Frontispiece from an old MS.

DYER'S (T. F. T.) British Popular Customs, Present and Past. An Account of the various Games and Customs associated with different Days of the Year in the British Isles, arranged according to the Calendar. By the Rev. T. F. Thiselton Dyer, M.A.

EARLY TRAVELS IN PALESTINE. Comprising the Narratives of Arculf, Willibald, Bernard, Sæwulf, Sigurd, Benjamin of Tudela, Sir John Maundeville, De la Brocquière, and Maundrell; all unabridged. With Introduction and Notes by Thomas Wright. Map of Jerusalem.

ELLIS (G.) Specimens of Early English Metrical Romances, relating to Arthur, Merlin, Guy of Warwick, Richard Cœur de Lion, Charlemagne, Roland, &c. &c. With Historical Introduction by J. O. Halliwell, F.R.S. Illuminated Frontispiece from an old MS.

ETHELWERD. Chronicle of.—*See Six O. E. Chronicles.*

FLORENCE OF WORCESTER'S Chronicle, with the Two Continuations: comprising Annals of English History from the Departure of the Romans to the Reign of Edward I. Trans., with Notes, by Thomas Forester, M.A.

GEOFFREY OF MONMOUTH. Chronicle of.—*See Six O. E. Chronicles.*

GESTA ROMANORUM, or Entertaining Moral Stories invented by the Monks. Trans. with Notes by the Rev. Charles Swan. Edit. by W. Hooper, M.A.

GILDAS. Chronicle of.—*See Six O. E. Chronicles.*

GIRALDUS CAMBRENSIS' Historical Works. Containing Topography of Ireland, and History of the Conquest of Ireland, by Th. Forester, M.A. Itinerary through Wales, and Description of Wales, by Sir R. Colt Hoare.

HENRY OF HUNTINGDON'S History of the English, from the Roman Invasion to the Accession of Henry II.; with the Acts of King Stephen, and the Letter to Walter. By T. Forester, M.A. Frontispiece from an old MS.

INGULPH'S Chronicles of the Abbey of Croyland, with the CONTINUATION by Peter of Blois and others. Trans. with Notes by H. T. Riley, B.A.

KEIGHTLEY'S (Thomas) Fairy Mythology, illustrative of the Romance and Superstition of Various Countries. Frontispiece by Cruikshank.

LEPSIUS'S Letters from Egypt, Ethiopia, and the Peninsula of Sinai; to which are added, Extracts from his Chronology of the Egyptians, with reference to the Exodus of the Israelites. By L. and J. B. Horner. Maps and Coloured View of Mount Barkal.

MALLET'S Northern Antiquities, or an Historical Account of the Manners, Customs, Religions, and Literature of the Ancient Scandinavians. Trans. by Bishop Percy. With Translation of the PROSE EDDA, and Notes by J. A. Blackwell. Also an Abstract of the 'Eyrbyggia Saga' by Sir Walter Scott. With Glossary and Coloured Frontispiece.

MARCO POLO'S Travels; with Notes and Introduction. Edit. by T. Wright.

MATTHEW PARIS'S English History, from 1235 to 1273. By Rev. J. A. Giles, D.C.L. With Frontispiece. 3 vols.—*See also Roger of Wendover.*

MATTHEW OF WESTMINSTER'S Flowers of History, especially such as relate to the affairs of Britain, from the beginning of the World to A.D. 1307. By C. D. Yonge. 2 vols.

NENNIUS. Chronicle of.—*See Six O. E. Chronicles.*

ORDERICUS VITALIS' Ecclesiastical History of England and Normandy. With Notes, Introduction of Guizot, and the Critical Notice of M. Delille, by T. Forester, M.A. To which is added the CHRONICLE OF St. EVROULT. With General and Chronological Indexes. 4 vols.

PAULI'S (Dr. R.) Life of Alfred the Great. To which is appended Alfred's ANGLO-SAXON VERSION OF OROSIUS. With literal Translation interpaged, Notes, and an ANGLO-SAXON GRAMMAR and Glossary, by B. Thorpe. Frontispiece.

RICHARD OF CIRENCESTER. Chronicle of.—*See Six O. E. Chronicles.*

ROGER DE HOVEDEN'S Annals of English History, comprising the History of England and of other Countries of Europe from A.D. 732 to A.D. 1201. With Notes by H. T. Riley, B.A. 2 vols.

ROGER OF WENDOVER'S Flowers of History, comprising the History of England from the Descent of the Saxons to A.D. 1235, formerly ascribed to Matthew Paris. With Notes and Index by J. A. Giles, D.C.L. 2 vols.

SIX OLD ENGLISH CHRONICLES: viz., Asser's Life of Alfred and the Chronicles of Ethelwerd Gildas, Nennius, Geoffrey of Monmouth, and Richard of Cirencester. Edit., with Notes, by J. A. Giles, D.C.L. Portrait of Alfred.

WILLIAM OF MALMESBURY'S Chronicle of the Kings of England, from the Earliest Period to King Stephen. By Rev. J. Sharpe. With Notes by J. A. Giles, D.C.L. Frontispiece.

YULE-TIDE STORIES. A Collection of Scandinavian and North-German Popular Tales and Traditions, from the Swedish, Danish, and German Edit. by B. Thorpe.

ILLUSTRATED LIBRARY.

78 Vols. at 5s. each, excepting those marked otherwise. (19*l.* 7*s.* 6*d. per set.*)

ALLEN'S (Joseph, R.N.) Battles of the British Navy. Revised edition, with Indexes of Names and Events, and 57 Portraits and Plans. 2 vols.

ANDERSEN'S Danish Fairy Tales. By Caroline Peachey. With Short Life and 120 Wood Engravings.

ARIOSTO'S Orlando Furioso. In English Verse by W. S. Rose. With Notes and Short Memoir. Portrait after Titian, and 24 Steel Engravings. 2 vols.

BECHSTEIN'S Cage and Chamber Birds: their Natural History, Habits, &c. Together with SWEET'S BRITISH WARBLERS. 43 Coloured Plates and Woodcuts.

BONOMI'S Nineveh and its Palaces. The Discoveries of Botta and Layard applied to the Elucidation of Holy Writ. 7 Plates and 294 Woodcuts.

BUTLER'S Hudibras, with Variorum Notes and Biography. Portrait and 28 Illustrations.

CATTERMOLE'S Evenings at Haddon Hall. Romantic Tales of the Olden Times. With 24 Steel Engravings after Cattermole.

CHINA, Pictorial, Descriptive, and Historical, with some account of Ava and the Burmese, Siam, and Anam. Map, and nearly 100 Illustrations.

CRAIK'S (G. L.) Pursuit of Knowledge under Difficulties: Illustrated by Anecdotes and Memoirs. Numerous Woodcut Portraits.

CRUIKSHANK'S Three Courses and a Dessert; comprising three Sets of Tales, West Country, Irish, and Legal; and a Mélange. With 50 Illustrations by Cruikshank.

—— **Punch and Judy.** The Dialogue of the Puppet Show; an Account of its Origin, &c. 24 Illustrations and Coloured Plates by Cruikshank.

DANTE, in English Verse, by I. C. Wright, M.A. With Introduction and Memoir. Portrait and 34 Steel Engravings after Flaxman.

DIDRON'S Christian Iconography; a History of Christian Art in the Middle Ages. By the late A. N. Didron. Trans. by E. J. Millington, and completed, with Additions and Appendices, by Margaret Stokes. 2 vols. With numerous Illustrations.

Vol. I. The History of the Nimbus, the Aureole, and the Glory; Representations of the Persons of the Trinity.

Vol. II. The Trinity; Angels; Devils; The Soul; The Christian Scheme. Appendices.

DYER (Dr. T. H.) Pompeii: its Buildings and Antiquities. An Account of the City, with full Description of the Remains and Recent Excavations, and an Itinerary for Visitors. By T. H. Dyer, LL.D. Nearly 300 Wood Engravings, Map, and Plan. 7*s.* 6*d.*

—— **Rome:** History of the City, with Introduction on recent Excavations. 8 Engravings, Frontispiece, and 2 Maps.

GIL BLAS. The Adventures of. From the French of Lesage by Smollett. 24 Engravings after Smirke, and 10 Etchings by Cruikshank. 612 pages. 6*s.*

GRIMM'S Gammer Grethel; or, German Fairy Tales and Popular Stories, containing 42 Fairy Tales. By Edgar Taylor. Numerous Woodcuts after Cruikshank and Ludwig Grimm. 3*s.* 6*d.*

HOLBEIN'S Dance of Death and Bible Cuts. Upwards of 150 Subjects, engraved in facsimile, with Introduction and Descriptions by the late Francis Douce and Dr. Dibdin.

INDIA, Pictorial, Descriptive, and Historical, from the Earliest Times. 100 Engravings on Wood and Map.

JESSE'S Anecdotes of Dogs. With 40 Woodcuts after Harvey, Bewick, and others; and 34 Steel Engravings after Cooper and Landseer.

KING'S (C. W.) Natural History of Precious Stones and Metals. Illustrations. 6*s.*

LODGE'S Portraits of Illustrious Personages of Great Britain, with Biographical and Historical Memoirs. 240 Portraits engraved on Steel, with the respective Biographies unabridged. Complete in 8 vols.

LONGFELLOW'S Poetical Works, including his Translations and Notes. 24 full-page Woodcuts by Birket Foster and others, and a Portrait.

—— Without the Illustrations, 3s. 6d.

—— **Prose Works.** With 16 full-page Woodcuts by Birket Foster and others.

LOUDON'S (Mrs.) Entertaining Naturalist. Popular Descriptions, Tales, and Anecdotes, of more than 500 Animals. Numerous Woodcuts.

MARRYAT'S (Capt., R.N.) Masterman Ready; or, the Wreck of the *Pacific*. (Written for Young People.) With 93 Woodcuts. 3s. 6d.

—— **Mission; or, Scenes in Africa.** (Written for Young People.) Illustrated by Gilbert and Dalziel. 3s. 6d.

—— **Pirate and Three Cutters.** (Written for Young People.) With a Memoir. 8 Steel Engravings after Clarkson Stanfield, R.A. 3s. 6d.

—— **Privateersman.** Adventures by Sea and Land One Hundred Years Ago. (Written for Young People.) 8 Steel Engravings. 3s. 6d.

—— **Settlers in Canada.** (Written for Young People.) 10 Engravings by Gilbert and Dalziel. 3s. 6d.

—— **Poor Jack.** (Written for Young People.) With 16 Illustrations after Clarkson Stanfield, R.A. 3s. 6d.

—— **Midshipman Easy.** With 8 full-page Illustrations. Small post 8vo. 3s. 6d.

—— **Peter Simple.** With 8 full-page Illustrations. Small post 8vo. 3s. 6d.

MAXWELL'S Victories of Wellington and the British Armies. Frontispiece and 4 Portraits.

MICHAEL ANGELO and RAPHAEL, Their Lives and Works. By Duppa and Quatremère de Quincy. Portraits and Engravings, including the Last Judgment, and Cartoons.

MUDIE'S History of British Birds. Revised by W. C. L. Martin. 52 Figures of Birds and 7 coloured Plates of Eggs. 2 vols.

NAVAL and MILITARY HEROES of Great Britain; a Record of British Valour on every Day in the year, from William the Conqueror to the Battle of Inkermann. By Major Johns, R.M., and Lieut. P. H. Nicolas, R.M. Indexes. 24 Portraits after Holbein, Reynolds, &c. 6s.

NICOLINI'S History of the Jesuits: their Origin, Progress, Doctrines, and Designs. 8 Portraits.

PETRARCH'S Sonnets, Triumphs, and other Poems, in English Verse. With Life by Thomas Campbell. Portrait and 15 Steel Engravings.

PICKERING'S History of the Races of Man, and their Geographical Distribution; with An Analytical Synopsis of the Natural History of Man. By Dr. Hall. Map of the World and 12 coloured Plates.

POPE'S Poetical Works, including Translations. Edit., with Notes, by R. Carruthers. 2 vols. With numerous Illustrations.

—— **Homer's Iliad**, with Introduction and Notes by Rev. J. S. Watson, M.A. With Flaxman's Designs.

—— **Homer's Odyssey**, with the Battle of Frogs and Mice, Hymns, &c., by other translators including Chapman. Introduction and Notes by J. S. Watson, M.A. With Flaxman's Designs.

—— **Life**, including many of his Letters. By R. Carruthers. Numerous Illustrations.

POTTERY AND PORCELAIN, and other objects of Vertu. Comprising an Illustrated Catalogue of the Bernal Collection, with the prices and names of the Possessors. Also an Introductory Lecture on Pottery and Porcelain, and an Engraved List of all Marks and Monograms. By H. G. Bohn. Numerous Woodcuts.

—— With coloured Illustrations, 10s. 6d.

PROUT'S (Father) Reliques. Edited by Rev. F. Mahony. Copyright edition, with the Author's last corrections and additions. 21 Etchings by D. Maclise, R.A. Nearly 600 pages.

RECREATIONS IN SHOOTING. With some Account of the Game found in the British Isles, and Directions for the Management of Dog and Gun. By 'Craven.' 62 Woodcuts and 9 Steel Engravings after A. Cooper, R.A.

RENNIE. Insect Architecture. Revised by Rev. J. G. Wood, M.A. 186 Woodcuts.

ROBINSON CRUSOE. With Memoir of Defoe, 12 Steel Engravings and 74 Woodcuts after Stothard and Harvey.

—— Without the Engravings, 3s. 6d.

ROME IN THE NINETEENTH CENtury. An Account in 1817 of the Ruins of the Ancient City, and Monuments of Modern Times. By C. A. Eaton. 34 Steel Engravings. 2 vols.

SHARPE (S.) The History of Egypt, from the Earliest Times till the Conquest by the Arabs, A.D. 640. 2 Maps and upwards of 400 Woodcuts. 2 vols.

SOUTHEY'S Life of Nelson. With Additional Notes, Facsimiles of Nelson's Writing, Portraits, Plans, and 50 Engravings, after Birket Foster, &c.

STARLING'S (Miss) Noble Deeds of Women; or, Examples of Female Courage, Fortitude, and Virtue. With 14 Steel Portraits.

STUART and REVETT'S Antiquities of Athens, and other Monuments of Greece; with Glossary of Terms used in Grecian Architecture. 71 Steel Plates and numerous Woodcuts.

SWEET'S British Warblers. 5s.—*See Bechstein.*

TALES OF THE GENII; or, the Delightful Lessons of Horam, the Son of Asmar. Trans. by Sir C. Morrell. Numerous Woodcuts.

TASSO'S Jerusalem Delivered. In English Spenserian Verse, with Life, by J. H. Wiffen. With 8 Engravings and 24 Woodcuts.

WALKER'S Manly Exercises; containing Skating, Riding, Driving, Hunting, Shooting, Sailing, Rowing, Swimming, &c. 44 Engravings and numerous Woodcuts.

WALTON'S Complete Angler; or the Contemplative Man's Recreation, by Izaak Walton and Charles Cotton. With Memoirs and Notes by E. Jesse. Also an Account of Fishing Stations, Tackle, &c., by H. G. Bohn. Portrait and 203 Woodcuts, and 26 Engravings on Steel.

—— **Lives of Donne, Wotton, Hooker,** &c., with Notes. A New Edition, revised by A. H. Bullen, with a Memoir of Izaak Walton by William Dowling. 6 Portraits, 6 Autograph Signatures, &c.

WELLINGTON, Life of. From the Materials of Maxwell. 18 Steel Engravings.

—— **Victories of.**—*See Maxwell.*

WESTROPP (H. M.) A Handbook of Archæology, Egyptian, Greek, Etruscan, Roman. By H. M. Westropp. Numerous Illustrations.

WHITE'S Natural History of Selborne, with Observations on various Parts of Nature, and the Naturalists' Calendar. Sir W. Jardine. Edit., with Notes and Memoir, by E. Jesse. 40 Portraits and coloured Plates.

CLASSICAL LIBRARY.

TRANSLATIONS FROM THE GREEK AND LATIN.

105 Vols. at 5s. each, excepting those marked otherwise. (25l. 13s. per set.)

ACHILLES TATIUS.—*See Greek Romances.*

ÆSCHYLUS, The Dramas of. In English Verse by Anna Swanwick. 4th edition.

—— **The Tragedies of.** In Prose, with Notes and Introduction, by T. A. Buckley, B.A. Portrait. 3s. 6d.

AMMIANUS MARCELLINUS. History of Rome during the Reigns of Constantius, Julian, Jovianus, Valentinian, and Valens, by C. D. Yonge, B.A. Double volume. 7s. 6d.

ANTONINUS (M. Aurelius), The Thoughts of. Translated, with Notes. Biographical Sketch, and Essay on the Philosophy, by George Long, M.A. 3s. 6d. Fine Paper edition on hand-made paper. 6s.

APOLLONIUS RHODIUS. 'The Argonautica.' Translated by E. P. Coleridge.

APULEIUS, The Works of. Comprising the Golden Ass, God of Socrates, Florida, and Discourse of Magic, &c. Frontispiece.

ARISTOPHANES' Comedies. Trans., with Notes and Extracts from Frere's and other Metrical Versions, by W. J. Hickie. Portrait. 2 vols.

ARISTOTLE'S Nicomachean Ethics. Trans., with Notes, Analytical Introduction, and Questions for Students, by Ven. Archdn. Browne.

—— **Politics and Economics.** Trans., with Notes, Analyses, and Index, by E. Walford, M.A., and an Essay and Life by Dr. Gillies.

—— **Metaphysics.** Trans., with Notes, Analysis, and Examination Questions, by Rev. John H. M'Mahon, M.A.

—— **History of Animals.** In Ten Books. Trans., with Notes and Index, by R. Cresswell, M.A.

—— **Organon**; or, Logical Treatises, and the Introduction of Porphyry. With Notes, Analysis, and Introduction, by Rev. O. F. Owen, M.A. 2 vols. 3s. 6d. each.

—— **Rhetoric and Poetics.** Trans., with Hobbes' Analysis, Exam. Questions, and Notes, by T. Buckley, B.A. Portrait.

ATHENÆUS. The Deipnosophists. Trans. by C. D. Yonge, B.A. With an Appendix of Poetical Fragments. 3 vols.

ATLAS of Classical Geography. 22 large Coloured Maps. With a complete Index. Imp. 8vo. 7s. 6d.

BION.—*See Theocritus.*

CÆSAR. Commentaries on the Gallic and Civil Wars, with the Supplementary Books attributed to Hirtius, including the complete Alexandrian, African, and Spanish Wars. Portrait.

CATULLUS, Tibullus, and the Vigil of Venus. Trans. with Notes and Biographical Introduction. To which are added, Metrical Versions by Lamb, Grainger, and others. Frontispiece.

CICERO'S Orations. Trans. by C. D. Yonge, B.A. 4 vols.

—— **On Oratory and Orators.** With Letters to Quintus and Brutus. Trans., with Notes, by Rev. J. S. Watson, M.A.

—— **On the Nature of the Gods,** Divination, Fate, Laws, a Republic, Consulship. Trans. by C. D. Yonge, B.A.

—— **Academics, De Finibus, and Tusculan Questions.** By C. D. Yonge, B.A. With Sketch of the Greek Philosophers mentioned by Cicero.

CICERO'S Offices; or, Moral Duties. Cato Major, an Essay on Old Age; Lælius, an Essay on Friendship; Scipio's Dream; Paradoxes; Letter to Quintus on Magistrates. Trans., with Notes, by C. R. Edmonds. Portrait. 3s. 6d.

DEMOSTHENES' Orations. Trans., with Notes, Arguments, a Chronological Abstract, and Appendices, by C. Rann Kennedy. 5 vols. (One, 3s. 6d.; four, 5s.)

DICTIONARY of LATIN and GREEK Quotations; including Proverbs, Maxims, Mottoes, Law Terms and Phrases. With the Quantities marked, and English Translations. With Index Verborum (622 pages).

DIOGENES LAERTIUS. Lives and Opinions of the Ancient Philosophers. Trans., with Notes, by C. D. Yonge, B.A.

EPICTETUS. The Discourses of. With the Encheiridion and Fragments. With Notes, Life, and View of his Philosophy, by George Long, M.A.

EURIPIDES. A New Literal Translation in Prose. By E. P. Coleridge. 2 vols.

EURIPIDES. Trans. by T. A. Buckley, B.A. Portrait. 2 vols.

GREEK ANTHOLOGY. In English Prose by G. Burges, M.A. With Metrical Versions by Bland, Merivale, and others.

GREEK ROMANCES of Heliodorus, Longus, and Achilles Tatius; viz., The Adventures of Theagenes and Chariclea; Amours of Daphnis and Chloe; and Loves of Clitopho and Leucippe. Trans., with Notes, by Rev R. Smith, M.A.

HELIODORUS.—*See Greek Romances.*

HERODOTUS. Literally trans. by Rev. Henry Cary, M.A. Portrait. 3s. 6d.

HESIOD, CALLIMACHUS, and Theognis. In Prose, with Notes and Biographical Notices by Rev. J. Banks, M.A. Together with the Metrical Versions of Hesiod, by Elton; Callimachus, by Tytler; and Theognis, by Frere.

HOMER'S Iliad. In English Prose, with Notes by T. A. Buckley, B.A. Portrait.

—— **Odyssey, Hymns, Epigrams, and Battle of the Frogs and Mice.** In English Prose, with Notes and Memoir by T. A. Buckley, B.A.

HORACE. In Prose by Smart, with Notes selected by T. A. Buckley, B.A. Portrait. 3s. 6d.

JULIAN THE EMPEROR. Containing Gregory Mazianzen's Two Invectives and Libanus' Monody, with Julian's Theosophical Works. By the Rev. C. W. King, M.A.

JUSTIN, CORNELIUS NEPOS, and Eutropius. Trans., with Notes, by Rev. J. S. Watson, M.A.

JUVENAL, PERSIUS, SULPICIA, and Lucilius. In Prose, with Notes, Chronological Tables, Arguments, by L. Evans, M.A. To which is added the Metrical Version of Juvenal and Persius by Gifford. Frontispiece.

LIVY. The History of Rome. Trans. by Dr. Spillan and others. 4 vols. Portrait.

LONGUS. Daphnis and Chloe.—*See Greek Romances.*

LUCAN'S Pharsalia. In Prose, with Notes by H. T. Riley.

LUCIAN'S Dialogues of the Gods, of the Sea Gods, and of the Dead. Trans. by Howard Williams, M.A.

LUCRETIUS. In Prose, with Notes and Biographical Introduction by Rev. J. S. Watson, M.A. To which is added the Metrical Version by J. M. Good.

MARTIAL'S Epigrams, complete. In Prose, with Verse Translations selected from English Poets, and other sources. Dble. vol. (670 pages). 7s. 6d.

MOSCHUS.—*See Theocritus.*

OVID'S Works, complete. In Prose, with Notes and Introduction. 3 vols.

PAUSANIAS' Description of Greece. Trans., with Notes and Index, by Rev. A. R. Shilleto, M.A., sometime Scholar of Trinity College, Cambridge. 2 vols.

PHALARIS. Bentley's Dissertations upon the Epistles of Phalaris, Themistocles, Socrates, Euripides, and the Fables of Æsop. With Introduction and Notes by Prof. W. Wagner, Ph.D.

PINDAR. In Prose, with Introduction and Notes by Dawson W. Turner. Together with the Metrical Version by Abraham Moore. Portrait.

PLATO'S Works. Trans. by Rev. H. Cary, H. Davis, and G. Burges. 6 vols.

—— **Dialogues.** A Summary and Analysis of. With Analytical Index to the Greek text of modern editions and to the above translations, by A. Day, LL.D.

PLAUTUS'S Comedies. In Prose, with Notes by H. T. Riley, B.A. 2 vols.

PLINY'S Natural History. Trans., with Notes, by J. Bostock, M.D., F.R.S., and H. T. Riley, B.A. 6 vols.

PLINY. The Letters of Pliny the Younger. Melmoth's Translation, revised, with Notes and short Life, by Rev. F. C. T. Bosanquet, M.A.

PLUTARCH'S Morals. Theosophical Essays. Trans. by Rev. C. W. King, M.A.

—— **Ethical Essays.** Trans. by Rev. A. R. Shilleto, M.A.

—— **Lives.** *See page 7.*

PROPERTIUS, The Elegies of. With Notes, translated by Rev. P. J. F. Gantillon, M.A., with metrical versions of Select Elegies by Nott and Elton. 3s. 6d.

QUINTILIAN'S Institutes of Oratory. Trans., by Rev. J. S. Watson, M.A. 2 vols.

SALLUST, FLORUS, and VELLEIUS Paterculus. Trans., with Notes and Biographical Notices, by J. S. Watson, M.A.

SENECA DE BENEFICIIS. Translated by Aubrey Stewart, M.A. 3s. 6d.

SENECA'S Minor Essays. Translated by A. Stewart, M.A.

SOPHOCLES. The Tragedies of. In Prose, with Notes, Arguments, and Introduction. Portrait.

STRABO'S Geography. Trans., with Notes, by W. Falconer, M.A., and H. C. Hamilton. Copious Index, giving Ancient and Modern Names. 3 vols.

SUETONIUS' Lives of the Twelve Cæsars and Lives of the Grammarians. The Translation of Thomson, revised, with Notes, by T. Forester.

TACITUS. The Works of. Trans., with Notes. 2 vols.

TERENCE and PHÆDRUS. In English Prose, with Notes and Arguments, by H. T. Riley, B.A. To which is added Smart's Metrical Version of Phædrus. With Frontispiece.

THEOCRITUS, BION, MOSCHUS, and Tyrtæus. In Prose, with Notes and Arguments, by Rev. J. Banks, M.A. To which are appended the METRICAL VERSIONS of Chapman. Portrait of Theocritus.

THUCYDIDES. The Peloponnesian War. Trans., with Notes, by Rev. H. Dale. Portrait. 2 vols. 3s. 6d. each.

TYRTÆUS.—*See Theocritus.*

VIRGIL. The Works of. In Prose, with Notes by Davidson. Revised, with additional Notes and Biographical Notice, by T. A. Buckley, B.A. Portrait. 3s. 6d.

XENOPHON'S Works. Trans., with Notes, by J. S. Watson, M.A., and Rev. H. Dale. Portrait. In 3 vols.

COLLEGIATE SERIES.

11 Vols. at 5s. each.   (2l. 15s. per set.)

DANTE. The Inferno. Prose Trans., with the Text of the Original on the same page, and Explanatory Notes, by John A. Carlyle, M.D. Portrait.

—— **The Purgatorio.** Prose Trans., with the Original on the same page, and Explanatory Notes, by W. S. Dugdale.

DOBREE'S Adversaria. (Notes on the Greek and Latin Classics.) Edited by the late Prof. Wagner. 2 vols.

DONALDSON (Dr.) The Theatre of the Greeks. With Supplementary Treatise on the Language, Metres, and Prosody of the Greek Dramatists. Numerous Illustrations and 3 Plans. By J. W. Donaldson, D.D.

GOETHE'S Faust. Part I. German Text, with Hayward's Prose Translation and Notes. Revised, with Introduction and Bibliography, by Dr. C. A. Buchheim. 5s.

KEIGHTLEY'S (Thomas) Mythology of Ancient Greece and Italy. Revised by Dr. Leonhard Schmitz. 12 Plates.

HERODOTUS, Notes on. Original and Selected from the best Commentators. By D. W. Turner, M.A. Coloured Map.

—— **Analysis and Summary of,** with a Synchronistical Table of Events—Tables of Weights, Measures, Money, and Distances—an Outline of the History and Geography—and the Dates completed from Gaisford, Baehr, &c.   By J. T. Wheeler.

NEW TESTAMENT (The) in Greek. Griesbach's Text, with the Readings of Mill and Scholz, and Parallel References. Also a Critical Introduction and Chronological Tables. Two Fac-similes of Greek Manuscripts. 650 pages. 3s. 6d.

—— or bound up with a Greek and English Lexicon to the New Testament (250 pages additional, making in all 900). 5s.

The Lexicon separately, 2s.

THUCYDIDES. An Analysis and Summary of. With Chronological Table of Events, &c., by J. T. Wheeler.

SCIENTIFIC LIBRARY.

48 Vols. at 5s. each, excepting those marked otherwise.   (12l. 19s. per set.)

AGASSIZ and GOULD. Outline of Comparative Physiology. Enlarged by Dr. Wright. With Index and 300 Illustrative Woodcuts.

BOLLEY'S Manual of Technical Analysis; a Guide for the Testing and Valuation of the various Natural and Artificial Substances employed in the Arts and Domestic Economy, founded on the work of Dr. Bolley. Edit. by Dr. Paul. 100 Woodcuts.

BRIDGEWATER TREATISES.

—— **Bell (Sir Charles) on the Hand;** its Mechanism and Vital Endowments, as evincing Design. Preceded by an Account of the Author's Discoveries in the Nervous System by A. Shaw. Numerous Woodcuts.

—— **Kirby on the History, Habits,** and Instincts of Animals. With Notes by T. Rymer Jones. 100 Woodcuts. 2 vols.

—— **Buckland's Geology and Mineralogy.** With Additions by Prof. Owen, Prof. Phillips, and R. Brown. Memoir of Buckland. Portrait. 2 vols. 15s. Vol. I. Text. Vol. II. 90 large plates with letterpress.

BRIDGEWATER TREATISES. *Continued.*

—— **Chalmers on the Adaptation of External Nature to the Moral and Intellectual Constitution of Man.** With Memoir by Rev. Dr. Cumming. Portrait.

—— **Prout's Treatise on Chemistry,** Meteorology, and the Function of Digestion, with reference to Natural Theology. Edit. by Dr. J. W. Griffith. 2 Maps.

—— **Roget's Animal and Vegetable Physiology.** 463 Woodcuts. 2 vols. 6s. each.

—— **Kidd on the Adaptation of External Nature to the Physical Condition of Man.** 3s. 6d.

CARPENTER'S (Dr. W. B.) Zoology. A Systematic View of the Structure, Habits, Instincts, and Uses of the principal Families of the Animal Kingdom, and of the chief Forms of Fossil Remains. Revised by W. S. Dallas, F.L.S. Numerous Woodcuts. 2 vols. 6s. each.

—— **Mechanical Philosophy, Astronomy, and Horology.** A Popular Exposition. 181 Woodcuts.

CARPENTER'S Works.—*Continued.*

— **Vegetable Physiology and Systematic Botany.** A complete Introduction to the Knowledge of Plants. Revised by E. Lankester, M.D., &c. Numerous Woodcuts. 6s.

— **Animal Physiology.** Revised Edition. 300 Woodcuts. 6s.

CHEVREUL on Colour. Containing the Principles of Harmony and Contrast of Colours, and their Application to the Arts; including Painting, Decoration, Tapestries, Carpets, Mosaics, Glazing, Staining, Calico Printing, Letterpress Printing, Map Colouring, Dress, Landscape and Flower Gardening, &c. Trans. by C. Martel. Several Plates.

— With an additional series of 16 Plates in Colours, 7s. 6d.

ENNEMOSER'S History of Magic. Trans. by W. Howitt. With an Appendix of the most remarkable and best authenticated Stories of Apparitions, Dreams, Second Sight, Table-Turning, and Spirit-Rapping, &c. 2 vols.

HOGG'S (Jabez) Elements of Experimental and Natural Philosophy. Being an Easy Introduction to the Study of Mechanics, Pneumatics, Hydrostatics, Hydraulics, Acoustics, Optics, Caloric, Electricity, Voltaism, and Magnetism. 400 Woodcuts.

HUMBOLDT'S Cosmos; or, Sketch of a Physical Description of the Universe. Trans. by E. C. Otté, B. H. Paul, and W. S. Dallas, F.L.S. Portrait. 5 vols. 3s. 6d. each, excepting vol. v., 5s.

— **Personal Narrative of his Travels** in America during the years 1799-1804. Trans., with Notes, by T. Ross. 3 vols.

— **Views of Nature; or, Contemplations of the Sublime Phenomena of Creation,** with Scientific Illustrations. Trans. by E. C. Otté.

HUNT'S (Robert) Poetry of Science; or, Studies of the Physical Phenomena of Nature. By Robert Hunt, Professor at the School of Mines.

JOYCE'S Scientific Dialogues. A Familiar Introduction to the Arts and Sciences. For Schools and Young People. Numerous Woodcuts.

JUKES-BROWNE'S Student's Handbook of Physical Geology. By A. J. Jukes-Browne, of the Geological Survey of England. With numerous Diagrams and Illustrations, 6s.

JUKES-BROWNE'S Works.—*Cont.*

— **The Student's Handbook of Historical Geology.** By A. J. Jukes-Brown, B.A., F.G.S., of the Geological Survey of England and Wales. With numerous Diagrams and Illustrations. 6s.

— **The Building of the British Islands.** A Study in Geographical Evolution. By A. J. Jukes-Browne, F.G.S. 7s. 6d.

KNIGHT'S (Charles) Knowledge is Power. A Popular Manual of Political Economy.

LILLY. Introduction to Astrology. With a Grammar of Astrology and Tables for calculating Nativities, by Zadkiel.

MANTELL'S (Dr.) Geological Excursions through the Isle of Wight and along the Dorset Coast. Numerous Woodcuts and Geological Map.

— **Petrifactions and their Teachings.** Handbook to the Organic Remains in the British Museum. Numerous Woodcuts. 6s.

— **Wonders of Geology; or, a Familiar Exposition of Geological Phenomena.** A coloured Geological Map of England, Plates, and 200 Woodcuts. 2 vols. 7s. 6d. each.

SCHOUW'S Earth, Plants, and Man. Popular Pictures of Nature. And Kobell's Sketches from the Mineral Kingdom. Trans. by A. Henfrey, F.R.S. Coloured Map of the Geography of Plants.

SMITH'S (Pye) Geology and Scripture; or, the Relation between the Scriptures and Geological Science. With Memoir.

STANLEY'S Classified Synopsis of the Principal Painters of the Dutch and Flemish Schools, including an Account of some of the early German Masters. By George Stanley.

STAUNTON'S Chess Works. — *See page 21.*

STÖCKHARDT'S Experimental Chemistry. A Handbook for the Study of the Science by simple Experiments. Edit. by C. W. Heaton, F.C.S. Numerous Woodcuts.

URE'S (Dr. A.) Cotton Manufacture of Great Britain, systematically investigated; with an Introductory View of its Comparative State in Foreign Countries. Revised by P. L. Simmonds. 150 Illustrations. 2 vols.

— **Philosophy of Manufactures,** or an Exposition of the Scientific, Moral, and Commercial Economy of the Factory System of Great Britain. Revised by P. L. Simmonds. Numerous Figures. 800 pages. 7s. 6d.

ECONOMICS AND FINANCE.

5 *Volumes*. (1*l*. 2*s. per set.*)

GILBART'S History, Principles, and Practice of Banking. Revised to 1881 by A. S. Michie, of the Royal Bank of Scotland. Portrait of Gilbart. 2 vols. 10*s*.

RICARDO on the Principles of Political Economy and Taxation. Edited by E. C. K. Gonner, M.A., Lecturer, University College, Liverpool. 5*s*.

SMITH (Adam). The Wealth of Nations. An Inquiry into the Nature and Causes of. Edited by E. Belfort Bax. 2 vols. 7*s*.

REFERENCE LIBRARY.

32 *Volumes at Various Prices.* (8*l*. 3*s. per set.*)

BLAIR'S Chronological Tables. Comprehending the Chronology and History of the World, from the Earliest Times to the Russian Treaty of Peace, April 1856. By J. W. Rosse. 800 pages. 10*s*.

—— **Index of Dates.** Comprehending the principal Facts in the Chronology and History of the World, from the Earliest to the Present, alphabetically arranged; being a complete Index to the foregoing. By J. W. Rosse. 2 vols. 5*s*. each.

BOHN'S Dictionary of Quotations from the English Poets. 4th and cheaper Edition. 6*s*.

BOND'S Handy-book of Rules and Tables for Verifying Dates with the Christian Era. 4th Edition. 5*s*.

BUCHANAN'S Dictionary of Science and Technical Terms used in Philosophy, Literature, Professions, Commerce, Arts, and Trades. By W. H. Buchanan, with Supplement. Edited by Jas. A. Smith. 6*s*.

CHRONICLES OF THE TOMBS. A Select Collection of Epitaphs, with Essay on Epitaphs and Observations on Sepulchral Antiquities. By T. J. Pettigrew, F.R.S., F.S.A. 5*s*.

CLARK'S (Hugh) Introduction to Heraldry. Revised by J. R. Planché. 5*s*. 950 Illustrations.

—— *With the Illustrations coloured*, 15*s*.

COINS, Manual of.—*See Humphreys.*

COOPER'S Biographical Dictionary. Containing concise notices of upwards of 15,000 eminent persons of all ages and countries. 2 vols. 5*s*. each.

DATES, Index of.—*See Blair.*

DICTIONARY of Obsolete and Provincial English. Containing Words from English Writers previous to the 19th Century. By Thomas Wright, M.A., F.S.A., &c. 2 vols. 5*s*. each.

EPIGRAMMATISTS (The). A Selection from the Epigrammatic Literature of Ancient, Mediæval, and Modern Times. With Introduction, Notes, Observations, Illustrations, an Appendix on Works connected with Epigrammatic Literature, by Rev. H. Dodd, M.A. 6*s*.

GAMES, Handbook of. Edited by Henry G. Bohn. Numerous Diagrams. 5*s*. (*See also page* 21.)

HENFREY'S Guide to English Coins. Revised Edition, by C. F. Keary, M.A., F.S.A. With an Historical Introduction. 6*s*.

HUMPHREYS' Coin Collectors' Manual. An Historical Account of the Progress of Coinage from the Earliest Time, by H. N. Humphreys. 140 Illustrations. 2 vols. 5*s*. each.

LOWNDES' Bibliographer's Manual of English Literature. Containing an Account of Rare and Curious Books published in or relating to Great Britain and Ireland, from the Invention of Printing, with Biographical Notices and Prices, by W. T. Lowndes. Revised Edition by H. G. Bohn. 6 vols. cloth, 5*s*. each, or in 4 vols., half morocco, 2*l*. 2*s*.

MEDICINE, Handbook of Domestic, Popularly Arranged. By Dr. H. Davies. 700 pages. 5*s*.

NOTED NAMES OF FICTION. Dictionary of. Including also Familiar Pseudonyms, Surnames bestowed on Eminent Men, &c. By W. A. Wheeler, M.A. 5*s*.

POLITICAL CYCLOPÆDIA. A Dictionary of Political, Constitutional, Statistical, and Forensic Knowledge; forming a Work of Reference on subjects of Civil Administration, Political Economy, Finance, Commerce, Laws, and Social Relations. 4 vols. 3*s*. 6*d*. each.

PROVERBS, Handbook of. Containing an entire Republication of Ray's Collection, with Additions from Foreign Languages and Sayings, Sentences, Maxims, and Phrases. 5s.

—— **A Polyglot of Foreign.** Comprising French, Italian, German, Dutch, Spanish, Portuguese, and Danish. With English Translations. 5s.

SYNONYMS and ANTONYMS; or, Kindred Words and their Opposites, Collected and Contrasted by Ven. C. J. Smith, M.A. 5s.

WRIGHT (Th.)—*See Dictionary.*

NOVELISTS' LIBRARY.

13 Volumes at 3s. 6d. each, excepting those marked otherwise. (2l. 8s. 6d. per set.)

BJÖRNSON'S Arne and the Fisher Lassie. Translated from the Norse with an Introduction by W. H. Low, M.A.

BURNEY'S Evelina; or, a Young Lady's Entrance into the World. By F. Burney (Mme. D'Arblay). With Introduction and Notes by A. R. Ellis, Author of 'Sylvestra,' &c.

—— **Cecilia.** With Introduction and Notes by A. R. Ellis. 2 vols.

DE STAËL. Corinne or Italy. By Madame de Staël. Translated by Emily Baldwin and Paulina Driver.

EBERS' Egyptian Princess. Trans. by Emma Buchheim.

FIELDING'S Joseph Andrews and his Friend Mr. Abraham Adams. With Roscoe's Biography. *Cruikshank's Illustrations.*

—— **Amelia.** Roscoe's Edition, revised. *Cruikshank's Illustrations.* 5s.

—— **History of Tom Jones, a Foundling.** Roscoe's Edition. *Cruikshank's Illustrations.* 2 vols.

GROSSI'S Marco Visconti. Trans. by A. F. D.

MANZONI. The Betrothed: being a Translation of 'I Promessi Sposi.' Numerous Woodcuts. 1 vol. 5s.

STOWE (Mrs. H. B.) Uncle Tom's Cabin; or, Life among the Lowly. 8 full-page Illustrations.

ARTISTS' LIBRARY.

9 Volumes at Various Prices. (2l. 8s. 6d. per set.)

BELL (Sir Charles). The Anatomy and Philosophy of Expression, as Connected with the Fine Arts. 5s. Illustrated.

DEMMIN. History of Arms and Armour from the Earliest Period. By Auguste Demmin. Trans. by C. C. Black, M.A., Assistant Keeper, S. K. Museum. 1900 Illustrations. 7s. 6d.

FAIRHOLT'S Costume in England. Third Edition, Enlarged and Revised by the Hon. H. A. Dillon, F.S.A. With more than 700 Engravings. 2 vols. 5s. each.
Vol. I. History. Vol. II. Glossary.

FLAXMAN. Lectures on Sculpture. With Three Addresses to the R.A. by Sir R. Westmacott, R.A., and Memoir of Flaxman. Portrait and 53 Plates. 6s.

HEATON'S Concise History of Painting. New Edition, revised by W. Cosmo Monkhouse. 5s.

LECTURES ON PAINTING by the Royal Academicians, Barry, Opie, Fuseli. With Introductory Essay and Notes by R. Wornum. Portrait of Fuseli. 5s.

LEONARDO DA VINCI'S Treatise on Painting. Trans. by J. F. Rigaud, R.A. With a Life and an Account of his Works by J. W. Brown. Numerous Plates. 5s.

PLANCHÉ'S History of British Costume, from the Earliest Time to the 10th Century. By J. R. Planché. 400 Illustrations. 5s.

LIBRARY OF SPORTS AND GAMES.

14 Volumes at 3s. 6d. and 5s. each. (2l. 18s. per set.)

BOHN'S Handbooks of Athletic Sports. With numerous Illustrations. In 8 vols. 3s. 6d. each.

Vol. I.—Cricket, by Hon. and Rev. E. Lyttelton; Lawn Tennis, by H. W. W. Wilberforce; Tennis, Rackets, and Fives, by Julian Marshall, Major Spens, and J. A. Tait; Golf, by W. T. Linskill; Hockey, by F. S. Creswell.

Vol. II.—Rowing and Sculling, by W. B. Woodgate; Sailing, by E. F. Knight; Swimming, by M. and J. R. Cobbett.

Vol. III.—Boxing, by R. G. Allanson-Winn; Broad-sword and Single Stick, &c., by R. G. Allanson-Winn and C. Phillipps-Wolley; Wrestling, by Walter Armstrong; Fencing, by H. A. Colmore Dunn.

Vol. IV.—Rugby Football, by Harry Vassall; Association Football, by C. W. Alcock; Baseball, by Newton Crane; Rounders, Field Ball, Baseball-Rounders, Bowls, Quoits, Curling, Skittles, &c., by J. M. Walker, M.A., and C. C. Mott.

Vol. V.—Cycling and Athletics, by H. H. Griffin; Skating, by Douglas Adams.

Vol. VI.—Practical Horsemanship, including Riding for Ladies. By W. A. Kerr, V.C.

Vol. VII.—Driving, and Stable Management. By W. A. Kerr, V.C. [*Preparing.*

Vol. VIII.—Gymnastics, by A. F. Jenkin; Clubs and Dumb-bells, by G. T. B. Cobbett and A. F. Jenkin. [*In the press.*

BOHN'S Handbooks of Games. New Edition, entirely rewritten. 2 volumes. 3s. 6d. each.

Vol. I. TABLE GAMES.

Contents:—Billiards, with Pool, Pyramids, and Snooker, by Major-Gen. A. W. Drayson, F.R.A.S., with a preface by W. J. Peall—Bagatelle, by 'Berkeley'—Chess, by R. F. Green—Draughts, Backgammon, Dominoes, Solitaire, Reversi, Go Bang, Rouge et noir, Roulette, E.O., Hazard, Faro, by 'Berkeley.'

Vol. II. CARD GAMES.

Contents:—Whist, by Dr. William Pole, F.R.S., Author of 'The Philosophy of Whist, &c.'—Solo Whist, and Poker, by R. F. Green; Piquet, Ecarté, Euchre, Bézique, and Cribbage, by 'Berkeley:' Loo, Vingt-et-un, Napoleon, Newmarket, Rouge et Noir, Pope Joan, Speculation, &c. &c., by Baxter-Wray.

CHESS CONGRESS of 1862. A collection of the games played. Edited by J. Löwenthal. New edition, 5s.

MORPHY'S Games of Chess, being the Matches and best Games played by the American Champion, with explanatory and analytical Notes by J. Löwenthal. With short Memoir and Portrait of Morphy. 5s.

STAUNTON'S Chess-Player's Handbook. A Popular and Scientific Introduction to the Game, with numerous Diagrams. 5s.

—— **Chess Praxis.** A Supplement to the Chess-player's Handbook. Containing the most important modern Improvements in the Openings; Code of Chess Laws; and a Selection of Morphy's Games. Annotated. 636 pages. Diagrams. 5s.

—— **Chess-Player's Companion.** Comprising a Treatise on Odds, Collection of Match Games, including the French Match with M. St. Amant, and a Selection of Original Problems. Diagrams and Coloured Frontispiece. 5s.

—— **Chess Tournament of 1851.** A Collection of Games played at this celebrated assemblage. With Introduction and Notes. Numerous Diagrams. 5s.

BOHN'S CHEAP SERIES.

Price 1s. each.

A Series of Complete Stories or Essays, mostly reprinted from Vols. in Bohn's Libraries, and neatly bound in stiff paper cover, with cut edges, suitable for Railway Reading.

ASCHAM (Roger). Scholemaster. By Professor Mayor.

CARPENTER (Dr. W. B.). Physiology of Temperance and Total Abstinence.

EMERSON. England and English Characteristics. Lectures on the Race, Ability, Manners, Truth, Character, Wealth, Religion. &c. &c.

—— **Nature**: An Essay. To which are added Orations, Lectures, and Addresses.

—— **Representative Men**: Seven Lectures on PLATO, SWEDENBORG, MONTAIGNE, SHAKESPEARE, NAPOLEON, and GOETHE.

—— **Twenty Essays on Various Subjects.**

—— **The Conduct of Life.**

FRANKLIN (Benjamin). Autobiography. Edited by J. Sparks.

HAWTHORNE (Nathaniel). Twice-told Tales. Two Vols.

—— **Snow Image**, and Other Tales.

—— **Scarlet Letter.**

—— **House with the Seven Gables.**

—— **Transformation**; or the Marble Fawn. Two Parts.

HAZLITT (W.). Table-talk: Essays on Men and Manners. Three Parts.

—— **Plain Speaker**: Opinions on Books, Men, and Things. Three Parts.

—— **Lectures on the English Comic Writers.**

—— **Lectures on the English Poets.**

—— **Lectures on the Characters of Shakespeare's Plays.**

—— **Lectures on the Literature of the Age Elizabeth,** chiefly Dramatic.

IRVING (Washington). Lives of Successors of Mohammed.

—— **Life of Goldsmith.**

—— **Sketch-book.**

—— **Tales of a Traveller**

—— **Tour on the Prairies**

—— **Conquests of Granada and Spain.** Two Parts.

—— **Life and Voyages of Columbus.** Two Parts.

—— **Companions of Columbus**: Their Voyages and Discoveries.

—— **Adventures of Captain Bonneville** in the Rocky Mountains and the West.

—— **Knickerbocker's History of New York**, from the beginning of the World to the End of the Dutch Dynasty.

—— **Tales of the Alhambra.**

—— **Conquest of Florida under Hernando de Soto.**

—— **Abbotsford & Newstead Abbey.**

—— **Salmagundi**; or, The Whim-Whams and Opinions of LAUNCELOT LANGSTAFF, Esq.

—— **Bracebridge Hall**; or, The Humourists.

—— **Astoria**; or, Anecdotes of an Enterprise beyond the Rocky Mountains.

—— **Wolfert's Roost**, and other Tales.

LAMB (Charles). Essays of Elia. With a Portrait.

—— **Last Essays of Elia.**

—— **Eliana.** With Memoir.

MARRYAT (Captain). Pirate and the Three Cutters. With a Memoir of the Author.

Bohn's Select Library of Standard Works.

Price 1s. in paper covers, and 1s. 6d. in cloth.

1. BACON'S ESSAYS. With Introduction and Notes.
2. LESSING'S LAOKOON. Beasley's Translation, revised, with Introduction, Notes, &c., by Edward Bell, M.A. With Frontispiece.
3. DANTE'S INFERNO. Translated, with Notes, by Rev. H. F. Cary.
4. GOETHE'S FAUST. Part I. Translated, with Introduction, by Anna Swanwick.
5. GOETHE'S BOYHOOD. Being Part I. of the Autobiography Translated by J. Oxenford.
6. SCHILLER'S MARY STUART and THE MAID OF ORLEANS. Translated by J. Mellish and Anna Swanwick.
7. THE QUEEN'S ENGLISH. By the late Dean Alford.
8. LIFE AND LABOURS OF THE LATE THOMAS BRASSEY. By Sir A. Helps, K.C.B.
9. PLATO'S DIALOGUES: The Apology—Crito—Phaedo—Protagoras. With Introductions.
10. MOLIÈRE'S PLAYS: The Miser—Tartuffe—The Shopkeeper turned Gentleman. Translated by C. H. Walt, M.A. With brief Memoir.
11. GOETHE'S REINEKE FOX, in English Hexameters. By A. Rogers.
12. OLIVER GOLDSMITH'S PLAYS.
13. LESSING'S PLAYS: Nathan the Wise—Minna von Barnhelm.
14. PLAUTUS'S COMEDIES: Trinummus — Menaechmi — Aulularia — Captivi.
15. WATERLOO DAYS. By C. A. Eaton. With Preface and Notes by Edward Bell.
16. DEMOSTHENES—ON THE CROWN. Translated by C. Rann Kennedy.
17. THE VICAR OF WAKEFIELD.
18. OLIVER CROMWELL. By Dr. Reinhold Pauli.
19. THE PERFECT LIFE. By Dr. Channing. Edited by his nephew, Rev. W. H. Channing.
20. LADIES IN PARLIAMENT, HORACE AT ATHENS, and other pieces, by Sir George Otto Trevelyan, Bart.
21. DEFOE'S THE PLAGUE IN LONDON.
22. IRVING'S LIFE OF MAHOMET.
23. HORACE'S ODES, by various hands. *[Out of Print.*
24. BURKE'S ESSAY ON 'THE SUBLIME AND BEAUTIFUL.' With Short Memoir.
25. HAUFF'S CARAVAN.
26. SHERIDAN'S PLAYS.
27. DANTE'S PURGATORIO. Translated by Cary.
28. HARVEY'S TREATISE ON THE CIRCULATION OF THE BLOOD
29. CICERO'S FRIENDSHIP AND OLD AGE.
30. DANTE'S PARADISO. Translated by Cary.
31. CHRONICLE OF HENRY VIII. Translated by Major M. A. S. Hume.

THE ONLY AUTHORIZED AND COMPLETE 'WEBSTER.'

WEBSTER'S INTERNATIONAL DICTIONARY.

An entirely New Edition, thoroughly Revised, considerably Enlarged, and reset in New Type.

Medium 4to. 2118 *pages,* 3500 *illustrations.*

Prices: Cloth, £1 11s. 6d.; half-calf, £2 2s.; half-russia, £2 5s.; calf, £2 8s. Also in 2 vols. cloth, £1 14s.

In addition to the Dictionary of Words, with their pronunciation, etymology, alternative spellings, and various meanings, illustrated by quotations and numerous woodcuts, there are several valuable appendices, comprising a Pronouncing Gazetteer of the World; Vocabularies of Scripture, Greek, Latin, and English Proper Names; a Dictionary of the noted Names of Fiction; a Brief History of the English Language; a Dictionary of Foreign Quotations, Words, Phrases, Proverbs, &c.; a Biographical Dictionary with 10,000 Names, &c.

This last revision, comprising and superseding the issues of 1847, 1864, and 1880, is by far the most complete that the Work has undergone during the sixty-two years that it has been before the public. Every page has been treated as if the book were now published for the first time.

SOME PRESS OPINIONS ON THE NEW EDITION.

'We believe that, all things considered, this will be found to be the best existing English dictionary in one volume. We do not know of any work similar in size and price which can approach it in completeness of vocabulary, variety of information, and general usefulness.'—*Guardian.*

'The most comprehensive and the most useful of its kind.'—*National Observer.*

'A magnificent edition of Webster's immortal Dictionary.'—*Daily Telegraph.*

'A thoroughly practical and useful dictionary.'—*Standard.*

'A special feature of the present book is the lavish use of engravings, which at once illustrate the verbal explanations of technical and scientific terms, and permit them to remain readably brief. It may be enough to refer to the article on "Cross." By the use of the little numbered diagrams we are spared what would have become a treatise, and not a very clear one. . . . We recommend the new Webster to every man of business, every father of a family, every teacher, and almost every student—to everybody, in fact, who is likely to be posed at an unfamiliar or half-understood word or phrase.'—*St. James's Gazette.*

Prospectuses, with Specimen Pages, on application.

London: GEORGE BELL & SONS, York Street, Covent Garden.

www.ingramcontent.com/pod-product-compliance
Lightning Source LLC
Chambersburg PA
CBHW032048220426
43664CB00008B/910